FROM THE GOLDEN GATE TO MEXICO CITY

THE U.S. ARMY TOPOGRAPHICAL ENGINEERS IN THE MEXICAN WAR, 1846–1848

by
Adrian George Traas

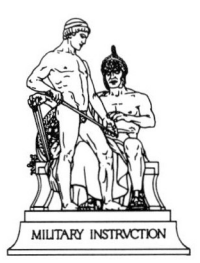

OFFICE OF HISTORY, CORPS OF ENGINEERS
and
CENTER OF MILITARY HISTORY

UNITED STATES ARMY
WASHINGTON, D.C., 1993

Library of Congress Cataloging-in-Publication Data

Traas, Adrian George, 1934–
From the Golden Gate to Mexico City : the U.S. Army Topographical Engineers in the Mexican War, 1846–1848 / by Adrian George Traas.
p.   cm. — (CMH pub ; 70–10)
Includes bibliographical references and index.
1. Mexican War, 1846–1848—Engineering and construction.
2. United States. Army.   Corps of Topographical Engineers—History.
3. Mexican War, 1846–1848—Regimental histories—United States.
4. Military Topography—United States—History—19th century.
I. United States. Army.   Corps of Engineers. Office of History.
II. Center of Military History.   III. Title.   IV. Series.
E409.2T73   1992
973.6'24—dc20   91–45500
                                                                                                        CIP

CMH Pub 70–10

First Printing

For sale by the Superintendent of Documents, U.S. Government Printing Office
Washington, D.C. 20402

Foreword

In performing its many civil-military missions throughout its history, the U.S. Army has often been a pioneer on the frontiers of technology. Army engineers in particular have been preeminent in developing and using new technologies to carry out their assignments. Even pre-dating their organization into a separate branch in 1838, the Army's topographical engineers carried on civil works programs, their work in road and harbor construction, waterway charting, and all the great innovations involved in creating a continental infrastructure quickly elevating them into a kind of quasi-independent federal civil works organization. Prominent among these missions was the exploration and mapping of the West.

Mapping in nineteenth century America had both a civilian and military dimension. Military and civilian explorers mapped the territories of the American West, providing one of the essential tools for agricultural expansion and urban development. As part of their traditional military responsibilities, Army engineers accompanied military forces in the field, making reconnaissances, planning the route of advance, and charting the terrain for the military commanders. Commanders also looked to the engineers for special kinds of intelligence involving the terrain and the military strength of the enemy.

Topographical Engineers in the Mexican War serves a twofold end. The book demonstrates how the engineers performed a valuable combat support mission in America's first foreign war. It describes their contribution to the Fremont and Kearney expeditions to California and their efforts during General Zachary Taylor's advance to Buena Vista. It also shows the engineers on the cutting edge of nineteenth century technology as they laid the communication routes throughout the southwest and California that would tie the new continental nation together.

In addition to the intrinsic interest found in an account of such adventures, today's military students can also learn much about the influence of terrain on campaigns and battles, encountering principles that still govern the use of geographical intelligence in our era of computer and satellite technology. What follows should also renew their pride in the knowledge that the Army has always stood on the forefront of science and technology during its two centuries of service.

HENRY J. HATCH	HAROLD W. NELSON
Lieutenant General, USA	Brigadier General, USA
Chief of Engineers	Chief of Military History

Washington, D.C.
7 June 1991

The Author

Lt. Col. Adrian G. Traas, U.S. Army Corps of Engineers, retired, received his commission and B.A. degree upon his graduation from Marquette University in 1957. He received a Master of Arts degree in history from Texas A&M University in 1971.

His military service included assignments as executive officer and commanding officer of the 64th Engineer Battalion (Base Topographic) in Italy, Ethiopia, Liberia, and Iran; staff officer and instructor at the Army Engineer School; professor of military science at Marquette; and assistant chief of Histories Division at the Center of Military History. He has also served as company commander of engineering units in Korea and Fort Belvoir, Virginia; as post engineer in Italy; and on ROTC duty at Texas A&M. He served two tours in Vietnam, the first with the 19th Engineer Battalion and 45th Engineer Group and the second as an adviser with a South Vietnamese engineer group and a deputy region engineer.

He is currently preparing a volume on military engineering operations in the Vietnam War series.

Preface

This publication analyzes and explains the role of the U.S. Army Topographical Engineer Corps in the war with Mexico, commencing with the activities of the Topographical Engineers in 1845 and tracing their evolution from a scientific, mapping, and construction agency of the federal government to their active participation in the war. Originally submitted as a master's thesis at Texas A&M University, the account begins with the role the Topographical Engineers played in military reconnaissances and explorations in anticipation of the hostilities between the United States and Mexico. Their role during the war is recounted, particularly the conquest and explorations of California, New Mexico, and Arizona. Included is Capt. John C. Fremont's third expedition, important for both its military and geographic contributions. Under the commands of Generals Scott and Taylor in Mexico, several officers of the corps assumed important leadership responsibilities in addition to their topographic duties. They contributed to the American military victory, and, of more lasting consequence, their reports provided basic scientific information about the little-known regions that became part of the United States as a result of the Mexican War.

The Corps of Topographical Engineers, or more informally identified as "topogs," was established as a separate corps in 1838, when some thirty-six authorized officers were placed on an equal footing with the Corps of Engineers. Their responsibilities were topography, mapping, and civil engineering works authorized by Congress. This realigning left the larger Corps of Engineers free to concentrate on its combat role as supporter of the Army in the field and builder of coastal fortifications.

The topographic responsibilities entailed exploring and surveying the territories on both sides of the Mississippi River. By 1845, John C. Fremont as a result of his second expedition, had pushed these explorations westward to California. The knowledge of the land and the scientific data that the Topographical Engineers brought back to Washington resulted in accurate mapping and provided information about people, plant and animal life, routes, minerals, and soil conditions.

Nearly two-thirds of the officers of the Corps of Topographical Engineers served with distinction in the Mexican War. Just as significant and more lasting were the results of their topographic and geographic studies. Even in the midst of a war, members of this scientifically oriented corps noted their geographic surroundings. The Topographical Engineers were as much at home in speaking before a group of scientists as in living in and exploring the rugged terrain or supervising boundary surveys, lighthouse surveys, river and harbor improvements, and construction projects. The efforts of this small corps of topogs resulted in more accurate maps of the newly acquired lands in the West and in portions of Mexico. The published travels of these officers, along with the other popular travel literature of the day, stimulated interest in westward migration.

This study outlines the activities of the Corps of Topographical Engineers and the diversity of its efforts in the only conflict in American history in which the corps served throughout as a distinctive branch of the Army. Because of the contribution of members of the Corps of Topographical Engineers, commanders were able to effectively use the reconnaissance information provided. These engineers played decisive roles in campaigns in California and Mexico, and provided the nation with maps of the newly acquired lands and vast amounts of valuable scientific findings.

In the course of research and writing the author has received generous support from many individuals. Deep appreciation and gratitude is extended to Dr. Herbert H. Lang, Texas A&M University, for his patient understanding in directing this research and his valuable suggestions for improving the style and form of this study when it was prepared in 1971. I am also most appreciative of the assistance rendered by Dr. Garry D. Ryan and other employees of the National Archives, and the constructive criticism of Drs. Allan G. Ashcraft and T.M. Stinnett, who graciously consented to serve on my thesis committee. A special word of appreciation is also due Mrs. E.I. Bailey for typing the original thesis manuscript and Mrs. Wyvetra B. Yeldell for her typing a portion of the initial revised manuscript for this publication. A word of thanks also goes to Dr. John T. Greenwood, the former Chief of the Office of History, U.S. Army Corps of Engineers, who believed this study had some merit for publication. The study also benefited greatly from the advice of reviewers of the Engineer Office of History including Drs. Frank N. Schubert and Paul K. Walker and Mr. Dale E. Floyd. I am also indebted to the thorough review given by Lt. Col. Richard O. Perry, former Chief, Histories Division, U.S. Army Center of Military History, and Dr. Jamie W. Moore, the Citadel.

A special word of thanks is also due to Morris J. MacGregor, Acting Chief Historian, and to John W. Elsberg, Editor in Chief of the Center. A large amount of praise is also owed to the editors: Kathleen Richardson for the original manuscript and Samuel Duncan Miller for the final editing. Barbara H. Gilbert, Diane Sedore Arms, and Joycelyn M. Canery skillfully carried the manuscript through to publication. Arthur S. Hardyman, Howell C. Brewer, Sherry L. Dowdy, and Linda M. Cajka ably handled graphics and cartographic support.

Of course, the author alone is responsible for all interpretations and conclusions drawn in this work, as well as any errors that may occur.

Washington, D.C.   ADRIAN G. TRAAS
7 June 1991

Contents

Chapter	Page
1. THE GENESIS OF A SMALL CORPS	3
The Military Situation on the Eve of War	4
The Corps' Contribution to the American Victory	4
The Two Engineering Corps	5
Training Army Topographers	7
Origin of Army Topographers	9
Service as a Subordinate Bureau, 1818–1831	11
The Corps as a Separate Bureau, 1831–1838	14
The Topographical Engineers Corps, 1838–1845	17
The Corps and Manifest Destiny	18
Colonel Kearny's Mounted Reconnaissance, 1845	20
The Corps on the Eve of War	22
2. ON TO THE GOLDEN GATE WITH FREMONT	25
Orders for Fremont's Third Expedition, 1845	26
Fremont Organizes His Expedition	29
The Route to California	30
Fremont Arrives in California	32
The Mysterious Rendezvous With Lieutenant Gillespie, USMC	35
Fremont and the Bear Flag Revolt	37
The Navy Joins Forces With Fremont	39
All of California Is Taken	40
Fremont's Dispute With Kearny	42
Fremont's Geographic Memoir	44
The Subsidiary Expedition of Lieutenants Abert and Peck, 1845	45
Abert's Map and Report, 1846	48

Chapter	Page
3. WITH THE ARMY OF THE WEST	63
Lieutenant Emory's Instructions	66
From Fort Leavenworth to Santa Fe	67
The Occupation of Santa Fe	70
Emory's Comments on New Mexican Society	71
Setting Out for California	73
News From California	74
Observing the Indians Along the Way	75
Still No Enemy	78
Arrival in California	79
The Battle of San Pasqual	80
Kearny Moves on to Los Angeles	83
Emory's Report of a Military Reconnaissance	84
4. LIEUTENANTS ABERT AND PECK IN NEW MEXICO	89
Lieutenant Abert's Stay at Bent's Fort	89
Abert's Route From Bent's Fort to Santa Fe	91
Arrival in Santa Fe and New Instructions	92
The Survey of Southern New Mexico	93
Orders To Return to Washington	95
Abert's Hard Trip Back	96
Peck Follows a Different Route	99
Lieutenant Abert's Report	100
5. WITH ZACHARY TAYLOR IN NORTHERN MEXICO	115
Topogs Join Taylor's Army	116
Military Surveys, Late 1845	118
Surveying a Route to the Rio Grande	120
The Move to the Rio Grande	122
Opposite Matamoros	123
Topogs in the First Battles of the War	124
Declaration of War and Strategy	127
Taylor Crosses Into Mexico	128
Military Reconnaissances Around Matamoros	130
The Move to Monterrey	131
The Battle of Monterrey	132
Meade Again Becomes Acting Chief Topog	137
Resumption of Operations	138

Chapter	Page
Meade Receives a New Assignment	140
The Battle of Buena Vista	142
Other Topographic Tasks in Northern Mexico	145
6. WOOL AND HIS TOPOGS JOIN TAYLOR	**149**
Wool's Army Assembles in San Antonio	149
The March to Mexico	150
The Crossing of the Rio Grande Into Mexico	152
From Monclova to Parras	154
Wool Joins Taylor at Buena Vista	155
Hughes Reports on the Future of Texas	156
Views on Northern Mexico	158
Hughes' Final Report	160
The Other Topographical Engineers	161
7. TO MEXICO CITY WITH SCOTT	**177**
Scott's Topogs Assemble	178
The Landing at Vera Cruz	181
The Two Engineering Corps Roles at Vera Cruz	182
Meade Departs	185
Cerro Gordo	186
Fewer Topogs After Cerro Gordo	191
On to Puebla	192
Reconnoitering the Approaches to Mexico City	193
The Battles of Contreras and Churubusco	195
A Short-Lived Armistice and Molino del Rey	197
The Storming of Chapultepec and Into Mexico City	198
Scott Praises His Engineers	200
Hughes and Emory Take on New Roles in Mexico	201
Mapping the Valley of Mexico and Final Reports	204
Later Careers of Scott's Topogs	206
8. SO MUCH BY SO FEW	**211**
Topographical Corps Work in 1846	211
Corps Projects in 1847	213
Colonel Abert's Overview of the Corps, 1848	216
Epilogue	218

Appendixes

	Page
A. Report of Captain Hughes of Wool's March Into Mexico.	229
B. Report of the Survey of the Valley of Mexico.	304
C. Report of the Chief, Topographical Engineers, 1848	318
BIBLIOGRAPHY.	337
INDEX	347

Tables

No.

1. Corps of Topographical Engineers Officers, 1845–1848.	8
2. Topographical Engineers Appointed Generals (U.S.A., Volunteers, Brevets) in the Civil War.	224

Maps

1. Western Exploration, 1845–1847	2
2. The Mexican War, 1846–1847.	64

Illustrations

The following illustrations appear between pages 50 and 62:

Colonel John J. Abert
Major Stephen H. Long
Long's Map of His 1819–1820 Expedition Depicting the "Great American Desert"
Snag Boat
Lieutenant Emory's 1844 Map of the West
William B. Franklin During the Civil War
Typical Uniforms of Regular Army Soldiers During the Mexican War
Section III of Fremont Map Based on the 1844 Expedition to California

Section IV of Fremont Map Based on the 1844 Expedition
  to California
Fremont at Snow Peak
Fremont's 1848 Map

The following illustrations appear between pages 102 and 114:

William H. Emory During the Civil War
Drawing of Santa Fe
Cereus Giganteus
Passing San Felippe, New Mexico
Drawing Made by Lieutenant Abert During His Convalescence at
  Bent's Fort in 1846
Abert and Peck Map of the Rio Grande Valley
Zachary Taylor
George Meade During the Civil War
Sketch of Palo Alto
Battle of Palo Alto
Sketch of Resaca de la Palma
View of Monterrey From Independence Hill
Meade's Map of Monterrey
Map of Buena Vista

The following illustrations appear between pages 164 and 176:

Brevet Major General John E. Wool
Young Robert E. Lee, 1838
Major General Winfield Scott
The Landing at Vera Cruz
Joseph E. Johnston During the Civil War
Lieutenant George H. Derby
Drawing the "Ass-sault"
View of Cerro Gordo
Scott's Army Taking Detour Around Lake Chalco
Map of Cerro Gordo
Map of the Valley of Mexico
Map of Battle of Molino del Rey
Map Prepared by Topographical Engineers of Battles for
  Mexico City
Scott's Entry Into Mexico City
Capture of the *tete de pont* at Churubusco

FROM THE GOLDEN GATE TO MEXICO CITY THE U.S. ARMY TOPOGRAPHICAL ENGINEERS IN THE MEXICAN WAR 1846–1848

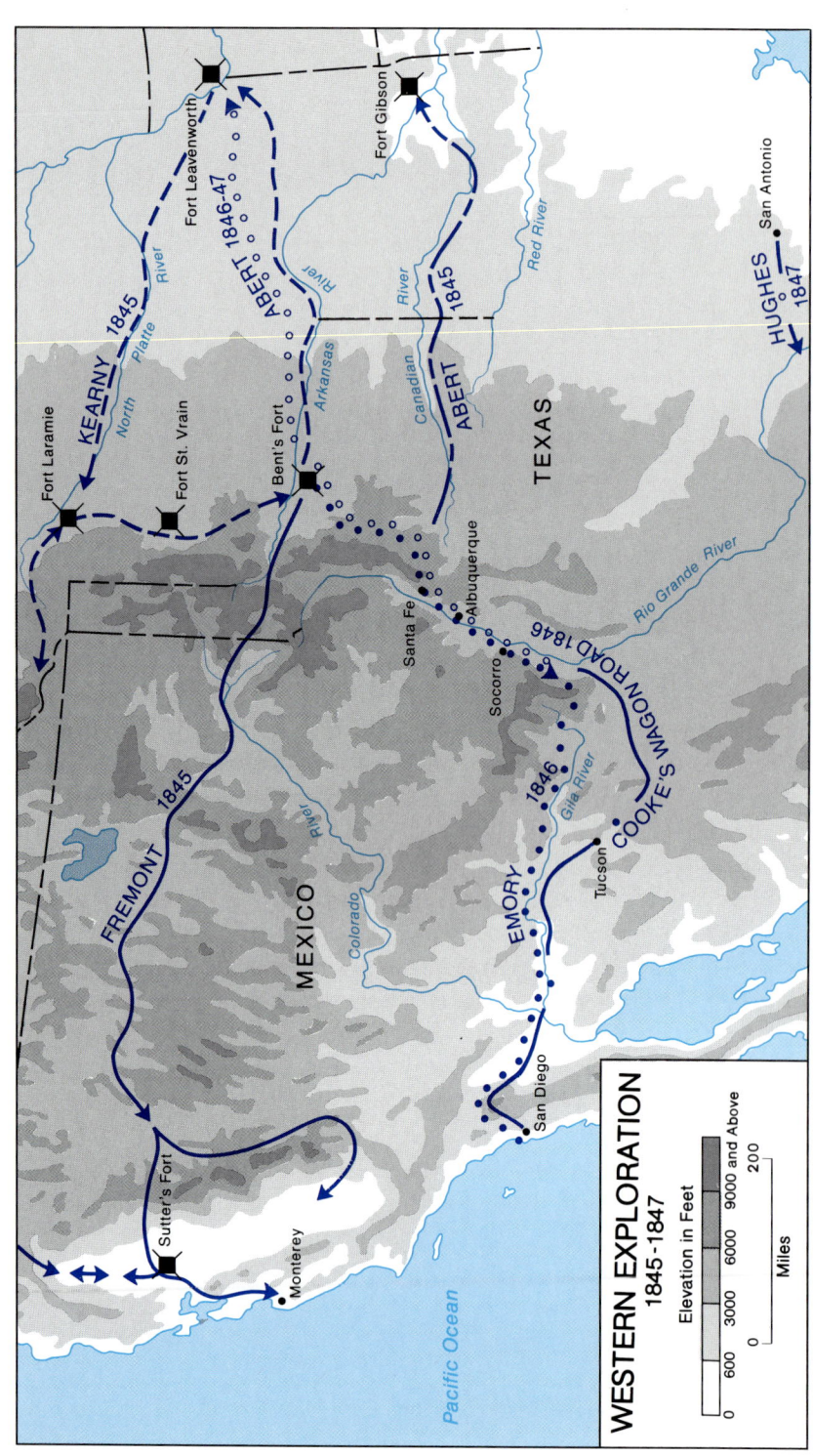

MAP 1

CHAPTER 1

The Genesis of a Small Corps

In 1845 the United States faced two international problems: a dispute with Great Britain over Oregon, and Mexico's opposition to the annexation of Texas. Either could have led to war. Fortunately, by the following year the United States reached an agreement with Great Britain over Oregon. But the quarrel with Mexico moved one step closer to war on 1 March 1845, when Congress resolved to admit Texas to the Union.[1]

Mexican resentment over American expansionism became a fundamental cause for war between the two nations. American settlers in Texas had rebelled in 1836 and set up an independent republic. The slaughter of Texans at the Alamo and Goliad by Mexican troops sent shudders of horror throughout the American public, and relations between the two countries deteriorated. Mexican anger further increased when the United States recognized Texas independence. Other incidents between the two nations added to Mexican ill-feeling. In 1842 an American naval task force, acting on a false rumor that war with Mexico had broken out, seized the coastal town of Monterey in Mexican ruled California. Although the embarrassed Americans relinquished the town and apologized, nothing could allay Mexican fear that Americans planned to seize California. With the election of James K. Polk to the presidency in 1844, relations between the two countries grew even worse. The new American president ran on a platform favoring the annexation of Texas, and, after Polk's inauguration, Congress acted to admit the republic of Texas to the Union.

---

[1] For background see K. Jack Bauer, *The Mexican War, 1846–1848* (New York: Macmillan, 1974), pp. 1–36, and John S.D. Eisenhower, *So Far From God: The U.S. War With Mexico, 1846–1848* (New York: Random House, 1989), pp. 1–26.

The Military Situation on the Eve of War

While Polk waited for Texas to accept the offer of statehood orders went out alerting military commanders to prepare for possible hostilities with Mexico. The Navy concentrated in Texan and Mexican waters, and the Pacific Squadron received instructions to prepare to seize ports along the California coast. In June, orders reached Bvt. Gen. Zachary Taylor and his "Corps of Observation" at Fort Jesup, Louisiana, to move to a position "on or near the Rio Grande well suited to repel any invasion." Instead, Taylor moved his army by land and sea to Corpus Christi, avoiding the disputed border region.[2]

In July Texas' agreement to annexation created more war jitters. Secretary of War William L. Marcy dispatched more troops to Texas, and authorized Taylor to call upon the governors of nearby states for militia. Polk sought to negotiate a settlement on American terms, seeking to define a Rio Grande boundary and to purchase Upper California and New Mexico. The Mexican government, however, had no intention of giving up half of its national territory.

When notified of the Mexican government's refusal to negotiate, Polk, in January 1846, ordered Taylor to move his force to the Rio Grande as soon as possible. Taylor, called "Old Rough and Ready" by his troops, acknowledged the order and its instructions not to consider Mexico as an enemy. He was not to take action unless a declaration of war took place or American forces came under attack.

Events, however, did lead to the Mexican War, America's first foreign war fought almost entirely in a strange and distant land. During the war a small group of uniformed topographers, or "topogs," of the U.S. Army Corps of Topographical Engineers served with distinction. This is the story of a unique organization, particularly its members, and its contribution to the nation, not only in the war with Mexico but as an agency for internal development.

The Corps' Contribution to the American Victory

Although the public knew little about the work of the Corps of Topographical Engineers during the war, the corps contributed significantly to the victory of U.S. forces. Besides the topogs' military

---

[2] Bauer, *The Mexican War,* p. 18.

THE GENESIS OF A SMALL CORPS 5

contributions, the small corps of officers (the corps did not have enlisted personnel) achieved geographic and scientific discoveries, products of more lasting consequence. Their investigations, carried out in the midst of the war, broadened geographic knowledge about the little-known regions of the Southwest. In essence, the corps served as sort of an intelligence gathering agency.

Most of the topogs, 26 of the 46 officers on Army rolls between 1846 and 1848, served in or near combat zones. Other members of the corps provided indirect support to the war effort. Although the topogs served meritoriously in the theaters of war, their topographic and geographic studies and maps resulted in a singular accomplishment among the branches of the Army. Even in the midst of a war the Topographical Engineers maintained their interest in the sciences. By the very nature of their backgrounds, they could not resist noting their geographic surroundings.[3]

The topogs' efforts resulted in the most up-to-date and accurate maps of the regions they crossed, before, during, and following the war. Published accounts of the Topographical Engineers' travels also added significantly to the popular travel literature of the day. Accounts of the curious ways and customs of the Mexicans and Indians, their languages and heritage, the climate, the wild and barren topography, and exotic vegetation and wildlife lent an air of romanticism never before experienced by Americans. The Army topographers' accounts outlined the routes to California, Oregon, and the Southwest, revealing at the same time the potential of these newly acquired territories. As a result, the hordes of pioneers heading west after the war put the writings of the Topographical Engineers to practical use.[4]

The Two Engineering Corps

Two separate engineering corps existed in the U.S. Army at the time. Robert E. Lee, P. G. T. Beauregard, Henry W. Halleck, and George B. McClellan, all well known Civil War commanders,

---

[3] Official Army Register for 1847, Adj. Gen. Off., Washington, 1847, p. 11; Henry P. Beers, "History of the U.S. Topographical Engineers," *Military Engineer* 34 (June 1942): 291; Thomas H. S. Hamersly, *Complete Army Navy Register of the U.S.A. From 1776 to 1887* (New York: Thomas H. S. Hamersly, 1888), p. 643.

[4] Robert W. Johannsen, *To the Halls of the Montezumas: The Mexican War in the American Imagination* (New York: Oxford Univ. Press, 1985), p. 12.

served in the Corps of Engineers as captains and lieutenants during the Mexican War. The Corps of Topographical Engineers included other prominent Civil War leaders to be. George G. Meade, Joseph E. Johnston, John Pope, and John C. Fremont served as topog captains and lieutenants during the conflict with Mexico. Other veteran engineering officers of the two corps who served in the Mexican War also went on to positions of responsibility in the Army, in business, and in education.

The responsibilities of the Corps of Topographical Engineers included not only topography and mapping, but, just as significant, civil engineering works authorized by Congress. The civil engineering projects—roads, canals, railways, lighthouses, and public buildings and works—were a great share of the topographical corps' efforts. When war broke out, the Corps of Topographical Engineers found itself in the midst of a large construction effort. Military engineering support to armies in the field, however, and construction of fortifications remained with the Corps of Engineers.[5]

Mapping was an important responsibility of the Topographical Engineers. From the military commander's viewpoint accurate knowledge of the terrain often means the difference between success or failure on the battlefield. A military agency is often given the task of mapping its own country and obtaining the latest information on the geography and topography of other nations, which in modern terms is referred to as terrain intelligence. The scientific side benefits gathered by the topographers—general information about people, plant and animal life, minerals, and soil conditions—was also especially significant during this period of United States' expansion.[6]

Many of the duties of the topographers assigned to field commands were similar to those conducted by the Corps of Engineers. Army regulations in force between 1840 and 1857 specified that armies in the field would always have Topographical Engineers to help

> ... in reconnaissances of the country through which an army has to pass, or in which it has to operate; in the examination of all routes of communication by land or by water, both for supplies and for military move-

---

[5] For an overview of the history of the Corps of Engineers including the Topographical Engineers see *The History of the US Army Corps of Engineers* (Washington, D.C.: U.S. Army Corps of Engineers, 1986).

[6] For an overview of corps activities in the West, see Frank N. Schubert, *Vanguard of Expansion: Army Engineers in the Trans-Mississippi West, 1819–1879* (Washington, D.C.: U.S. Army Corps of Engineers, 1980).

ments; in the construction of military roads and permanent bridges connected with them, and in the absence of an officer or officers of the Corps of Engineers, of military bridges, and of field works, for the defense of encampments, fords, ferries, and bridges.[7]

Although Army topographers worked for field commanders, they regularly forwarded reports to the chief of their corps. These reports covered matters of geographic, topographic, and other scientific studies, all items of the utmost interest to the topogs' headquarters in Washington. The high esprit de corps and personal scientific interests among members of the corps also served as an incentive to gather vast amounts of information about the regions they crossed.

Training Army Topographers

In this period, in which the Topographical Engineers operated as a corps and separate branch of the Army, all but 8 of the 72 Army topographers who served between 1838 and 1863 obtained their commissions from the Military Academy. The majority of the Topographical Engineer officers also received their training in military engineering at West Point. Since the Corps of Engineers had responsibility for the Military Academy's operation, engineering and engineering-related subjects predominated in the school's curriculum. Courses included mathematics, drawing, military and civil engineering, history, geography, ethics, military science, some law, and French and Spanish. Officers graduated well versed in surveying; in the construction of buildings, roads, bridges, canals, and railroads; and in the improvement and building of harbors. Usually the top graduates received commissions in one of the two engineering branches.[8]

---

[7] War Department, "General Regulations for the Army, 1841," Art. LXXV, par. 878, p. 159, quoted from Garry D. Ryan, *War Department Topographical Bureau, 1831–1863: An Administrative History* (Doctoral dissertation, American University, 1968), p. 149.

[8] Archie P. McDonald, "West Point and the Engineers," *Military Engineer* 57 (May–June 1965): 187–89; James A. Morrison, Jr., *"The Best School in the World": West Point, the Pre-Civil War Years, 1833–1866* (Kent, Ohio: Kent State Univ. Press, 1986), pp. 23–24, 91–101. Other historical studies on West Point include Stephen E. Ambrose's *Duty, Honor, Country: A History of West Point* (Baltimore: Johns Hopkins Press, 1966), R. Ernest Dupuy's *Men of West Point: The First 150 Years of the United States Military Academy* (New York: William Sloan Associates, 1951), and Thomas J. Fleming's *West Point: The Men and Times of the United States Military Academy* (New York: William Morrow and Co., 1969).

TABLE 1—CORPS OF TOPOGRAPHICAL ENGINEERS OFFICERS, 1845–1848
(Regular Grades as of 31 August 1847)

Colonel
John J. Abert

Lieutenant Colonel
James Kearney

Majors

Hartman Bache	Stephen H. Long
James D. Graham	William Turnbull [4]

Captains

Augustus Canfield	Joseph E. Johnston [4]	John McClellan [4]
Thomas J. Cram [4]	Thomas J. Lee	Howard Stansbury
Campbell Graham	Thomas B. Linnard [4]	William H. Swift
George W. Hughes [4]	John Mackay	William G. Williams [1,4]

First Lieutenants

Jacob E. Blake [1,4]	Charles N. Hagner [4]	James H. Simpson
William H. Emory	Andrew A. Humphreys	Lorenzo Sitgreaves
John C. Fremont [2,4]	John N. Macomb	William H. Warner
John W. Gunnison	Eliakim P. Scammon [4]	Israel C. Woodruff

Second Lieutenants [5]

James W. Abert [4]	William R. Palmer	William F. Smith
Francis T. Bryan [4]	William G. Peck [4]	George Thom [4]
George H. Derby [4]	John Pope [4]	Joseph D. Webster [4]
William B. Franklin [4]	William F. Raynolds	Amiel W. Whipple
Edmund L. F. Hardcastle [4]	Martin L. Smith [4]	Thomas J. Wood [3,4]
George Meade [4]		

[1] Killed in action.
[2] Resigned Mar 1848.
[3] Reassigned Oct 1846.
[4] Mexican War service.
[5] Does not include two brevet second lieutenants appointed on 1 July 1848.

Sources: *Official Army Register for 1847*, Adj. Gen. Off., Washington, 1847, p. 11; Henry P. Beers, "History of the U.S. Topographical Engineers," *Military Engineer* 34 (June 1942): 291; Thomas H. S. Hamersly, *Complete Army Navy Register of the U.S.A. From 1776 to 1887* (New York: Thomas H. S. Hamersly, 1888), p. 643; Wilcox, *History of the Mexican War*, p. 615.

Two of the eight officers had attended the military academy but left before graduation to work in civilian life. One, Stephen H. Long, graduated from Dartmouth, however, he did serve at West Point as an instructor. John C. Fremont was also in this group. He received his credentials in the field and under the expert guidance of Joseph N. Nicollet and Ferdinand Hassler. Of these eight Topographical Engineers, only Fremont seemed to resent West Point's apparent domination of the Army.[9]

The Corps of Topographical Engineers did not have a service school to provide further training to its officers. The topogs obtained their expertise in mapping and construction by on-the-job training, by travel, and by association with the scientists and engineers of the day. In addition, the corps instructed its supervisors to ensure that their junior officers received training in the skills of their trade. For example, in 1845 Bvt. Captain Fremont received specific instructions from Colonel John James Abert, the chief of the corps, on this point before setting out on his third trans-Mississippi expedition.[10]

Origin of Army Topographers

The Topographical Engineers date back to the American Revolution when Robert Erskine received an appointment as "geographer" for General George Washington. Erskine died in 1780, and two positions were established, one for the northern wing of the Army and the other for the southern wing. As a result, the topographers served as a distinct group of engineers from the earliest days of the United States. Following the American Revolution, Congress retained one of the geographer positions, that of surveyor of the public lands, to comply with the provisions of the Land Ordinance of 1785. Although the Army did not have a topographic branch at the time, the expeditions of Captains Meriwether Lewis and William Clark, Lieutenant Zebulon Pike, and others served as models. The later expeditions of the Corps of

---

[9] William H. Goetzmann, *Army Exploration in the American West, 1803–1863* (New Haven: Yale Univ. Press, 1959), pp. 12–16, 69–74; *Dictionary of American Biography* (New York: Charles Scribner's Sons, 1964), VIII, p. 514; and XIII, pp. 385–86. Nicollet was a brilliant French scientist who undertook topographical surveys sponsored by the Topographical Bureau. Fremont accompanied Nicollet on two surveys in 1838 and 1839 that produced a map of the upper Mississippi valley. These surveys resulted in a publication by the government after Nicollet's death in 1843 entitled *Report Intended To Illustrate a Map of the Hydrographical Basis of the Upper Mississippi River.* Hassler served as superintendent of the Coast Survey.

[10] Goetzmann, *Army Exploration*, pp. 16–17.

Topographical Engineers resembled in many ways these earlier Army ventures in the West.[11]

During the War of 1812 the Army greatly increased its number of military topographers. On 3 March 1813 an act of Congress authorized for the Army General Staff 16 topographical officer positions with ranks of brevet major and captain.[12] This act, however, did not authorize a corps or any administrative capability. During the war the topographers served as staff officers in both the northern and southern wings of the Army. Significantly, two of the topogs who served in the war, Isaac Roberdeau and John James Abert, later went on to serve as chiefs of the Army topographers.[13]

Instructions issued to topogs during the war also served as a model for future operations. When assigned to armies in the field these officers were

> To make such surveys, and exhibit such delineations of these as the commanding general shall direct; to make plans of all military positions (which the Army may occupy) and of their respective vicinities, indicating the various roads, rivers, creeks, ravines, hills, woods, and villages to be found therein; to accompany all reconnoitering parties sent out to obtain intelligence of the movements of the enemy or of his position, etc.; to make sketches of their route, accompanied by written notes of everything worthy of observation thereon; to keep a journal of every day's movements, when the Army is on march, noticing the varieties of ground, of buildings, of culture, and the distances and state of the road between given points throughout the march of the day and, lastly, to exhibit the positions of contending armies on fields of battle, and disposition made, whether for attack or defense.[14]

---

[11] Beers, "History of the Topographical Engineers," p. 287; Goetzmann, *Army Exploration*, pp. 6–7; Ryan, *Topographical Bureau Administrative History*, pp. 3–12; Edward Burr, "Historical Sketch of the Corps of Engineers, U.S. Army," *Occasional Papers of the Engineer School, No. 71* (Washington, D.C.: Government Printing Office, 1939), pp. 33–34; Frank N. Schubert, ed., *The Nation Builders: A Sesquicentennial History of the Corps of Topographical Engineers, 1838–1863* (Washington, D.C.: U.S. Army Corps of Engineers, 1988), p. 3.

[12] Since there were no medals to speak of, brevet ranks, temporary promotions without an increase in pay, became the common form of recognition for heroism or service.

[13] Goetzmann, *Army Exploration*, p. 7; Burr, "Historical Sketch," p. 35; Ryan, *Topographical Bureau Administrative History*, pp. 13–19.

[14] Quoted from Beers, "History of the Topographical Engineers," p. 287.

THE GENESIS OF A SMALL CORPS

The conclusion of the war led to the usual reduction in military personnel. In authorizing the smaller military establishment following the war, Congress provided for a Corps of Engineers but made no mention of Topographical Engineers. Two topogs (including Isaac Roberdeau) remained on active duty to complete surveys on the northern frontier and Lake Champlain. The two topogs saw an immense task ahead after the border survey. In their report they recommended "the completion of a frontier military survey of the whole interior and exterior of the United States."[15]

Recognizing the need for Topographical Engineers in military operations, Congress in 1816 passed a law authorizing ten officers. Significantly, this legislation provided for the first time several Army topographers during peacetime. Unlike the Corps of Engineers the topographical officers continued to lack a central office or branch status as a separate corps. Generally, the War Department assigned them as staff officers to the two military departments. A few topographers also found themselves working for the Board of Engineers for Fortifications. In this role the Army topographers surveyed the sites for seacoast and inland fortifications. A side benefit of these surveys also resulted in later improvements to navigation. Farther inland Major Stephen H. Long, one of the noted topogs of the period, established Fort Smith in Arkansas and explored the Old Northwest for future fortification sites.[16]

Service as a Subordinate Bureau, 1818–1831

In 1818 the War Department consolidated the Corps of Engineers, the Topographical Engineers, the U.S. Military Academy, and the Board of Engineers for Fortifications into a single Engineer Department headed by the senior Corps of Engineers officer. Under

---

[15] Burr, "Historical Sketch," p. 38. The entire report by Majors I. Roberdeau and John Anderson is reproduced on pages 36–38; Schubert, *The Nation Builders*, pp. 4–5.

[16] Goetzmann, *Army Exploration*, pp. 8–9; Beers, "History of the Topographical Engineers," pp. 287–88; Burr, "Historical Sketch," pp. 38–39; Ryan, *Topographical Bureau Administrative History*, pp. 22–23, 35–36; Schubert, *The Nation Builders*, pp. 5–6. For more on the Board of Engineers on Fortifications see Jamie W. Moore, *The Fortifications Board, 1816–1828, and the Definition of National Security*, The Citadel, Monograph Series, no. XVI (Charleston: The Citadel, Jan 1981).

the direction of Major Roberdeau the topogs became part of a subordinate Topographical Bureau. Located in Washington, the bureau's main duties consisted of housekeeping tasks but not control over programs or personnel. The bureau collected and preserved the specimens brought back by scientific expeditions, compiled maps, and stored and cared for the topogs' survey instruments.[17]

Under the Engineer Department the Topographical Engineers continued their normal work, in some cases working on related or identical projects with Corps of Engineers' officers. In 1819 and 1820 Major Stephen Long led an expedition to the Rocky Mountains, but his somewhat negative report of the high plains region created the "Great American Desert" myth. While Long explored the trans-Mississippi West, two Engineer officers surveyed the lower Mississippi. A topographer served on General Andrew Jackson's military operation against the Seminole Indians in Florida. Several topogs and Engineers surveyed harbors and bays, formally known as the Survey of the Coast, a joint effort that continued for several years thereafter. The topogs dominated the boundary surveys. In 1823 Major Long determined the northern boundary between the United States and Canada at the 49th parallel in Minnesota.[18]

The placement of the Army topographers under the Engineer Department heightened the already strained relations with the Corps of Engineers. Some problems between the two groups of Army engineers had occurred while working on similar or related projects. This partly stemmed from the class standing upon graduation from West Point; the top ranks of the graduating class received assignments to the Corps of Engineers closely followed by the second ranking group, the topogs. Corps of Engineers' officers tended to believe that greater skills were necessary in the planning and construction of fortifications than for public works. Engineer officers also made sure they ran the Engineer Department. In the absence of the Chief of Engineers an Engineer captain or sometimes even a lieutenant, not Major Roberdeau, took over the department. Stephen Long took a dim view of the topogs' apparent

---

[17] Burr, "Historical Sketch," p. 39; Ryan, *Topographical Bureau Administrative History*, pp. 28–32, 41; Schubert, *The Nation Builders*, p. 6.

[18] Beers, "History of the Topographical Engineers," p. 288; Schubert, *The Nation Builders*, pp. 6–7.

THE GENESIS OF A SMALL CORPS

second-class status, and he believed Engineer officers "cordially hate or more probably are jealous of our rising reputation."[19]

By 1824 the importance of waterways became paramount in the development of the young nation's commerce. By this time too the federal government, following the Supreme Court decision in the Gibbons versus Ogden case, had asserted its role in interstate commerce and the improving of the country's transportation system, particularly the rivers, canals, and harbors. In order to better develop the vast lands beyond the Appalachians, the young nation desperately needed to improve navigable passageways. Congress, in recognition of an increased government commitment to internal improvements, passed legislation which involved using the Army's engineers to do the work. The General Survey Act of 1824 initially called for field surveys, plans, and estimates of roads and canals, but within a month a second law appropriated funds and authorized the employment of necessary Army engineers to improve the navigation of the Ohio and Mississippi rivers. Besides, Congress believed the soldier-engineers would obtain experience and do something useful to enhance the country's defenses and development. From that point both the Corps of Engineers and the Topographical Engineers became deeply involved in civil works.[20]

By the end of May President James Monroe appointed a Board of Engineers for Internal Improvements to administer the General Survey Act. Its members included Corps of Engineers' officers but no Topographical Engineers. The topogs felt frustrated by the lack of recognition, and Major Long asked Roberdeau if the topographers were "to be mere chain bearers in the giant work of internal improvement." Three topogs, however, were attached to the board to lead survey parties to evaluate canal routes. The survey work dramatically influenced the topogs' outlook on their mission. Authorized ten officers to do military reconnaissances and make maps, the topogs instead devoted almost all their efforts to inter-

---

[19] Statement made in 1824 and quoted from Schubert, *The Nation Builders*, pp. 8–9; James L. Morrison, Jr., "The Best School in the World," *West Point, the Pre-Civil War Years, 1833–1866* (Kent, Ohio: Kent State Univ. Press, 1986), pp. 8, 142.

[20] Schubert, *The Nation Builders*, pp. 9–13; Ryan, *Topographical Bureau Administrative History*, p. 36.

nal improvements. By 1830 topogs led 10 of the 13 surveys for canal, road, and railroads, while civilians headed the other 3. Although the Engineer Department took care of general supervision of the surveys and the navigation work on the Mississippi and Ohio rivers, the topogs accomplished the great share of the field work. Scattered as they were throughout the interior of the country, the topographers began to earn a national reputation for their internal improvement work.[21]

In 1826 further legislation added more surveys for harbor and river improvements and significantly the authorization to carry out the actual work. On the Ohio River near Henderson, Kentucky, Major Long supervised the construction of a wing dam which reduced a sandbar and raised the water for navigation. Later the engineers supervised commercially developed steam-powered snagboats to clear the rivers of hazardous limbs and debris, thereby improving navigation. Now for the first time boats could be safely operated at night. Other survey work included the Chesapeake and Ohio Canal, a trans-Florida canal, and the Cumberland Road. Demands for similar services were so great that the War Department employed civil engineers and detailed additional officers with engineering skills from other branches of the Army.[22]

The Corps as a Separate Bureau, 1831–1838

In January 1829 Bvt. Lt. Col. Isaac Roberdeau suddenly died, and after some deliberation Major John J. Abert took over the reins of the Topographical Bureau. The following year he succeeded in gaining representation on the Board of Internal Improvements. The board's usefulness, however, had diminished once it had identified the required survey work, and in 1831 the Secretary of War abolished the board. In a dramatic move for the

---

[21] Quoted from Schubert, *The Nation Builders*, pp. 8–9, 13–15; Ryan, *Topographical Bureau Administrative History*, pp. 36–38.

[22] Beers, "History of the Topographical Engineers," p. 288; Burr, "Historical Sketch," p. 49; Ryan, *Topographical Bureau Administrative History*, p. 62; Goetzmann, *Army Exploration*, p. 8; Schubert, *The Nation Builders*, pp. 15–17. For a detailed account of the corps contributions in transportation, see Forest G. Hill, *Roads, Rails and Waterways: The Army Engineers and Early Transportation* (Norman: University of Oklahoma Press, 1957).

topogs the secretary also transferred the board's responsibilities to the Topographical Bureau and elevated the bureau to independent status within the War Department.[23]

When Brevet Colonel Abert took over the Topographical Bureau, he began working in earnest to establish first an independent bureau followed by the establishment of a separate Corps of Topographical Engineers. He argued that the distinct duties between both kinds of engineers—topographers and fortifications engineers—were important enough to justify two separate corps. The Chief Engineer, Colonel Charles Gratiot, did not agree, arguing that surveys and construction were inseparable. As a slight concession, however, Abert received an appointment as assistant to the Chief Engineer for topographic matters. The following year he became a member of the Board of Engineers for Internal Improvements. At first Abert's role as an assistant chief still denied him complete control over topographic operations until his appointment to the Board of Engineers for Internal Improvements as coordinator of its operations. With the closing down of the board two years later Abert finally succeeded in getting the War Department to make the bureau a separate office directly responsible to the Secretary of War. Now free of direct Engineer Department control, Abert came one step closer to his goal of establishing a Corps of Topographical Engineers.[24]

Now for the first time a centralized Topographical Bureau controlled its own personnel and stood on an equal footing with the Engineer Department and the other elements of the Army staff. The duties of the bureau as outlined by the War Department were both military and civil. It continued to act as a topographic repository and took charge of military surveys and reconnaissances and the management of internal improvements. To overcome the limited officer strength authorization, the bureau continued the prac-

---

[23] Ryan, *Topographical Bureau Administrative History*, pp. 40, 72–75, 78–83; Schubert, *The Nation Builders*, pp. 17–19.

[24] Beers, "History of the Topographical Engineers," p. 289; Goetzmann, *Army Exploration*, pp. 9–10; Burr, "Historical Sketch," pp. 39–40; Ryan, *Topographical Bureau Administrative History*, pp. 76–83; Schubert, *The Nation Builders*, pp. 19–20.

tice of hiring civilian surveyors and borrowing infantry and artillery officers to do the surveys. The responsibilities taken over from the Board of Engineers for Internal Improvements included the supervision of over 50 personnel—12 civil engineers, 30 line officers, and Abert's own 10 topogs and a few attached Engineers. Up until 1836 the Corps of Engineers handled all river and harbor construction projects, but that year the War Department transferred several Great Lakes and Lake Champlain projects to the Topographical Bureau. In this manner Abert's mixed force of topogs proceeded to accomplish field surveys and some of the construction responsibilities for internal improvements.[25]

Soon the small bureau became overloaded with civil engineering projects. By 1838 construction activities had increased immensely and surpassed surveying in importance. The topogs were also helping the new railroads, a somewhat controversial practice, by doing surveys and supervising some construction. The system of detailing officers from other branches to the hard-pressed Topographical Bureau began to reveal drawbacks, particularly when requirements for the Seminole War resulted in the withdrawal of the detailed officers from the internal improvements work. The campaign against the Indians in Florida also demanded the services of topogs in the field and the preparation of a map of the peninsula. Several topogs remained in Florida through the 1840s, working on roads and improving the map.[26]

Other engineering requirements drew on the skills of the Topographical Engineers. In 1834 the bureau took on the construction of coastal lighthouses for the Treasury Department. The Treasury Department also reestablished the Coast Survey in 1836, and the project absorbed more of the Topographical Bureau's limited capability. Thereafter, until the abolishment of the Corps of Topographical Engineers in 1863 as a separate corps, one or more officers remained assigned to this survey.[27]

---

[25] Schubert, *The Nation Builders*, pp. 20–21; Ryan, *Topographical Bureau Administrative History*, pp. 83–84, 88, 91–93, 96, 102.

[26] Ryan, *Topographical Bureau Administrative History*, pp. 88, 94–96, 102–10, 115–16; Beers, "History of the Topographical Engineers," p. 290; Schubert, *The Nation Builders*, p. 23.

[27] Beers, "History of the Topographical Engineers," pp. 289–90; Schubert, *The Nation Builders*, pp. 27–28.

THE GENESIS OF A SMALL CORPS

The Topographical Engineers Corps, 1838–1845

In the meantime, Abert continued to pursue his goal to elevate his bureau to corps status. Although the bureau assumed the responsibility for the surveys for internal improvements, Congress and the War Department had failed to delineate the duties of the Corps of Engineers and the Topographical Bureau. Measures in Congress to establish the separate corps failed in 1836 and 1837 before finally passing in 1838. The Seminole War and the expansion of the western frontier prompted Congress to enact legislation to increase the size and improve the efficiency of the military establishment. This logically led to the establishment of the Corps of Topographical Engineers, and the law defined the duties of the two engineering corps. The topogs took on all the civil engineering works directed by the federal government, especially the improvements for rivers and harbors. The Corps of Engineers retained military construction projects, primarily the construction of coastal fortifications. In turn, the Topographical Engineers transferred to the Corps of Engineers its plans and drawings of fortifications.[28]

The act of 5 July 1838 establishing the new corps authorized a total of 36 officers but no enlisted personnel. More specifically, the act of Congress authorized a 36-man topographical engineering corps to "consist of one colonel, one lieutenant colonel, four majors, ten captains, ten first lieutenants, and ten second lieutenants." Colonel Abert became the chief of the corps and as such became equal in rank to all the other heads of Army services, including the Chief of Engineers. The act also ended the corps' dependence on civilian engineers.[29]

As a result of this reorganization, the operations of the Topographical Engineers expanded rapidly. The topogs assumed all responsibility for river and harbor improvements on the Mississippi, Ohio, Missouri, Arkansas, and Red rivers and in many harbors on the

---

[28] Ryan, *Topographical Bureau Administrative History,* pp. 111–42; Beers, "History of the Topographical Engineers," p. 348; Schubert, *The Nation Builders,* pp. 23–26.

[29] Quoted from Burr, "Historical Sketch," p. 40; Schubert, *The Nation Builders,* p. 24. Yearly rosters may be found in the Official Army Register. For a roster of the officers of the corps from its original complement upon formation in 1838 and changes prior to the Civil War, see Beers, "A History of the Topographical Engineers," p. 291; or Goetzmann, *Army Exploration,* pp. 435–37.

Atlantic and Gulf coasts and on the Great Lakes. Surveying of the Great Lakes intensified on a systematic basis in 1841. Topogs supervised the road-building projects in Wisconsin, Iowa, Michigan, Arkansas, and Florida. Ostensibly built for military purposes, these roads also eased the westward migration and delivery of mail, agriculture produce, and other commerce. Several topogs also reported to the State Department to work on various boundary surveys along the international borders, including the Texas Boundary Survey (1840–1841) and the Northeast Boundary Survey (1840–1850). By 1845 seven topogs were at work surveying the New Brunswick–Maine boundary. Other members of the corps supervised the construction of new military roads in the territories. In Washington the corps embarked on several important public works projects. Topogs resumed work on the long-delayed Washington Monument, began constructing an aqueduct in the Georgetown area of the District of Columbia, and started paving Pennsylvania Avenue between the Capitol and the White House. The topographers also found time to help the Corps of Engineers' military construction program by surveying potential fortification sites and reconnoitering strategic locations.[30]

In the 1840s the Topographical Engineers began a long series of military surveys. Surveys for defensive purposes were underway for the harbor at Portsmouth, New Hampshire, and roads to and from Washington, D.C. Very extensive surveys were also made around New Orleans and in Florida to include the Dry Tortugas and Key West harbor. Although well established in its public works role, the corps increased its role in western exploration and mapping.[31]

The Corps and Manifest Destiny

As the tension increased between the United States and Mexico in 1845, one of the topogs, Bvt. Captain John C. Fremont, prepared to depart on his third expedition to the West. Although strong American expansionist aspirations prompted the acquisition of the

---

[30] Beers, "History of the Topographical Engineers," pp. 348–49, 351; Ryan, *Topographical Bureau Administrative History,* pp. 143, 146, 148–49; Goetzmann, *Army Exploration,* pp. 11–12; Schubert, *The Nation Builders,* pp. 55–56; see also W. Turrentine Jackson, *Wagon Road West: A Study of Federal Road Surveys and Construction in the Trans-Mississippi West, 1846–1869* (New Haven, CT: Yale University Press, 1965).
[31] Schubert, *The Nation Builders,* p. 57.

THE GENESIS OF A SMALL CORPS 19

territories of California and New Mexico either by negotiation or by force, very little information and few reliable maps were available for military operations. The United States still knew very little about its own lands west of the Mississippi, a vast expanse of territory acquired years earlier as a result of the Louisiana Purchase in 1803.[32]

This requirement for geographic information turned the corps' attention to increasing its mapping of the West, and this in turn presented new opportunities for exploration. Except for Stephen H. Long, now an older major engaged in river improvement work, only Fremont had any significant exploration experience west of the Mississippi. East of the river the corps had paid particular attention to its role as a government engineering, public works, and construction agency. Now necessity prompted the corps' involvement westward.

Several concerns in the West confronted President Polk's new administration. First, restless Indian tribes needed to be appeased. In particular, the mobile, horse-mounted Indians of the western plains preyed on unescorted settlers and traders passing through their territories. Second, accurate maps for military purposes were either lacking or inadequate. As a result, an urgent requirement induced military planners to launch a series of military expeditions to gather information about the areas in contention with Mexico. Third, the movement of armies and their logistical trains required a knowledge of existing and proposed routes for transporting supplies.

At the time the corps had only a single map of the entire trans-Mississippi West, an unpublished 1844 map of Texas compiled by 1st Lt. William H. Emory from available sources. Josiah Gregg's *Commerce of the Prairies* (1844) and Tanner's *American Atlas* (1839) offered some reliable information, but generally the commercial maps, largely based on hearsay and conjecture, were woefully inaccurate. Even Emory's map relied on less than accurate information. The forthcoming maps resulting from Fremont's 1843–1844 expedition tracing the route along the Oregon Trail were still in preparation. For the most part the available maps proved unsatisfactory for use by military commanders in the field. As a result, the Army had to rely on military expeditions to reconnoiter and map the terrain, a responsibility of the Corps of Topographical Engineers.

---

[32] Unless otherwise indicated the following paragraphs are based on Goetzmann, *Army Exploration,* pp. 109–11.

During this period the Corps of Topographical Engineers had evolved into an agency in support of Manifest Destiny—the manifestation of the American urge to expand the nation's boundaries westward to the Pacific Ocean. It was during this stage of collecting topographic and geographic data in the West that members of the Corps of Topographical Engineers, particularly Fremont, were drawn into the conflict with Mexico.[33]

That the members of the corps became involved in efforts to expand the nation seemed only natural—their exploration and mapping simply became the by-product of any new territorial gains. Fremont, one of the more illustrious members of the corps, has been both accused of and credited with being the agent of Manifest Destiny in the seizure of California. Historian William H. Goetzmann, in his seminal work on the topogs' explorations in the West, writes that the corps was a central institution of Manifest Destiny as well as the focus for a national spirit of romanticism. In the drive westward, he states, the corps served as the agent of a democratic collective will.[34]

By 1845 Manifest Destiny provided the impetus for deploying the Topographical Engineers in areas close to the Mexican border. Three Army expeditions, two composed entirely of topogs, were dispatched westward. Although their chief task directly related to the threat of war, the Army topographers also received instructions to gather scientific information.

Colonel Kearny's Mounted Reconnaissance, 1845

On 23 May 1845, Colonel Stephen Watts Kearny's dragoon force of mounted infantrymen set out from Fort Leavenworth, Kansas. The expedition headed south to Bent's Fort (located in southeastern Colorado) and returned to Fort Leavenworth via a route paralleling the Arkansas River. By following this route Kearny's troopers provided some security to the wagon trains traveling between Santa Fe and St. Louis, and the presence of the horse soldiers on the plains also offered some measure of protection to the wagon trains moving along the Oregon Trail. Besides gathering

---

[33] For a discussion of this phrase see Ray A. Billington, *The Far Western Frontier, 1830–1860* (New York: Harper and Row, 1950), pp. 148–50.

[34] Goetzmann, *Army Exploration*, pp. 4–6, 17–21, and 429; Schubert, *The Nation Builders*, pp. 54, 56–57.

THE GENESIS OF A SMALL CORPS 21

geographic information of the border regions the reconnaissance succeeded in making a strong show of force and impressed the Indians, deterring them from any outbursts if war did break out with Mexico. In the end, Kearny's military reconnaissance proved the worthiness of American cavalry mobility.[35]

The Topographical Engineers attached 2d Lt. William B. Franklin to the expedition to record the information gained and to map the region. Franklin arrived at Fort Leavenworth after Kearny's departure, and he joined the column eight days later. The dragoons had headed northwest along the Oregon Trail toward Fort Laramie, then following the North Platte River, they passed Chimney Rock on 10 June. When the expedition arrived at the fort on the 18th, Kearny called for an immediate council with the Sioux Indians. Franklin recorded the colonel's use of pageantry and strength to impress and deter the Indians from attacking the wagon trains along the Oregon Trail. The young topographer observed that during the parley the Indians exhibited feelings of guilt and knew that the arrival of the dragoons meant possible punishment for past misdeeds. Kearny left Fort Laramie with an agreement from the temporarily awed Indians to refrain from attacking the Oregon-bound settlers. The dragoons resumed their march west to South Pass, passing such landmarks as Independence Rock and Red Buttes. After returning to Fort Laramie, the column turned south and arrived at Bent's Fort in late July. The soldiers resumed the march the next day and returned to Fort Leavenworth by 24 August 1845.[36]

The reconnaissance achieved impressive results. The mobile force marched some 2,200 miles in 99 days, and in his report

---

[35] Stephen W. Kearny, "Report of a Summer Campaign to the Rocky Mountains... in 1845," Sen. Exec. Doc. 1. 29th Cong., 1st sess., 1846, p. 210; Goetzmann, *Army Exploration,* pp. 111–12. This report contains a map and abstract of the journal of the accompanying Topographical Engineer, Lieutenant William B. Franklin. Franklin's journal has also been reprinted. See Frank N. Schubert (ed.), *March to South Pass: Lieutenant William B. Franklin's Journal of the Kearny Expedition of 1845,* 1, Engineer Historical Studies (Washington, D.C.: U.S. Army Corps of Engineers, 1979).

[36] National Archives, Record Group 77, Records of the Office of the Chief of Engineers. Letters Received by the Topographical Bureau (hereafter cited as RG 77, Records of the OCE, LR, TE 77), Franklin to Abert, 5 Nov. 1845, LR 150, TE 77. This letter contained Franklin's full report, which was abstracted for inclusion in Kearny's report.

Kearny suggested repeating such excursions in lieu of establishing "expensive" forts. His ideas differed quite a bit from those of Fremont and other topographers. The topogs viewed the establishment of forts as an inducement to frontier settlement and protection along key trade and emigration trails.[37]

Franklin prepared a careful map and report of the route for publication as part of Kearny's report. The printed report included abstracts of the topographer's journal along with those of other officers on the reconnaissance, but they did not provide much new information. The map, however, proved of value since it provided the corps with an exercise in western map-making. In addition, most of Franklin's map incorporated the information Fremont had obtained in his 1843 and 1843–1844 expeditions. In any case, the information gathered on the plains country served as a useful guide to settlers moving westward over the route.[38]

Much broader in scope were the two topographical expeditions that set forth that year. Both originated from orders issued to Bvt. Captain Fremont—his and an ancillary expedition under 2d Lt. James W. Abert, Colonel Abert's son. In these cases, however, Topographical Engineer officers, not line officers, commanded the expeditions. Besides the military missions assigned to the topographers, the soldier-scientists of the corps also received instructions to gather scientific data on the areas they passed through.

The Corps on the Eve of War

For the most part the topogs moved easily from their role as civil engineers and scientists to their primary duties of map-making, intelligence, and military assignments in support of the Army under wartime conditions. To improve the work of the corps Colonel Abert persistently urged establishing a unit of topographical enlisted men to help in surveys and military duties. Doing so would relieve the corps from detailing soldiers from other branches, particularly from the artillery, and save on the cost of hiring civilians. Congress, how-

---

[37] Goetzmann, *Army Exploration*, pp. 113–15.

[38] Ibid., pp. 115–16; Franklin to Abert, 5 Nov. 1845, LR 150, TE 77; Carl I. Wheat, *Mapping the Trans-Mississippi West, 1540–1861*, II (San Francisco: The Institute of Historical Cartography, 1958), pp. 191–92. A reproduction of this map is opposite page 192.

THE GENESIS OF A SMALL CORPS

ever, did not act on this recommendation. The corps, therefore, remained composed entirely of officers, and the topogs continued the practice of contracting with civilians.[39]

Once his topogs joined a field command Colonel Abert lost direct control over them. At best, Abert could request the commanders to allow his Topographical Engineers to do additional tasks desired by his bureau. From a strictly military standpoint, the topographers assigned to a command became staff officers. During the course of the war nearly half of the members of the corps served under the commands of Generals Stephen W. Kearny, Winfield Scott, Zachary Taylor, and John E. Wool. However, the majority of these topogs kept their technical lines of communication open to the bureau. Throughout the war the topogs in the field consistently submitted letters and copies of reports to Colonel Abert in Washington.[40]

The United States entered this war like many others, unprepared. Campaign plans did not exist. The small and inexperienced Army needed to be expanded, trained, equipped, and deployed great distances to operate in vast unknown lands. The Army did not have an intelligence system, and an urgent need arose for reliable information on the geography and topography of the envisioned war zone. Commanders appointed to lead campaigns in Texas and Mexico (including the future American Southwest) lacked information on roads, sources of supplies, facilities, obstacles, and even the climate. This ignorance of geography and lack of military intelligence dramatically increased the work of the corps as soon as its members joined their field commands.[41]

---

[39] Ryan, *Topographical Bureau Administrative History*, p. 147.

[40] Ibid., pp. 150–51. Several of the reports cited in this publication have copies filed in the Topographical Bureau and are housed in the National Archives.

[41] George L. Rives, *The United States and Mexico, 1921–48*, II (New York: Charles Scribner's Sons, 1913), p. 195.

CHAPTER 2

On to the Golden Gate With Fremont

Among the Topographical Engineers, John Charles Fremont stands out as a well-known explorer and the conqueror of California. Biographers and historians have subjected his career to the closest scrutiny and criticism. Fremont was not as much an explorer of the unknown as he was a scientist and cartographer. Allan Nevins, in his biography of Fremont, used an appropriate sobriquet: the "Pathmarker." Following his successful and highly acclaimed expedition to the West in 1843–1844, Fremont returned to Washington. With the help of his wife and Charles Preuss, his principal topographic assistant, he began to prepare a report and map of his route to Oregon.[1]

---

[1] Biographies on Fremont are numerous. The most reliable is Allan Nevins, *Fremont, Pathmarker of the West* (New York: Longmens, Green and Co., 1955). Another biography that outlines his explorations in detail is Frederick S. Dellenbaugh, *Fremont and '49* (New York: Knickerbocker Press, 1914). Other biographies include Herbert Bashford and Harr Wagner, *A Man Unafraid: The Story of John Charles Fremont* (San Francisco: Harr Wagner Publishing Corp, 1927); Alice Eyer, *The Famous Fremonts and Their America* (n.p.: Fine Arts Press, 1948); Cardinal Goodwin, *John Charles Fremont: An Explanation of His Career* (Stanford, CA: Stanford University Press, 1930). Several biographies were published in 1856 at the time of his campaign for the presidency and are highly laudatory in nature: John Bigelow, *Memoir of the Life and Public Service of John Charles Fremont* (Boston: Ticknor and Fields, 1856). This work is valuable for the correspondence and orders included. All of the foregoing biographies are pro-Fremont; however, Nevins and Dellenbaugh's works do not hesitate to criticize Fremont. The Fremont papers have been published by Donald Jackson and Mary Lee Spence (eds.), *The Expeditions of John Charles Fremont*, 3 vols., by the University of Illinois Press. Fremont wrote *Memoirs of My Life* (Chicago: Belford, Clarke and Co., 1887). Portions of this work and his "Geographical Memoir" were published by Allan Nevins in *Narratives of Exploration and Adventure* (New York, 1956). Besides the biographies, the explorations are outlined in Goetzmann, *Army Exploration*, p. 117.

Orders for Fremont's Third Expedition, 1845

On 12 February 1845 Colonel Abert sent to the newly breveted Captain Fremont a letter of instructions and orders for his next expedition. The colonel assigned two lieutenants as assistants and granted authority for the topographer to hire civilians. Abert instructed Fremont to survey the Arkansas and Red rivers within the U.S. boundary, particularly noting the navigable properties of each. Fremont was also to survey the area within a reasonable distance of Bent's Fort.[2]

Abert's instructions also gave some indication of further exploration. The same paragraph stated that the general outline of Fremont's duties was previously indicated in the chief topographer's annual report of the corps in 1844. In that report to Congress, Abert had also recommended an expedition into the still unexplored regions of the West to survey the Great Basin. From there the expedition would move from the Great Salt Lake to the lakes in Oregon, with a return route to follow the Colorado River toward Santa Fe to the headwaters of the Canadian River and then to its junction with the Arkansas River.[3]

No evidence exists that Fremont received direct orders to proceed to California. Instead he believed that "President Polk entered on his office with a fixed determination to acquire California, if he could acquire it in an honorable and just manner." Fremont's close association with his father-in-law, Senator Thomas Hart Benton of Missouri, had made him aware of the problems with Mexico and the fear of a British plot to seize California. Even before his marriage to Jessie Benton in 1839, Fremont became attracted to the cause of Manifest Destiny as espoused by the senator. The new Secretary of the Navy, George Bancroft, also professed an

---

[2] These orders can be found in Donald Jackson and Mary Lee Spence (eds.), *The Expeditions of John Charles Fremont*, I (Urbana, IL: University of Illinois Press, 1970), pp. 395–97; National Archives, 77, Records of the OCE, Letters Sent by the Topographical Bureau, Abert to Fremont, 12 Feb 1845, LS 211, TE 77 (hereafter cited as LS, TE 77). See also Goetzmann, *Army Exploration*, p. 117.

[3] "The Annual Report of the Chief of Topographical Engineers," Report of the Secretary of War, Sen. Doc. 1, 28th Cong., 2d sess., 1844, pp. 218, 221–22. Colonel Abert's words are "The general outline of Captain Fremont's duties are indicated in the annual report from this office."

eager interest to add California and the entire Southwest to the United States.[4]

Thus, regardless of Colonel Abert's 12 February instructions, Fremont already had decided on another expedition to California. He could count on support by Senator Benton, Secretary Bancroft, and other government officials. Association with his father-in-law and other influential persons, coupled with his recently acquired fame, gave Fremont wide latitude in his next mission.[5]

Fremont's writings following the expedition made no mention of secret orders for the conquest of California. In defending his actions in a magazine article some 46 years later, he wrote: "The distance was too great for timely communication, but failing this, I was given discretion to act."[6] No evidence exists, however, that Fremont's immediate supervisor confirmed these instructions. Colonel Abert's guidance seemed clear enough in that Fremont should explore regions "within reasonable distance of Bent's Fort."[7] However, Fremont's magazine article claimed: "But in arranging this expedition the eventualities of war had to be considered. My private instructions were, if needed, to foil England carrying the war now imminent with Mexico into its territory of California. At the fitting moment that territory was seized, and held by the United States." The Topographical Bureau's files do not reveal these "private instructions." If they were known to Colonel Abert, all he could do, considering the powerful supporters of Fremont, was tactfully ignore them.[8]

By 10 April Colonel Abert, possibly prescient to Fremont's intentions, issued supplemental instructions to the explorer. The colonel ordered his son, 2d Lt. James W. Abert, and 2d Lt. William G. Peck to accompany the expedition. Using the worsening relations with Mexico as a basis, the chief topographer advised:

On arriving at Bent's Fort, if you find it desirable, you will detach a lieutenant and party to explore the Southern Rocky Mountains and the regions

---

[4] Fremont, *Narratives*, p. 435. Background information on this subject is included in Goetzmann, *Army Exploration*, pp. 102–03; Nevins, *Pathmarker*, pp. 192–204; Bauer, *The Mexican War*, p. 165.

[5] Fremont, *Narratives*, p. 435.

[6] John Charles Fremont, "The Conquest of California," *The Century Magazine*, 41 (Apr 1891): 920.

[7] Quoted in Jackson and Spence (eds.), *Fremont*, I, pp. 407–08; Abert to Fremont, 12 Feb 1856, LS 211, TE 77.

[8] Fremont, "The Conquest of California," *The Century Magazine*, 919.

south of the Arkansas under such instructions as your experience shall suggest.... It is extremely desirable that you should be in before the adjournment of the next session of Congress in order that if operations should be required in that country the information obtained may be at command.[9]

Fremont's only recorded letter to Colonel Abert during this planning stage was a request for small arms and a mountain howitzer. Abert concurred, although it was not usual practice for a scientific expedition to have artillery. Fremont, never at a loss for well placed words, defended his request by adding: "The uncertain and frequently hostile disposition of the people inhabiting the countries along the line of exploration render every advantage of arms which can be afforded material to the safety of our very small party." [10]

Colonel Abert also issued more guidance before the party's departure. On 14 May the colonel provided guidelines for the training of the two lieutenants. On the 26th he informed the explorer to use his own discretion as to the size of the expedition. This seems to add more credence to the colonel's possible knowledge of the "private instructions" and may explain his decision to order a detached party. He wrote to Fremont that Lieutenant Abert's party should return as soon as it had finished its work "in order that the expenses of the expedition may be reduced, and funds be left to meet the events of your own efforts for more distant discoveries, which will probably keep you some time longer in the field than he [Abert] will be." [11]

The chief Army topographer, however, never raised the issue of any direct violation of official orders. No doubt he realized that the arguments of the opposing power structure, if charges were made against Fremont for insubordination, would be insurmountable. The colonel most likely knew that his subordinate's plans had the sanction of high government officials. It is strange, however, that he did not incorporate that knowledge in later correspondence to the explorer. Indeed, by the end of May, the news of Fremont's extended expedition even appeared in a Washington newspaper:

[9] Jackson and Spence (eds.), *Fremont*, I, pp. 407–08; Abert to Fremont, 10 Apr 1845, LS 118, TE 77.
[10] Jackson and Spence (eds.), *Fremont*, I, p. 419; Abert to Fremont, 9 May 1845, LR 130, TE 77.
[11] Jackson and Spence (eds.), *Fremont*, I, pp. 422–23; Abert to Fremont, 14 May 1845, LS 133, TE 77; Abert to Fremont, 26 May 1845, LS 136, TE 77.

Captain Fremont has gone on his third expedition, determined upon a complete military and scientific exploration of the vast unknown region between the Rocky Mountains and the Pacific, and between the Oregon River and the Gulf of California. The expedition is expected to continue nearly two years. Its successful results are regarded with the highest degree of interest by all the friends of Science in America and Europe.[12]

Fremont Organizes His Expedition

In May 1845 Fremont left Washington for St. Louis, where he assembled his expedition. There the topog captain recruited an exceptional group of men. He hired Edward M. Kern, a young Philadelphia artist and naturalist, in place of Charles Preuss as his topographic assistant. All the other members of the party except Abert and Peck were civilians. Many of this group had been with Fremont before, and they included experienced guides Joseph Walker, Alexis Godey, Basil Lajeunesse, Lucien Maxwell, and Theodore Talbot. Kit Carson, the famed frontier scout, his partner, Dick Owens, and an exotic escort of 12 Delaware Indians later joined the expedition at Bent's Fort.[13]

Several historians have stressed that the large number of people and the armaments of the expedition are evidence of Fremont's intention to conquer California. Allan Nevins noted that "Obviously, sixty men were an excessive force for a mere topographical party, and sharpshooting is not a topographical necessity." Frederick S. Dellenbaugh concurs. Fremont's devotees, such as Herbert Bashford and Harr Wagner, however, wrote that the

---

[12] Washington *Union News*, May 1845, as quoted in Eyer, *The Famous Fremonts and Their America*, p. 137.

[13] Goetzmann, *Army Exploration*, p. 118. Preuss stayed behind and prepared a map based on data from Fremont's second expedition, which was actually a series of large-scale maps carefully depicting all necessary information along the line of travel. For a detailed discussion and reproductions of these maps see Wheat, *Mapping the Trans-Mississippi West*, III, pp. 24–29. Some of the maps may also be seen reproduced in Goetzmann, *Army Exploration*, back cover in original edition; and in Jackson and Spence (eds.), *Fremont*, Map Portfolio and "Commentary," pp. 14–15. For more on Kern and Talbot see Robert V. Hine, *Edward Kern and American Expansion* (New Haven, CT: Yale University Press, 1982); and Robert V. Hine and Savoie Lottinville (eds.), *Soldier in the West: Letters of Theodore Talbot During His Services in California, Mexico and Oregon 1845–53* (Norman, OK: University of Oklahoma Press, 1972).

weaponry "was a great acquisition to topographical work, marksmanship being essential qualification."[14]

The Route to California

On 20 June 1845, the topographic party set out from St. Louis and headed toward Bent's Fort to rendezvous with Kit Carson and the others. When Fremont made clear his intention to maintain strict discipline, 13 men quickly dropped out. He moved his men at a rapid pace, and by 2 August they reached Bent's Fort. While outfitting his party and waiting for Carson and Owens to come up from Taos, New Mexico, Fremont issued instructions to Lieutenant Abert for conducting the auxiliary expedition. By 16 August both parties had set out, Abert down the Arkansas and Fremont up that river to the west. Fremont noted as he left the fort that he had "a well appointed compact party of sixty, mostly experienced and self-reliant men, equal to any emergency likely to occur, and willing to meet it."[15]

Fremont carried with him some of the most up-to-date topographic equipment of the period. The topographic tools included a portable transit for measuring horizontal and vertical angles, two sextants for measuring the altitudes of celestial bodies, and two pocket chronometers for precisely measuring time, an important factor in determining the longitude. The delicate barometers used for meteorological observations and measuring elevations received some damage along the way.[16]

By 20 August Fremont's party had encamped along the Arkansas near present-day Pueblo, Colorado. Fremont later recalled the topographic capabilities of his expedition:

I had me good instruments for astronomical observations, among them a portable transit instrument. This I set up, and established here one of the four principal positions on which depend the longitudes of the region

---

[14] Nevins, *Pathmarker*, p. 207; Dellenbaugh, *Fremont and '49*, p. 288; Bashford and Wagner, *A Man Unafraid*, p. 157.
[15] Fremont, *Narratives*, p. 437; Goetzmann, *Army Exploration*, p. 118.
[16] John C. Fremont, "Geographic Memoir upon Upper California, in Illustration of his Map of Oregon and California: Addressed to the Senate of the United States by John C. Fremont," Sen. Misc. Doc. 148, 30th Cong., 1st sess., 1848, p. 46; James W. Abert, "Journal of Lieutenant James A. [*sic*] Abert, from Bent's Fort to St. Louis in 1845," Sen. Exec. Doc. 438, 29th Cong., 1st sess., 1846, pp. 7–8. For a description of mapping techniques see Goetzmann, *Army Exploration*, pp. 438–39.

embraced by the expeditions. The longitude was determined by moon culminations and the latitude by sextant observation of Polaris and stars in the south.[17]

Next the party headed across Colorado and Utah. On 26 August they camped at the Royal Gorge of the Arkansas and arrived at the headwaters of that river in Mexican territory on 2 September. Fremont and his group pushed on through the Tennessee Pass and across the Continental Divide. On the 4th they reached the Piney River, a tributary of the Colorado, and by 13 October the party arrived at the south shore of the Great Salt Lake. The expedition next struck west across the desert toward the mountains and California. Fremont aimed his march toward a mountain, which he named Pilot Peak. This desert route later gained fame among the westward emigrants and became know as the Hastings Cutoff.[18]

On 5 November Fremont split his force into two parties. Winter was approaching, and he expected to encounter snow in crossing the Sierras into California. Considering it "imprudent to linger long in the examination of the Great Basin," he decided to divide the party and use the interval of good weather to run two separate survey lines across the Basin. Walker guided the larger, main group under Theodore Talbot. With Kern serving as topographer, the group followed the more familiar route along the Humboldt River to Carson's Sink, then moved southward to the rendezvous point at Walker Lake. Meanwhile, Fremont's smaller party moved through central Nevada from the Humboldt to Franklin Lake, then southwest skirting the Alkali Desert. He continued westward to Walker Lake in western Nevada, thereby blazing the most feasible trail of the time across Nevada. As a result the topog dispelled the idea that the Great Basin from the Great Salt Lake to the Sierras was the sandy, barren plain described by others. Instead Fremont found the area traversed by parallel mountain ranges covered with adequate timber, grass, and wildlife. The group reached

---

[17] Fremont, *Narratives,* pp. 440–41.
[18] Fremont, *Narratives,* pp. 441–43, 446–47; Dellenbaugh, *Fremont and '49,* pp. 291–92; Goetzmann, *Army Exploration,* p. 119. Nevins noted that Fremont apparently did not know of Jediah Smith's crossing in 1827. Walker and Peter S. Ogden crossed over north of the Great Salt Lake to the Humboldt, and the Bartleson-Bidwell party crossed over in 1841. See Nevins, *Pathmarker,* pp. 472–73 fn.

the Walker Lake rendezvous point on 24 November, and three days later the main party joined them.[19]

Still concerned about the difficulties of leading the entire party and its baggage through snow covered passes in the Sierras, Fremont again divided his party. This time he lead a selected group of 15 via the shorter route through the mountains, while Kern and the main body followed a southerly route around the mountains. A blanket of snow covered the peaks and ridge lines, but Fremont's party succeeded in finding a clear pass and safely descended into the California valley. This pass, later named for the ill-fated Donner pioneer party, became part of a new trail from the Great Salt Lake to California. The topog captain could also take credit for blazing this route, though not through the pass, and rightfully deserved the appellation of "Pathfinder."[20]

Fremont Arrives in California

On 10 December Fremont reached John Sutter's settlement at New Helvetia, better known as Sutter's Fort and the future site of Sacramento. Sutter, who was away when the topogs arrived, returned the following day, and the settler extended the same hospitality given to the explorer the year before. Four days later Fremont departed in the direction of the San Joaquin Valley to link up with Kern. The main party had not arrived, and the topog decided to rove around the valley. After a while he concluded that the main party had elected to take its time to ease the burden on their pack animals. Since they had experienced guides, Fremont did not become overly concerned for the larger party's safety. By mid-January he decided to return to Sutter's Fort to await their arrival.[21]

Now that he was in California, legally part of Mexico and foreign territory, Fremont felt obliged to contact the authorities there and stock up on provisions for the winter. Resting until late Jan-

---

[19] Fremont, *Narratives,* pp. 448–54; Nevins, *Pathmarker,* p. 213. Kern's journal was published more than 20 years later. Edward M. Kern, "Journal of an Exploration of Mary's of Humbolt River, Carson Lake, and Owens River and Lakes in 1845," appendix to James H. Simpson, *Report of Explorations across the Great Basin of the Territory of Utah . . . in 1859* (Washington, D.C.: Government Printing Office, 1876), pp. 477–80.
[20] Fremont, *Narratives,* pp. 454–57; Nevins, *Pathmarker,* pp. 215–16.
[21] Fremont, *Narratives,* p. 458–64.

uary, he then traveled to Monterey to call on the American consul, Thomas O. Larkin, and the Mexican Commandant, Don Jose Castro. Fremont arrived at a time of internal tension, for Castro and the governor of California, Don Pio Pico, were at odds. In addition, the previous governor had been ousted earlier, and contacts outside California were virtually nonexistent. The presence of the well armed topographic party aroused Castro's attention and suspicions about American intentions in California. He had reason to be concerned, for only a few years earlier an American naval force had temporarily occupied Monterey.[22]

Castro treated the American explorer with courtesy, giving him permission to resupply but not any written consent to stay in California. The topographer told Castro of his peaceful intent, and assured him that his party only carried weapons to hunt game and for protection against the Indians. His purpose for being in the area, Fremont explained, had to do with finding a shorter route to Oregon and other "scientific purposes," but winter had caught him in the mountains. He told Castro he had come to Monterey seeking permission to set up a winter camp in the San Joaquin Valley. With Castro's verbal approval for the Americans to stay for a while in the Sacramento Valley, Fremont moved his party to Laguna, a vacant ranch 13 miles southeast of San Jose, for refitting. During this period the main party rejoined the expedition.[23]

The courtesy extended to the expedition to remain in California dwindled as the Americans appeared to linger in the area. Fremont's men appeared to get along well with the local Spanish speaking Californians, drawn by curiosity to visit the encampment. During these gatherings the Californians impressed Fremont and his colleagues with their fine horsemanship. Near the end of February Fremont moved his 60-man party southwest toward the settled Santa Clara valley. On 3 March they encamped on the Hartwell ranch near present-day Salinas, only 25 miles from Monterey. Two days later the

---

[22] Ibid., pp. 464–66.
[23] Fremont, *Narratives*, pp. 465–68; H.H. Bancroft outlines the details of the Californians' internal problems in *History of California* (San Francisco: A.L. Bancroft and Co., 1886), IV, pp. 518–45, V, pp. 30–53. See also Justin H. Smith, *War With Mexico* (New York: Macmillan Co., 1919) I, pp. 315–30; Nevins, *Pathmarker*, p. 218; Eisenhower, *So Far From God*, p. 211.

disturbed Castro dispatched one of his cavalry officers with an ultimatum ordering the expedition to leave California.[24]

The Mexican authorities had every right to demand Fremont's withdrawal. He had marched into settled regions under the guise of a peaceful scientific expedition during times of difficult relations between Mexico and the United States. Men like Carson, Walker, Owens, the other mountain men, and the Delaware Indians hardly looked like peaceful scientific types. Historians generally hold the view that Fremont was biding his time and waiting for the expected news that war had been declared. Bernard De Voto wrote of Fremont in *The Year of Decision, 1846,* that "destiny was stirring in his soul."[25]

Fremont's supporters portray the topographer's later actions as an example of the American spirit that nothing could interfere with Manifest Destiny. The topog boldly retired to Hawk's Peak, a rough mountain overlooking the plains of San Juan and Monterey. There he chose a strong position near the summit, strengthening it with a rude fort of fallen oak trees. By defiantly hoisting the American flag above the fort, Fremont put Larkin in a difficult position. The U.S. government entrusted the consul, as a confidential agent, to work behind the scenes to win over the population, thereby easing the way to attach California to the Union. Fremont's actions seemed inconsistent with Larkin's policy of conciliation. The consul's correspondence with Washington, however, did suggest some sympathy for Fremont's unusual mission.[26]

For all the outspokenness on both sides, no epic conflict occurred at Hawk's Peak. The flagpole fell down late on the third day. This provided Fremont with a good excuse to retire north to Lassen's Meadows. The party traveled in short stages, hardly the

---

[24] Fremont, *Narratives*, pp. 467–71; Eisenhower, *So Far From God*, p. 211.

[25] Fremont, *Narratives*, pp. 467–71; Bancroft, *History of California*, V, pp. 7 and 102; Dellenbaugh, *Fremont and '49*, pp. 310–11; Nevins, *Pathmarker*, p. 227; Bernard De Voto, *The Year of Decision 1846* (Boston: Houghton Mifflin Co., 1943), p. 42. The letters from the California officials are contained in Thomas O. Larkin, *The Larkin Papers*, IV (Berkeley, CA: University of California Press, 1951), pp. 228–29.

[26] Bigelow, *Memoir of the Life and Public Service of John Charles Fremont*, p. 133; Bancroft, *History of California*, V, pp. 12–13; Rives, *The United States and Mexico, 1821–48*, p. 174; Bauer, *The Mexican War*, p. 166.

flight described by boasting Mexican officials. By 22 March they encamped on the American River not far from Sutter's Fort. Since Fremont planned to retire to the Klamath Indian country and Oregon, he aptly justified his decision to leave the Hawk's Peak:

> The protecting favor which the ways of all civilized governments and peoples accords [*sic*] to scientific expeditions impaired on me, even here, a corresponding obligation; and I now felt myself bound to go on my way, having given General Castro sufficient time to execute his threat. Besides, I kept always in mind the object of the Government to obtain possession of California and would not let a proceeding which was mostly personal put obstacles in the way.[27]

The Mysterious Rendezvous With Lieutenant Gillespie, USMC

After moving around the Sacramento valley for about a month, Fremont next headed toward Oregon's Klamath Lake to make topographic observations. He could easily have resumed his march via his old trail to the Columbia River. Instead he elected to push westward into the unexplored Cascade Range fully aware that this route ran through hostile Klamath Indian country. The party reached the lake on 6 May. On the evening of the 8th two horsemen rode into camp and informed him that a Lieutenant Archibald Gillespie, U.S. Marine Corps, was approximately 100 miles away and was bearing dispatches for Fremont. The topog hastily decided to rendezvous with the Marine Corps courier. He picked ten of his best men, including Kit Carson, Owens, four other seasoned men, and four of the Delawares, and quickly set forth.[28]

Lieutenant Gillespie had just completed an incredible and perilous journey by way of Mexico to deliver secret messages to Larkin and Fremont and to relay information to the Pacific fleet. The planning in Washington, particularly on the part of Polk, Bancroft, and Benton, was charged with intrigue. Secretary of State James Buchanan had forwarded only one official dispatch, dated 17 October 1845, along with a letter of introduction. These documents were directed to Larkin, and instructed him to pursue plans for

---

[27] Fremont, *Narratives,* pp. 472, 477.
[28] Ibid., pp. 494–96.

peaceful secession and later annexation of California by the voluntary act of its inhabitants.[29]

Bancroft instructed Gillespie to bring Fremont up to date on recent international developments. Fremont and Gillespie became instant allies. In addition to facing a common danger, both were quite compatible as energetic and impetuous individuals and contemptuous of the Spanish speaking Californians. After Gillespie informed him of Buchanan's instructions to Larkin, Fremont felt the time had arrived to act:

> The information through Gillespie had resolved me from my duty as an explorer, and I was left to my duty as an officer of the United States Army, with the further authoritative knowledge that the Government intended to take California. I was warned by my government of the new danger against which I was bound to defend myself; and it had been made known to me now on the authority of the Secretary of the Navy that to obtain California was the chief object of the President.[30]

Fremont also used the personal correspondence from Benton and his family to reinforce his decision. According to Fremont and his wife, the correspondence (which has not been preserved) contained a family cipher warning him to be prepared to act. As Fremont later wrote:

> The letter from Senator Benton, while apparently of friendship and family details, contained passages and suggestions which, read by the light of many conversations and discussions with himself and others at Washington, clearly indicated to me that I was required by the Government to find out any foreign schemes in relation to California and, so far as might be in my power to counteract them.

Fremont pondered and reached the conclusion that night: "The time has come. England must not get a foothold. We must be first. Act—discreetly, but positively."[31]

---

[29] The letters were dated 17 October and 1 November 1845. Buchanan's instructions in the 17 October letter were committed to memory by Gillespie and destroyed because he was subject to search while passing through foreign territory. Larkin, *The Larkin Papers*, IV, pp. 44–47, 82. Also see Werner H. Marti, *Messenger of Destiny: The California Adventures 1846–1847, of Archibald H. Gillespie, U.S. Marine Corps* (San Francisco, CA: John Howell Books, 1960), pp. 8–9.

[30] Fremont, *Narratives*, p. 497; Eisenhower, *So Far From God*, pp. 212–13.

[31] Ibid., p. 498. For a detailed discussion of the cipher and dispatch from Buchanan see Josiah Royce, *California from the Conquest in 1848 to the Second Vigilance Committee in San Francisco* (Boston and New York: Houghton Mifflin Co., 1914), pp. 123–50. Senator Benton also gave his views on this subject in support of Fremont. Thomas Hart Benton, *Thirty Years View* (New York: D. Appleton and Co., 1854), II, pp. 689–91.

Fremont reasoned correctly that the United States and Mexico were at war, although the news of the declaration of war by the United States probably had not reached California. At the time Fremont received his communiques, however, the first major battles of the war were taking place in Texas. He later explained, "I saw the way opening clear before me. War with Mexico was inevitable; and a grand opportunity now presented itself to realize in their fullest extent the farsighted views of Senator Benton, and make the Pacific Ocean the western boundary of the United States." The topog next formulated the first steps toward the conquest of California, which summarized his actions for the balance of that fateful year of 1846:

> I resolved to move forward on the opportunity and return forthwith to the Sacramento Valley in order to bring to bear all the influences I could command. Except myself, then and for nine months [actually six months; Brig. Gen. Stephen W. Kearny arrived in December] afterward, there was no other officer of the Army in California. The citizen party under my command was made up of picked men, and though small in number, constituted a formidable nucleus for frontier warfare, and many of its members commanded the confidence of the emigration.[32]

Fremont had to deal first with another problem. That night a band of Klamath Indians attacked the party's camp, and the Americans suffered several casualties. When Fremont and his entire party returned to the Klamath Lake region in California, they exacted vengeance on the Indians there.[33]

Fremont and the Bear Flag Revolt

Fremont returned to Lassen's ranch on 24 May. Upon arriving he received word of a recent Mexican proclamation expelling all aliens who had not taken up Mexican citizenship. The edict also prohibited any further emigration of Americans from the United States. This

---

[32] Ibid., p. 499.

[33] Ibid., pp. 499–507. Kit Carson gave his version in a later interview in the Washington *Union News*, 16 June 1846; Kit Carson, *Kit Carson's Autobiography*, Milo M. Quaife (ed.) (Lincoln, NE: University of Nebraska Press, 1935), pp. 96–99. See also Edwin L. Sabin, *Kit Carson Days 1809–1868*, I (n.p.: Press of the Pioneers, Inc., 1935), pp. 443–44.

measure gave Fremont further justification to remain in California: to protect American lives and stand ready to strike in case of war.[34]

On 24 May he wrote to Benton, ostensibly giving reasons for returning to the United States via California. Larkin supported Fremont and wrote that the heavy snow inhibited the explorer from taking an alternative return route through Oregon. At that time of the year, the snow and the hostile Indians in Oregon gave a good pretext for venturing again into California.[35]

By 30 May Fremont encamped at the Buttes of the Sacramento, and there the American settlers informed him of the latest rumors that Mexican authorities would enforce the laws excluding unauthorized immigrants and carry out their threats to expell those already there. Although there appeared to be no real basis for the rumors, the Americans believed them. Fremont's return and presence added to the commotion, thereby lending encouragement to the settlers to act on their own to solidify their resistance to Mexican authority.[36]

Fremont took no action against the Mexicans, but retaliated against hostile Indians in the area. In assessing the young Army topographer's actions during this stage in his stormy career, historians' views of Fremont are varied—either he acted too aggressive or too hesitant and overcautious. Typically, his actions could be described as impulsive, a trait Fremont exhibited all his life. Considering these divergent views, one could also conclude that the topog simply became confused. He made conflicting statements to different settlers. One, William B. Ide, claimed that Fremont had outlined a plan of conquest by the settlers while he would stand aloof. Jessie Fremont later wrote that her husband did not know of the war, abhorred it, and returned to California for personal reasons. All this suggests that the orders carried by Gillespie were far less extensive than Fremont himself claimed.[37]

---

[34] Nevins, *Pathmarker*, pp. 281–86.

[35] Portions of letters in Bancroft, *History of California*, V, p. 26.

[36] Ibid., pp. 85–109; Nevins, *Pathmarker*, pp. 259–61. Nevins noted that the revolution could well have started without Fremont's presence. Also see Billington, *The Far Western Frontier*, pp. 164–65; and K. Jack Bauer, *The Mexican War, 1846–1848* (New York: Macmillan Co., 1974), p. 168.

[37] Nevins, *Pathmarker*, pp. 264–66; Letter quoted in Goetzmann, *Army Exploration*, pp. 122–23; Simeon Ide, *A Biographical Sketch of the Life of William B. Ide* (Glorieta, NM: Rio Grande Press, 1967), pp. 114–15.

ON TO THE GOLDEN GATE WITH FREMONT

In June 1846 the Bear Flag Revolt took place. It began with Eye-kid Meritt's seizure of Mexican horses on 9 June. Five days later, with advice from Fremont, the settlers took Sonoma. On 16 June the Americans occupied Sutter's Fort and proclaimed an independent Republic of California. By the 25th Fremont and his ninety-man force had come out in the open to join the settlers at Sonoma to do battle with the scanty Mexican forces. By now Fremont was coordinating his efforts with Commander John B. Montgomery of the U.S.S. *Portsmouth* now lying offshore in San Francisco Bay.[38]

Soon most of northern California was in American hands. Fremont then organized the California Battalion with himself serving as its commander. With an organization consisting of 234 men from the topographic party, settlers, and other adventurers, Fremont forged the strongest disciplined force in that theater of war.[39]

The Navy Joins Forces With Fremont

Having heard of the first battles of the war in Texas, Commodore John D. Sloat of the U.S. Navy's Pacific squadron ordered Montgomery to take San Francisco, and he sent word to Fremont to report to him. Sloat seized Monterey on 7 July, and prepared to join forces with Fremont to take the rest of California. When the American flag flew over Sutter's Fort a few days later, the Bear Flag Revolt ended as quickly as it started.[40]

Almost immediately, the British ship *Collingwood* arrived at Monterey. Having discovered that California had been formally annexed by the United States and somewhat chagrined that the Americans got there first, a British officer aboard the *Collingwood* later penned a rather descriptive account of Fremont's dramatic entrance in the port town:

A vast cloud of dust appeared first, and then in long file emerged this wildest wild party. Fremont rode ahead, a spare, active-looking man, with such an eye! He was dressed in a blouse and leggings, and wore a felt hat.

---

[38] Fremont to Montgomery, 16 June 1846, as quoted in Nevins, *Pathmarker*, pp. 273–74. Also see Bancroft, *History of California*, V, pp. 101–31, 145–90.

[39] Nevins, *Pathmarker*, pp. 275–79. Bauer states the battalion numbered 224, *The Mexican War*, p. 169.

[40] Nevins, *Pathmarker*, pp. 279–80; Bauer, *The Mexican War*, p. 170.

After him came five Delaware Indians, who were his body guard.... The rest, many of them blacker than the Indians, rode two and two, the rifle held by one hand across the pommel of the saddle.[41]

Sloat appeared shocked when he learned that Fremont had acted without formal orders. He recalled the disgrace that had befallen the naval commander who seized the town four years earlier. Fortunately for Fremont, Sloat's successor, Commodore Robert F. Stockton, described by historian Justin Smith as "a smart, but vain, selfish, lordly and rampant individual thirsting for glory," arrived to take over the naval command. On 23 July Stockton placed Fremont and his men under his command. He also appointed the topog a major and left him in command of the California Battalion.[42]

All of California Is Taken

The conquest of California involved a series of movements and occupation of key points, usually without opposition, and the internal strife among the Mexican officials in California added to the relative ease of the American operations. Fremont and his battalion landed at San Diego and marched toward Los Angeles to join forces with Stockton and Larkin, who landed at San Pedro. Los Angeles fell without opposition on 13 August, and on the 17th the Americans declared the region a territory of the United States. Stockton now appointed Fremont military commandant of northern California and ordered him to return north to recruit more personnel.[43]

Shortly after Stockton and Fremont departed, the native Californians, prompted by the poor conduct of the American garrison under Gillespie's command, rebelled and retook southern California. Los Angeles fell to a band of insurgents on 22 September. Between 1 October to 15 December Stockton's forces made a series of petty marches and countermarches. In October Fremont re-

---

[41] Frederick Walpole, *Four Years in the Pacific*, as quoted in Dellenbaugh, *Fremont and '49*, pp. 351–52.

[42] Smith, *War With Mexico*, I, p. 336; Dellenbaugh, *Fremont and '49*, pp. 353–54; Bauer, *The Mexican War*, pp. 172–73; Eisenhower, *So Far From God*, pp. 214–15.

[43] Smith, *War With Mexico*, I, pp. 336–37; Dellenbaugh, *Fremont and '49*, pp. 356–57; Nevins, *Pathmarker*, pp. 291–93; Bancroft, *History of California*, V, pp. 255–87.

ceived orders to move south with reinforcements. He soon reached Santa Barbara but unexpectedly returned to Monterey. There the topog learned of his promotion to lieutenant colonel of the Mounted Rifles as of 26 May.[44]

In late November, Fremont set out for Los Angeles with a force of more than 400 men. In San Luis Obispo his troops captured Don Jesus Pico, one of the Californian resistance leaders. Pico had violated his parole and faced a death sentence, but an emotional plea by Pico's family swayed Fremont, and he pardoned the Californian. Such compassionate acts on Fremont's part also gained the favor of the Californians, and Pico became one of his strongest devotees.[45]

After very hard traveling, Fremont reached Santa Barbara on 27 December. Following a few days rest, his battalion moved on and reached San Buenaventura on 5 January 1847. The next day they heard news that an army commanded by Commodore Stockton and General Kearny had marched into Los Angeles. By the 12th he encamped his force near the mission of San Fernando. As usual, Fremont took the initiative and began negotiations with Don Andres Pico, leader of the Californian resistance.[46]

On 13 January the parties came to an agreement, and Fremont, on his own authority, signed the Treaty of Couenga. The terms were liberal and had the effect of appeasing the southern Californians. Even one of Fremont's greatest critics, historian H. H. Bancroft, conceded that the explorer had acted wisely. Perhaps Justin Smith best summed it up

It was a singular denouement. Men defeated, without a hope left, dictated terms to the conquerors. A brevet captain, just blossoming into a lieutenant colonel, eclipsed a commodore and a brigadier general; and the arch-ruffian of the Bear cult reappeared as a fairy godmother to save and bless the Californians, who detested him. But the ending was after all a happy one. The Americans felt a new respect for the people, and they were able to see that, although destitute of gunpowder, the insurgents, if driven to extremities, could have done much harm with lance, dagger and torch, and could have sown the seeds of perennial hate.[47]

---

[44] Bancroft, *History of California*, V, pp. 314–15; Nevins, *Pathmarker*, p. 294; Bauer, *The Mexican War*, pp. 183–84; Eisenhower, *So Far From God*, pp. 217–18.
[45] Nevins, *Pathmarker*, pp. 295–96; Dellenbaugh, *Fremont and '49*, pp. 365–68.
[46] Nevins, *Pathmarker*, p. 296; Dellenbaugh, *Fremont and '49*, pp. 369–71.
[47] Nevins, *Pathmarker*, pp. 299–300; Bancroft, *History of California*, V, pp. 405–07; Smith, *War With Mexico*, I, p. 346; Bauer, *The Mexican War*, pp. 193–94.

Fremont's Dispute With Kearny

Fremont quickly became involved in a controversy with General Kearny. Both Stockton and Kearny claimed overall command in California. Fremont supported Stockton, who, in return, promised him the governorship of the newly acquired territory. Later orders confirmed Kearny's claim. A despondent Fremont lamented, "Each gave men an order to act under him. I remained with Stockton as I had agreed. When Stockton sailed for Mexico I was made to feel the revenge of Kearny." Fremont's short term as governor under Stockton's authority legally ended on 1 March 1847, when Kearny, after receiving authority from Washington, proclaimed himself governor.[48]

Fremont further angered his new commander over the issue of mustering of the California Battalion into federal service. Ignoring the great distance between Los Angeles and Monterey, the young topog decided to deal directly with the general. In a display of his usual rashness, Fremont covered the distances to Los Angeles on horseback at record speed, managed to almost fight a duel with one of Kearny's officers (postponed when the general found out about the prearranged combat), and eventually was ordered to accompany Kearny on his return to the East. Upon arrival at Fort Leavenworth the general charged Fremont with mutiny and insub-

---

[48] Quoted in Fremont, "Conquest of California," *The Century Magazine,* 41 (April 1891): 927. There are many views on this controversy. Nearly all of Fremont's biographers, especially Upham and Bigelow, portray Fremont as an innocent and Kearny as the villain. Nevins and Dellenbaugh are more objective. Kearny is strongly supported by his biographer, Dwight L. Clarke, *Stephen Watts Kearny, Soldier of the West* (Norman, OK: University of Oklahoma Press, 1961), pp. 256–87. Another western historian wrote, "it was a rather stupid mistake because an army officer should have known it was wiser to obey a superior of his own branch of service." Edward S. Wallace, *The Great Reconnaissance: Soldiers, Artists and the Scientists on the Frontier, 1848–1861* (Boston: Little, Brown and Co. 1955), p. 173. Justin Smith also commented that Fremont was a provokingly unprincipled and unsuccessful schemer, and that Kearny showed himself grasping, jealous, domineering and harsh," *War With Mexico,* II, p. 454. Also see Theodore Griva, *Military Governments in California, 1846–1850* (Glendale, CA: Arthur H. Clark Co., 1963), pp. 56–103.

ordination. As a result of his impending court-martial Fremont did not see any further action in the war.[49]

The court-martial commenced on 2 November 1847 at Fort Monroe, Virginia. By then the War Department had ruled that the topographic officer would not be tried on matters taking place before the war, conveniently precluding an examination concerning Fremont's presence in California at the outbreak of war. The topog also received the strong and influential backing of Senator Benton, who viciously attacked Kearny's role in California. (Benton's personal vendetta continued the following year in a vain attempt to deny Kearny's confirmation to brevet major general.) During the course of the trial, Fremont's father-in-law also charged that the Army's West Point clique was persecuting a successful officer who did not attend or graduate from that institution. On 31 January 1848, Fremont was found guilty of mutiny and disobeying a lawful command and conduct prejudicial of good order. Two of Fremont's colleagues, Bvt. Colonel Stephen H. Long (also not a graduate of West Point) and Major James D. Graham, were on the 13-man court-martial board which returned the verdict. The court sentenced Fremont to dismissal from the service but recommended clemency. After intensive consultation with his cabinet, President Polk pronounced Fremont innocent of the charge of mutiny but guilty of disobedience and conduct prejudicial to good order and military discipline. The President then remitted all punishment, and Fremont, still a lieutenant colonel, received orders to report to duty. Considering himself a victim of a great injustice, Fremont submitted his resignation on 19 February. The Army accepted it on 15 March 1848, thus ending the topog's military career for the time being. He did not submit a formal report of his third expedition to the Topographical Bureau.[50]

---

[49] Correspondence between Fremont and Kearny regarding Fremont's request to join his regiment in Mexico, Kearny's refusal of the request, and a later request from Fremont to return separately are contained in Bigelow, *Life and Public Service of John Charles Fremont*, pp. 189–214; Nevins, *Pathmarker*, pp. 320–21; Dellenbaugh, *Fremont and '49*, pp. 375–77.

[50] Bauer, *The Mexican War*, pp. 367–68; Nevins, *Pathmarker*, pp. 327–42; Clarke, *Stephen Watts Kearny, Soldier of the West*, pp. 338–73. Extracts of the trial are contained in Bigelow, *Life and Public Service of John Charles Fremont*, pp. 217–318. Benton's comments are contained in his *Thirty Years View*, II, pp. 715–19.

Fremont's Geographic Memoir

Fremont's third expedition resulted in significant geographic findings. He had shown that the Great Basin was not the formidable desert described earlier by Major Long, and could be crossed. He also had traced a new overland route. Thanks to the famous botanist John Torrey, the explorer's collection of plants appeared in a Smithsonian Institution publication as "Plantae Fremontianae." Congress, which had postponed the publication of Fremont's narrative, somewhat belatedly authorized the publication of his "Geographical Memoir" along with Charles Preuss' important 1848 map.[51]

In its day, Preuss' map was the most accurate portrayal of western America between the Rockies and the Pacific. It represented a compilation of the best sources available at the Topographical Bureau which were based on the surveys of Fremont and his military colleagues and several western explorers. The Great Salt Lake was depicted more accurately, and the map included more geographic data and names for the northern reaches of the Great Basin. Fremont's famous appellation "Golden Gate" for the entrance to San Francisco Bay appeared for the first time on Preuss' map. When word of the gold discoveries reached the East, Fremont added the term "El Dorado or Gold Regions" to the appropriate locations. According to the former topog the map was preliminary only, and he made himself available for any future government-sponsored explorations.[52]

The "Geographical Memoir" itself was not a journal but rather a geographic description of the region from New Mexico to the Pacific Coast. Fremont described each region separately—the Sierra Nevadas, the Great Basin, and the maritime regions west of the Sierra Nevadas. There could hardly be any doubt about his conclusion: "Geographically, the position of California is one of the best in the world; lying on the coast of the Pacific, fronting Asia, on the line of an American road to Asia, and possessed of advantages to give full effect to its grand geographical position."[53]

---

[51] Goetzmann, *Army Exploration*, p. 122.

[52] Fremont, "Geographic Memoir," Sen. Misc. Doc. 148, Goetzmann, *Army Exploration*, p. 106. A detailed discussion of the map may be found in Wheat, *Mapping the Trans-Mississippi West, 1540–1861*, III, pp. 55–62. Reproductions of two editions of this map are located opposite pages 56 and 57.

[53] Fremont, "Geographic Memoir," Sen. Misc. Doc. 148, p. 44.

In a statistically important appendix to the memoir Fremont included the astronomical observations of Professor Joseph C. Hubbard of the Naval Observatory, tables of latitude and longitude for specific locations from Bent's Fort to the Buttes of Sacramento, and meteorological observations of the Great Basin and San Joaquin valley. The factual data dispelled the desert myth and later had great agricultural importance.[54]

Senator Benton saw to it that his son-in-law's "Geographical Memoir" obtained wide readership. In 1848 the Senate authorized the printing of 20,000 copies, and the House produced another edition the following year. These were the last official publications of Fremont's writings as a Topographical Engineer. The corps had lost its most distinguished and at the same time most impetuous representative.[55]

Fremont's impulsiveness and youthful arrogance were unfortunate for him, but the Corps of Topographical Engineers benefited. While wearing his topog uniform, Fremont had distinguished himself as a geographer, scientific collector, and explorer. His glamorous career served as a model for the other officers, and their reports often reflected his influence. And Fremont had made a direct contribution to the war effort.[56]

The Subsidiary Expedition of Lieutenants Abert and Peck, 1845

Naming the expedition after Abert and Peck is ironic; after all, the two Topographical Engineers assigned to Fremont as assistants ended up exploring what had been, at least officially, assigned to Fremont. As noted earlier, Colonel Abert had modified his instructions to give Fremont authority to assign the exploration of the Rockies to his assistants. The two lieutenants accompanied Fremont as far as Bent's Fort. Upon arriving at the fort in early August 1845, Fremont paused to outfit his party. Before starting on his trek to California on the 16th, Fremont took the time to make sure the two young topographers knew how to use their surveying instruments.

---

[54] Ibid., pp. 45–65.

[55] Jackson and Spence (eds.), *Fremont*, Map Portfolio and "Commentary," pp. 15–16; Wheat, *Mapping the Trans-Mississippi West, 1540–1861*, III, fn, p. 56.

[56] Goetzmann, *Army Exploration*, p. 123. Robert Selph Henry also discusses Fremont's impulsiveness in *The Story of the Mexican War* (New York and Indianapolis: Bobbs-Merrill Co., 1950), p. 113.

As Colonel Abert had noted, "Both Lieutenants Abert and Peck will be found well versed in the theories and the mathematics, which the duties require, and in need only of practice in the use of the sextant, which I have no doubt they will soon acquire under your able superintendence." He added that Lieutenant Abert should return directly to Washington after completing his survey.[57]

During his stay at Bent's Fort, the young Abert displayed his artistic ability. Cheyenne Indians often visited the fort and the adjacent explorers' camp, and Abert put his skills to work by making sketches of these visitors. While sketching their portraits the personable lieutenant quickly struck up friendships with several of the Indian leaders, who even allowed the squaws to pose. Old Bark and Yellow Wolf, two of the Cheyenne leaders, also provided Abert with information about their culture, language, and habits. The topog later incorporated this information in a later report of his 1846 expedition to New Mexico.[58]

On 12 August, four days before Fremont departed to the west, Abert set out with a thirty-three-man party downstream along the Arkansas River. Besides Peck, Abert also had as a guide the able Tom Fitzpatrick, Caleb Greenwood, and John Hatcher, veteran mountain men, who served as hunters. Provisions obtained at the fort included sufficient flour, sugar, and coffee to last two months, and as a treat, Abert packed several boxes of macaroni and rice. The party also had 4 wagons, 56 mules, 7 horses, and 8 cows for emergency food. Scientific equipment included a sextant and chronometer, but Fremont had taken all the other equipment, leaving Abert without any barometers.[59]

Abert initially moved east from Bent's Fort along the Arkansas River. On the 16th the topographic party swung south down the Purgatory River. With the Rockies in the background they continued in this direction for three days before joining the Santa Fe Trail, following it through to the Raton Pass. The group then left the trail and

---

[57] Col Abert to Fremont, 14 May 1845, LS 133, TE 77; Jackson and Spence (eds.), *Fremont*, I, pp. 422–23; Goetzmann, *Army Exploration*, pp. 117–18, 123; Lt Abert, "Journal," Sen. Exec. Doc. 438, p. 2. The following account is primarily based on Lt. Abert's journal.

[58] Abert's 1846 expedition is discussed in the next chapter. Abert, "Journal," Sen. Exec. Doc. 438, pp. 3–5.

[59] Ibid., pp. 2, 7–8; Goetzmann, *Army Exploration*, p. 124.

moved along the headwaters of the Canadian River. By 1 September Abert and Peck had descended the steep slopes to the Canadian and entered the Llano Estacado, a plain stretching from New Mexico into West Texas. Several days later they were in dangerous Comanche country and could see campfires in the distance. On the eighth they noticed Indian scouts observing them. Fortunately, Greenwood and Hatcher were adopted members of the Kiowa tribe, and the Indians treated the explorers well. To preclude any mistaken identity, the Kiowa chiefs provided an Indian guide and his squaw to accompany the party eastward along the Canadian.[60]

On the 15th Greenwood and Hatcher turned back toward Bent's Fort, and the party continued along the Canadian River. The following day the Indian escort departed. Abert's group proceeded south of the Canadian to seek out the headwaters of the False Washita River. Reaching what they believed to be the False Washita (actually a few miles to the north) they traveled some 70 miles eastward in the Texas panhandle along the North Fork of the Red River. Off on the horizon the travelers saw Indians observing them, but they reached the Canadian on the 24th without incident. Proceeding rapidly eastward, the Americans safely left Comanche and Kiowa territory. They moved through the Canadian River valley and further saved some time by simply following the well-beaten buffalo paths.[61]

By 10 October Abert and his men were past buffalo country, and they soon reached the ruins of Fort Holmes in eastern Oklahoma. They followed old dragoon trails, with thick vegetation and forests slowing the party's progress. Three days later they killed a marked hog, a sign they were nearing civilization. As the party passed through friendly Creek Indian settlements, Abert's well traveled group had taken on a fearsome appearance compared, as he put it, to the "tastefully" dressed Indians.[62]

---

[60] Abert, "Journal," Sen. Exec. Doc. 438, pp. 3–5, 14–45.

[61] Ibid., pp. 47–49, 55–58. Distance and latitude cited in Gouverneur K. Warren, "Memoir to Accompany the Map of the Territory of the United States from the Mississippi River to the Pacific Ocean (1858) . . . Exploring Expeditions since AD 1800," U.S. War Department, *Reports of the Explorations and Surveys . . . for a Railroad from the Mississippi River to the Pacific Ocean, 1853–6*, XI, House Exec. Doc. 91, 33d Cong., 2d sess., 1861, p. 52.

[62] Ibid., pp. 65–69.

On reaching the North Fork of the Canadian, most of the party moved straight on to Fort Gibson. Abert headed toward Webber Falls, some four miles from the juncture of the Arkansas and Canadian, while Peck made exact astronomical observations of the juncture of the two rivers. With their survey now tied into known points, the lieutenants reached Fort Gibson on 21 October. The topographers then moved on to St. Louis in the next leg of their return to Washington.[63]

Abert's Map and Report, 1846

Once back in Washington, Abert and Peck prepared their report and a map of the region they had traversed. These results were published in June 1846 and provided the latest authoritative information on North Texas and the Canadian River region. Besides their findings, the topogs compiled their map from the best available sources including the earlier maps done by Fremont, William B. Franklin, and Josiah Gregg. Local Indian sources provided some information on the terrain between the Canadian and Arkansas rivers, which the topogs duly noted. In addition to tracing the Canadian River region from New Mexico to its juncture with the Arkansas, the map depicted the Platte, the Arkansas, several portions of other rivers, and the mountain region west of Fort Laramie and Bent's Fort to Santa Fe. Published to a scale of 32 miles to an inch, the map embraced the country from the 94th meridian to the Rocky Mountains and between the Platte River and the 35th parallel.[64]

Abert's report also included many sketches, geographic observations, and appropriate descriptions. While his report provided valuable intelligence for the Army, the information in it, especially the location of water and wood, also proved useful information to later travelers and settlers. He also included significant descriptions of the Kiowa and Comanche Indians, the first time these tribes received attention in an official government report. While his description of the Indians may have sounded discouraging for

---

[63] Ibid., pp. 72–75.
[64] Wheat, *Mapping the Trans-Mississippi West*, II, pp. 192–93. A reproduction of this map is opposite page 193. Warren, "Memoir," House Exec. Doc. 91, p. 52.

future settlers moving west across the region, it did serve a practical purpose as ethnological source material of the tribes encountered by the expedition.[65]

Like many other Topographical Engineers, Abert did not concentrate in a specific scientific field; he left the analysis of the data to the experts. Publication of Abert's report turned out to be especially timely for military purposes. War had just been declared, and his information and map were put to practical use for future military operations in the Southwest.

The exploratory efforts of the Topographical Engineers on the eve of the Mexican War were, of course, only part of the tasks being undertaken by the corps. And virtually all of the corps' peacetime activities ceased when war broke out. The Topographical Bureau itself would have little to do with the war effort, but some two-thirds of the corps' officers would deploy to the field commands. Lieutenant Abert would again head west, this time to serve for a time with Lieutenant Emory in General Kearny's force gathering at Fort Leavenworth.

---

[65] Abert, "Journal," Sen. Exec. Doc. 438; Goetzmann, *Army Exploration,* p. 126.

Colonel John J. Abert. (National Archives)

Major Stephen H. Long. (National Archives)

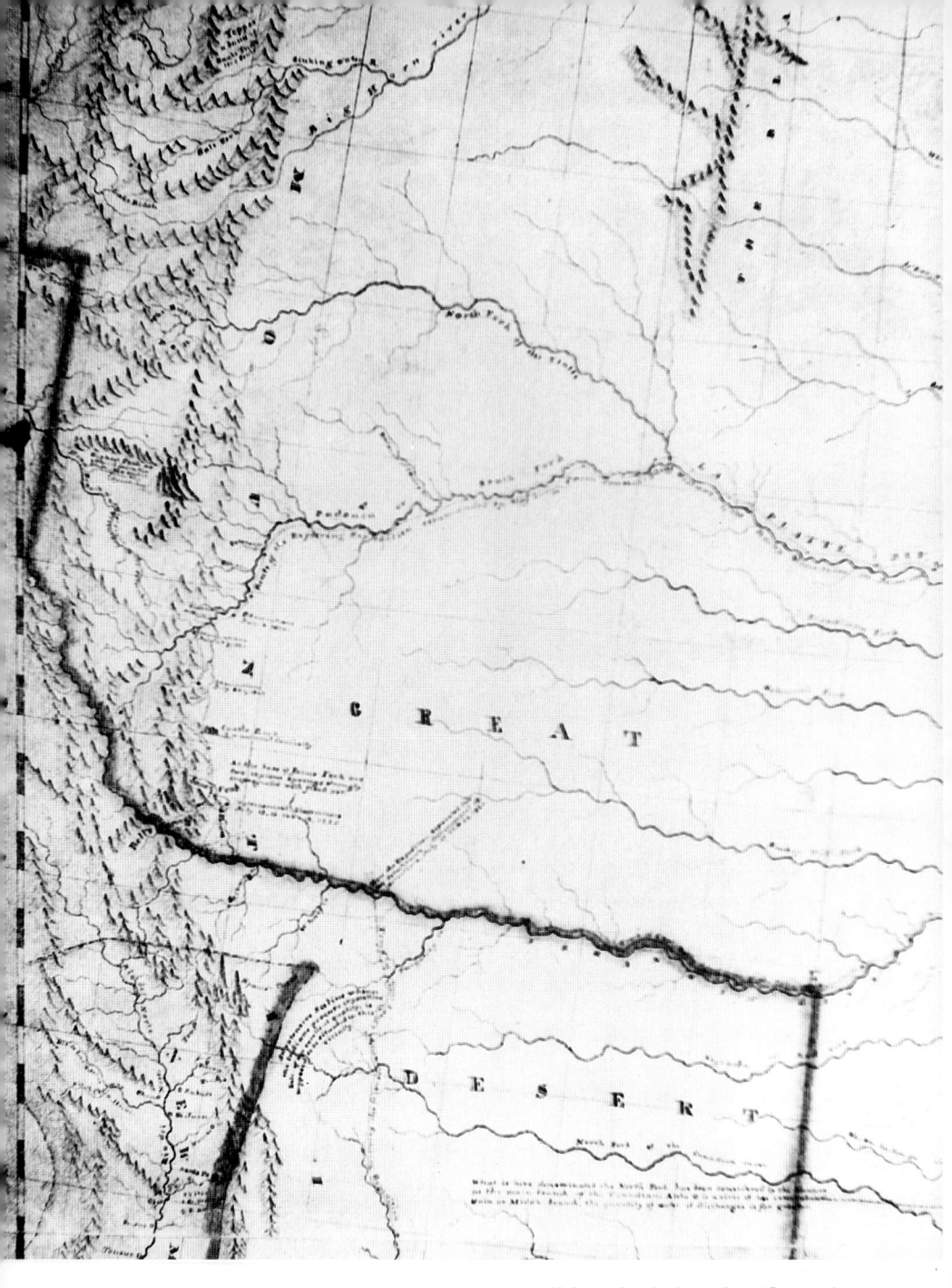

A portion of Long's map of his 1819–1820 expedition depicting the "Great American Desert." (National Archives)

One of the snag boats built after Long took charge of the snag boat fleet. (National Archives)

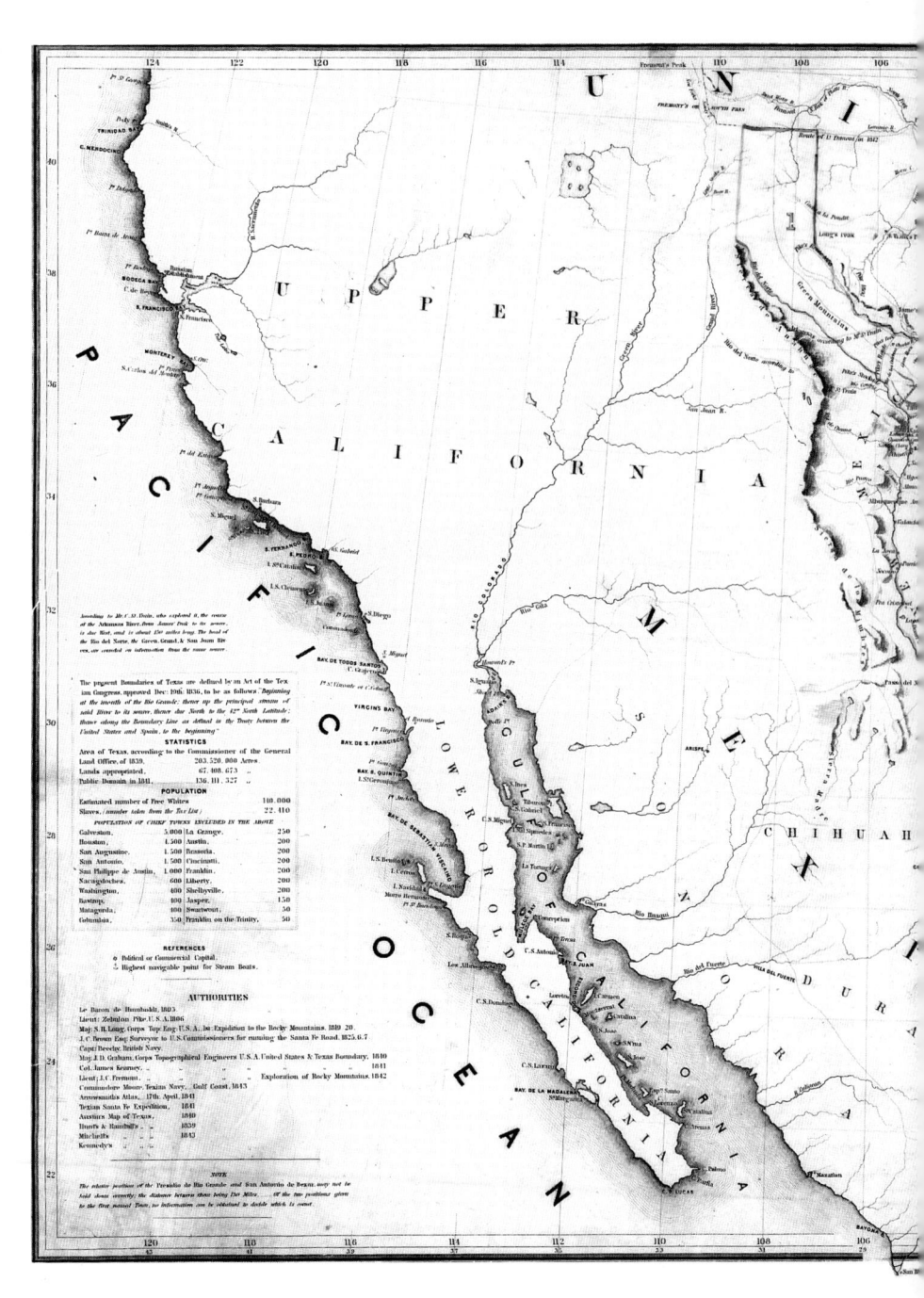

Lieutenant Emory's 1844 map of the West. (National Archives)

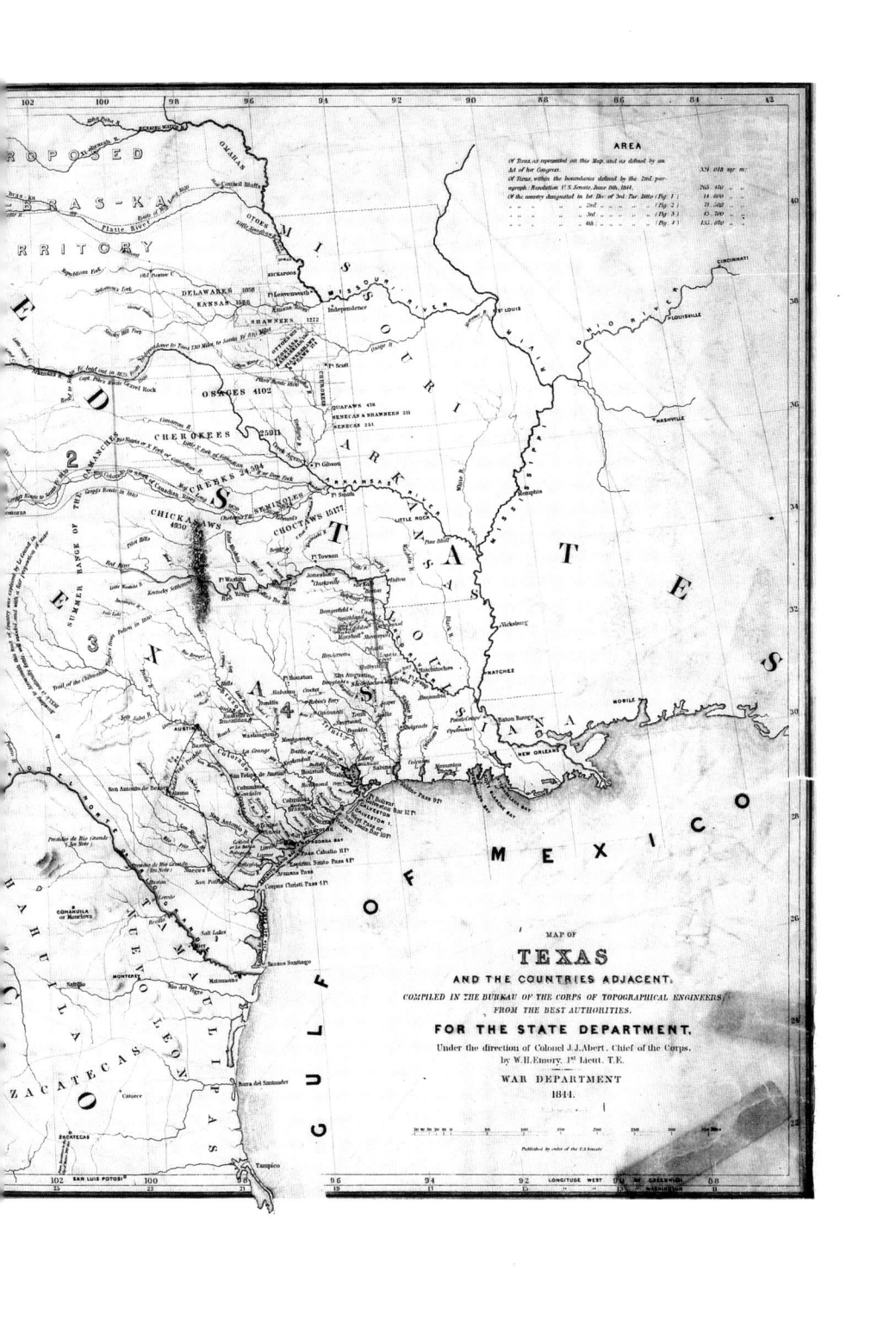

MAP OF
TEXAS
AND THE COUNTRIES ADJACENT.
COMPILED IN THE BUREAU OF THE CORPS OF TOPOGRAPHICAL ENGINEERS,
FROM THE BEST AUTHORITIES.
FOR THE STATE DEPARTMENT.
Under the direction of Colonel J.J. Abert, Chief of the Corps,
by W.H. Emory, 1st Lieut. T.E.

WAR DEPARTMENT
1844.

William B. Franklin during the Civil War. (U.S. Military Academy Archives)

Typical uniforms of Regular Army soldiers during the Mexican War. (U.S. Army Center of Military History)

Section III of Fremont map based on the 1844 expedition to California. (National Archives)

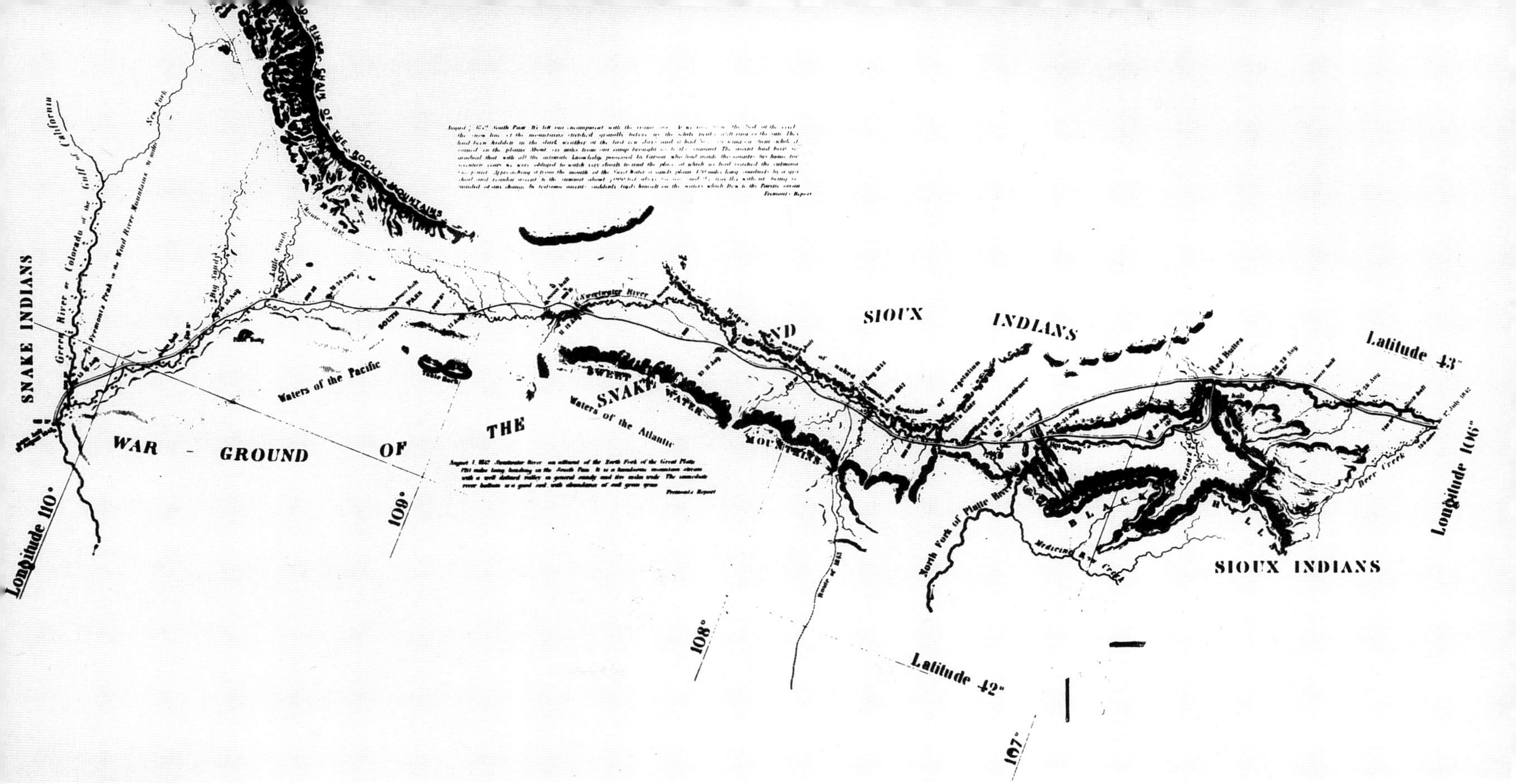

Section IV of Fremont map based on the 1844 expedition to California. (National Archives)

Fremont at Snow Peak, a romanticized version used in Republican campaign literature during the 1850s. (Library of Congress)

Fremont's 1848 map. (National Archives)

CHAPTER 3

With the Army of the West

In late spring 1846, in anticipation of war with Mexico, Colonel Stephen Watts Kearny readied an army of 1,700 regulars and volunteers at Fort Leavenworth for a possible campaign to seize New Mexico and California. By the end of June Kearny, newly promoted to brigadier general, had assembled a mixed force, grandly called "the Army of the West," consisting of his own 1st Dragoons, a volunteer force of artillery and infantry, some mounted plainsmen, and several Delaware and Shawnee scouts. When news of the war and orders to move out arrived, the army began its long march, advancing by detachments to conserve water and grass. The Army of the West did not face much in the way of Mexican opposition. The major deterrent along the route of march turned out to be the vast western distances and resupply difficulties. By August the expeditionary force had advanced 850 miles, and seized Santa Fe, New Mexico, without firing a shot. After establishing a military government, Kearny and his expeditionary force, now cut back to 300 mule-mounted dragoons, set out in late September toward California.

A small group of topographical engineers under 1st Lt. William Hensley Emory accompanied the army through the hitherto uncharted region of the Southwest. Emory's vivid account of the expedition, formally entitled "Notes of a Military Reconnoissance" [sic], provides a day-by-day journal of the army's march and a description of the country's geography and people. After his return to the Topographical Bureau, he prepared the first accurate map of the region.[1]

---

[1] William H. Emory, "Notes of a Military Reconnoissance [sic] from Fort Leavenworth, in Missouri to San Diego, in California Including Part of the Arkansas, Del Norte, and Gila Rivers," House Exec. Doc. 41, 30th Cong., 1st sess., 1848. See also Ross Calvin (ed.), *Lieutenant Emory Reports: A Reprint of Lieutenant W.H. Emory's Notes of a Military Reconnoissance* [sic] (Albuquerque: University of New Mexico Press, 1951). Many quotations from Emory's "Notes" also appear along with other

THE MEXICAN WAR
1846-1847

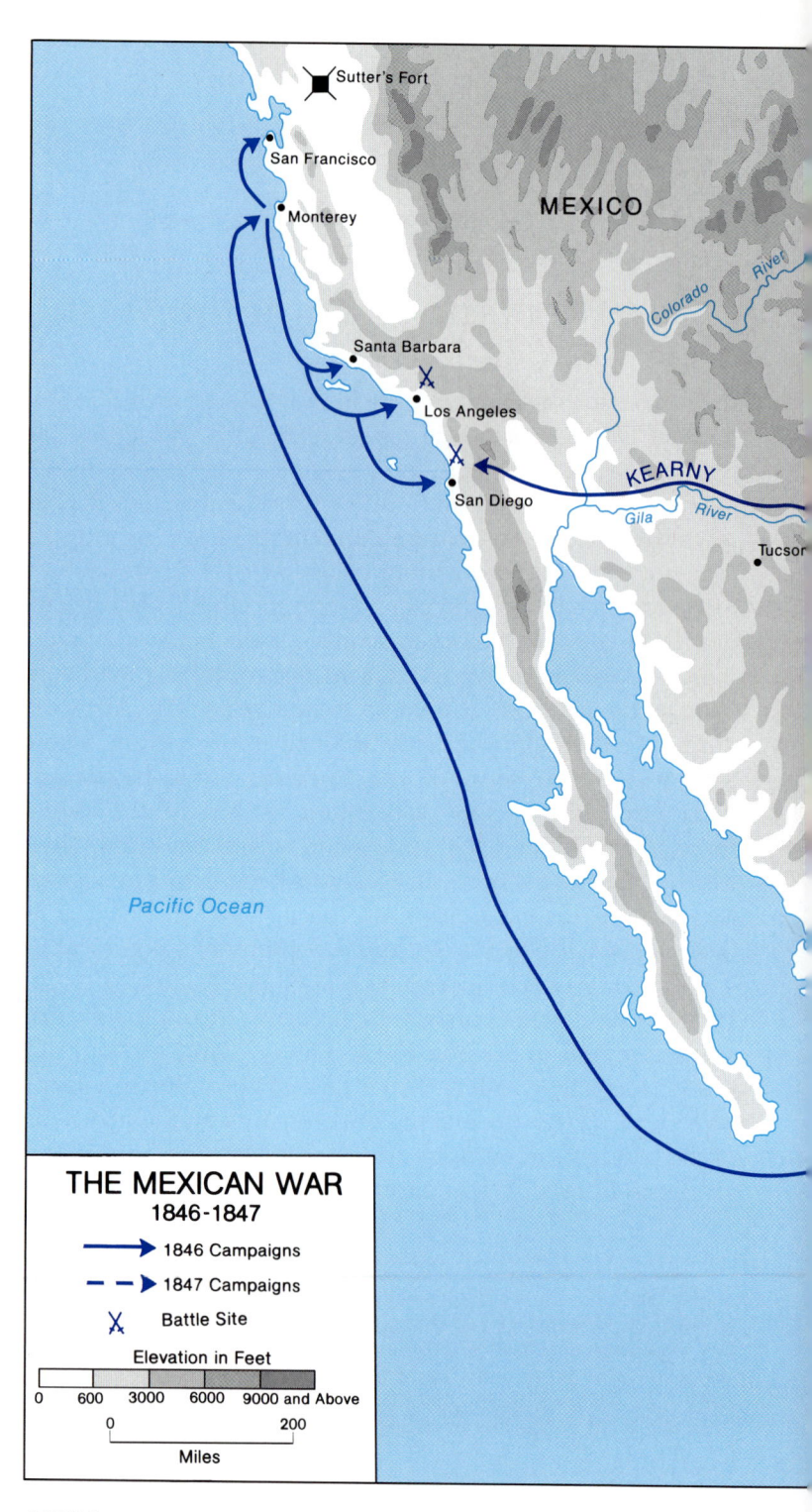

→ 1846 Campaigns
--▶ 1847 Campaigns
✗ Battle Site

Elevation in Feet
0   600   3000   6000   9000 and Above

0 — 200
Miles

MAP 2

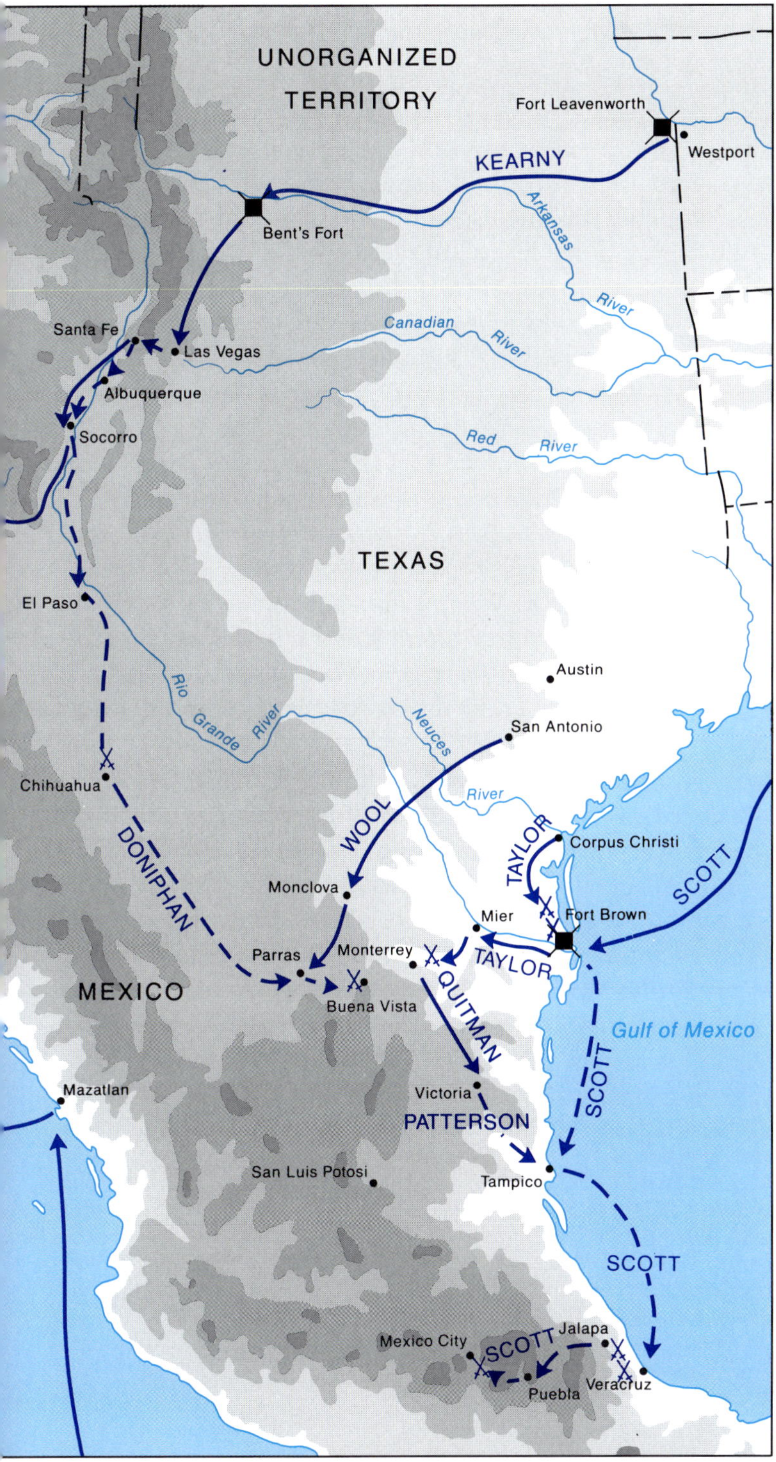
UNORGANIZED
TERRITORY
Fort Leavenworth
Westport
KEARNY
Arkansas
River
Bent's Fort
Santa Fe
Las Vegas
Canadian
River
Albuquerque
Socorro
Red
River
TEXAS
El Paso
Rio
Grande
River
Austin
San Antonio
Neuces
River
Chihuahua
DONIPHAN
WOOL
TAYLOR
Corpus Christi
SCOTT
Monclova
Mier
Fort Brown
Parras
Monterrey
TAYLOR
Buena Vista
QUITMAN
MEXICO
Gulf of Mexico
SCOTT
Mazatlan
Victoria
PATTERSON
San Luis Potosi
Tampico
SCOTT
Mexico City
SCOTT
Jalapa
Puebla
Veracruz

Lieutenant Emory's Instructions

Emory's wide ranging interests and his career following the campaign in the Southwest made him as well known as Fremont. Through his active interest in the sciences, Emory had developed close associations with notable astronomers, mathematicians, and geologists. Whenever possible he attended the yearly meetings of the American Association for the Advancement of Science. His image, however, was that of a red-whiskered veteran frontier cavalryman, and his associates referred to him as "Bold Emory."[2]

On 5 June 1846 Emory received orders to join Kearny's army. The military members of his party included 1st Lt. William H. Warner, a seasoned topographer, and 2d Lts. Abert and Peck, both now veterans of western exploration. Emory also had two civilians attached to his topographic section: Norman Bestor, a statistician, and John M. Stanley, a landscape painter. Except for Peck the selected topogs were already in Washington and ready to move on short notice. When notification came Emory had less than 24 hours to collect instruments and make other preparations. Peck, then assigned at West Point, received his orders to proceed directly to St. Louis to join Emory's party.[3]

Emory received clear and concise orders from Colonel Abert: "Although ordered to report as field and topographical engineer, under the regulations, you will not consider these in light of exclusive duties, but will perform any military duty which shall be assigned to you by Colonel Kearny in accordance with your rank."[4] Emory obeyed, of course, but also turned the orders neatly around. Emory later noted, "in all cases where it did not interfere with other and more immediate military demands of the service, the attention

---

journals and reports in James M. Cutts, *The Conquest of California and New Mexico* (Philadelphia: Cary and Hart, 1847). Portions of a slightly different version of Emory's reconnaissance journal also appeared in W. H. Emory, "Extracts from the *Journal*," *Niles [Ohio] National Register*, 71 (31 Oct, 7 Nov, 14 Nov 1846): 138–40, 157–59, 174–75.

[2] Goetzmann, *Army Exploration*, pp. 128–30; George W. Cullum, *Biographical Register of the Officers and Graduates of the United States Military Academy* (Boston: Houghton Mifflin Co., 1891), I, pp. 481–83; *DAB*, III, pp. 153–54.

[3] Emory, "Notes," House Exec. Doc. 41, pp. 7–8; Goetzmann, *Army Exploration*, pp. 130–31.

[4] Abert to Emory, 5 June 1846, LS 337, TE 77.

of myself, and the officers assigned to duty with me, should be employed in collecting data which would give the government some idea of the regions traversed."[5]

During the short time allotted for preparations, Emory managed to gather instruments and other supplies. These he recalled proved "sufficient for all the objects appertaining directly to our military wants, but insufficient for the organization and outfit of a party intended for exploration." The bureau provided two 8½-inch Gambey sextants and some other equipment, and he borrowed two excellent box chronometers from the Navy. When the party departed on 6 June the topographer still lacked a pocket chronometer and telescope of sufficient power to observe eclipses.[6]

The sensitive instruments required extreme care during transport, but the topogs' best efforts were not enough. Initially, the topographers placed the chronometers in a basket and transported them by wagon. The instruments' rates changed materially after the rough crossing over the Allegheny Mountains, and the jarring motion of an Ohio River steamer further aggravated their condition. To preclude any further damage, Bestor resorted to carrying the chronometers. This turned out to be a fortuitous move, because on one occasion the wagon formerly used to transport the delicate instruments overturned. Fortunately, the instruments still worked satisfactorily when the party reached Fort Leavenworth. After arriving at the fort Emory managed to borrow a Bunton syphon barometer from the post medical department.[7]

From Fort Leavenworth to Santa Fe

Emory's topographic party did not linger long at Fort Leavenworth. On 27 June 1846 Emory led an advance party in the direction of Bent's Fort. A day later the main body of Kearny's Army of the West departed in the same direction. The topog began his

---

[5] Emory, "Notes," House Exec. Doc. 41, p. 7.

[6] Emory took the latest available publications and maps; two copies of Fremont's report of his 1843–1844 expedition; Mitchell's map of Texas, Oregon, and California; four copies of his own 1844 map of Texas; a copy of Abert's 1845 map; Gregg's *Commerce of the Prairies*; two sets of Hasswell's tables; and two nautical almanacs. Emory, "Notes," House Exec. Doc. 41, pp. 8–9.

[7] Emory, "Notes," House Exec. Doc. 41, pp. 8–9; Goetzmann, *Army Exploration*, pp. 130–31.

journal of the reconnaissance by briefly noting the well known route between Fort Leavenworth and Santa Fe. He did, however, take detailed scientific and astronomical observations. The topographers reached the trading post on 29 July. After the main force arrived, Kearny allowed a brief rest and awaited reinforcements. Lieutenant Abert, however, became ill and remained behind when the army resumed its march.[8]

On 2 August, the Army of the West departed Bent's Fort and headed southwest toward Santa Fe, the capital of New Mexico and the first major objective. Emory's journal entries now became more detailed. His vivid description of the column's dramatic departure sets the tone and style of his account of the expedition:

> I looked in the direction of Bent's Fort, and saw a huge United States flag flowing to the breeze, and straining every fiber of an ash pole planted over the center of a gate. The mystery was soon revealed by a column of dust to the east, advancing with about the velocity of a fast walking horse—it was the "Army of the West." I ordered my horses to be hitched up, and the column passed, took my place with the staff.[9]

The column proceeded along the Arkansas and then followed the Timpas River southwest. At the end of the first day's march Emory recorded the route of the army and the distance it covered, a routine he would follow daily. As the army made its way to California, he included entries on elevation, astronomical observations on latitude and longitude, and remarks about vegetation, water, wildlife, climate, and the topographic features of the land they crossed.[10]

The topographer also began to describe the hardships facing the dragoon force. The column pushed on through the dry and dusty Timpas valley, passing "the hole in the rock"—a stagnant pool of water. After passing "hole in the prairie," he wrote, "We passed a dead horse belonging to the infantry, black with crows, and a wolf in their midst, quietly feeding on the carcass. This gave us unpleasant forebodings for our noble, but now attenuated horses." In one day the army covered thirty-six miles, but the horses were already beginning to fail. The sturdy mules, however, fared much better.[11]

---

[8] Emory, "Notes," House Exec. Doc. 41, pp. 10–14.
[9] Ibid., p. 15.
[10] Ibid., pp. 15–16.
[11] Ibid., pp. 16–17.

The following day the army reached Purgatory Valley, and on 6 August ascended the Raton Pass into New Mexico. "The view from our camp is inexpressibly beautiful," Emory wrote in his journal, "and reminds persons of the landscapes of Palistine" [*sic*]. On the 7th they reached the top of the 7,500–foot pass and could observe many mountains, including Pike's Peak. Excited by the vista, Emory noted the changes in the landscape: "For two days our way was strewed with flowers; exhilarated by the ascent, the green foliage of the trees in striking contrast with the deserts we had left behind, they were the most agreeable days of the journey."[12]

Kearny's army rapidly descended the pass and proceeded along the old road to Santa Fe. Along the route the Americans encountered Mexicans for the first time. The natives they met seemed rather unimpressive, giving rise to some premature views of their enemy's military prowess. Observing some Mexicans who were detained, Emory noted, "They were mounted on diminutive asses, and presented a ludicrous contrast by the side of the big men and horses of the first dragoon." Fitzpatrick, the guide, who seldom laughed, became almost convulsed whenever he turned his well-practiced eye in their direction. Word also reached Kearny that the Mexican governor had proclaimed martial law and ordered all Mexicans to arms. More prisoners were detained the next day but Kearny ordered their release as soon as the rear guard had passed.[13]

On the 13th the Army of the West entered Watrous, New Mexico, the first town the army had seen after 775 miles of traveling. The next day messengers from the Mexican governor informed Kearny he intended to do battle but suggested negotiations as an alternative. Despite rumors that a strong Mexican force had occupied the pass on the far side of Las Vegas, on 15 August the Americans entered the town without opposition.

Kearny conciliated the local populace. Addressing the inhabitants from a rooftop in the main square of the town, the general proclaimed the area's annexation to the United States, and offered something to the people that the Mexican government had not delivered—protection against the marauding Apaches and Navahos. The American commander also promised that the people would not be harmed, nor would churches be burned or dese-

---

[12] Ibid., pp. 18–19.
[13] Ibid., pp. 20–23.

crated by his soldiers. Kearny then required the alcalde and other officials to swear oaths of allegiance to their new government.[14]

With the town peacefully occupied, Kearny prepared his army to meet a Mexican force rumored to be in a gorge two miles to the west. Filled with all the proper glory and excitement of an attack, the troopers unfurled the unit guidons and colors, bugles sounded. Emory described the charge: "All wore the aspect of a gala day; and as we approached the gorge, where we expected to meet the enemy, we broke into a full gallop, preceded by a squadron of horses." But there was no battle. As the American troops safely crossed good defensive strongpoints it became evident the enemy had fled. The Army of the West had a clear, unopposed route to Santa Fe.[15]

As the army neared Santa Fe, Emory began to take detailed notes describing the peoples and antiquities of the Southwest. When the Americans entered the ancient fortified town of Pecos, Emory, noted the influence of Christianity upon the inhabitants. After observing the ruins of a Catholic church in the town, he wrote that it typified the "engraftment of the Catholic church upon the ancient religion of the country." His crude study in western anthropology and archaeology also embraced the popular view that an Aztec or Mayan civilization existed in New Mexico.[16]

The Occupation of Santa Fe

Following the occupation of each town along the way Kearny repeated his speech and promises of protection and imposed his oath-swearing requirements. On 18 August the army began a forced march to reach Santa Fe by sundown. Emory again noted his surprise at the lack of Mexican resistance, particularly after observing the many excellent defense positions along the Americans' line of march. The topog described one spot where, with a skilled engineer and a hundred resolute men, the Mexicans could have made the position impregnable. As the Army of the West approached the provincial capital, the governor and his forces fled Santa Fe without offering any resistance. Wisely the officials left in

---

[14] Ibid., pp. 24–28.
[15] Ibid., p. 28.
[16] Ibid., p. 30. See also Goetzmann, *Army Exploration,* pp. 132–33, for a discussion on this subject.

charge decided to graciously welcome Kearny and his troops. After the American flag was hoisted, a prominent citizen of the town extended an invitation to several of the American officers to his house where they feasted on a splendid meal.[17]

Following the occupation of Santa Fe, Emory, in cooperation with Lieutenant Jeremy F. Gilmer of the Corps of Engineers, reconnoitered the town and selected a site for a fort. Within five days they obtained approval for the site and the construction plans to build Fort Marcy. The topographer also prepared a map of the region for General Kearny and Colonel Abert. Emory also dispatched eight separate reports of the army's progress along with his scientific observations to the Topographical Bureau between 18 June and 24 August. And before the mail express departed east on the 25th he managed to complete and forward a map of the army's line of march to that point. Emory also proceeded to fill his journal with remarks of this hitherto almost unknown region, some predicting the practical and theoretical economic, social, political, and religious future of the Southwest. He correctly foretold the importance of New Mexico as an American possession, mentioning the feasibility of running a rail line through the region to the West coast.[18]

For the time being Emory was now the sole effective Army topographer in Kearny's army. Abert had come down earlier with a debilitating illness during the stop at Bent's Fort and remained behind; later Peck also became ill; and, Warner received orders detaching him to ordnance duty. This lack of military assistants did not deter the intrepid topog from reconnoitering the region around Santa Fe on his own. On 2 September, taking only Bestor, Emory accompanied a force led by Kearny south along the Rio Grande River to challenge a Mexican force rumored moving north. On reaching Santo Domingo the following day, Kearny took the occasion to meet with the Pueblo Indians in the area.[19]

Emory's Comments on New Mexican Society

The stopover in Santo Domingo presented another opportunity for the astute topographer to record more observations and in-

---

[17] Emory, "Notes," House Exec. Doc. 41, pp. 30–32.
[18] Ibid., pp. 32, 35–36.
[19] Ibid., pp. 36–38.

sights about the local Indians and New Mexican society. The Indians' relationship with the local Catholic priest particularly impressed Emory. The cleric invited him and several other officers to his home, where the ever observant topog seemed to delight in commenting about the attractive girls seen glancing into the windows and doors of the padre's parlor. Soon a cautious play of glances ensued between the young officers and the girls; a "little exchange of the artillery of eyes," Emory recorded in his journal. But he was very glad "to see the padre move towards the table, and remove the pure white napkin from the grapes, melons, and wine." [20]

Before departing Santo Domingo, Kearny gave his usual speech to the inhabitants, and Emory made notes on the population and the amount of ground under cultivation. By 4 September Kearny neared Bernalillo, where the American force learned that the rumors regarding the Mexican force were false. Here, too, the Americans were received with hospitality; this time a local wealthy man invited the officers to his home. Emory often participated in these repasts and took the time to record his impressions of the furnishings, food, and utensils found within the dwellings of their hosts, typically homes belonging to the wealthy or clergy. He also commented on one of the New Mexicans' more popular foods: "Chile the Mexicans consider the *chef d'oeuvre* of the cuisine, and seem really to revel in it; but the first mouthful brought the tears trickling down my cheeks, very much to the amusement of the spectators with their leather-lined throats." [21]

Because the clergy wielded considerable influence among the people, the Americans were fortunate that the priests considered them as friends. After their entry in Padilla the soldiers received another invitation to a prominent citizen's home. Playing their role as proper guests, the Americans went out of their way to attend a mass before breakfast. The mixed odor of people and incense at the service, however, caused some discomfort. Emory recalled that their attendance "proved anything but an appetizer." After their stay in Padilla, the army moved on to Isleta.[22]

By the 7th they reached Peralta. After a night of taking astronomical observations of the stars, Emory accompanied the army to Tome, arriving there just in time to witness a feast honoring the

---

[20] Ibid., p. 38.
[21] Ibid., pp. 38–40.
[22] Ibid., p. 41.

WITH THE ARMY OF THE WEST   73

Virgin Mary. Emory found the event novel and striking. He accidentally moved into the path of the procession and had a candle thrust into his hand by a grave Mexican. Emory later wrote, "It was thought proper that the officers should show every respect to the religious observances of the country, consequently they did not decline participation in these ceremonies."[23]

The army returned to Santa Fe on 11 September, and Emory assigned more work to his staff before departing with Kearny for California. He ordered Warner and Peck to Taos to determine its latitude and the topography along the road. Three days later he drafted instructions for Lieutenants Abert and Peck. Both lieutenants, now sufficiently recovered from their illnesses, received word to remain with the occupation force. During their stay in New Mexico the two topogs made a separate topographic survey of the newly acquired American territory.[24]

Setting Out for California

With reinforcements on the way and New Mexico relatively pacified, Kearny now turned his attention to continue the march to California. He divided his expeditionary force into three columns. First, he directed the Missouri volunteers under Colonel Alexander W. Doniphan, who recently arrived with his regiment, to move to Chihuahua in Northern Mexico. Doniphan would then proceed to the southeast to join forces with General Taylor's army moving in the direction of Monterrey. The second column, his own Army of the West, began preparations to depart westward along a northern route. A third force, a battalion of Mormon infantry, received orders to march overland to California along a separate southern route. The Mormon Battalion, under the command of Lt. Col. Philip St. George Cooke, was en route to Santa Fe and not expected to arrive before Kearny's departure. Meanwhile, another American force had also left for Santa Fe to relieve Kearny.[25]

---

[23] Ibid., pp. 41–42.
[24] Ibid., pp. 43–44.
[25] Ibid., p. 45. See also Bauer, *The Mexican War,* pp. 135–41, for a discussion of the New Mexico occupation. Cooke's report is attached to Emory's report. Also see P. St. George Cooke, *The Conquest of New Mexico and California: An Historical and Personal Narrative* (New York: G.P. Putnam's Sons, 1878).

On 25 September 1846 Kearny's force of 300 dragoons set out on the long march to California. Emory's topographic party, now less Abert and Peck, consisted of fourteen men. He had one officer, Lieutenant Warner, and no enlisted personnel. The rest of his staff included civilians: Bestor, Stanley, and two other civilian assistants, drivers for the instrument wagon and a transportation wagon, one man in charge of instruments, two men in charge of the mules, an assistant teamster, and two private servants for the officers.[26]

In order to avoid covering the same ground, Emory elected to follow a route a little west of Kearny's army, which at the time was heading in a southerly direction. This he figured on doing for a few days, but almost immediately he became seriously ill. By the sixth day of his illness (1 October) the weakened topographer finally rose from his cot without any help. By then news had reached the American force of Navaho and Apache attacks on nearby settlements. Emory speculated that the Mexican governor, Armijo, permitted these depredations in retaliation to the New Mexicans who opposed him. This lack of protection, Emory concluded, revealed the former regime's fearful and arbitrary rule.[27]

The army moved past Valencia and on to Socorro. Emory longed to cross the mountains and explore the haunts of the Apaches and Comanches and perhaps find a shorter return route via the Red River. "But onward to California was the word," he recorded in his journal, "and he who deviated from the trail of the army must expect a long journey for his jaded beast and several days separation from his baggage. We were not on an exploring expedition; war was the object; yet we had now marched one thousand miles without flashing a saber." [28]

News From California

Before reaching the town of Valverde, word reached Kearny of the American victory in California. Kit Carson, on his way to Washington to deliver a message from Fremont, had stopped at the dragoon encampment and relayed the latest information to Kearny.

---

[26] Emory, "Notes," House Exec. Doc. 41, p. 45.
[27] Ibid., pp. 47–48.
[28] Ibid., p. 50. Colonel Abert also corresponded with Emory on the exploration of the Red River, but this would require the approval of Kearny. Abert to Emory, 21 Aug 1846, LS 420; and 16 Sep 1846, LS 444, TE 77.

Based on this news the American commander made a fateful decision the following day. No longer feeling the need to move on to California with his full force, Kearny sent 200 dragoons back to Santa Fe and pushed on with the remaining 100 men. Emory and his party remained with Kearny. The general then assured Carson that the dispatches would be delivered to Washington, and he ordered the unhappy scout to act as his guide.[29]

On 7 October the now almost minuscule Army of the West passed the last Rio Grande settlement. It then continued along the left bank, departing from the southward main road. Between the 10th and the 13th Kearny held up his dragoon force to await the arrival of pack saddles, a course of action advised by Carson who was aware of the deteriorated road conditions ahead. When the pack saddles arrived, the army switched from wagons to mules. Everybody in the command seemed happy about the switch, except Emory; "My chronometers and barometer, which before rode so safely, were now in constant danger. The trip of a mule might destroy the whole." Emory now regretted all the more that he had not had time in Washington to obtain a pocket chronometer, because the large ones were unsuitable for carrying on foot or by mule. The viameter, an instrument attached to a wagon to measure mileage, was removed from the wagon and attached to a wheel of one of the small towed howitzers. At this point Emory had recorded the distance from Santa Fe as 203 miles. The march westward continued, and soon the American force began its descent from the New Mexican plateau.[30]

Observing the Indians Along the Way

On 15 October the army left the Rio Grande and turned west to the Black Mountains. Three days later Kearny's column reached the deserted copper mine of Santa Rita de Cobre, where the Apaches, under the notorious chief Magnus Colorado, had driven

---

[29] Emory, "Notes," House Exec. Doc. 41, p. 53. See also Goetzmann, *Army Exploration*, p. 134; Charles L. Dufour, *The Mexican War; A Compact History, 1846–1848* (New York: Hawthorn Books, 1968), pp. 145–46; Eisenhower, *So Far From God*, p. 220.

[30] Emory, "Notes," House Exec. Doc. 41, pp. 53–56; Dufour, *Mexican War; A Compact History*, p. 146.

off the inhabitants. On the 20th, at a location just a few miles from the Gila River, Emory witnessed the meeting of his general, Magnus Colorado, and the other Apache chiefs. He observed that the Apaches swore friendship to the Americans and eternal hatred to the Mexicans, but "Carson with a twinkle of his keen hazel eye, observed to me, 'I would not trust one of them.' " Still, the meeting and later trading session impressed the topographer. He recorded in his journal: "Several wore beautiful helmets, decked with black feathers, which, with the short skirt, waist belt, bare legs and buskins, gave them the look of ancient Greek warriors." The army reached the Gila River later that day. As usual Emory took notes about the local geology, vegetation, and wildlife.[31]

Kearny then moved on westward past ruined Indian pueblos and remnants of aqueducts. Emory saw evidence of broken and scattered pottery, and he duly recorded his findings. By 28 October the army cleared the Black Mountains and moved through the valley of the Gila not far from Mount Graham. Here Emory observed quantities of agate and obsidian fragments. He recalled that William H. Prescott, in writing his history of the Americas, had described the stones as those used by the Aztecs to cut out the hearts of victims at ceremonial sacrifices. Moving on, they passed Mount Turnbull on the last day of the month. The soldiers found further evidence of Indian ruins, and Emory prepared sketches and site plans of the various dwellings. The topographer's expectations now heightened at the prospect of seeing the well publicized Indian structures at Casa Montezuma (Casa Grande).[32]

On the first day of November Kearny's army moved from the Gila River to follow Carson's old trail. The column followed it for some sixty miles over rough terrain before again striking the river route. Along the route they encountered more Apaches. At that point the army's mules had worn down. The Indians promised a trade, but the number of mules they provided proved disappointingly few. By the 4th the expedition descended toward the Gila in a southerly direction. Because of the southward shift, the army made only meager progress to the west—one degree and four seconds in seven days. When the expedition made its next stop Emory's jour-

---

[31] Ibid., pp. 56–62.
[32] Ibid., pp. 63–71.

nal entry reflected: "We are yet 500 miles from the nearest settlement, and no one surveying our cavalry at this moment would form notions favorable to the success of the expedition." Sores and scars covered every animal.[33]

As the army moved west again along the Gila River, Emory attached appropriate names to landmarks. He named Mineral Creek and speculated on the presence of copper and gold. The army also passed through the wide plain country of the Pima and Maricopa Indians, and Emory observed that the Gila's current had slowed considerably. By 9 November, as they passed near modern-day Florence, Arizona, they saw more ruined Indian settlements. The army reached Casa Grande the following day, and Emory, his wish now fulfilled, explored the famed dwellings. During the course of his investigation he had Stanley prepare detailed sketches for use in his final report.[34]

Emory expressed considerable admiration for the Pimas and Maricopas. The Indians possessed well-cultivated lands with irrigated fields of wheat, corn, and other staples. The topog noted that these remote people yet did not know the evils of the white man's liquor. He also found them a peace-loving, religious people who believed in one overruling spirit. Despite their rather passive nature Emory concluded they were not helpless, for both peoples often defeated the dreaded Apaches, the evidence being warriors just returned from a battle with scalps and prisoners.[35]

By mid-November the army completed its trek through the Gila Bend region and moved on from the valley to another tableland. Emory wrote that most of his mules had traveled some 1,800 miles, and somehow they managed to revive after each stop. He observed more signs of former Indian habitations, and the topographer surmised that the Maricopas were moving eastward in juxtaposition with the Pimas. He observed boulders with hieroglyphic symbols beside more modern inscriptions, and Carson discovered several American names. In this more dismal stretch leading to the Colorado River, remains of former settlements were still present though fewer in number.[36]

---

[33] Ibid., pp. 71–76.
[34] Ibid., pp. 77–82.
[35] Ibid., pp. 82–89.
[36] Ibid., pp. 89–93.

Still No Enemy

One week later the American force became aware of possible contact with the enemy. On the 22d the straggling column came upon a recently occupied camp estimated to have accommodated a Mexican force of 1,000. Although Kearny's force numbered only 110 men, with men and beasts so run down that even the general had to switch from his exhausted horse to a mule, the American commander prepared to order an attack. He ordered Emory to set off with a fifteen-man reconnaissance party. Near the juncture of the Gila and Colorado rivers, the patrol soon encountered a small group of Mexicans who were driving about five hundred horses from California to Sonora for the Mexican army. They offered no resistance. Because the captured horses appeared wild and useless, the Americans later decided to release their captives. The army then prepared for the ninety-mile march across the California desert. Meanwhile, Emory, Warner, and Stanley took astronomical observations at the juncture of the two rivers. The topog's next journal entries described the impressive canyon region. Emory also reflected on the possibility of steamboat navigation on the lower Colorado and the feasibility of flatboat navigation up the Gila to the Pima villages. On the way back to camp they met a Mexican courier carrying dispatches from California to Sonora containing news of the uprisings in Los Angeles and Santa Barbara. This information, dated 15 October, stirred Kearny to hasten his column's march westward.[37]

On the 25th the Americans forded the Colorado River and crossed into California. The army now began a memorable eight-day trek across the desert to Warner's ranch at the base of the Sierra Madres. Emory described the barrenness of the region. Midway across the desert men and animals could not quench their thirst because they could only find brackish water. The topog did not find any evidence that one of the areas they crossed, the Imperial valley, would later become a famous and rich agricultural area. The heavy sand made travel difficult for the animals, but the army moved as fast as possible, covering fifty-four miles in two days. Rations ran low, and the men resorted to eating their animals. Emory wrote that one of the officers "found in a concealed place one of

---

[37] Ibid., pp. 93–97.

the best pack mules slaughtered, and the choice bits cut from his shoulders and flank, stealthily done by some mess less provident than others." Wolves could be heard fighting over the abandoned, worn-out horses and mules. Thorns from desert thickets cut man and beast. Four days after setting out, the troops slaughtered a horse and ate it with great relish.[38]

Arrival in California

Despite the hardships the army plodded westward in anticipation that the long trek was almost over. The weary troopers advanced through an ever-narrowing valley ridged by gray granite and quartz mountains. By the first day of December they reached the deserted Indian village of San Felippe. In this final stage of the long march the men, according to Emory, repeatedly ascended "divides" in the anticipation of seeing "the glowing pictures drawn of California." On the following day the soldiers sighted the first large trees of evergreen oak since leaving the States. Then emerging from yet another pass they sighted the beautiful valley of Agua Caliente, which Emory ecstatically described as "waving with yellow grass." Crossing over another ridge the hungry and exhausted army feasted its eyes on Warner's ranch.[39]

As Kearny's men descended toward the ranch, they could see inhabitants driving off the cattle and horses, apparently in fear that the advancing column was Mexican. On arriving at the ranch and establishing their identity, the American force learned that the Mexicans had imprisoned the owner and established a stronghold nearby. By their presence at Warner's ranch, the Americans also discovered that they now sat astride the pass to Sonora—the Mexican main supply route to California. Before moving on to San Diego, however, Kearny decided to refit his weary force and sent word to the American garrison requesting an escort. The army rested and feasted for two days. Emory's topographic party alone devoured a fat, full-grown sheep in a single meal.[40]

---

[38] Ibid., pp. 99–113. Emory also advised against using slaves to develop the area as opposed to the existing system of peonage. Later, opponents of slavery were to quote his remarks. See Charles D. Hart, "Slavery Expansion to the Territories, 1850," *New Mexico Historical Quarterly*, 41 (Oct 1966): 269–86.

[39] Emory, "Notes," House Exec. Doc. 41, pp. 104–05.

[40] Ibid., p. 105.

The Battle of San Pasqual

On 4 December the Army of the West, now somewhat rejuvenated, set out toward San Diego. Kearny encamped in the valley of the Rio Isabel near Stokes's ranch. Stokes had advised Kearny earlier of the latest news, and the general sent the rancher to San Diego to inform Commodore Stockton of the need for reinforcements. The following morning the troops marched out in cold and rainy weather to the Santa Maria ranch. On the way they met their escort, Captain Gillespie of the Marines in command of a party of thirty-five. Along with this joining of the two small American contingents came word that a Mexican force was some nine miles distant. For the first time in its long march, the American army sensed a distinct possibility of encountering the enemy. A reconnaissance party reported that the mounted Mexican force numbered approximately 160 men. As the Mexicans apparently knew of the presence of the reconnaissance party, Kearny decided to attack immediately. Emory recalled the excitement of the forthcoming action, "We were now on the main road to San Diego, all the 'by-ways' being in our rear, and it was therefore deemed necessary to attack the enemy, and force a passage. About 2 o'clock, a.m., the call to horse was sounded."[41]

Early in the cold, wet, and foggy morning of 6 December 1846, the small American army moved out to meet the Mexican lancers. A small advance guard mounted on the best horses led the way followed by Kearny and the main force of dragoons, mostly mounted on mules. The balance of the column, including the two mountain howitzers, brought up the rear. Kearny invited Emory and Warner to accompany him. In turn, the chief topog took four other members of his topographic party. He told Bestor, Stanley, and the others to move with the rear echelon and take care of the party's baggage, instruments, and notes.[42]

By daybreak the approaching Americans saw the enemy's campfires. Quickly alerted to the arrival of Kearny's combined force, the Mexicans, armed with their deadly lances, moved out to do battle. Emory recorded the events that followed in dramatic

---

[41] Ibid., pp. 107–08.
[42] Ibid., p. 108. See also Dufour, *Mexican War; A Compact History*, p. 149; Bauer, *The Mexican War*, p. 188; Eisenhower, *So Far From God*, pp. 222–23.

style. He recalled that Kearny "ordered a trot, then a charge, and soon we found ourselves engaged in a hand to hand conflict with a largely superior force." As the advance party lunged forward, the enemy fired a heavy volley and then fell back faking a retirement. Kearny's main force, mounted on horses and slower mules, soon found itself cut off and under attack by the expert Mexican horsemen. In the end, however, the Mexicans retired from the battlefield, thus concluding the so-called Battle of San Pasqual as a costly "victory" for the Americans.

The battle amounted to hardly more than a skirmish. Kearny had no more than 150 men, including Gillespie's force, and perhaps 80 took part in the fighting. The Americans lost one of the howitzers when the mules towing it panicked and fled to the enemy lines. According to Emory the Americans lost 18 men killed and 13 wounded while their opponents suffered only 2 killed and a few wounded. The wounded included Kearny, Warner (in three places), Gillespie, and several key officers—one-third of all the American officers present. Emory also claimed to have saved the general from being finished off by a lancer ready to strike the American commander from behind. The topog rushed in and drove the assailant away with his sword.[43]

That night the Americans buried their dead while the foe hovered about. The military situation had become quite desperate for the victors. Provisions were exhausted, all the horses were dead, and the mules were in poor condition. The Americans, besides being fewer in number, were ragged, worn down by fatigue, and emaciated. Early the following day Kearny urgently dispatched several men to make their way to San Diego for help and carriages to transport the wounded.[44]

Emory's journal entry that morning grimly reported: "Day dawned on the most tattered and ill-fed detachment of men that ever

---

[43] Emory, "Notes," House Exec. Doc. 41, pp. 108–09, 168. Kearny's report is contained in Cutts, *The Conquest of California and New Mexico*, pp. 199–201. Other accounts of the battle are in Goetzmann, *Army Exploration*, pp. 139–40; Smith, *War With Mexico*, I, pp. 341–42; Dufour, *Mexican War; A Compact History*, pp. 149–50; and Clarke, *Stephen Watts Kearny, Soldier of the West*, p. 214; Bauer, *The Mexican War*, p. 188; Eisenhower, *So Far From God*, pp. 222–26. Fremont obtained the lost howitzer as a result of the Treaty of Couenga, and it was mentioned in Fremont's court-martial that he refused to transfer the gun along with other property to Kearny's command.

[44] Emory, "Notes," House Exec. Doc. 41, p. 109.

the United States mustered under her colors." They arranged the wounded and the pack animals in the middle of the column and straggled toward San Diego. As the weary force headed toward the ranch of San Bernardo, the Mexicans gave way. After the Americans departed the ranch, their adversaries threatened to take a hill in their path and simultaneously attack from the rear. Some of Kearny's troops charged the hill, an exchange of shots took place, and their opponent withdrew from the high ground. The now desperate American force proceeded to occupy the hill for a last-ditch stand.[45]

Fortunately for the Americans, further fighting did not take place the following day. That morning Kearny selected Emory to act as the American representative to a truce called by the Mexican commander, Don Andres Pico, to trade prisoners. By evening Kit Carson, leading a party of three, slipped out of the besieged encampment and headed toward San Diego, twenty-nine miles distant, to repeat the general's message for help. As usual Emory, regardless however bad things looked at the time, routinely continued recording his astronomical observations of the camp's position.[46]

The battered Americans waited for the relief force. During the siege the Mexicans drove a band of wild horses to harass the surrounded encampment. The Americans dexterously turned aside the animals, and took advantage of the encounter: "Two or three of the fattest were killed in the charge, and formed, in the shape of a gravy-soup, an agreeable substitute for the poor steaks of our worn down brutes, on which we had been feeding for a number of days." By the evening of the 10th a force of 180 marines and sailors from San Diego finally arrived.[47]

The relief force caused the Mexicans to back off, and on the following day the combined American forces moved on toward the Pacific unopposed. Anticipation of sighting the ocean swelled within the fatigued men of the Army of the West. Approximately seventeen miles northeast of San Diego they were rewarded with a magnificent panorama. "The Pacific opened for the first time to our view," Emory noted in his journal, "the sight producing strange but agreeable emotions. One of the mountain men who had never seen the ocean before exclaimed: 'Lord! there is a great prairie without

---

[45] Ibid., pp. 109–10.
[46] Ibid., pp. 110–11.
[47] Ibid., pp. 111–12.

a tree.'" They reached San Diego on 12 December, thus completing an epic journey. According to Emory, the Army of the West had marched 1,912 miles from Fort Leavenworth to the public square in San Diego, successfully covering the long distance through the entire trans-Mississippi Southwest along a route previously negotiated by only a few trappers and Indians.[48]

Kearny Moves on to Los Angeles

On 12 December Emory entered a few comments in his journal. They would influence the Topographical Bureau's activities and national policies for the next ten years. He extolled the fine harbor of San Diego: "The harbor of San Francisco has more water, but that of San Diego has a more uniform climate, better anchorage, and perfect security from winds in any direction." While San Francisco would become a commercial metropolis, because of the rich lands and the rivers of the surrounding area, "San Diego should be made the terminus of a railroad leading by the route of the Gila to the Del Norte [Rio Grande], and thence to the Mississippi and the Atlantic." Emory's strong advocacy of a southern transcontinental railroad route would form the basis of the bureau's later recommendations, and the Topographical Bureau would become one of the key backers of the southern route.[49]

At the end of December Emory received orders to report to General Kearny as his Adjutant General. He began his new duties just as the campaign to retake Los Angeles got underway. With a nondescript command of soldiers, sailors, marines, and irregulars, Stockton and Kearny joined forces and set out on the 29th. The topog in his new capacity directed the placement of defensible camp sites along the route of march. Although Emory had embarked on new duties, he still inserted topics of topographic interest in his journal. He included interesting comments about the missions of San Luis Rey, Flores, and San Juan Capistrano, and on the Santa Anna and San Gabriel rivers. On 8 January 1847 Kearny's force reached the San Gabriel River where a short skirmish took place. The next day the American force moved on to Los Angeles

---

[48] Ibid., pp. 112–13, 178; Goetzmann, *Army Exploration,* p. 141.
[49] Emory, "Notes," House Exec. Doc. 41, p. 113; Goetzmann, *Army Exploration,* pp. 141, 268.

where another abortive Mexican attack took place. By the 10th the joint force reoccupied the town. The Mexicans had dispersed, and the Americans took complete possession of all California, this time for good. Thus, some six weeks before the Battle of Buena Vista and over two months before Scott's landing at Vera Cruz, the rich region was securely in American hands.[50]

Emory then returned to his engineering duties. He selected a site for a fort, drew up the necessary plans, and saw to the beginning of its construction. Several weeks later he received orders to return to Washington to prepare his report. Breveted twice in the battles in California, Brevet Major Emory returned to San Diego on 25 January to sail for the States.[51]

Emory's Report of a Military Reconnaissance

Upon Emory's return to Washington, his journal and map were incorporated into a final report and prepared for printing. Like Fremont's earlier expeditions, the U.S. government considered these reports important enough for widespread dissemination to the public. In December 1847, the Senate authorized the printing of Emory's epic "Notes of a Military Reconnoissance." The House followed suit the next month. Even a New York publisher took advantage of the public domain government publications and reprinted a commercial version. Of the two Congressional publications, the House document turned out to be more comprehensive in scope. Not only did it contain Emory's "Notes," but also Lieutenant Abert's journal (of 27 June to 29 July 1846) and map of New Mexico, Colonel Philip St. George Cooke's report of his march to California, and many sketches and drawings.[52]

---

[50] Emory, "Notes," House Exec. Doc. 41, pp. 114–21.

[51] Ibid., pp. 121–26. Emory returned after having traveled 6,900 miles by ship and 3,600 miles on land, including 2,500 miles on horse or mule. See *Niles [Ohio] National Register,* 72 (14 Aug 1847): 372.

[52] During this period Emory was also involved in Fremont's court-martial board. Because Emory was Kearny's Adjutant General, several letters were signed by him for the general. The defense thus tried to implicate Emory in an alleged conspiracy against Fremont; see Clarke, *Stephen Watts Kearny, Soldier of the West,* p. 358. One letter to Fremont used in the court-martial concerned the requirement of Kearny's approval in any organizational changes in the California Battalion; see Bigelow, *Memoir of the Life and Public Service of John Charles Fremont,* p. 262.

Emory's report added significantly to scientific geography, particularly of the newly acquired Southwest. His map became the first professional and accurately drawn representation of the region. Included were data and topography that only he and his party observed, plus information reported by Cooke along his route. Carl Wheat wrote in his study of western maps that it "is a document of towering significance in the cartographic history of the West."[53]

The map immediately made all commercial atlases obsolete. With the single exception of the area of Gila Bend, Emory's map of the Gila River is accurate to this day. The gold-seekers on their way to California in 1849 used it widely along with the topog's "Notes." The Topographical Bureau later based its mapping and exploration efforts in the region on this map. When used with data collected by Fremont and other Topographical Engineers and explorers, the map became even more significant. "It tied the country together on a route at its extreme south," Wheat wrote, "and was to become of great value when the boundary of the United States and Mexico was traced a few years later."[54]

Emory's report alone had five lengthy appendices. The first consisted of three pages of correspondence between Emory and Albert Gallatin, a former Secretary of the Treasury, about the Indian ethnology of the Southwest. The ex-Secretary had helped to found the American Ethnological Society in 1842. Whatever Emory could furnish by way of descriptions and drawings of the pueblos, archaeological remains, and their locations were of considerable benefit to the society. In his exchange of correspondence with Gallatin the topographer regretted that he did not have the opportunity to pursue his findings about any connections between the Pimas and the Mexican Indians. Still, Emory's findings were among the first serious steps in the study of the pueblo tribes and their mysterious past. Coupled with this he provided thorough de-

---

[53] Wheat, *Mapping the Trans-Mississippi West*, III, p. 6. Cooke later wrote, "My rude map covered four hundred and seventy-four miles, and it chanced to get into Captain Emory's hands while he was finishing his own map in Washington. The tests which he was able to apply to it, proved its singular accuracy, and he incorporated it with his own. It appears in atlases as Colonel Cooke's wagon route." Cooke, *The Conquest of New Mexico and California*, p. 158.

[54] Goetzmann, *Army Exploration*, p. 142; Wheat, *Mapping the Trans-Mississippi West*, III, p. 8.

scriptions of the Maricopas and the Apaches. Only Josiah Gregg's *Commerce of the Prairies,* published in 1844, had thus far touched on the fields of Indian ethnology and contemporary life.[55]

Emory's second appendix contained twenty-five pages on the botany of the Southwest. The noted botanist John Torrey studied the cactus specimens sent back from the expedition and listed eighteen new species and one new genus as Emory's findings. He even named one of the plants *Quercus Emoryi* in honor of the topographer. Dr. George Englemann, a leading authority on the plants, prepared a special section on cacti. He identified fifteen species and rendered the first scientific report of the giant cactus. Emory's drawing of the plant helped to make it an item of scientific interest for years.[56]

The remaining three appendices in the more detailed House published report contained information which would be of great help to the Army and future travelers. One had sixteen pages of meteorologic observations. Another appendix contained several pages of geographic positions depicting the distances from camp to camp, the total distances from Fort Leavenworth, and the precise latitude and longitude at each place of observation. A huge fifth appendix, a 205-page "Table of Astronomical Observations," contained more than 2,000 astronomical observations of precise locations on the earth's surface. A total of 357 separate barometric observations also showed the elevations along the route. Many of these readings differed only slightly from more accurate modern readings, a remarkable feat considering the rough treatment given to the instruments.[57]

Emory's report was a significant geographic achievement. Despite the lack of time and instruments, he had prepared an interesting and lively description of the topography, animals, plants, inhabitants, archaeology, and geology of the Southwest. Like Fremont, he described the possibilities and limitations for future development of the regions traversed. For example, the topog touched upon the potential mineral resources of the territory. Like his more famous colleague, Fremont, however, he did not consider the subject to be

---

[55] Emory, "Notes," House Exec. Doc. 41, pp. 127–385. See also Goetzmann, *Army Exploration,* pp. 142–43.
[56] Emory, "Notes," House Exec. Doc. 41, pp. 135–59. See also Goetzmann, *Army Exploration,* p. 143.
[57] Emory, "Notes," House Exec. Doc. 41, pp. 160–385. See also Goetzmann, *Army Exploration,* p. 142.

the principal purpose of his examination of the region. Even today Emory's "Notes of a Military Reconnoissance" is of value because of the firsthand picture it provides of the Southwest in 1846.

Emory also included the account of Lieutenant Abert's travels to Bent's Fort. Abert's appendix incorporated a nine-page list of plants, all in their proper Latin terms, and noted the location of collected specimens.[58]

---

[58] James W. Abert, "Notes of Lieutenant J.W. Abert," House Exec. Doc. 41, 30th Cong., 1st sess., 1848, pp. 386–414.

CHAPTER 4

Lieutenants Abert and Peck in New Mexico

After Emory set off to California with the Army of the West, Lieutenant James W. Abert, with the assistance of Lieutenant William G. Peck, embarked on a three month survey and examination of the newly acquired New Mexican territory. Guided by Emory's detailed instructions, the two topogs and their party rode out through the Rio Grande valley, taking topographic readings and making a meticulous inquiry into the uses and possibilities of the region. They constantly scrutinized and recorded their surroundings, going from town to town noting agriculture production, estimating the population, and examining mineral resources. Finishing their survey around Christmas of 1846, Abert and Peck returned to Washington via separate routes. The return trip proved much more severe than the work in New Mexico. In particular, Abert proved his mettle during that grueling winter.

Lieutenant Abert's Stay at Bent's Fort

During the first leg of Kearny's march from Fort Leavenworth Lieutenant Abert had become quite ill and remained behind at Bent's Fort to recuperate. Three weeks later he felt well enough to at least resume his journal. With a copy of Horace, a Greek testament, and his ever-ready sketch book, the topog optimistically wrote, "I served to make the hours of confinement pass pleasantly." By 27 August he felt well enough to make it down the stairs from his room without help. As time passed Abert regained his strength. He began making preparations to rejoin the Army of the West and purchased mules for the journey to Santa Fe. During his stay at the trading post, the residents of the fort, aware of Abert's interest in natural history, provided the inquisitive officer with samples of plants and minerals and a wildcat hide—all of which he avidly added to his growing collection.[1]

Abert also displayed the same keen interest as Emory in the culture of the American Indians. While recuperating at Bent's Fort he took the opportunity to renew his friendship with the Cheyenne Chief Old Bark. When the topog later prepared his report he commended the Cheyennes, particularly because of the rare number of offenses committed against the whites and their honesty in trading. The report also reflected Abert's sympathy for the tribe's desperate condition at the time. The Cheyennes were beset with hunger, shortage of game, and severe epidemics of measles and whooping cough. Abert placed some of the blame for the Indians' plight on Washington:

> As the people of the United States have been, and are, the greatest cause of the diminution in the quantity of game, by continually travelling through the country, by multiplying roads, and thus destroying the quiet ranges where the animals breed; by killing many of them, and by the immense numbers that they induce the Indians to destroy for their robes, it seems but fair that the United States should assist the Cheyennes. At this moment a very beneficial influence might be exerted upon them, as they have their minds now full of this plan of ... forming permanent habitations, and of living like the whites, by tilling the ground and raising cattle.[2]

The Indian visitors to the trading fort, in turn, took an interest in Abert and his drawing skills. After seeing his plant sketches, they insisted that he draw their portraits. In return he had the Indians bring in more plant and wildlife specimens. With the aid of an interpreter, the topog began to take copious notes. One topic of interest, not surprising considering his own health at the time, included Indian folk medicine. He contrasted the Cheyenne's use of the juice of a root to treat rattlesnake bites with the typical cure of the frontiersmen who frequented the fort. "At Bent's Fort," Abert wrote, "the usual remedy is alcohol. They say that if they can make a person drunk, soon after the bite he is safe."[3]

---

[1] James W. Abert, "Report of the Secretary of War, Communicating in Answer to a Resolution of the Senate, a Report and Map of the Examination of New Mexico, made by Lieutenant J. W. Abert of the Topographical Corps," Sen. Exec. Doc. 23, 30th Cong., 1st sess., 1848, pp. 3–5.
[2] Ibid., pp. 6–7.
[3] Ibid., p. 9.

Abert also compiled a Cheyenne dictionary during his stay at the fort. Unfortunately, this portion of his papers disappeared during his hard winter journey back to St. Louis later that year. His final report, however, did include several pages of the Cheyenne vocabulary based on letters he forwarded earlier to the Topographical Bureau and notes he kept in his sketch book.[4]

Abert's Route From Bent's Fort to Santa Fe

After a stay of over a month Abert felt well enough to travel. He set out on the afternoon of 9 September 1846 with a small party bound for Santa Fe. He seemed happy to be back on the open prairie again, and the party made eight miles the first day. Once encamped after a long day's journey, the stylistic Abert added more observations and insights to his journal. "At night," he recalled, "we had a serenade from a full choir of prairie wolves; they collected around our camp in great numbers, and broke forth in sudden bursts of their inimitable music."[5]

One week later the party approached Raton Pass. Excited by the increasing signs of wildlife, Abert moved quickly ahead of his companions, crossed over the pass, and left his ox team far behind. By now his growing specimen collection included a gopher, a horned lizard, and a centipede. Reunited the following day, the party continued to descend the pass over a rocky trail lined with the wreckage of wagons of earlier travelers.[6]

Several times the topographer and his companions met travelers passing in the opposite direction, and they passed on the latest news of Kearny's peaceful occupation of Santa Fe. As the party neared Las Vegas on the 23d, signs of civilization began to appear in the form of homes and grazing sheep and cattle. They arrived in the town the following day and immediately moved on in the direction of Santa Fe through a succession of small New Mexican towns. Abert, however, did find some time to investigate and describe the adobe construction and irrigation systems of the region they crossed. By the 27th they reached a point only 27 miles from Santa Fe and hurriedly pushed on to their destination. The ex-

---

[4] Ibid., pp. 10–11. Abert also provided a detailed description of Bent's Fort.
[5] Ibid., p. 17.
[6] Ibid., p. 22.

hausted topog later noted that he "was soon seated amongst my friends, who looked upon me as one awakened from the dead."[7]

Arrival in Santa Fe and New Instructions

After arriving in Santa Fe Abert received new instructions to conduct another independent survey. Before Emory departed with Kearny's Army of the West on 25 September, he left instructions for Abert and Peck to continue the survey of New Mexico. Peck had also suffered an illness, and Emory decided after consulting with Kearny that both lieutenants should make the map of New Mexico based upon his preliminary observations. In addition, the two lieutenants were instructed to furnish "an account of the population and resources, military and civil, of the province."[8]

Emory's orders specified that completing the survey depended on the two men doing other duties as required by the local commander. Fortunately, these were minimal. Abert and Peck continued the survey's triangulation based on six astronomical positions set by Emory. Upon completion of this task, they proceeded to comply with Emory's instructions to plot "the course of the Del Norte, that of its tributaries to the base of the mountains or beyond the settlements; the quantity of land under cultivation; the position of towns, churches, hills," and other topographic features. Specifically, Emory wanted data to include

The population, number of cattle, horses, and sheep, and the quantity of grain and other agricultural products, the facilities and best localities for water power to propel machinery, and also the mineral resources of the country, it is very desirable to know. You will, therefore, give particular attention to acquiring all the information on these subjects which the present statistical knowledge in the country will afford.[9]

Before setting out on his next venture, Abert took time to explore Santa Fe and comment in his journal about the town's people and customs. He visited the marketplace and attended a local fandango, where the young officer noted the New Mexicans' love of music and display of good manners. "For a Mexican," he wrote, "never even lights his cigaritto without asking your consent."[10]

---

[7] Ibid., pp. 26–31.
[8] Emory, "Notes," House Exec. Doc. 41, p. 43.
[9] Ibid., p. 44.
[10] Ibid., p. 32.

On 29 September Abert and Peck headed south to investigate the gold mining region along Galisteo Creek. There they found primitive mines, and within a week the lieutenants returned to Santa Fe with a variety of samples. Then they packed the mineral samples and wildlife specimens for shipment to Washington. Abert followed this with further exploration of Santa Fe. He drew sketches of the town and its churches. Along with a description of the town he also wrote a laudatory account of the construction of Fort Marcy. Abert liked to visit the marketplace for a daily promenade because as he noted, "one sees more of character displayed in the market place than at any other public assembly." He also began to compare his notes with those of Lieutenant Zebulon Pike, who explored the same region in 1807.[11]

The Survey of Southern New Mexico

On 8 October Abert and Peck and their small party set out to begin their topographic survey. Their survey lasted over two months until their return to Santa Fe on 23 December. Initially, the topogs followed the Rio Grande south as far as Valverde, a distance of 150 miles. Then they moved northwest of the river seventy-five miles opposite Albuquerque. In the final leg of their exploration the topographers turned eastward for the final fifty miles.[12]

After its departure from Santa Fe the party passed Sandia on 14 October and arrived in Albuquerque the following day. Before their arrival Abert heard news of a Navaho Indian raid. In an area not far from the topographer's route the marauding Indians devastated an entire valley and drove away a large number of sheep. Still Abert wanted to press toward the fabled cities of Cibola. A few days later they entered Navaho country, where the explorers, without the benefit of a military escort, proceeded with caution. His party moved on unmolested and soon reached the first cities of Cibola—Cibolleta, Moquino, Pajuate, Covero, Laguna, Rito, and Acoma—clustered on the banks of the Rio de San Jose or its branches. Abert and Peck

---

[11] Abert, "Report and Map of the Examination of New Mexico," Sen. Exec. Doc. 23, pp. 32–39. Peck's notes of his earlier reconnaissance with Lieutenant Warner to the Taos region were included in Abert's report, pages 40–44. Pike ended up being taken into custody by Spanish cavalry.

[12] Warren, "Memoir," House Exec. Doc. 91, pp. 53–54.

spent two days in Laguna and Acoma, and on the 22d headed east again, about five miles north and parallel to the Laguna-Acoma road. They visited the ruins of Rito and encamped again on the Rio Puerco. By the 26th they were back in Albuquerque.[13]

The so-called Seven Cities of Cibola did not impress the Americans. The disappointed topogs found Rito a pile of adobe ruins. The other towns were simple one- and two-story pueblos occupied by primitive Indians who practiced simple agricultural methods similar to those of Indians east of the Rio Grande. Acoma, located on a high limestone rock, appeared somewhat more pretentious. The topographers reached the town by a narrow stairway cut out of the rock face.[14]

Local officials and wealthy citizens usually greeted and provided quarters to the unescorted party. By the time an American escort did show up, Abert believed that his party had already ventured through the most dangerous areas. He elected to move on without troop protection. When Abert reached the Rio Grande, news of General Zachary Taylor's victory at the northern Mexican city of Monterrey began to reach New Mexico.[15]

The next leg of Abert's survey led his party to Valverde. Between 27 and 31 October the topographers traveled up and down the banks of the Rio Grande, crossing several times between Peralta and Padilla and again at the Canon Inferno and continuing eastward through the Sierra Blanca to Chilili. The party discovered Chilili abandoned and in ruins. Apparently a stream changed its course thereby forcing the inhabitants to establish a new settlement nearby. On 6 November the group again joined the Rio Grande at Casa Colorado and proceeded along the banks of the river south through La Joya de Ciboletta and Socorro. By the 15th they reached the American dragoon camps at Valverde, part of Colonel Alexander W. Doniphan's expeditionary force gathering for the move into northern Mexico to join forces with Taylor. While investigating the ruins of Valverde, Abert learned that Doniphan and his Missouri volunteers had encamped nearby in Socorro.[16]

---

[13] Abert, "Report and Map of the Examination of New Mexico," Sen. Exec. Doc. 23, pp. 49–60.
[14] Ibid., pp. 54–55.
[15] Ibid., pp. 53, 60.
[16] Ibid., pp. 67–83.

Abert found Valverde a hub of American activity in anticipation of Doniphan's march to Chihuahua. Many trading wagons and their civilian teams had already gathered in town to support the assembling army. Abert and his party remained near Valverde for nearly a month to conduct astronomical observations, gather more specimens, and visit Doniphan and the nearby army camps. The topog lieutenant also took advantage of the army's communications link with Washington and forwarded several reports of his activities to the Topographical Bureau.[17]

Orders To Return to Washington

By 12 December Abert had completed the survey and made preparations to return to Washington. Orders received from Colonel Abert directed the two lieutenants to return to the topographic headquarters to prepare a map and report of their New Mexico surveys. The two had accumulated information of great interest in the capital, and their orders insured that topographers would not accompany Doniphan's army. Apparently, neither Kearny nor Colonel Abert saw fit to assign Topographical Engineers to Doniphan, and he in turn did not make a request to assign even one topog to his staff. Abert considered joining Doniphan, but he did not know where that expedition, or another army assembling in Texas under Brigadier General John E. Wool, would go after reaching Chihuahua.[18]

As a result, the topog decided to return to the United States via Santa Fe along a route he knew was open to travel despite the impending arrival of winter. "Many of my friends represented the undertaking as almost impossible," he later wrote, "but there was one

---

[17] Ibid., pp. 85–90. The Topographical Bureau registered four letters in all from Abert: 7 Oct 1846, LR 1004; 25 Dec 1846, LR 165; 24 Feb 1847, LR 170; 19 Apr 1847, LR 300, TE 77. Only copies of the last two are on file. Lieutenant Abert's correspondence of 19 April was his handwritten version covering the period 15 November 1846 through 21 March 1847 (the day of his return to Washington). This journal was slightly different from the printed report.

[18] Abert, "Report and Map of the Examination of New Mexico," Sen. Exec. Doc. 23, p. 90. Colonel Abert advised his son to return to Washington and recommended an alternative return route. He suggested either the Rio Grande or Red River; however, he concluded, "positive instructions cannot be given from such a distance, and reliance is placed upon your discretion and intelligence, as well in what relates to the safety of your command, as to the results it will collect." Abert to Abert, 18 Nov 1846, LS 504, TE 77.

trader who had crossed the prairies in the winter; and as he had done it, I did not see why it might not be done again, moreover, my orders to return had to be obeyed."[19]

Abert then organized a party for the return trip. During his stay at Valverde he hired eighteen men recently discharged from the trade caravans and interested in returning to the United States. On 23 December 1846, after a nine day trip, his party reached Santa Fe. Upon arriving they heard news of a planned New Mexican insurrection. Adding to the negative tone of his return trip, news had arrived of the latest Comanche depredations along the Canadian River. These dire warnings did not deter the intrepid topographer from spending the next five days preparing for the long journey. With his valuable notes and specimens packed, Abert and his party departed Santa Fe on the 28th amidst an ominous snow storm. Meanwhile, Peck had made separate plans to depart later along a slightly different route.[20]

Abert's Hard Trip Back

Both of the topographers endured many trials and hardships on their return trips. The weather turned very cold on the prairie, and the snow at Raton Pass reportedly reached depths of five feet. In one instance Abert's foot froze to the stirrup on his mule. The cold and weary party also had to haggle over the price of corn with the inhabitants along the New Mexican portion of their route. Abert abruptly put a stop to this and made the New Mexicans accept the standard quartermaster rate. Wagons broke down and required expedient repairs. Fortunately, the wagons could be readily patched up because of the availability of materials from the many abandoned wagons along the route. They trudged on and along the way passed one party of wagoners who had decided to remain in one spot throughout the winter. Icy conditions also plagued the cold and fatigued travelers, particularly when crossing streams and climbing and descending the slippery banks. The descent to the fording sites usually resulted in wagons skidding down the slope, dragging men and ani-

---

[19] Abert, "Report and Map of the Examination of New Mexico," Sen. Exec. Doc. 23, p. 90.
[20] Ibid., pp. 91–96.

mals into cold streams or across icy surfaces. Reluctant ox teams and mules had to be dragged through the freezing water.[21]

Such conditions began to take toll of Abert's party. The men riding either in the wagon boxes or on the mules exposed themselves to frostbite. To keep warm they trudged through the deep snow. In one instance, however, this effort so fatigued two members of the party that they could not walk any farther. Seven men contracted measles, and Abert noted, "Many of the men were getting sick and nearly all had dreadful coughs." It became increasingly difficult for the weakening group to hunt game. By the time the exhausted party reached Bent's Fort, on 20 January 1847, most of the men were very sick. Little did they realize that their ordeal had only begun.[22]

The harsh trip thus far did not convince the topog to hole up at the fort until spring. He hastily made plans to push on eastward across present-day Colorado and Kansas toward Fort Leavenworth. After exchanging wagons and obtaining provisions for forty days, Abert left the seven sick men and pushed on through Indian country. The smaller party proceeded along the Santa Fe Trail watchful for roving bands of Pawnees and Arapahos known to have raided wagon trains along the trail. The Cheyennes they encountered appeared friendly; however, in one instance Indians stole some axes but their chief returned the pilfered items. Although Abert remained on guard while passing through Arapaho country, he did accept an invitation to visit the lodge of Chief Long Beard for a feast. The topog nonchalantly observed that the dog meat being consumed was considered "bon bouche" for festive occasions. Considering the less than fastidious appetite of his men, Abert added, "It was well he kept his fat dogs under his eye, or some of my party might have been tempted to commit similar extravagances."[23]

By 1 February the weather took a turn for the worse. A blizzard struck their camp, and members of the party arose the next morning to discover several men buried in the heavy snowfall. Only by tracing cracks on the snow's surface did the searchers find their buried comrades. According to Abert these cracks were "caused by the movements of the restless sleepers; covered by a heavy mantle

---

[21] Abert, "Report and Map of the Examination of New Mexico," Sen. Exec. Doc. 23, pp. 97–110.

[22] Ibid.; Abert to Abert, 19 Apr 1847, LR 300, TE 77, p. 12.

[23] Ibid., pp. 110–12.

of snow they had kept extremely warm, and now the chill air felt to them more intolerable." They also found three of the mules frozen to death. Abert speculated that the same fate would have befallen the remainder of the party if the storm had lasted much longer. When the party proceeded to dig out its belongings, one of the men suffering from snow blindness and sitting off to the side suddenly shouted an alarm. He felt something tugging at his buffalo robe, and panicking he somehow scared off some famished wolves. The following day a less fortunate mule wandered off, and this time the wolves succeeded in getting a meal.[24]

On the morning of the 6th Abert and his men discovered that all the mules were missing. Abert wrote angrily, "There was no doubt that the Pawnees had driven the animals off; we were on their hunting grounds, where no other tribe of Indians dare venture without fear." He knew it was impossible to track down the Indians, and now without pack animals Abert considered caching his collection of geological and wildlife specimens. He decided, however, against such a drastic course of action. Abert also had to overrule some members of the party who wanted to leave a sick man behind with provisions they hoped would last until another caravan came along. Fort Leavenworth still remained some 348 miles away.[25]

Some good fortune and spirit, however, persisted within the jaded company of travelers. They found two abandoned oxen and hitched them to the party's remaining wagon. Abert's journal vividly described how his men exerted incredible effort to move on. "Then attaching ourselves in a line with long ropes," he wrote, "we moved off from the scene of all our miseries, with more cheerful hearts, than for many a long day; the air was rent with shouts and laughter as we rejoiced in thus triumphing over our disasters." They moved off at a rate of two miles per hour during this "ne plus ultra" phase of the trek to their destination.[26]

Some of the topog's party, however, did not make it to the fort. They reached Pawnee Fork on the 12th, but one of the men became too ill to go on. He remained along the side of the road with two guards. Another blizzard struck the party a week later at Turkey Creek. After thirty-six hours of heavy snow Abert and his

[24] Ibid., pp. 112–17.
[25] Abert to Abert, 19 Apr 1847, LR 300, TE 77, pp. 23–24.
[26] Ibid.; Abert's rate of speed is noted on page 25 of the letter.

men again dug themselves out. They found two men buried in six feet of snow. This time one of them did not survive.[27]

The worst was over. Abert made arrangements with another wagon train to ship most of the specimens and baggage to Washington. Leaving all but two of his men with the wagon train, Abert, now outfitted with a horse, rode swiftly eastward. Three weeks later he finally reached Washington, over two months after his departure from Santa Fe.[28]

Peck Follows a Different Route

Lieutenant Peck's return trip back to Washington also featured some excitement. He delayed his departure until the American army of occupation put down an insurrection in the northern New Mexican town of Taos in early 1847. A few days out of Santa Fe the topographer's small party lost ten horses and mules to Comanche raiders. The following day the Indians made off with the remaining thirty-five animals. In the ensuing gunfight a musket ball reportedly struck Peck's pistol at the point of the manufacturer's stamped impression, thus creating a similar impression on the ball. When the shooting ended one of the men next to the topog had been wounded, and Peck noticed his own uniform had several bullet holes.[29]

The trek to St. Louis held further adventures for the young topog. That evening, however, he had the good fortune to meet another party of Americans, including Kit Carson, now resuming his trek east after marching with Kearny to California. During the meeting Peck acquired several replacement horses. Farther along the Arkansas, another Indian attack, this time by Pawnees, attempting to capture the horses. This time they easily drove off the marauders. By the time Peck reached St. Louis on 16 May 1847, U.S. troops were being dispatched to secure the Santa Fe route.[30]

Peck did not submit a formal report of his return from Santa Fe, but his return trip did contribute to the geographic knowledge of the West. His change in routes allowed him to hastily survey the adjacent Cimarron route. "It is nothing but a reconnaissance," he

---

[27] Abert, "Report and Map of the Examination of New Mexico," Sen. Exec. Doc. 23, pp. 123–25.
[28] Ibid., pp. 127–30.
[29] Cutts, *Conquest of California and New Mexico*, pp. 236–37.
[30] *Niles [Ohio] National Register*, 72 (29 May 1847), p. 205.

later wrote, "and was made in the same manner that all other reconnaissances have been made in that country, except that I had no means of establishing astronomical positions. The country is eminently favorable to a compass line, and I think it may give a fair idea of the route." Later the Topographical Bureau incorporated Peck's survey into Emory's map.[31]

Lieutenant Abert's Report

In 1848 the Senate and House ordered Abert's "Report and Map of the Examination of New Mexico" printed. Because Abert and Peck had also incorporated the surveys of Emory and Warner, their's was an up-to-date, accurate, and significant report and map of the region. When the United States obtained the territory of New Mexico in 1848 by the Treaty of Guadalupe-Hidalgo, a professional piece of cartography depicting terrain, settlements, waterways, and routes already existed. Along with the work done by Emory, the resultant map would serve as the framework for further surveys of the Southwest. In addition, the bureau incorporated Abert's map into Fremont's more complete 1848 map of the West. The written portion of Abert's report and map comprised 130 pages of printed text, two pages of comments on geology of New Mexico, and many beautiful sketches that included representations of Santa Fe, Indians, towns, the ruins of Pecos and Acoma, and natural wonders such as Canon Inferno.[32]

Both Abert and Peck returned to other topographic duties, thus ending their direct involvement in the war with Mexico. The following year Abert assumed duties at West Point as a drawing instructor and later taught English literature and moral philosophy. Peck also took up instructor duties at the Military Academy as a professor of mathematics until 1855 when he left the Army. Abert stayed on and served as a staff officer during the Civil War. In later

---

[31] Quoted in Warren, "Memoir," Report of Explorations and Surveys . . . for a Railroad, XI, House Exec. Doc. 91, p. 54; Wheat, *Mapping the Trans-Mississippi West*, III, p. 5.

[32] In addition to the survey, map, and specimens, Abert also collected valuable data on population, governmental organization, and economic production. He included the 1844 official census, which gave the population of New Mexico as 100,964. Abert, "Report and Map of the Examination of New Mexico," Sen. Exec. Doc. 23, pp. 61–63.

years, the two former topogs took on civilian college teaching careers—Abert as a professor of English literature at the University of Missouri at Rolla and Peck as a professor of physics and civil engineering at the University of Michigan and later as a professor of mathematics, astronomy, and mechanics at Columbia University. He authored several textbooks on mathematics and mechanics and translated a physics textbook from French to English. Abert died in 1897 at the age of 77 after a long and distinguished career. Peck died in 1892.[33]

The campaign in the Southwest resulted in the acquisition by the United States of the coveted southwestern region. Accompanying Kearny's Army of the Southwest, Emory, Abert, and Peck produced comprehensive reports of the region. Their maps and surveys would later serve as a solid foundation of geographic knowledge for later surveys made by the Corps of Topographical Engineers. In turn, the topographic surveys would provide valuable information to travelers and for the future development of the territory.

---

[33] Cullum, *Biographical Register*, II, 151–52, 192.

William H. Emory during the Civil War. (U.S. Military Academy Archives)

Drawing of Santa Fe, from Emory's report. (National Archives)

Cereus giganteus, from Emory's report. (National Archives)

Passing San Felippe, New Mexico, from Emory's report. (National Archives)

Drawing made by Lieutenant Abert during his convalescence at Bent's Fort in 1846, from his report. (National Archives)

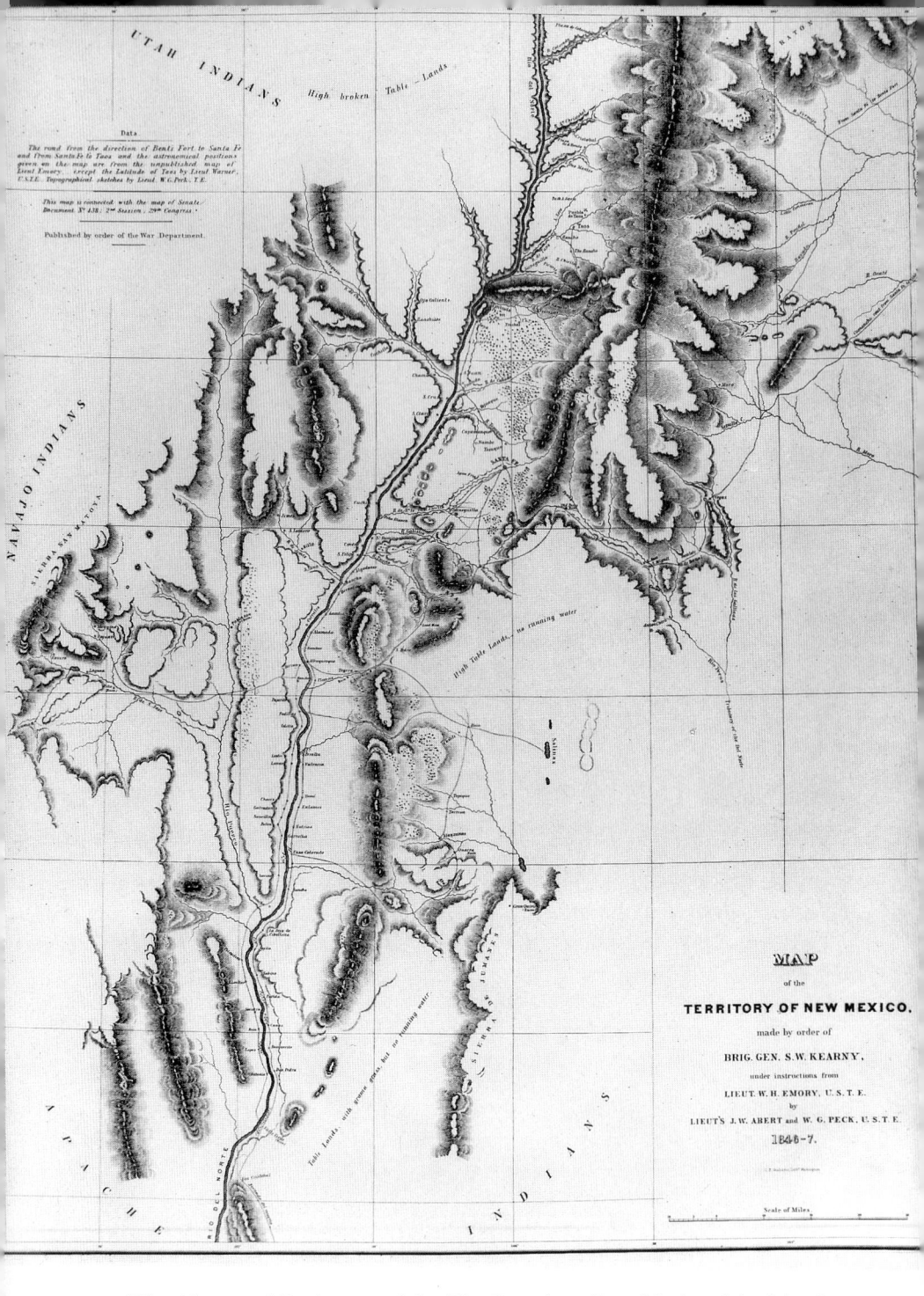

The Abert and Peck map of the Rio Grande valley. (National Archives)

Zachary Taylor. (Library of Congress)

George Meade during the Civil War. (National Archives)

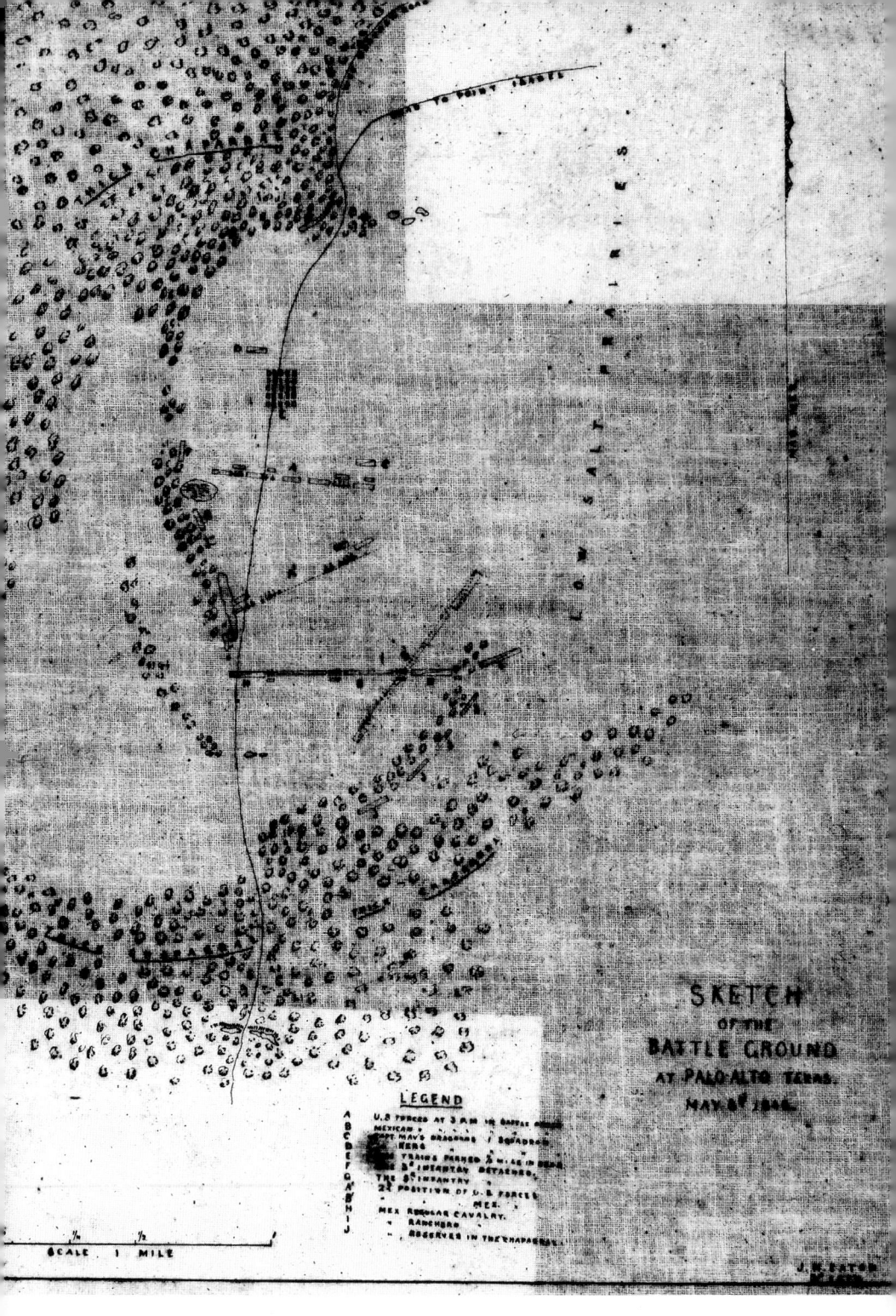

Sketch of Palo Alto. (National Archives)

Battle of Palo Alto, Taylor's astride "Old Whitey." (Library of Congress)

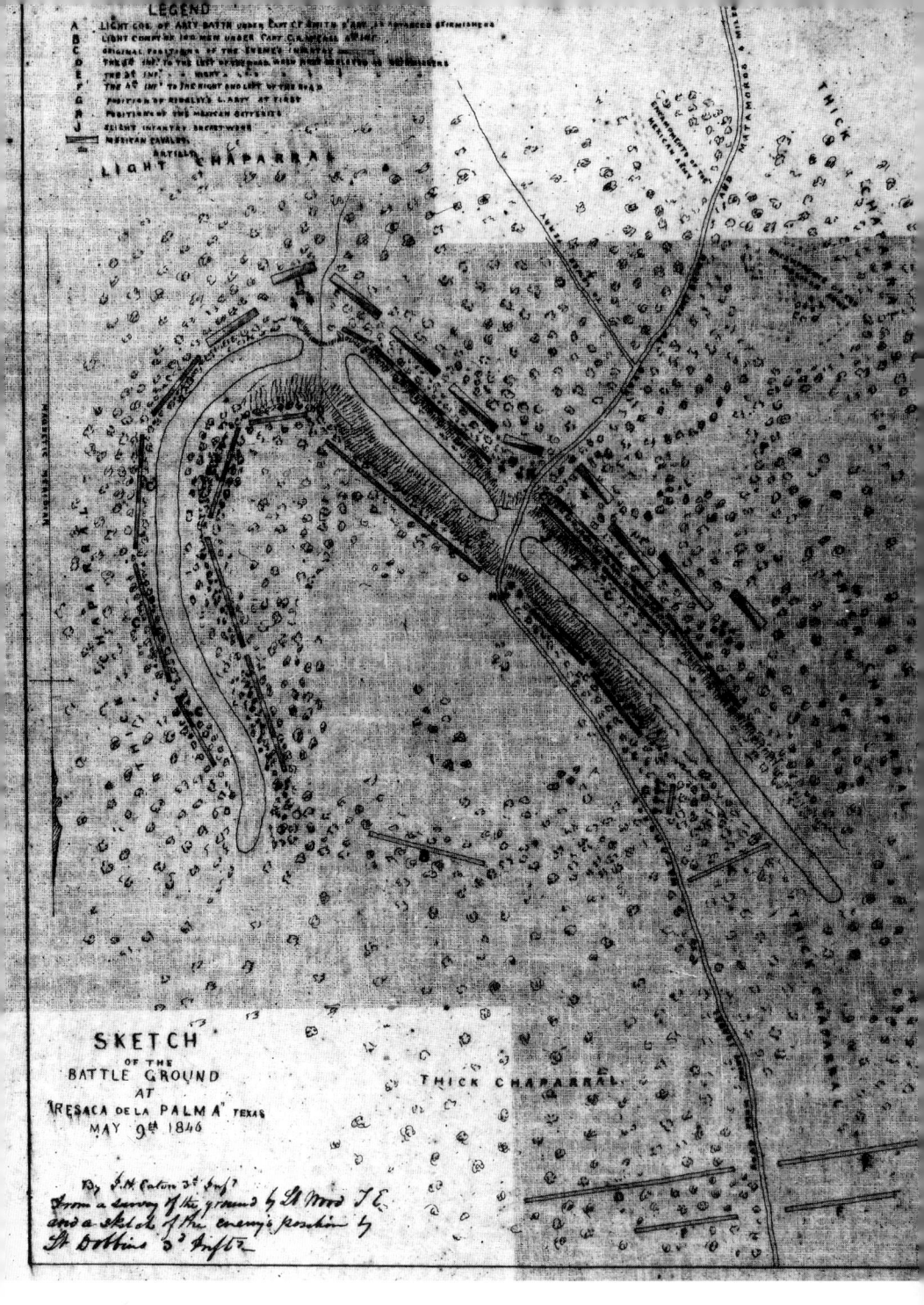

Sketch of Resaca de la Palma. (National Archives)

View of Monterrey from Independence Hill in the rear of the Bishop's Palace. (Library of Congress)

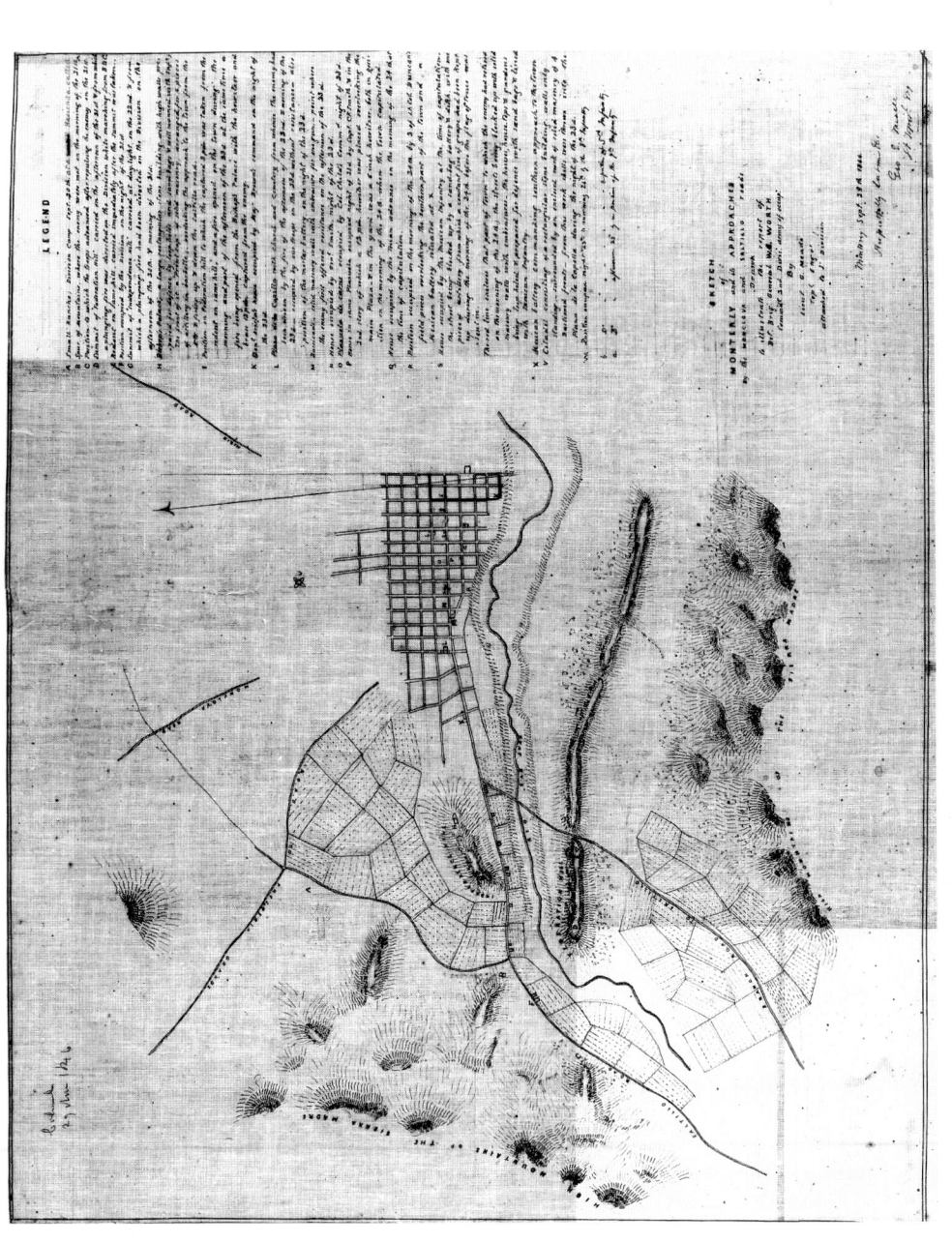

Meade's map of Monterrey. (National Archives)

Map of Buena Vista surveyed by Captain Linnard and Lieutenants Pope and Franklin and drawn by Lieutenant Sitgreaves. (National Archives)

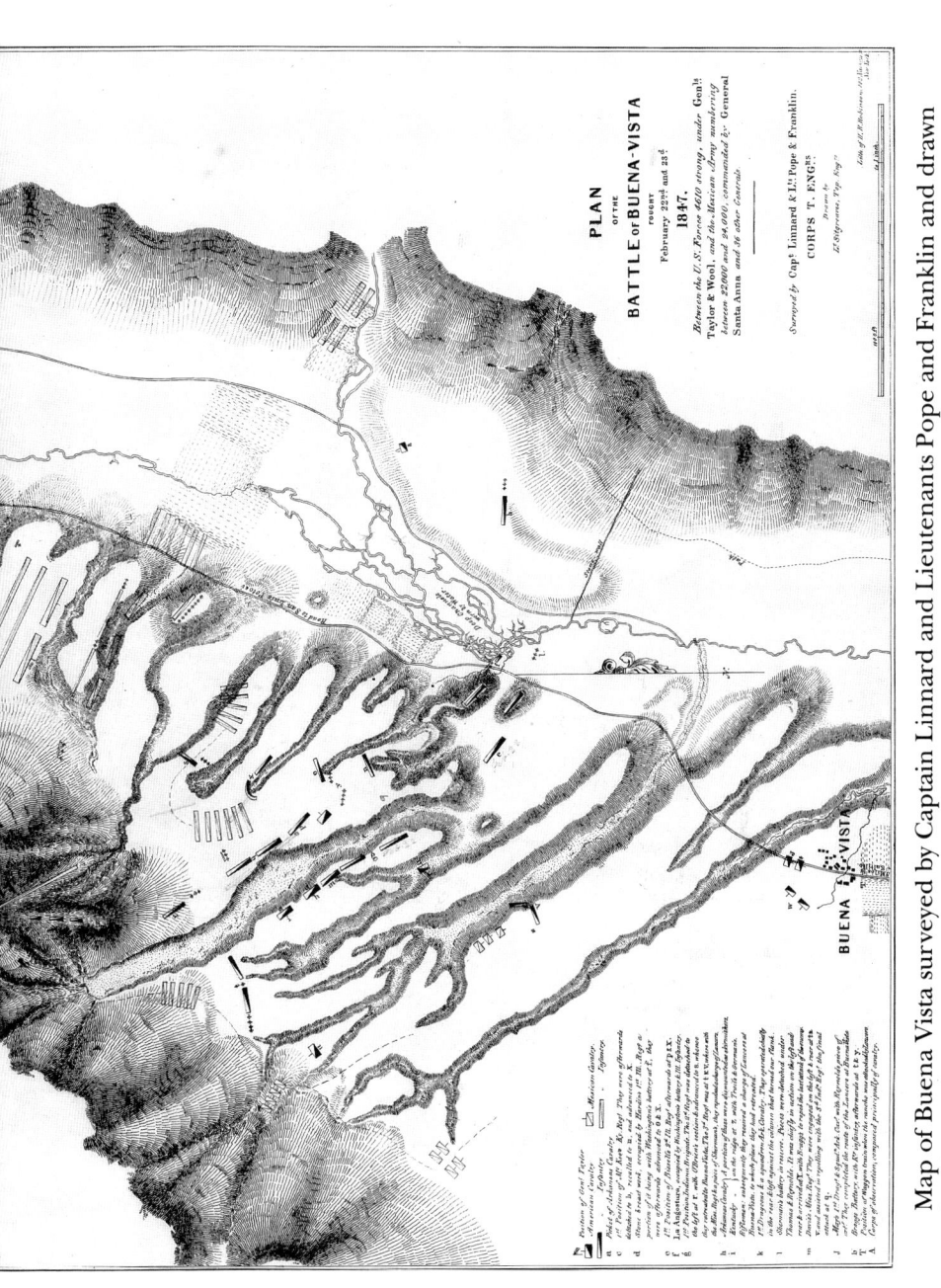

CHAPTER 5

With Zachary Taylor in Northern Mexico

Following the official incorporation of Texas into the Union and as international relations with Mexico deteriorated in the spring of 1845, the U.S. government determined to put troops in Texas. In June Washington alerted Brig. Gen. Zachary Taylor to prepare to move his army from Fort Jessup, Louisiana, into Texas. He concentrated his forces at New Orleans, and before the month was out Old Rough and Ready received orders to move into Texas after the state officially accepted annexation. While portions of his army went overland, Taylor accompanied the first troops, which set out on 23 July by sea for Corpus Christi. They reached the coast of St. Joseph's Island on the 26th and shortly thereafter moved by small boats to Corpus Christi.[1]

Immediately, Taylor's staff became aware of the need for up-to-date maps. Lt. Col. Ethan Allen Hitchcock, Taylor's Inspector General, aptly described the Army's lack of access to geographic and intelligence information: "My sickness is partly disgust at the state of things here—the haste and ignorance displayed in this movement. The government has actually no information of the coast, harbors, bars, etc. and as little of the interior." The best available map of Texas and adjacent country—drawn up by Lieutenant Emory and compiled at the Topographical Bureau in 1844—reached Taylor on 29 August. Hitchcock angrily noted in his diary that the map added "a distinct boundary mark to the Rio Grande. Our people ought to be damned for their impudent arrogance and domineering pre-

---

[1] Bauer, *The Mexican War*, pp. 18–19, 32; Smith, *War With Mexico*, I, pp. 138–42; Dufour, *The Mexican War; A Compact History*, pp. 32–35; Eisenhower, *So Far From God*, pp. 30–33.

sumption! It is enough to make atheists of all to see such wickedness in the world whether punished or unpunished."[2]

Emory had actually prepared his map of the Southwest for the Department of State, and it was based on available information from the best authorities at the time. This included the explorations and maps prepared by Baron Von Humboldt, Lieutenant Zebulon Pike, and Major Stephen Long; from Fremont's 1842 expedition; and from various naval sources, atlases, and local materials. Although excellent for political purposes, Emory's small-scale map did not meet the needs of a military commander. Taylor's army needed a map with significant military information based on military reconnaissance patrols. To remedy the deficiency, the Topographical Bureau ordered several experienced topogs to report to General Taylor.[3]

One was 2d Lt. George Gordon Meade, who received his orders at home in Philadelphia on 12 August 1845 to report at once to Texas. Meade graduated from West Point in 1835, left the Army in October 1836, but then returned to active duty in 1842 as a second lieutenant in the Topographical Engineers. After an assignment as a topographer for the northeast boundary survey, he took on duties as a construction engineer to design and build lighthouses on Delaware Bay. The orders to report to Taylor's army came as an unexpected surprise to the young topographer.[4]

Topogs Join Taylor's Army

Meade followed a well-traveled route to his new assignment. From Washington he went by rail to Cumberland, Maryland. Next he took a mail stage to Wheeling in western Virginia, then continued his journey by land to Zanesville, Ohio. After reaching the Ohio River port town (where he took note of low river conditions), Meade boarded a river steamer which took him past Louisville and Cincinnati to the Mississippi River. After another river voyage,

---

[2] Ethan Allen Hitchcock, *Fifty Years in Camp and Field: Diary of Major General Ethan Allen Hitchcock, USA*, W.A. Croffut (ed.) (New York: G.P. Putnam's Sons, 1909), pp. 195, 198.

[3] Wheat, *Mapping the Trans-Mississippi West*, II, pp. 190–91. A reproduction of this map is opposite page 184.

[4] George Meade (ed.), *The Life and Letters of George Gordon Meade*, I (New York: Charles Scribner's Sons, 1913), pp. 1–18.

Meade arrived in New Orleans on 4 September. The journey from Philadelphia took approximately nineteen days.[5]

Other topographers were reporting to what was being grandly called Taylor's "Army of Occupation." The newly designated chief Topographical Engineer for the command, Captain Thomas J. Cram, joined Meade in New Orleans, and on 12 September they met up with the third member of the topographic staff, Bvt. 2d Lt. Thomas J. Wood, at St. Joseph's Island. On the 15th, the three traveled twenty-five miles by steamboat to Corpus Christi. Meade recorded his initial impressions of the elderly Taylor in one of his many letters to follow to his wife: "I found [General Taylor] to be a plain, sensible old gentleman, who laughs very much at the excitement in the Northern States on account of his position, and thinks there is not the remotest probability of there being any war."[6]

Cram was an experienced topographer. Wood was just reporting to his first assignment. Cram received his commission as an Artillery officer from West Point in 1826; resigned from the Army in 1836, then returned to active duty as a topog in 1838. He had worked on a variety of internal improvements projects in the Midwest and was engaged in surveys of the Mississippi River near Cape Girardeau, Missouri, and harbor improvements in St. Louis before reporting to Texas. Wood, also a West Point graduate, received his commission in 1845 and reported directly to Taylor's army.[7]

Meade felt some uneasiness about his future assignment. He wrote to his wife, "I find matters pretty much as expected here; Colonel Abert's grand plan to carry out which, I was added to the number of officers asked for, is an entire failure, as General Taylor has his own views and plans, and does not intend to trouble himself with those of other people, so that there was not use in my coming, and I might have been of more services at the Tortugas." Apparently the old general's staff shared the same views. Meade, however, contended, "Now that I am here I want to see it out." Despite Taylor's failure to make full use of his staff, Meade grew to revere him.[8]

---

[5] Meade, *Letters*, I, pp. 20–24.
[6] Ibid., pp. 25–26.
[7] Cullum, *Biographical Register*, I, p. 366, II, p. 211.
[8] Meade, *Letters*, I, p. 26.

Military Surveys, Late 1845

Taylor had definite plans to employ his topographers. Sending them forth to reconnoiter the region southward toward the Rio Grande, on 14 September he reported to Washington that he had directed his army to examine the nearby country in the direction of the contested river border. The general added that the reconnaissance would soon include surveys "of the Nueces and the Laguna Madra [sic] ... in the event of a forward movement to the Rio Grande."[9]

Within a few days of their arrival at Corpus Christi, the three topogs were out in the field. Accompanied by a military escort they began systematic topographic surveys of the Nueces River, the Laguna de la Madre, and Aransas Bay. On the second day of their initial reconnaissance along the Nueces River to San Patricio, Wood became ill and returned to camp. The burden of work over the course of the thirteen day outing fell to Meade. The party struggled through tall prairie grass, described by the topog "as high as a man almost, which breaks you down marching through it." Roads in the area "are rendered impassable by a heavy rain; the soil is so soft they become boggy after a few hours, so that traveling and particularly marching large bodies of men, will be a very difficult operation."[10]

Upon his return to Taylor's encampment at Corpus Christi Meade felt a sense of accomplishment. On 10 October he wrote his wife, "I find my position here most agreeable." Regarding his topographic duties Meade added, "I have been much occupied in making drawings, which, as it has been done under the eyes of all the army, has enabled us to show them we are no idlers and mere civilians, but that, in anticipation of war, we are the first employed, and our duties of a most important nature."[11]

Shortly thereafter, the topog changed his heretofore positive views on the local climate. Meade had a mild bout with dysentery, this delayed a second reconnaissance to the Brazos Santiago, and a few days later all three topographers were seriously ill—Cram with

---

[9] Taylor to the Adjutant General, 14 Sep 1845, quoted from Robert H. Thornhoff, "Taylor's Trail in Texas," *Southwest Historical Quarterly*, 70 (July 1966): 9.

[10] Meade, *Letters*, I, pp. 27–29.

[11] Ibid., p. 29.

dysentery and Wood with a violent fever. Recovering, Meade said of the local environment, "Though I should not call the climate bad, I by no means call it good, for it is very changeable, the midday sun excessively hot, the nights cold, with very heavy dews." Meade also found it difficult to adjust to the "Northers" and the resultant violent temperature changes. He reported a forty degree change in a few hours and noted that "having been burned by the sun, you are frozen by the cold air, so that it requires a pretty stout constitution to stand the racket." [12]

Meade persevered, looked to the brighter side of his military duties, and tried to downplay the monotony and usual illnesses that plagued camp life. He believed he would remain in the area for quite a while even without a war. If negotiations improved, he thought he and the other topographers would be assigned to do the boundary survey. He cheerfully wrote his wife: "I have the pleasant prospect of spending a year here, at the least, if not more." Having regained his health, he began to tire of "A camp where there is not active service is a dull and stupid place, nothing but drill and parades, and your ears are filled all day with drumming and fifeing [*sic*]. All this is very pretty for such as have never seen it, but fifteen years of such business takes off the edge of novelty." [13]

On 13 November Meade began a reconnaissance of the Laguna de la Madre. He appeared to be the only effective topographer in Taylor's army, for Cram remained ill and Wood had departed for his home in Kentucky on two months' sick leave. This time Meade stayed out ten days exploring the area between the mainland and Padre Island. Illness again struck the young topog, this time he came down with a serious case of jaundice. By 9 December he managed to write his wife, "I have been as yellow as an orange, and although not sick enough to keep [to] my bed, yet I have felt very badly, and have been under the influence of medicine all the time." He refused sick leave and by the end of the month had recovered.[14]

As 1846 began Old Rough and Ready's Army of Occupation of regulars and volunteers had grown to nearly 4,000, almost half the strength of the entire U.S. Army. Units arriving over the course of

---

[12] Ibid., pp. 31–34.
[13] Ibid., pp. 34–35.
[14] Ibid., pp. 36–39, 42.

the six-month encampment at Corpus Christi settled down to a training routine, but the arrival of winter and its wet, miserable, and unhealthful weather, however, adversely affected training. The cold and often ill soldiers were forced to huddle in their tents, awaiting developments.[15]

Surveying a Route to the Rio Grande

Meanwhile, President Polk finally made his decision to move Taylor's army to the disputed Rio Grande boundary. On 3 February 1846, Old Rough and Ready received instructions to move, but he remained ignorant of the most direct land route to Matamoros almost until the last moment. During the preceding six months Taylor had directed the reconnaissances of the various routes, but unusually harsh winter weather inhibited good road surveys. By the 16th, however, he reported to the War Department that

> Examinations are now in progress of the two routes to Point Isabel—that by the mainland and that by Padre island. The reports of the officers charged with these will determine the route of march. Our train, which is necessarily very heavy, is rapidly organizing, and we shall be to commence the movement by the 1st of March.[16]

Meade, now Taylor's Chief Topographical Engineer, busied himself doing field surveys. He accompanied Captain Joseph Mansfield, the senior Corps of Engineers staff officer, on a marine expedition near Corpus Christi to examine a coastal route along the Gulf of Mexico from Aransas Bay to Matagorda. The topog preferred to go by land on horseback, but he rationalized, "I would rather go in boats than be doing nothing." In another of his letters to his wife dated 18 February, Meade described what he had accomplished in the last month: "Since then we have been knocking about the bays between Corpus Christi and this place [Matagorda], making surveys, and visiting towns, and places where towns are to be." By the time he got back to Corpus Christi on 1 March, he learned of the orders for Taylor to march south to the Rio Grande.[17]

---

[15] Bauer, *The Mexican War*, p. 34; Russell F. Weigley, *History of the United States Army* (New York: Macmillan, 1967), pp. 173, 182; Eisenhower, *So Far From God*, p. 50.

[16] Taylor to the Adjutant General, 16 Feb 1846, as quoted in Thornhoff, "Taylor's Trail in Texas," p. 11.

[17] Meade, *Letters*, I, pp. 46–47.

Also in Taylor's camp now was another Topographical Engineer, 1st Lt. Jacob E. Blake. He outranked Meade, though the latter still had the distinction of remaining as Taylor's chief Topographical Engineer. A graduate of the West Point class of 1833, Blake became an Infantry officer and then a Topographical Engineer in 1838. He served as a topog in Florida, worked on Lake Erie harbor construction between 1839–1841, surveyed the United States–Mexico boundary in 1841, and followed that with a series of military reconnaissance patrols of the approaches to New Orleans. He returned to Florida in 1842 as a command topographer and served there until reporting to Texas in September 1845.[18]

Blake reported his arrival at Corpus Christi to the Topographical Bureau on 27 September 1845, and regularly provided monthly reports of his activities. He scrupulously sent all available information back to the bureau, taking care on 25 January to send Meade's sketch of Laguna de la Madre to Colonel Abert. By 6 February Blake reported to the colonel of plans to reconnoiter Padre Island, and within three weeks he forwarded a copy of his completed report to the bureau.[19]

Blake's reconnaissance provided a detailed description of the route to Matamoros and the Rio Grande via Padre Island, and his report is a good example of providing crucial information to a tactical commander before the disposition of troops is decided. Blake reported on fording sites, the availability of wood, and the lack of grass—an important consideration in those days for an army's horses, mules, and oxen. After describing a feasible fording site across the Laguna de la Madre to Padre Island, Blake said that the next 106 miles down the island along the beach "were adapted to transportation by wagon, and for movement of Infantry." [20]

Blake also provided a detailed picture of Brazos Island, including comparisons between the port settlements of Brazos Santiago and Point Isabel. He determined that vessels with a draft of seven to eight feet could negotiate the narrow channel between Padre and Brazos islands near Brazos Santiago, where he observed sev-

---

[18] Ibid., p. 51; Cullum, *Biographical Register*, I, pp. 558–59.
[19] Blake to Abert, 27 Sep 1845, LR 1298; Blake to Abert, 25 Jan 1846, LR 168. Both in RG TE 77. Several of Blake's reports are no longer on file; however, they are listed in the Topographical Bureau's Register of Letters Received.
[20] Blake to Abert, 25 Feb 1846, LR 246, TE 77.

eral Mexican vessels. He believed boats stood a better chance of not being blown ashore when compared to Point Isabel on the other side of the channel on the mainland. The topog added that barges could be used along the beaches around Brazos Santiago whereas only shallow draft vessels could navigate within 250 yards of Point Isabel. Blake also observed an American vessel at Point Isabel taking on a load of cotton and hides. One problem with Brazos Santiago, the topog noted, appeared to be its susceptibility to storms. Only the previous August a storm had virtually destroyed the town. Blake did not find suitable building materials for fortifications nor grass for the animals, and he concluded that the island "is merely a series of shifting sand hills or knolls liable to be washed or blown away by the violent gales." [21]

By contrast, Point Isabel had a good road leading to Matamoros. Grass, driftwood for fuel, and water appeared sufficient, and the area could be secured with a minimum of troops. Farther south, however, a shallow channel at Boca Chica between the mainland and Brazos Island seemed unfit for navigation or fording. Having continued up the mouth of the Rio Grande to Burrita, Blake reported that vessels with a five-foot draft could travel several miles up the river.[22]

The Move to the Rio Grande

About one month after receiving notification to move his army, and after carefully examining the various engineer reconnaissance reports, Taylor selected the mainland route over some 200 miles of sun-baked prairie. In retrospect, his decision appeared to be the right one. Meade was given the responsibility to examine the line of march and select and lay out positions for camps. He departed on 8 March with the advance guard under Colonel David E. Twiggs.[23]

Blake kept Colonel Abert and the Topographical Bureau informed of Colonel (Brevet Brig. Gen) William J. Worth's march to the Rio Grande. He inclosed a copy of the orders for the march, a sketch map, and pertinent remarks. His report also included a copy of orders he received near the Arroyo Colorado on the 22d

---

[21] Ibid.
[22] Ibid.
[23] Thornhoff, "Taylor's Trail in Texas," p. 14; Meade, *Letters*, I, p. 51.

delineating the combat duties of a Topographical Engineer: "A subaltern and fifteen men of Dragoons will be kept about a mile in advance of the columns to communicate, at least hourly, intelligence of the enemy and of any obstructions to the march. The Topographical Engineer attached to the cavalry will accompany this advance." Following these orders, Blake recorded information on locations; the distances from Corpus Christi to Matamoros; the intermediate distances; appropriate information on the availability of water, wood, and grass; road conditions; and a geographic description of the route of advance.[24]

Opposite Matamoros

After reaching the disputed river boundary, Taylor set about fortifying his position opposite Matamoros and establishing supply lines to Point Isabel, now determined to be his base of supply. Under the supervision Captain Mansfield, the Americans hastily constructed an earthwork. By 2 April, Meade could describe "our position with the Mexicans on the opposite side of the river" as the "status quo." It was a grim land, "the most miserable desert, without wood or water, that I ever saw described, and perfectly unfit for the habitation of man." Listening to accounts of attractive women and congenial people on the other side of the river, a growing number of Americans deserted. Taylor ordered drastic measures to stop a mass desertion.[25]

As the American and Mexican armies faced each other across the river, Meade provided his wife his views on the tactics best suited each side. He pointed out the American army's tenuous link to its supplies saying, "if they [the Mexicans] have a general worth a sixpence he will attack Point Isabel, help himself to our provisions, forage, and money-chest, and then establish himself in our rear and oblige us to cut our way through him to get to our pork and beans." The Mexican commander (General Mariano Arista) acted otherwise, dispatching a cavalry unit across the river to cut off Taylor's supply route. When it

---

[24] Blake to Abert, 27 Mar 1846, LR 444, TE 77. The items mentioned were enclosed in his 27 March correspondence.

[25] Meade, *Letters*, I, pp. 52, 56. Meade's other letters written to his wife between 5 March and 2 April were not received. For a discussion on deserters see Bauer, *The Mexican War*, pp. 41–42, and Eisenhower, *So Far From God*, pp. 61–62.

ambushed and captured a small American force of dragoons, Taylor reported the opening of hostilities to Polk.[26]

Topogs in the First Battles of the War

Leaving behind enough men to defend the earthen fortification, Taylor set off on 1 May with the bulk of his army to secure Point Isabel. He returned on the eighth to find his garrison besieged and a Mexican army blocking his way at a watering hole called Palo Alto. Stretched out for more than a mile, at least 4,000 Mexicans faced 2,300 Americans. Taking the initiative, Taylor ordered an assault with bayonets. The advancing American infantry moved through knee-high, sharp edged grass, dodging solid cannon balls from smaller and ineffective Mexican artillery. Volleys from one of Taylor's infantry regiments repulsed a Mexican cavalry attack on the right, and mobile horse drawn "flying artillery" blasted the lancers as they tried to reform. By this time the gunfire had set the dry grass ablaze, and Taylor, using the cover afforded by the dense smoke, redeployed most of his force to the Mexican left. Heavy cannon barrages followed by enfilading fire from Taylor's mobile artillery threw back a Mexican counterattack. Next morning, the Mexicans, who had suffered heavy casualties, withdrew. Taylor had essentially won the battle by deadly effective use of his artillery.[27]

Lieutenant Blake had his moment of honor just before the Battle of Palo Alto. Because of the distance and the chaparral, General Taylor lacked intelligence of the enemy's disposition of troops and artillery. As the two armies drew opposite each other, Blake volunteered his services to the general to reconnoiter the enemy's positions. Captain James Duncan of the artillery described what happened:

To obtain the important information, Lieutenant J. E. Blake, of the Topographical Engineers, dashed off from the right of our line to within musket-shot of the enemy's left. Here he dismounted, and with his field-glass coolly counted the number of men in one of the enemy's squadrons, which, of course, enabled him accurately to estimate the enemy's entire

---

[26] Ibid., I, pp. 60, 66–69.
[27] Bauer, *The Mexican War,* pp. 49–57; Eisenhower, *So Far From God,* pp. 76–80. For an analysis of the battle see K. Jack Bauer, "The Battles on the Rio Grande: Palo Alto and Resaca de la Palma, 8–9 May 1846," in Charles E. Heller and William A. Stofft, eds., *America's First Battles, 1776–1965* (Lawrence, Kans.: Univ. of Kansas Press, 1986), pp. 57–74.

cavalry force. Lieutenant Blake then remounted his horse, and galloped from left to right of the enemy's line, stopping from time to time, and carefully observing the formation and number of his infantry, as well as the position, number, and calibre of his field guns, all of which information was fully verified by the subsequent events of the day.[28]

Blake reportedly rode to within eighty yards of the enemy lines, where he dismounted. Two Mexican officers rode out to see if Blake intended to parley, but Blake remounted and went along the line. Incredibly, no shots came from the opposing line until he had returned to the American lines and had given his report to General Taylor. Another officer, riding next to Blake, later wrote that because of their nearness to the enemy lines: "Had they thought proper, they could have fired a volley from their main line, and swept us to Guinea; but they did not."[29]

The probability of a bright career for Lieutenant Blake ended tragically the morning after the battle. While riding with the general's train back to camp, he dismounted to get some refreshments and rest. When the topog unbuckled his holsters, they quickly fell to the ground accidentally discharging one of the pistols. The shot severely wounded him, and he died before evening. Blake's last thoughts expressed regret that he did not instead fall at Palo Alto. Taylor noted the sad news in his report of the battle and specifically mentioned Blake's valuable reconnaissance, which resulted in the discovery of at least two batteries of artillery amidst the Mexican cavalry and infantry.[30]

---

[28] Quoted from *General Taylor and His Staff* (Philadelphia: Grigg, Elliot and Co., 1848), pp. 243–44.

[29] Quoted from *Niles [Ohio] National Register*, 70 (13 June 1846): 230. Accounts of Blake's daring reconnaissance are also found in Dufour, *Mexican War; A Compact History*, p. 70; Nathan C. Brooks, *A Complete History of the Mexican War* (Chicago: Rio Grande Press, 1965), p. 127; J. Reese Fry, *A Life of General Zachary Taylor* (Philadelphia: Grigg, Elliot and Co., 1847), p. 121; J. Frost, *The Mexican War and Its Warriors* (New Haven, CT: H. Mansfield, 1849), p. 40; John S. Jenkins, *History of the War Between the United States and Mexico* (Auburn: Derby and Miller, 1850), p. 109; *Taylor and His Generals, a Biography . . . Together with a Sketch of the Life of Major General Winfield Scott* (Hartford, CT: Silas Andrews and Son, 1848), pp. 58, 73; and Oliver O. Howard, *Great Commanders, General Taylor* (New York: D. Appleton and Co., 1897), p. 107.

[30] Cited from General Taylor Reports of 12 and 16 May 1846, in Fry, *Life of General Zachary Taylor*, pp. 129, 163; Frost, *Mexican War and Its Warriors*, p. 47; Jenkins, *War Between the United States and Mexico*, p. 109.

Taylor set out in the afternoon of 9 May with 2,000 men. The Americans again met the Mexican army a few miles to the south at Resaca de la Palma. This time they fought in a dry river bed on the road to the American encampment opposite Matamoros. Pushing units forward, Taylor directed assaults on both sides of the road. Dense chaparral forced the units into small groups, and fighting turned into an infantry battle with brutal hand-to-hand combat. The advancing infantry forced the Mexicans to abandon their positions east of the road, and soon the demoralized and leaderless Mexican soldiers turned about in panic and fled back toward Matamoros. The experienced American regulars and the leadership of the junior officers helped to carry the day. Again the Mexican army suffered much larger losses. Many Mexican soldiers, fleeing across the Rio Grande, either drowned in the swift current or died from the guns fired from the American earthwork, later named Fort Brown (now Brownsville) in honor of its fallen commander, Major Jacob Brown.[31]

Meade described the encounters at Palo Alto and Resaca de la Palma and of his role at Palo Alto. "I was in the action during the whole time, at the side of General Taylor, and communicating his orders," he told his wife, "and I assure you I may justly say I have had my 'bapteme de feu!' An officer of the General's staff had his horse shot under him, not two yards from me, and some five horses and men were killed at various times close to me." Describing the Battle of Resaca de la Palma the following day, he sadly reported the wounding of Lieutenant Blake. Meade advised his wife, "Say also to him [Major Hartman Bache, a Topographical Engineer stationed in the area] that poor Blake, of ours, after having gallantly borne himself through the conflict yesterday, unfortunately shot himself accidentally today, just as we marched, and it is feared the wound is mortal."[32]

Shortly after the two battles, Taylor reported the details to Washington. He commended Blake and Meade for "promptly conveying my orders to every part of the field." After Resaca de la Palma, Taylor also wrote of Lieutenant Wood's help in setting up and firing of the artillery's eighteen pounder. Because of their as-

---

[31] Bauer, *The Mexican War,* pp. 59–62; Eisenhower, *So Far From God,* pp. 80–85. Also see Bauer, "The Battles on the Rio Grande," pp. 74–80.
[32] Meade, *Letters,* I, pp. 80–82.

sortment of military skills, several other topogs had found also themselves later pressed into service as artillery officers.[33]

Declaration of War and Strategy

On 9 May 1846 President Polk received Taylor's report. Upon receipt of Polk's message that fighting had broken out in Texas, Congress approved a declaration of war and also passed a bill appropriating funds and authority to raise 50,000 volunteers.[34]

Surprisingly, the Regular Army was somewhat prepared for war. Though reduced to a strength of only 8,500 men, the cuts had not eliminated units. By this curious route, the expandable army envisioned long before by Secretary of War John C. Calhoun existed ready to be filled with new recruits. Congress also authorized the establishment of a regiment of mounted riflemen and a company of sappers, miners, and pontoniers, the latter an engineering unit equipped with a new type of rubber floating bridge. The Topographical Engineers, however, remained unchanged; still to be a small branch composed completely of officers without any units or enlisted personnel. Altogether in the Mexican War, over 30,000 men served in the Regular Army and over 70,000 in the militia and volunteer units. The total number in service at a given time probably never exceeded 50,000.[35]

The U.S. government also began to formulate some rough strategic plans. President Polk, Secretary of War William L. Marcy, and Maj. Gen. Winfield Scott, the Commanding General of the U.S. Army, worked out a three-pronged strategy to defeat the enemy and acquire territory. Polk made clear his policy objective—to seize Mexican territory north of the Rio Grande and the Gila River and westward to the Pacific Ocean. Taylor's army opposite Matamoros would advance to the northern Mexican city of Monterrey; another army under Brig. Gen. John E. Wool would march from San Antonio to Chihuahua; and Colonel Stephen Kearny's Army of the West would depart Fort Leavenworth, occupy Santa Fe and New Mexico, and proceed to San Diego on the California coast. Later plans also

---

[33] Cited from General Taylor Reports of 12 and 16 May 1846, in Fry, *Life of General Zachary Taylor*, p. 147. In October Wood transferred to the 2d Dragoons. Beers, "A History of the U.S. Topographical Engineers, 1813–1863," p. 291.
[34] Bauer, *The Mexican War*, pp. 66–78.
[35] Weigley, *History of the United States Army*, pp. 182–83.

called for a force to land at Vera Cruz on the Gulf of Mexico, for a direct advance on Mexico City.[36]

Taylor Crosses Into Mexico

When the Mexican army fled across the Rio Grande, Taylor lost an opportunity to destroy the demoralized enemy army. Instead, he delayed for over a week, blaming the War Department for not providing him with pontoon equipment back at Corpus Christi. Finally when the army did cross over the river to Matamoros, it discovered the enemy force had abandoned the town. Instead of pursuing the enemy, Old Rough and Ready elected to remain in the area to await the laborious effort to bring up supplies and their transport. July came before the first shallow-draft steamboat reached Camargo, a supply base established on a tributary of the Rio Grande. The wagons did not arrive until November, forcing Taylor to use Mexican pack mules and some native oxcarts to supplement his wagon train.[37]

Meade described the 18 May crossing of the Rio Grande and his duties. Exuding confidence he wrote his wife, "We shall beat them wherever we meet them, and in whatever numbers." Most of his time, however, consisted of the more mundane duties of a topog officer: "I have been in the saddle all day, making a reconnaissance of the environs of the town, with a view to select suitable sites for encampments and for the defense of the place." A letter dated the 25th to his wife described these duties:

> You may probably ask, "What have you to do?" Well, after the battles I had to make surveys of each field; then I had to reconnoitre [*sic*] the river, eight miles above and five miles below our camp, to select a crossing place; and as soon as we entered Matamoros, instead of squatting down, as the rest have done, for a few days' quiet, I was immediately required to make an exact survey of the town and the adjacent country for one and a half miles. Upon this I am presently engaged.[38]

---

[36] Maurice Matloff (ed.), *American Military History* (Washington, D.C.: Office of the Chief of Military History, rev. 1973), pp. 166–67; Bauer, *The Mexican War*, pp. 127, 145, 169, 232–37; Eisenhower, *So Far From God*, p. 105.

[37] Matloff, *American Military History*, p. 168; Weigley, *History of the United States Army*, pp. 180–81.

[38] Meade, *Letters*, I, pp. 85–86, 90.

Two days later he had finished his survey and expected to take about a week to prepare the drawing.[39]

Regardless of his esteem for Taylor, the topog became somewhat frustrated with the old man's administrative inadequacies. Meade exclaimed in another of his frequent letters home that his commanding general's chief weakness

> ... is the entire and utter ignorance of the use to which the staff department can be put, and especially my own corps. ... Did he have his own way, we should be perfectly useless; not from any unfriendly feeling on his part, but from absolute ignorance of what we can be required to do, and perfect inability to make any use of the information we do obtain.[40]

The topog also cited the general's failure to properly plan the bridging over the Rio Grande although he had more than ample time. Old Rough and Ready simply appeared to ignore his engineers' advice, and a nine-day delay resulted when he finally decided to cross the river. After the Mexican army quit Matamoros the engineers resorted to expedient measures by simply seizing some Mexican boats and the regular ferry. Meade cited this example as illustrative of the general's ignorance of the proper use of the command's engineers (both Corps of Engineers and Topographical Engineers):

> Here is the General's defect. Had he knew [*sic*] how to use his engineers the month we were lying in camp, he would have had us at work experimenting, and when any plan proved successful, had a bridge constructed and put in depot, and then on the tenth, in three or four hours, the whole army, artillery and all, could have been crossed, and the Mexican army prevented from retreating with some twelve pieces of artillery.[41]

Also in late May Meade launched into one of his frequent diatribes against the volunteer troops now arriving in large numbers.

---

[39] Ibid., p. 90.

[40] Ibid., p. 101.

[41] Ibid. This delay caused numerous recriminations. Taylor blamed the Quartermaster Department for having ignored an earlier request for a pontoon bridge, and further blame was passed to Congress for not appropriating funds. A pontoon bridge arrived in October 1846—long after the initial requirement. See James A. Huston, *The Sinews of War: Army Logistics, 1775–1953*, Army Historical Series (Washington, D.C.: Office of the Chief of Military History, 1966), pp. 133–34, 139. After Matamoros, bridges were not required in northern Mexico. See Harry Burgess, "The Influences of Bridges on Campaigns," *Military Engineer*, 19 (Mar 1927): 148; and Ivor D. Spencer, "Rubber Pontoon Bridges—in 1846," *Military Engineer*, 37 (Jan 1945): 24–27.

"The volunteers continue to pour in," he wrote, "and I regret to say I do not see it with much satisfaction. They are perfectly ignorant of discipline, and most restive under restraint. They are in consequence a most disorderly mass, who will give us, I fear, more trouble than the enemy." A few weeks later he also observed the volunteers' mistreatment of the indigenous population and added that this would prompt the Mexicans to rise en masse and obstruct progress into the country. Quite concerned, the observant topog added, "and if, when we reach the mountains, we have to fight the people as well as the soldiers, the game will be up with us."[42]

Military Reconnaissances Around Matamoros

Meanwhile, Meade received instructions to examine the Rio Grande to Reynosa. He hopped aboard a steamboat and conducted the usual military reconnaissance along the way and jotted down more commentary of the country. The agricultural possibilities of the areas along the river impressed the topog. He believed the soil equaled that along the Mississippi and was particularly well suited for growing cotton and sugar. He correctly prophesied:

> It is without doubt the finest part of Texas (if it belongs to Texas!) that I have seen and I anticipate its being densely populated, one day, when its resources are made available by the means of transporting its products to the sea. It has one advantage over the Mississippi Valley, which is its perfect salubrity.[43]

By July more Topographical Engineers reported for duty. Captain William G. Williams, another West Point graduate, arrived from his previous duty assignment as supervisor of the Great Lakes surveys. Williams, a member of the Class of 1824, received his commission in the Infantry and became a topog in 1834. His wide range of topographical duties included various surveys in the East, a reconnaissance of Cherokee lands in 1837–1838, and supervision of harbor work on Lake Erie.[44]

---

[42] Ibid., pp. 91, 110. His comments regarding the volunteers were extensive. See also pages 92, 94, 102–04, and 108–10. For a further and interesting evaluation of the volunteers see Johannsen, *To the Halls of the Montezumas*, pp. 22–44.

[43] Meade, *Letters*, I, p. 106.

[44] Cullum, *Biographical Register*, I, pp. 330–31.

Second Lieutenant John Pope was also commissioned at West Point. He went directly into the Topographical Engineers in 1842 and served his first tour in Florida. Before reporting to Mexico the future Union general served as an assistant in the Northeast Boundary Survey.[45]

With Williams now as the senior topographer, Meade had hopes of serving in the same capacity in General Wool's army then gathering in San Antonio. Meade, however, remained with Taylor. On 9 July Williams and Meade received orders to reconnoiter the region from Camargo toward Monterrey. Delays prevented departure, and they did not reach Camargo until the 13th. On the 19th Meade got part of his wish to be a command topographer when orders attached him to Worth's division. Taylor had finally started to move his army deeper into the interior of Mexico with Monterrey as the next major objective. Now part of the vanguard again, the topog appeared contented. By the 26th they reached Cerralvo, about halfway to Monterrey from Camargo.[46]

The Move to Monterrey

Other reasons besides pressure from Washington forced Taylor to move on. By August his army had swelled to 15,000 men, but Camargo's unhealthy and hot climate began to take toll of the troops, especially the volunteers. Since the army's arrival on the Rio Grande a number of soldiers had deserted, some lured away by Mexican offers of land, and others, who were Catholics, by Mexican appeals to their common religion. Others found attractive senoritas as a good excuse to quit. The remainder simply found Army life distasteful and harsh. Now faced with a serious disciplinary problem among the volunteers, Old Rough and Ready decided to send many back home.[47]

Despite such distractions, most men remained loyal, and by the end of the month Taylor's army was heading toward Monterrey. With about 3,000 regulars and the same number of volunteers, Taylor organized the regulars augmented by some volunteers into

---

[45] Cullum, *Biographical Register*, II, p. 126.
[46] Meade, *Letters*, I, pp. 106, 109–25.
[47] Matloff, *American Military History*, p. 168; Weigley, *History of the United States Army*, pp. 41–42; Bauer, *The Mexican War*, pp. 83–87.

two divisions, and the balance of volunteers into a third division. A little more than a quarter of the American expeditionary force consisted of mounted troops, armed with the percussion-cap rifles. The infantry still carried flintlock muskets with fixed bayonets, the latter highly preferred by Old Rough and Ready as an assault weapon. His artillery consisted of four field batteries, two 24-pounder howitzers, and one 10-inch mortar, which remained the only weapon suitable for the forthcoming siege against strongly fortified Monterrey.[48]

Meanwhile, Meade roamed out front of Worth's column and reconnoitered the road to Monterrey. On one occasion he nearly encountered Mexican cavalry, and in a letter to his wife dated 3 September he outlined his next move:

> Tomorrow I go forward in advance of the army with a strong working party and escort, to repair the road previously examined. The army will commence their march the next day, and in ten days from now we shall know whether Monterey is ours, by hard knocks or not.[49]

His road working party, however, did not depart until the 12th. The small mixed force, otherwise known as the Pioneer Advance consisting of ninety pioneers, cavalry, and rangers, made necessary road repairs for wagon traffic. A few days later, feeling confident that there would be little Mexican resistance, Meade confidently noted, "I have . . . pretty well made up my mind they will not fight." By the 19th the engineer work party and Worth's advance column reached the outskirts of Monterrey.[50]

The Battle of Monterrey

Taylor's engineering staffs probed the city's defenses for soft spots. Major Mansfield, the chief of the engineer staff, informed Taylor of the town's strong fortifications, but they appeared vulnerable in the direction of Saltillo. Captain Williams' topog reconnaissance confirmed the weaker defenses. He reported the presence of makeshift fortresses on the two hills—Independence and Federation—protecting the western edge of town and overlooking the road to Saltillo. In addition, he reported that these positions ap-

---

[48] Matloff, *American Military History*, pp. 168–69.
[49] Meade, *Letters*, I, p. 127.
[50] Ibid., p. 130.

peared difficult to reinforce. Based on these reports, Taylor decided to cut off Monterrey from this direction.[51]

On 20 September Old Rough and Ready ordered a double envelopment of the city. He sent Worth's division to the west, while the other two divisions struck from the east. The following day Worth succeeded in taking Federation Hill and cut the Mexican supply route to Saltillo. Two days later he moved his division up Independence Hill and captured the fortified ruins of the Obispado, an abandoned bishop's palace about halfway down the slope overlooking the city. Meanwhile, the main force made several feints followed by a series of assaults on the eastern edge of Monterrey and advanced into the city on the 23d. By midday the two attacks with bitter house-to-house and hand-to-hand street fighting closed in on the center of the city.[52]

Meade, of course, wrote a full description of his part in the battle for the city. He did not hesitate to alert his wife to the dangers of his reconnaissance duties and his close calls from the moment the first Mexican artillery rounds rained down on the Americans:

... one ball I assure you, came closer to me than I desire it to do again, just passing about two feet on one side of my knee. The remainder of the day was spent by the engineer officers in reconnoitering the positions of the enemy, a duty, I assure you, sufficiently hazardous, as they were obliged to go with small parties and far from the camp, giving enterprising enemy opportunity to cut them off.[53]

Meade continued to explain what happened the following day (20 September). While investigating enemy artillery positions, he received orders to accompany General Worth's flanking column. As the column advanced artillery began firing from Independence Hill, but the Americans managed to ensconce themselves near the

---

[51] Edward J. Nichols, *Zach Taylor's Little Army* (New York: Doubleday, 1963), p. 143; Brainerd Dyer, *Zachary Taylor* (Baton Rouge: Louisiana State University Press, 1946), p. 199; Fry, *Life of General Zachary Taylor*, pp. 219–20; Smith, *War With Mexico*, I, p. 239; David Lavender, *Climax at Buena Vista: The American Campaign in Northeastern Mexico, 1846–47* (Philadelphia: J.B. Lippincott Co., 1968), p. 107; Bauer, *The Mexican War*, pp. 92–93; Eisenhower, *So Far From God*, p. 128.

[52] Bauer, *The Mexican War*, pp. 93–99; Eisenhower, *So Far From God*, pp. 128–43.

[53] Meade, *Letters*, I, pp. 132–33. This hazardous duty is also noted in George W. Smith and Charles Judah (eds.), *Chronicles of the Gringos: The U.S. Army in the Mexican War, 1846: Accounts of Eyewitnesses and Combatants* (Albuquerque: University of New Mexico Press, 1968), pp. 79–80.

Saltillo road. Meade escorted Worth and a small party to the key road, and described the following action:

> Our advance was covered by about fifty Texans, and we proceeded along the road for two miles, till we came into the gorge through which the Saltillo road runs, where the enemy were reported in large force to our front. Having seen all we wanted, we were about retiring, when they opened a fire upon us from a fence alongside of the road, where some of the rascals had sneaked up to cut us off, but it was promptly returned by the Texans, and we came quietly back to camp.[54]

On the 21st the Mexicans sallied out to attack Worth's flanking force along the Saltillo road. Meade recalled, "The Mexican cavalry charged on our people most gallantly, but were received with so warm a fire as to throw them into confusion." The attackers fled, and Worth pushed on to take Federation Hill. That afternoon the Americans captured the hill and its key fortification, Fort Soldado.[55]

During this time, Taylor moved the remainder of his attacking forces toward the city. The diversionary attack on the eastern part of town on 21 September met with stiff resistance from the defenders, who barricaded the streets and turned the stone houses into fortifications. The probe unexpectedly developed into a full-scale assault, and the Americans were raked with heavy fire from the Citadel, the fortified ruins of an uncompleted cathedral about 1,000 yards north of the city, and other defensive positions in the city. The Mexicans repulsed the American attack on the Citadel, and La Teneria, an earthwork on the northeast corner of the city, fell only after heavy losses.[56]

Officers of both engineering corps directly participated in the assaults on the city's northeastern defenses. The Topographical Engineers fought alongside their Corps of Engineers colleagues, often helping Engineer officers in reconnaissances and assaults. Mansfield used a map prepared by Meade, consulting it to designate points of attack on the town's defenses. When the diversionary attack developed into an assault, Mansfield called on Williams

---

[54] Meade, *Letters*, I, p. 133.

[55] Ibid., pp. 133–34. See also Smith, *War With Mexico*, I, pp. 239–46; Dufour, *Mexican War; A Compact History*, pp. 116–20; Bauer, *The Mexican War*, p. 97; Eisenhower, *So Far From God*, pp. 131–33.

[56] Meade, *Letters*, I, pp. 134–35; Smith, *War With Mexico*, I, pp. 248–55; Dufour, *Mexican War; A Compact History*, pp. 120–24; Bancroft, *History of Mexico*, V, p. 383; Bauer, *The Mexican War*, pp. 95–96; Eisenhower, *So Far From God*, pp. 133–38.

and Pope to help him pick out other locations for the attacking units. As one participant later recalled, "Major Mansfield and Captain Williams were far in our front."[57]

Taylor's assault on the city turned out to be poorly executed, and many brave officers, including Williams, fell that day. "Captain Williams, of the topographical corps," recalled one observer, "lay on one side of the street, wounded; the gallant Major Mansfield, wounded in the leg, still pressed on with unabated ardor, cheering the men, and pointing out the places of attack."[58] At the end of the first day only La Teneria remained in American hands. The attackers had to withdraw from other forward positions, and no major action occurred the following day. The critically wounded Williams remained in a Mexican hospital until his death on 23 September. Pope, at his side at the time, later wrote to Abert of this latest tragic loss to the Topographical Engineers, "he wished it to be made known, he fell while leading the advance and in the discharge of his duty."[59]

On the 21st Worth's division on the western edge of the city prepared for an assault on Independence Hill. Just before dark the assault force moved out in a rain storm to their attack position at the base of the hill. Meade helped guide these troops to their proper places. At three in the morning of the 22d the Americans moved up the steep, rough slope of the hill, and following a brief fight took Fort Libertad. After Captain John Sanders of the Corps of Engineers located a suitable path up to the fort, troops dismantled a 12-pounder howitzer and dragged it up to a position overlooking the city. Worth's men next seized the fortified ruins of the Obispado, and by late afternoon the western approaches to the city were firmly in American hands.[60]

---

[57] Quoted from Smith and Judah (eds.), *Chronicles of the Gringos*, p. 80; Smith, *War With Mexico*, I, p. 251; Howard, *General Taylor*, p. 158; Fry, *Life of General Zachary Taylor*, pp. 243–44; Bauer, *The Mexican War*, p. 95.

[58] Quoted from William S. Henry, *Campaign Sketches of the War With Mexico* (New York: Harper and Brothers, 1847), p. 195; Bauer, *The Mexican War*, p. 96.

[59] Pope to Abert, 28 Sep 1846, LR 999, TE 77. This letter was enclosed in correspondence that Meade sent to Colonel Abert the same day. Eisenhower, *So Far From God*, p. 136.

[60] Meade, *Letters*, I, pp. 135–36; Smith, *War With Mexico*, I, pp. 246–48; Dufour, *Mexican War; A Compact History*. pp. 123–26; Bauer, *The Mexican War*, p. 97; Eisenhower, *So Far From God*, pp. 139–40.

By the 23d the Americans pushed into the city from two directions. As Taylor's main force cautiously advanced toward Monterrey's defense, Worth's artillery shelled the city from the west. Worth sent Meade to reconnoiter the Mexican artillery facing the hill, and the topog found that the enemy had abandoned that portion of the town. By the afternoon the Americans moved through the city, street by street, burrowing from house to house. Meanwhile, to their pleasant surprise they discovered that the Mexicans had abandoned their strong outer defenses, except the Citadel, and concentrated around the Cathedral in the town's central area.[61]

On 24 September an armistice was reached. The Mexican commander, fearing that his munitions would be detonated by the constant shelling, surrendered in return for an eight-week armistice. That evening Taylor agreed to the lenient terms because of his own critical condition, and he believed that peace now could be worked out between the two nations. Meade approved of the general's generous terms, and noted, "Here was an army of six-thousand men giving up to us a town with twenty-two pieces of artillery and a vast amount of the munitions of war, and retiring eighty miles to the interior and leaving us in a place they had attempted to defend." [62]

Reports prepared by the commanders reaching Washington after the battle also singled out the topogs contributions. Meade and Pope received brevet promotions to first lieutenant. Colonel Abert also recommended brevets for the deceased Williams and Blake, the latter for his heroic service at Palo Alto.[63]

---

[61] Meade, *Letters,* I, pp. 136–37; Smith, *War With Mexico,* I, pp. 256–59; Dufour, *Mexican War; A Compact History,* pp. 126–27; Bauer, *The Mexican War,* p. 99; Eisenhower, *So Far From God,* pp. 141–42.

[62] Meade, *Letters,* I, p. 139. Meade also discussed several other advantages. See pages 138–40.

[63] Ibid., p. 155; Abert to Scott, 20 Oct 1846, LS 483, TE 77; "Report of the Chief of Topographical Engineers," Report of the Secretary of War, House Exec. Doc. 4, p. 141. The official reports of the battle are consolidated in Report of the Secretary of War, House Exec. Doc. 4, 29th Cong., 2d sess., 1846, pp. 90, 108. Lieutenant Wood transferred to the Second Dragoons on 19 October 1846, thus ending his topographical career. He served with distinction in the war, later served with the cavalry on the frontier, and rose to brevet major general in the Union Army during the Civil War. Cullum, *Biographical Register,* I, p. 235; *DAB,* X, pp. 474–75.

Meade Again Becomes Acting Chief Topog

With Williams' death, Meade again became Taylor's Chief Topographical Engineer. As the Mexican army began its withdrawal from Monterrey, the topogs started to prepare detailed maps of the battle which Taylor included in his report to the War Department. Meade continued mapping the town and the surrounding area, but he received orders to report again to Worth's command for operations along the Saltillo road. Pope remained behind to continue the triangulation survey around Monterrey.[64]

By now Meade could see some credence to a morbid story then circulating among the officers about the topog and his unlucky superiors:

> They have a joke among the officers, that it is bad business for any officer to be sent here to command me, for he will be sure to be killed; and it is strange. Of the three superior officers who have been sent here at various times, the first (Captain Cram) had to leave the country soon after his arrival, on account of ill-health; the second (poor Blake) shot himself; and the third (Captain Williams) fell in recent operations against Monterey; leaving me each time the senior officer of the Topographical Engineers.[65]

In any case, Colonel Abert appreciated Meade's reports and maps. As noted, the topogs assigned to a field command did not have to report to the Topographical Bureau, but Colonel Abert insisted on receiving useful topographic information. In late November Abert acknowledged Meade's efforts: "The sketch and legends are highly creditable to you, and have been examined by the President and the Secretary of War." The colonel also verified the receipt of Williams' personal effects and accounts, which Meade took the time to administer.[66]

During their stay in Monterrey the topogs took advantage of the better living conditions afforded in the city. Meade, Pope, and an Engineer officer moved into a Mexican general's home. The topog boasted, "We each of us have our own servants, one of whom is cook, the other hostler, and the third plays waiter; so that we are quite comfortable, and from our luxurious quarters, the envy of the army." [67]

---

[64] Meade to Abert, 28 Sep 1846, LR 999; and 20 Oct 1846, LR 1031, TE 77.
[65] Meade, *Letters,* I, p. 144.
[66] Abert to Meade, 25 Nov 1846, LS 510, TE 77.
[67] Meade, *Letters,* I, p. 147.

Meade also wrote his wife about the condition of the troops after the battle. He expressed concern over the increasing incidence of illness among the soldiers, a threat more serious to an army even than battle. On a more positive note, however, the topog noted that control over the volunteer troops seemed to improve. His superiors knew how the volunteers could antagonize the local populace, and they acted accordingly. Taylor, to avoid incidents between his troops and the people, established his camp with most of the army three miles from town. Worth kept only a few troops in Monterrey.[68]

Meade continued to pen his thoughts on the strategy of the war. The future Civil War general and Union commander at Gettysburg advocated a landing at Vera Cruz and a march on Mexico City. On 5 October he wrote his wife that a plan merely to hold the northern Mexican provinces would result in a long-term occupation and the needless sacrifice of American lives. He concluded,

> We may go on in this way for five years, and not conquer peace. The loss of a few soldiers, and the temporary occupation of her frontier towns, is no embarrassment to Mexico; her capital and vital parts must be touched. Once occupy these (and we can do it as readily as we operate here, if we have the proportionate means), and she will be brought to terms.[69]

Resumption of Operations

Taylor's armistice in Mexico did not meet with President Polk's approval. Learning of the terms, the president ended the armistice, declaring angrily that another opportunity to defeat the enemy and conclude the war had been lost. Major James D. Graham, a Topographical Engineer, arrived in early November with dispatches from Washington directing Old Rough and Ready to end the armistice and resume operations. Meade wrote home of his support for the "old gentleman" and the wisdom of the armistice terms as he saw it:

> For myself, individually, you know my sentiments; opposed, at first, to this war, brought on by our injustice to a neighbor, and uncalled for aggression, she, in her stupidity and folly, giving our rulers plausible excuses for their conduct; but when once in it, I should and have desired to see it

---

[68] Ibid., pp. 146–47. For an account of the medical aspects of the war see Mary C. Gillett, *The Army Medical Department, 1818–1865* (Washington, D.C.: U.S. Army Center of Military History, 1987).

[69] Ibid., p. 143.

conducted in a vigorous manner, and brought to a speedy conclusion by its being carried on with energy well directed. But such has not been the case, nor will it ever be so, as long as generals are made in the counting-houses and soldiers on farms.[70]

The struggle resumed with American forces occupying more of Mexico. In November, Taylor marched southwest to take Saltillo, the U.S. Navy seized the port of Tampico on the Gulf, and General Wool's army of 3,400 men began a long march from San Antonio to join Taylor's army. By December another column, the 850-man 1st Missouri Mounted Volunteers under Colonel Alexander W. Doniphan, set forth from Valverde, New Mexico, crossing some 1,800 miles of difficult country, also to join Taylor. As the year ended the American forces occupied nearly all northeastern Mexico.[71]

Meade found Saltillo "a very pretty place, though not so beautifully situated as Monterey [*sic*]." He immediately noted a great difference in the agriculture of the newly occupied region which brought forth fields of wheat instead of orange and banana groves. The topog had little time to investigate the town, and he departed the next day on a three day reconnaissance. During the operation he covered twenty-five miles and boasted that such duties were "keeping up with my reputation of always being among those who penetrate farthest into the country."[72]

Meade returned with Taylor to Monterrey, where he prepared more sketches for the general's reports. There he noted that problems with the volunteer units had again surfaced. The astute lieutenant believed attaching regular officers and enlisted men to every volunteer regiment would bring order to the volunteers:

> Let the colonel be taken from the lieutenant colonels, and the captains from the lieutenants. The army can well spare these officers, for it is organized for such a purpose. Then in each regiment you would have enough practical knowledge to give a tone to it, and the volunteer regiments would soon be as efficient as regular troops. But, as it is, the generals know no more than the privates, and it is only by attaching regular officers, as staff officers, that they get along at all.[73]

---

[70] Ibid., pp. 150–52, quotation from p. 154.
[71] For accounts of Doniphan's march see Bauer, *The Mexican War*, pp. 151–59; Eisenhower, *So Far From God*, pp. 244–50.
[72] Meade, *Letters*, I, pp. 157–58.
[73] Ibid., p. 163. He discussed specific incidents involving the volunteers, but he also believed they were brave soldiers and lacking in leadership. See pages 161–66.

Meanwhile, Meade's tenure as Taylor's chief topog nearly ended again. Captain Thomas B. Linnard, a West Point graduate with sixteen years service, arrived in November to take over as the command's senior topographer. Linnard graduated in 1830 and received a commission in the artillery and served in combat in Florida during the Seminole War. He became a topog in 1838 and worked on harbor improvement projects in Delaware Bay, New York, and Mobile between 1843–1846. This time the bad fortune that seemed to afflict Meade's superiors did not strike the new chief topog too severely. Linnard soon came down with a fever rendering him unfit for immediate duty, but he soon recovered.[74]

Meade Receives a New Assignment

In December Taylor, under orders from Washington, expanded his operations southeastward to Victoria to meet American forces at Tampico. By then Wool's army had reached Parras to the west of Monterrey, and an army task force under the command of Maj. Gen. Robert Patterson had occupied Tampico. Worth would remain at Saltillo, and Maj. Gen. William O. Butler and a force of volunteers would remain at Monterrey. With his rear secured Taylor set out on the 15th with a task force consisting of Brig. Gen. David E. Twiggs' division of regulars and Brig. Gen. John A. Quitman's division of volunteers. Meade came along as the topographer. Three days out on the march, Taylor received information that General Antonio Lopez de Santa Anna had regained the presidency of Mexico and raised a new army. The wily Mexican leader appeared to be leading this army on a long march toward Monterrey. Taylor rushed back leaving Quitman to proceed to Victoria. The threat to Monterrey turned out to be a false alarm, and Old Rough and Ready resumed his march to Victoria.

Meade remained behind with Quitman. The lieutenant noted that Taylor "being very anxious to know the nature of the mountain passes, has detailed me to go with General Quitman to Victoria, where, upon meeting General Patterson, I shall be furnished with an escort of cavalry, and will then reconnoiter the whole country in front of the line of Tampico and this place [Montemorelos]." They reached Victoria on the 29th to await the arrival of Patterson.

[74] Ibid., p. 155; Cullum, *Biographical Register*, I, pp. 452–53.

Meanwhile, Quitman had the Topographical Engineer reconnoiter the road southward to Tula. Based on information obtained from a local native the topog decided to turn back short of his destination. "I found the rascally Mexican had deceived me," Meade later wrote, "and that I was within six miles of one hundred and fifty Mexicans. The object of my expedition was, however, fully accomplished—the examination of the road—and I satisfied myself that the road was impractical for wagons or artillery."[75]

A change in U.S. strategy, however, shifted the bulk of American forces to a new theater of operations. Mexican leaders still had not come to terms. President Polk, realizing the impracticality of moving south from Saltillo over inhospitable terrain, decided to go ahead with the operation to land at Vera Cruz and march inland to take Mexico City. General Scott set into action his plans to assemble a force for the amphibious operation and march the shorter route overland to the Mexican capital. Upon arriving in Mexico Scott proceeded to take more than half of Taylor's army and almost all his regulars, including Meade. Scott then ordered Old Rough and Ready to deploy his remaining force to defensive positions around Monterrey.[76]

While excited over his new assignment, Meade admitted he "regretted exceedingly parting with the old man." The topog also heard that Scott had six Topographical Engineers with him at Brazos Santiago, and four of the officers outranked him. After serving several times as command topographer, he would now "have to play fifth fiddle."[77]

For a short time Meade served as Patterson's chief topog with orders to reconnoiter a healthful site for an encampment near Tampico. On 3 February Captain John McClellan reported to Patterson and became his chief Topographical Engineer. Although disappointed to be subordinate again, Meade did appreciate getting three extra pairs of spectacles that McClellan picked up from Mrs. Meade. "I was on my last pair," he wrote his wife, "and I have had some terrible frights lately when I thought I had lost them."[78]

---

[75] Meade, *Letters*, I, pp. 170–73.
[76] Bauer, *The Mexican War*, pp. 232–34, 237–38; Eisenhower, *So Far From God*, pp. 161–65, 170–72.
[77] Meade, *Letters*, I, p. 175.
[78] Ibid., pp. 176–77.

John McClellan was an experienced topographer with twenty years of Army service. He received his commission at West Point as an Artillery officer in 1826, resigned in 1836, but returned to active duty as a Topographical Engineer in 1838. He served in various topographic assignments including two tours of duty in Florida during the Seminole War, harbor improvements in North Carolina, and duty at the bureau. Before reporting to Mexico McClellan supervised harbor improvement projects on Lake Michigan.[79]

While McClellan and Meade waited in Tampico for the next move, Meade continued his flow of letters. He filled his correspondence with the latest rumors and his feelings on the conduct of the war. He noted, "We are in a complete state of ignorance as to what is to be done," but when he learned of events the topog unleashed strong views. When Meade heard that Mexican troops retook Victoria and punished citizens who had cooperated with the Americans, he presented some perceptive thoughts on occupying and pacifying a country:

> This I considered cruel treatment on the part of our government, to send troops to occupy a place, hoist our flag, give appearances of protection to all, threatening those who are unwilling to serve you, thus making and forcing them to perform acts for which they are punished by their own armies, on our evacuating the place. Either let the people alone, or when you once have taken a place, hold it and protect those who compromise themselves by serving you. When is the Government of the United States going to awaken from its lethargy and send into Mexico force *sufficient to prosecute the war vigorously?* [80]

Soon Meade departed to another theater of war. By 24 February Scott passed through Tampico en route to Lobos Island in preparation for the Vera Cruz landing. McClellan and Meade, both now officially in Scott's command, departed Tampico on 1 March aboard a ship destined for Lobos Island. They departed amidst news of a large Mexican force approaching Taylor's positions near Saltillo.[81]

The Battle of Buena Vista

Meanwhile, Old Rough and Ready had disregarded his instructions and moved his smaller forces too far forward. Earlier Scott had ordered him to remain passive, noting, "I must ask you to

---

[79] Cullum, *Biographical Register,* I, p. 367.
[80] Meade, *Letters,* I , pp. 177–81.
[81] Ibid., pp. 184–87.

abandon Saltillo, and to make no detachments, except for reconnaissances and immediate defense, beyond Monterrey." Advice or order, Taylor ignored it and moved about 4,500 of his remaining troops to advanced positions some twenty miles farther south of Saltillo to Agua Nueva on the San Luis Potosi road.[82]

About this time General Santa Anna had intercepted a message from Scott to Taylor revealing the American plans. He decided to march his army over the desert wastelands first to strike the weakened Taylor and then return south to deal with Scott. On 21 February news reached a surprised Taylor of an approaching Mexican army estimated at some 15,000 men. Withdrawing up the Saltillo road to a better defensive position about a mile south of Buena Vista Ranch, Taylor positioned his troops in a region of mountain spurs, deep ravines, many gullies, and high hills.[83]

Near Buena Vista Wool deployed troops in a strong defensive position that he and Taylor had agreed on earlier. His topogs examined the defensible terrain features and seemed quite pleased to observe a network of deep gullies, ravines, and heights overlooking the road. The road itself traversed three miles of a narrow corridor called La Angostura, or "Narrows." Shortly after midnight of the 22d, the remaining forces at Agua Nueva withdrew to the defenses outside Buena Vista.[84]

A bitter and complicated battle followed on the 23d. After a day of inconclusive fighting, Santa Anna launched an attack on the American left, sending the defenders reeling backward. U.S. infantry and mobile artillery crossed over from the right and reestablished the defense line. Taylor, returning from Saltillo with reinforcements, sent the Mississippi Rifles, a regiment commanded by Jefferson Davis, to halt the next attack. Joined by the 3d Indiana, the two regiments, reinforced by the mobile artillery, formed a wide angle—the "V" of Buena Vista and halted another assault, thereby marking the turning point of the battle. After another bloody day the exhausted Americans still held the field as nightfall

---

[82] Scott to Taylor 26 Jan 1847, quoted in Smith, *War With Mexico*, I, p. 547. Smith also discusses Taylor's reply and reasons for his actions, pp. 368–69, 547–49.
[83] Bauer, *The Mexican War*, pp. 204–08; Eisenhower, *So Far From God*, pp. 173–76, 181.
[84] Bauer, *The Mexican War*, pp. 209–10; Eisenhower, *So Far From God*, p. 181; Smith, *War With Mexico*, I, pp. 373–83; Dufour, *Mexican War; A Compact History*, p. 169.

approached. Early the next morning they saw the dispirited Mexican columns heading south. As a result Taylor claimed another victory, this one by default.[85]

The topogs received due recognition for their part in the battle. Both Linnard and Pope, along with their Corps of Engineers colleagues and the topogs serving with Wool, went out on hazardous reconnaissance patrols and served as couriers. Taylor commended the topogs in his official report; Linnard received a promotion to brevet major and Pope became brevet captain.[86]

Another account reported that Linnard also helped Lt. Col. R. S. Dix to rally men of the retreating 2d Indiana. Dix took the unit's standard and derided the fleeing men for deserting their colors. Linnard joined him, and soon both officers had men gathering around the flag. Dix somehow found a fife and drum and had the national quickstep played, and the troops marched off behind him with Linnard bringing up the rear. They directed the Indianans toward the Mississippi Rifles, thereby bringing the once-fleeing men back into the battle.[87]

Buena Vista also became Taylor's last major battle. During the fighting he acted in his usual manner. He conspicuously perched himself on his horse "Old Whitey" in the center of the battle, disregarded the Mexican bullets, and calmly offered encouragement to the troops. The battle brought major campaigning in northern Mexico to an end. Santa Anna turned his battered army to the south. Following a long, harsh forced march the Mexican leader soon gathered another army to deal with Scott, then in the process of moving his army inland from Vera Cruz. During the remainder

---

[85] A few of the accounts of this battle are found in Smith, *War With Mexico*, I, pp. 384–400; Dufour, *Mexican War; A Compact History*, pp. 171–84; Singletary, *Mexican War*, pp. 48–53; Bauer, *The Mexican War*, pp. 208–18; Eisenhower, *So Far From God*, pp. 178–91. Reports of General Taylor and other commanders are found in Report of the Secretary of War, Sen. Exec. Doc. 1, 30th Cong., 1st sess., 1847, pp. 132–213.

[86] Report of the Secretary of War, Sen. Exec. Doc. 1, 30th Cong., 1st sess., 1847, pp. 132–213; Linnard to Abert, 20 Mar 1847, LR 248, TE 77; Heitman, *Historical Register*, I, pp. 634, 798. Also see Henry, *Campaign Sketches*, p. 313; James H. Carleton, *Battle of Buena Vista* (New York: Harper and Brothers, 1848), pp. 38, 58, 60, 62–63, 112–14; Lavender, *Climax at Buena Vista*, pp. 187–92, 207–09; Smith, *War With Mexico*, I, pp. 388, 390–91; Dufour, *Mexican War; A Compact History*, pp. 173–76; Report of the Secretary of War, Sen. Exec. Doc. 1, pp. 139, 159–61.

[87] Carleton, *Battle of Buena Vista*, pp. 81–82; R. S. Ripley, *War With Mexico*, 2 vols. (New York: Harper and Brothers, 1849), 1:411.

of the war Taylor's army remained on the defensive. Operations consisted mainly of securing the roads, controlling Mexican guerrillas and bandits, and administering the occupied territories.

Other Topographic Tasks in Northern Mexico

Taylor's Topographical Engineers settled down to more mundane tasks for the duration of the war. They mapped northern Mexico, drew up battlefield maps for the commanders' reports, and accomplished detailed reconnaissances of the area. By the end of March Linnard, using Lieutenants Franklin (who had arrived earlier as part of Wool's command) and Pope to help, completed a survey of the Buena Vista battlefield. In forwarding the finished map to the Topographical Bureau, Linnard confidently noted that it "may be relied on for accuracy." He considered this a significant accomplishment because the topographic instruments inherited from Meade turned out to be in poor condition. Linnard lamented, "The prismatic compasses are disabled, the pocket chronometer and theodolite also. The latter when I received it had no legs. The telescopes are utterly worthless—far inferior to the common ships glasses."[88]

Linnard's topogs also had to satisfy other requirements for Colonel Abert. Because the original copies of reconnaissance reports prepared during Wool's march to Mexico did not reach Washington, Franklin began the laborious process of making new copies for the bureau. He also had the thankless job of deciphering the nearly illegible handwriting of their author, Captain George W. Hughes', Wool's chief topographer at the time. By August 1847, 1st Lt. Lorenzo Sitgreaves, also one of Wool's topographers, began a project to satisfy Abert's request for maps. Sitgreaves sketched a map of Wool's march to Saltillo and another from Saltillo to the mouth of the Rio Grande by way of Monterrey and Matamoros. The colonel also desired a detailed reconnaissance to the south toward San Luis Potosi.[89]

The topogs also faced difficulties in getting the required specialized equipment and materials to do their work. Linnard had re-

---

[88] This is the same Franklin who served with Kearny's 1845 military reconnaissance. Linnard to Abert, 20 Mar 1847, LR 248, TE 77.

[89] Franklin to Abert, 15 Feb 1847, LR 172; 22 Mar LR 283, TE 77; Abert to Sitgreaves, 9 Aug 1847, LS 180, TE 77; Sitgreaves to Abert, 25 Oct 1847, LR 686, TE 77.

quested replacement instruments from New Orleans, but without success. Getting the delicate, hard-to-replace, and expensive equipment appeared almost impossible, and he complained to Colonel Abert, "An order for a reconnaissance is now before me, and we have not a prismatic or even a common pocket compass. It is very desirable that instruments should be sent out." His request included a theodolite, six prismatic compasses, a box of colors, good tracing paper, note books, mapping pens, pencils, a pocket chronometer, and a small spring wagon to carry instruments. He also needed funds to carry on his work. Logistically, the frustrated topogs found themselves much worse off than the rest of the Army in Mexico.[90]

Colonel Abert also succeeded in exerting some influence from far off Washington to insure an orderly flow of topographic information. With the resultant lull in the northern theater, the amount of information forwarded to the bureau had decreased. Abert could not understand this, and he prodded Linnard to get his topogs to use their time more productively. In November the colonel wrote, "I cannot forbear expressing to you my surprise at the little information from your command since you have been attached to the Army in North Mexico." To this he added his concern about the lack of topographic information received since the Buena Vista report.[91]

The Chief of the Corps of Topographical Engineers sternly suggested to Linnard that he should embark on a program. Colonel Abert wrote, "A complete survey should have been made of the road from Monterrey to Saltillo with plans of intricate passes on a more extensive scale; also the road from Saltillo to Agua Nueva, with details of passes, with memoirs describing the military, agricultural, manufacturing and fiscal resources of the country." He concluded that the area should be accessible and that surely enough Topographical Engineers were available to accomplish the work.[92]

This friendly advice spurred the topogs of the Army of North Mexico to increase their efforts. Linnard cautiously responded that not all the requested work could be accomplished. By April 1848, however, the brevet major forwarded a detailed report along with sketches of a reconnaissance that he and Pope made of the

---

[90] Linnard to Abert, 20 Mar 1847, LR 248, TE 77.
[91] Ibid.; Abert to Linnard, 19 Nov 1847, LS 268, TE 77.
[92] Abert to Linnard, 19 Nov 1847, LS 268, TE 77.

roads from Saltillo to Mayapil. Pope enclosed a separate report of a reconnaissance that he made along the San Luis Potosi road to Cedral. Colonel Abert, happy to get whatever information he could, gratefully acknowledged Linnard's reports.[93]

This episode showed the little control that Abert had over the activities of his Topographical Engineers once they were assigned to the field commands. Abert normally depended on the topogs in the field to use their discretion in forwarding useful information to him. Strong admonitions to officers in the field, as in the case of Linnard, were rare.[94]

By the spring of 1847 the war appeared to be going well for the United States. Around the time Mexican forces departed from Buena Vista, American forces had successfully occupied California, the American Southwest, and northern Mexico. The U.S. Navy blockaded the Pacific and Gulf ports, and U.S. Army and naval forces occupied several ports. Peace, however, was still not at hand.

---

[93] Linnard to Abert, 18 Apr 1848, LR 238, TE 77; Abert to Linnard, 12 May 1848, LS 382, TE 77.

[94] If Colonel Abert did desire to propose something for his Topographical Engineers, he usually suggested that his officers tactfully approach their commanders. See Ryan, *Topographical Bureau Administrative History*, p. 151. Generally, the colonel only indicated his displeasure if financial accounts of his Topographical Engineers were not submitted on time or if improperly maintained. Fremont was especially delinquent, and Abert wrote, "Allow me to call to your attention your accounts. These delays in their adjustment may prove embarrassing to you." Abert to Fremont, 26 Nov 1847, LS 273, TE 77.

CHAPTER 6

Wool and His Topogs Join Taylor

In August 1846, at about the same time Taylor was making preparations to depart Camargo and march on Monterrey, Brig. Gen. John E. Wool assembled another army in Texas to march into Mexico and join forces with Old Rough and Ready. Wool's march from San Antonio did not match the more sensational campaign of Colonel Doniphan's Missouri Volunteers, nor did the column encounter any significant opposition or march as far as Doniphan who set out from Missouri in June 1846, and after pausing at Valverde, New Mexico, resumed his march in December. The topogs who accompanied Wool's army, however, put their time to good use. As a result more geographic information along Wool's route became available as contrasted to Doniphan who did not have any topographers.

Wool's Army Assembles in San Antonio

By September 1846 a Topographical Engineer staff with orders to serve in Wool's army assembled in San Antonio. A month earlier Colonel Abert ordered Captain George W. Hughes to report to Wool as the "Chief of Staff of Topographical Engineers to the Army of the Centre." Other topogs assigned to help the captain included 1st Lt. Lorenzo Sitgreaves, 2d Lt. William B. Franklin, and 2d Lt. Francis T. Bryan.[1]

Captain Hughes and his three assistants had varied backgrounds. Hughes attended West Point for four years but did not graduate, and before entering active duty had worked for the government as a civil engineer. Before reporting to Texas he worked in Washington on a highly visible civil works project to improve Pennsylvania Av-

---

[1] Abert to Hughes, 6 Aug 1846, LS 400, TE 77.

enue between the White House and the Capitol. Sitgreaves received his commission from West Point in 1832; however, he began his service in the artillery. After a two-year separation from the army, he joined the Topographical Engineers in 1838 and later served in various construction and survey projects. Sitgreaves received his instructions to report to Texas while surveying the Florida reefs. After his tour with Colonel Kearny's dragoon reconnaissance, Franklin served for a while at the Topographical Bureau. He then moved on to do survey work at Ossabow Sound in Georgia, where he received his orders. Bryan had just graduated from West Point.[2]

Wool and his staff had very little geographic information on the route the army would take toward Chihuahua. As a result, the topogs' duties would not differ much from those accomplished by Emory and his staff in support of Kearny's march across the Southwest. The route the 3,400-man army planned to take ran from San Antonio to Presidio in Mexico, then in turn passing through Monclova and Parras. Hughes also had somewhat different views compared to Emory as far as gathering scientific specimens along the way. Unlike Fremont, Emory, and the young Abert, he did not have an interest in such matters nor did he maintain close connections with American scientists in the East. Instead, the pragmatic Hughes felt more inclined to associate himself mainly with his military and tactical duties. As a result, he focused his attention on preparing a map, but his memoir of the regions he crossed nevertheless described many of the same interesting topics.[3]

The March to Mexico

Hughes also reconnoitered supply routes in Texas. Before arriving in San Antonio in early September, he and Sitgreaves investigated the road from Port Lavaca, Wool's base of supply, which ran through Goliad. Franklin and Bryan reconnoitered a second route

[2] *DAB*, III, pp. 601–02, V, pp. 348–49; Cullum, *Biographical Register*, I, pp. 518–19, II, pp. 152–54, 261; *Appleton's Cyclopaedia of American Biography*, V (New York: D. Appleton and Co., 1888–1901), p. 543.

[3] Goetzmann, *Army Exploration*, pp. 149–50; George W. Hughes, "Report of the Secretary of War, Communicating . . . a Map Showing the Operations of the Army of the United States in Texas and the Adjacent Mexican States on the Rio Grande; Accompanied by Astronomical Observations, and Descriptive and Military Memoirs of the Country," 1 Mar 1849, Sen. Exec. Doc. 32, 31st Cong., 1st sess., 1850, pp. 5, 8; Hughes to Abert, Dec 1846, LR 1093, TE 77.

diverging from Victoria and passing through Seguin to San Antonio. In his report Franklin pointed out a serious disadvantage to travel in South Texas. "As it was mid-summer," he wrote, "to save our horses we left Victoria just at dusk. During the day the flies are so numerous that the horses are set nearly frantic, and humanity as well as his own comfort will dictate to the traveler in this part of Texas that he must lie by during the day and travel at night." As a result of these surveys Hughes recommended the shorter Goliad route.[4]

Before departing San Antonio Hughes did make some interesting observations of the recently annexed state of Texas. "The Alamo," he reported to Colonel Abert, "if placed in a suitable state of repair, would accommodate a regiment, and might at the same time be rendered a strong defensive work, well supplied with water." Somewhat familiar with agricultural methods, he recorded some astute observations of the once intensely farmed region and its irrigation works. He cautioned that it should "well be questioned whether this operation is not injurious rather than beneficial to the lands; for the soil being highly calcareous, and the water being nearly saturated with the same substance too much carbonate of lime must, in the course of years, be deposited in the fields." He suggested that "The remedy for this excess may be found in deep plowing, following in the rotation of crops." He also commented on the potential of grazing lands, adding "The cows are bad milkers, but might be easily improved by a cross on the Durham or Devon." The topog followed up with facts on population, climate, and health conditions of the area he saw in Texas.[5]

On 23 September 1846, Hughes departed San Antonio as head of the army's advance party. Suddenly the topogs became the envy of the whole camp, because even Corps of Engineers officers, including Captain Robert E. Lee, Wool's chief engineer, had to stay farther back to supervise pick and shovel work on the road and bridges. Hughes' well-armed party consisted of the four Topographical Engineers, an interpreter, a hunter-guide, two wagoners, four laborers, and two servants.[6]

---

[4] Quoted in Hughes to Abert, 20 Jan 1849, LR 129, TE 77. Hughes enclosed reports and memoirs from Sitgreaves and Franklin in his report submitted to the Topographical Bureau. See also Hughes, "Report," Sen. Exec. Doc. 32, pp. 9, 49.
[5] Hughes, "Report," Sen. Exec. Doc. 32, p. 10.
[6] Douglas Southall Freeman, *Robert E. Lee, a Biography*, I (New York: Charles Scribner's Sons, 1933), pp. 205–06; Hughes, "Report," Sen. Exec. Doc. 32, p. 12.

As the party moved south toward Mexico Hughes kept a running commentary of his observations. On the 24th the topog passed the French-German settlement of Castroville. Impressed by what he observed, Hughes praised the settlers, "who have brought with them to this wilderness the habits of industry, sobriety, and economy of their father-land." Later he touched on the weather and in particular the Texas "norther." Hughes noted that when storms hit the area, "The greater parts of Texas and the adjacent Mexican provinces are subject to these sudden and extreme transitions of climate; which often prove deleterious to animal life." Ironically, the following week the topog came down with dysentery.[7]

Along the route to the Rio Grande the other topogs continued with their duties. Franklin scouted ahead to pick camp sites for the moving army, and Sitgreaves continued to record observations for eventual use in determining latitudes and longitudes. They also kept a wary eye on the movements of Comanche Indians near the army's route. Eleven days and 164 miles after setting out, the engineers reached the Rio Grande, some five miles from Presidio. Hughes proudly asserted that when "the glorious flag of the stars and stripes was for the first time displayed in that far-off wilderness, many an eye glistened with patriotic emotion, and many a pulse beat high with the hope of future expectation."[8]

The Crossing of the Rio Grande Into Mexico

By 12 October the army began crossing the Rio Grande into Mexico. The Corps of Engineers contingent supervised the assembly of a "flying bridge," prefabricated in San Antonio for the crossing. Wool, unlike Taylor, had the foresight not to wait for pontoon bridging to arrive from the East. Escorted by a squadron of dragoons, the Topographical Engineers moved out again ahead of the army toward Santa Rosa, their next objective. According to Hughes: "The object was to reconnoiter the country, especially in reference to supplies, water, and encampments, with directions to communicate the information thus obtained daily to the commanding general."[9]

---

[7] Hughes, "Report," Sen. Exec. Doc. 32, pp. 12–13.
[8] Ibid., p. 16.
[9] Ibid., p. 18. See also Smith, *War With Mexico*, I, p. 270; Bauer, *The Mexican War*, p. 147.

The route led them some 105 miles to Santa Rosa. The topogs led the army past the settlements of Nava, San Fernando, and Santa Rita Springs, reaching Santa Rosa on the 20th. Along the way Hughes noted abandoned farms, the result of depredations by Comanches and Apaches. He wrote that the Indians "have driven the timid inhabitants from their rural dwellings, and cooped them up within the precincts of the villages, converting this once smiling garden into a howling wilderness." [10]

The small advance guard moved into Santa Rosa with no opposition. Hughes recalled, "It was quite amusing to see how soon they fraternized, and it was evident that the population hailed us as protectors and deliverers; and, in fact, more than one proposition was made to me to encourage a pronunciamento against the Mexican government." Santa Rosa presented a slight improvement over the other towns they passed, but Wool's chief topog observed that "the town wears that appearance of decay so common in Mexico." [11]

The next leg of Wool's march took the army deeper in Mexico to Monclova. The Topographical Engineers continued to survey the surrounding country, took astronomical observations, and made long distance reconnaissances. They also drew hasty maps, calculated their astronomical observations, laid out encampments, and chose camp sites for the troops. Wool made Monclova his base of supply, and no longer had to depend on a long supply route from San Antonio. While in Monclova, Hughes and his party also had time to prepare reports for Wool and the Topographical Bureau.[12]

Because of Taylor's armistice arrangements following the capture of Monterrey, Wool's army sat out the entire month of November in Monclova. The topogs kept busy reconnoitering the surrounding area, and near the end of the month Franklin made the more than 100 mile trip to Monterrey as a courier. Within the limited time allowed he also made a hasty reconnaissance of the route between the two cities. Upon reaching Monterrey Franklin had to proceed on to Saltillo to locate General Taylor. Returning with dispatches intended for Wool, the widely traveled topog found Wool's column already on the move southwest toward its next objective, the city of Parras.[13]

---

[10] Hughes, "Report," Sen. Exec. Doc. 32, p. 19.
[11] Ibid., pp. 23–24.
[12] Ibid., pp. 26–28.
[13] Ibid., p. 26. Franklin's reconnaissance report is on pages 57–59.

From Monclova to Parras

By 25 November Hughes rode out again in front of Wool's army on the road to Parras. He made journal entries of terrain, vegetation, and wildlife, but his somewhat plain prose paled when compared to the more colorful writings of Fremont, Emory, and Abert. Along the way he stopped off at the hacienda of San Lorenzo de Oboja on 3 December. The topogs found an efficiently managed establishment under American-educated owners, and this visit appeared to be the only item to impress him on this leg of the march. Hughes, considering himself to be a connoisseur of wine, praised the high quality of the vineyards, noting "They are all pure juice of the grape." He also commended the grain, cotton, and fruit crops.[14]

As the army wended its way unopposed to Parras, Hughes perceived a difference in the nature of the people of this more prosperous region. He considered them "industrious, sober, thrifty, intelligent, and unfriendly to the present form of their government," and also "favorably inclined to our government and its institutions." At Nadadores, sixteen miles to the south of Monclova, he quoted one wealthy Mexican, who on one occasion visited the United States, as saying, "sir, we have a glorious country and a good population, but our government is the worst in the world. I would rather be under the domination of the Comanche Chief." On arriving unopposed at their destination, Hughes found Parras to be "a collection of haciendas," where "the vineyards and gardens separate the homes from each other except on the principal streets." [15]

While waiting for further instructions from Taylor, Wool settled down in Parras, again making good use of the time. He kept his army in a high state of readiness and made sure that sufficient reconnaissance patrols roamed the area, especially toward Saltillo. Hughes commended his commander for fostering good relations with the local populace, thereby reducing any threat from that quarter. The topog further praised Wool's efficient handling of the march thus far over a difficult 700-mile trek, and at the same time maintaining its excellent fighting condition.[16]

---

[14] Ibid., p. 32.
[15] Ibid., pp. 33, 45–46, 48.
[16] Ibid., p. 33. See also Smith, *War With Mexico*, I, pp. 273–74.

Wool Joins Taylor at Buena Vista

Wool's preparedness paid off when suddenly on 17 December he received orders to move out to join Taylor's threatened and outnumbered force near Buena Vista. Within two hours the troops began marching down the well-known routes, thanks to the earlier reconnaissance patrols of the Topographical Engineers. Four days later, and nearly 120 miles to the east, Wool joined General William J. Worth's force. At a place called Agua Nueva, about twenty miles south of Saltillo, the Americans prepared for the arrival of Santa Anna, now reported moving north with a new army.[17]

Hughes, on a reconnaissance to Durango at the time the army suddenly moved, rejoined the army on its third day out. That evening Wool, Hughes, Robert E. Lee, and their staffs carefully checked the terrain in the darkness and fog. The general immediately noted the disadvantages of his assigned position and returned to Saltillo to confer with Taylor. Santa Anna, however, did not show; it would be several months before the Mexican leader moved north.[18]

By early January 1847 a large portion of Taylor's command including some of the topogs had marched off to join Scott's expeditionary force. This, of course, left Old Rough and Ready faced with defending northern Mexico. Hughes joined Worth's staff and departed with the division on the 9th. During the redeployment several Corps of Engineers officers, particularly Robert E. Lee, also departed. Meanwhile, Wool, now with one less topographer on his staff, found terrain near Buena Vista more advantageous for defense.[19]

By the third week in February Santa Anna's army suddenly appeared. The ensuing battle swirled around the undulating terrain, and Buena Vista became one of the most vicious engagements of the war. During the battle Sitgreaves and Franklin went out on frequent reconnaissance patrols and served as couriers. Bryan served with a three-piece mobile artillery detachment under Lieutenant John Paul Jones O'Brien. Early in the battle the artillery detach-

---

[17] Hughes, "Report," Sen. Exec. Doc. 32, pp. 33–34. Wool's professional attributes are also based on the account of his march in Smith, *War With Mexico*, I, pp. 269–76.

[18] Hughes, "Report," Sen. Exec. Doc. 32, p. 34; Smith, *War With Mexico*, I, pp. 275–76.

[19] Lavender, *Climax at Buena Vista*, p. 148.

ment deployed forward with the 2d Indiana Regiment to halt a Mexican advance. The attack, however, proved too strong, and the Indiana regiment retreated, leaving O'Brien, Bryan, and their gunners alone. They maintained fire with double charges of canister for as long as possible, leaving their guns only after suffering heavy casualties. The delaying action allowed the Mississippi Rifles, other reinforcements, and additional artillery to deploy and repulse the Mexican attack.[20]

Wool's topogs also received glowing comments in his reports of the battle. The general spoke highly of Sitgreaves and O'Brien praised Bryan. O'Brien wrote, "I saw him [Bryan] when exposed to a close and murderous cross fire of grape and canister on one side, and musketry in front, direct the fire of his piece, and give his commands with the same coolness as if he were on parade. He received a flesh wound in the arm." As a result of their services in battle, Sitgreaves received a promotion to brevet captain and Bryan and Franklin to brevet first lieutenants.[21]

Hughes Reports on the Future of Texas

Although Hughes rode off to join Scott's command, the topog later prepared a series of revealing reports which encompassed geographic and military affairs. Colonel Abert consolidated these and others submitted by the other topogs serving under Wool into one document and map, which the Senate published in 1850. The published report focused on military concerns, more than the all-encompassing reports of Fremont, Emory, and Abert. Wool, with his reputation for form and discipline, may have had some influence in keeping the Topographical Engineers from spending more time investigating the flora, fauna, and cultures of the regions. In addition, Hughes took a slightly different approach to his topographic duties. Wool employed his engineers to the maximum on military duties, thereby ensuring him the intelligence to meet any situation.

---

[20] Report of the Secretary of War, Sen. Exec. Doc. 1, 30th Cong., 1st sess., 1847, pp. 132–213; Henry, *Campaign Sketches*, p. 313; Carleton, *Battle of Buena Vista*, pp. 38, 58, 60, 62–63, 112–14; Lavender, *Climax at Buena Vista*, pp. 187–92, 207–09; Smith, *War With Mexico*, I, pp. 388, 390–91; Dufour, *Mexican War; A Compact History*, pp. 173–76; Heitman, *Historical Register*, I, pp. 257, 434, 634, 798, 890.

[21] Report of the Secretary of War, Sen. Exec. Doc. 1, 30th Cong., 1st sess., 1847, pp. 140, 161; Heitman, *Historical Register*, I, pp. 257, 798, 890.

Hughes' letters and final report made several recommendations regarding the defense of the Texas frontier. In February 1847, he wrote to Abert suggesting the building of a line of forts along the newly surveyed route between San Antonio and Presidio to protect settlers against robbers and predatory Indians. He also incorporated this recommendation in his formal report published by Congress. Such a plan required a regiment of mounted troops stationed at key posts at San Antonio, on the Quihi River, on the Leona River, and at the Rio Grande crossing near Presidio. The topog believed this measure need only be temporary, stating, "there can be no question that the protection which they [the army] would afford would be the means of rapidly settling the country with a population that soon would be able to defend itself." As a result, the army would serve as the spearhead for advancing settlement, similar to the Spanish presidios, except that mobile troops rather than infantry garrisons would be employed. By 1850 the government adopted this concept and established an inner ring of forts in western Texas.[22]

This measure also required facing up realistically to the hostile plains Indians. Hughes wrote, "It must be obvious to even the most superficial observer that hostilities with the Comanches and Lipans, the most warlike of the native tribes, are neither remote nor contingent." He also correctly predicted: "I regard it as inevitable, and believe we shall never establish cordial relations with them until they have been severely punished—an affair, by-the-by, not easy of accomplishment."[23]

The topog also noted the possible results of marauding Indians on the Mexicans. He believed clearing the border area might force the hostile tribes to prey "upon the northern provinces of Mexico, which they would assuredly desolate—a consequence which we may deplore, but cannot avert." This became a genuine concern of the Mexican government, and the resultant peace treaty incorporated a clause making the United States responsible for preventing Indian raids into Mexico.[24]

---

[22] Hughes, "Report," Sen. Exec. Doc. 32, p. 35; Hughes to Abert, 12 Feb 1847, LR 152, TE 77; Goetzmann, *Army Exploration,* p. 150.

[23] Hughes, "Report," Sen. Exec. Doc. 32, p. 35.

[24] Ibid.; Goetzmann, *Army Exploration,* pp. 194, 211. Goetzmann also discusses the problems that the Boundary Commission encountered after the war and the interest of the Topographical Bureau and other parties in the southern railroad route.

Hughes believed that Texas had immense potential despite some of the new state's obvious disadvantages. After describing the fertility of the eastern region, he agreed that "tis all barren" beyond the Rio Antonio and Nueces rivers. Although the state had pleasant rolling country with plenty of game, Hughes remarked, "The reverse of the picture is, that it abounds with venomous reptiles, snakes, scorpions, centipedes, and the tarantulas, and also annoying to the traveler were the innumerable crowds of ticks and red bugs, who fasten and prey upon him with an instinctive avidity." [25]

According to Hughes the line of forts he recommended could also exploit the potential of the large state. If the Army built the forts, he felt sure that "the natural advantages of the country could not fail to attract the attention of foreign immigrants, and of our own roving and adventurous countrymen." Almost prophetically the topog revealed the future greatness of Texas

> But it requires only a slight effort of the imagination to fancy it peopled with an industrious and teeming population, its heights crowned with human habitation, its fertile valleys in cultivation, and its plains covered with bleating flocks and lowing herds. It remains but for the government to will it, and this picture will be realized.[26]

Views on Northern Mexico

Hughes' comments on the social, religious, political, and economic aspects of Mexican life may not appear as fascinating as those crafted by Emory, but he still presented several significant points. Although Wool emphasized the military mission of his attached topogs, Hughes acknowledged that he did have instructions authorizing him to operate "independently of such duties as might be assigned by the commanding general." Therefore, he could, like Emory, gather whatever information he deemed relevant, but he admitted, "I only regret that these important duties have not been more satisfactorily performed." [27]

His report also reflected popular opinion in some quarters to rationalize the seizure of even more land from the defeated nation. "Nothing can be imagined," he maintained in reflecting his disdain

---

[25] Hughes, "Report," Sen. Exec. Doc. 32, pp. 35–36.
[26] Ibid.
[27] Ibid., p. 8.

of Mexican political affairs, "in a country pretending to be civilized, so inefficient, despotic, capricious, and oppressive as the government of the (so called) Mexican republic." The topog pointed out the Mexican government did not appear concerned with the welfare of the population in the northern provinces nor did it protect the people from marauding Indians. For the first time, Hughes noted, the people felt secure when the American army occupied the region. The topog detected an inclination of the inhabitants to either become an independent state under the protection of the United States or to join the Union. Presenting a case for further expansion, he suggested: "With the slightest encouragement during the last summer, the whole State of Coahuila would have pronounced against the existing government of Mexico."[28]

Hughes' comments on the Mexican people, however, ran counter to popular American beliefs disparaging its southern neighbor. The topographer rebutted the popular notion that the Mexicans exhibited an unusual degree of treachery and cruelty. "I should say," he wrote, "that they are naturally hospitable, kind-hearted, and amiable. In their manners they are extremely courteous, and the most civil people I have ever known." When out in front of Wool's army with his vulnerable advance party, the topog recalled, "Wherever I went, whether to the princely hacienda or the humble rancho, I was treated with kindness and hospitality; and I must confess that the impression made upon me was greatly in their favor." He never felt fearful in such situations and noted any acts of barbarity by the Mexicans were often committed in retaliation for acts committed by American soldiers. Hughes believed that the depredations of the rear or quartermaster troops, not Taylor's fighting men, caused ill feeling among the local inhabitants. His observations of the people did not derive solely from his service with Wool, but mainly through his later experiences under Scott as a commander of a volunteer infantry unit and as military governor.[29]

The pragmatic Hughes, however, provided some otherwise interesting vignettes in his report. He occasionally sprinkled in light comments on Mexican food and women. "Mexican cooking is," he wrote, "to my taste, detestable; but many Americans, less fastidious perhaps, affect to like it." In describing female costumes, he con-

---

[28] Ibid., pp. 38, 44.
[29] Ibid., p. 43.

cluded an interesting dialogue on the "chemise which exposes more of the person than is in most countries considered to be consistent with a due regard to modesty; but this is the custom of the country, and I am not disposed to criticize it."[30]

Hughes' Final Report

While accomplishing his topographic duties and later preparing his map and report of Wool's march, Hughes presented the military situation from his perspective. He supported the decision for Taylor's army to go on the defensive rather than attempt the long overland march to Mexico City. Noting the geographic obstacles to such a venture, the topog assumed that a disaster not unlike that of Napoleon's drive to Moscow could have resulted. The lines of operation and supply would have been longer, and the terrain was very rugged. Hughes, however, did not make the point that Santa Anna did succeed in moving his army over the same ground, albeit with much suffering by his troops, before and after Buena Vista.[31]

In his own line of work Hughes could claim that mapping of northern Mexico improved significantly. When Wool set forth in September 1846 little was known of the region. "The jealousy of the Spaniards, and the indolence of the Mexicans," Hughes wrote, "had prevented the publication of maps based upon reliable authority, and, owing to the excursions of the savage tribes, the present race of Mexicans were but imperfectly acquainted with it, and therefore but little information could be procured from them." Except along the main route, the Topographical Engineers literally groped their way taking astronomical observations like a ship at sea. As they headed into the interior of the strange country the topogs determined distances and located good camp sites for the army based on the availability of water, forage, and fuel. Hughes and Sitgreaves primarily reconnoitered the surrounding area, while Franklin concentrated on astronomical observations to determine latitude and longitude. The Topographical Engineers, according to Hughes, had "been able to collect a vast amount of geographical information, which may prove useful and interesting."

---

[30] Ibid., pp. 41–42.
[31] Ibid., p. 5. A copy of the report is reproduced in Appendix A.

All these facts went into the preparation of a high quality map depicting the region from San Antonio to Saltillo.[32]

Hughes final report also added a variety of appendices. These included the journals and memoirs of Franklin and Sitgreaves; recapitulations of latitudes and longitudes; drawings of San Antonio, the Alamo (including a site plan), and the cathedrals of Monclova; and a report and map by Josiah Gregg, the famous prairie traveler. Gregg's memoir and map traced the march of an Arkansas regiment to its rendezvous at San Antonio. Though not a Topographical Engineer, Gregg's interesting account added to the geographic knowledge of the region along a route that ran past the Texas towns of Washington and Seguin and along the Brazos River. His journal also included a history of San Antonio.[33]

Thus, Hughes' report and map, like those of his colleagues, brought a new understanding in the United States of hitherto practically unknown regions. Although his report and map did not entirely relate to the geography of the American West, they became the subject of primary interest to later historians of the war. Hughes brought geographic knowledge of areas in Texas and another region of northern Mexico to the attention of the American public for the first time. Along with the other Topographical Engineers, he emphasized the potential of the West at a propitious time in American history.[34]

The Other Topographical Engineers

Except for Hughes and Meade, the other Topographical Engineers finished their Mexican War service in the northern theater, and following the war many of them continued to serve the Corps in a variety of assignments. Captain Linnard and Lieutenant Franklin returned to assignments in the East where they remained. Lieutenants Sitgreaves, Bryan, and Pope remained in the West, where they concentrated on further topographic surveys.

Linnard's later career, however, was cut short by an early death. Returning from the war he assumed construction duties in Philadelphia as supervisor of lighthouse construction at Carysfort Reef and Sand Key, Florida, from 1849 to 1851. He died in Philadelphia in 1851.[35]

---

[32] Ibid., pp. 6, 8. By then Bryan had been attached to an artillery unit.
[33] Ibid., pp. 47–62, 51–57, 65–67.
[34] Goetzmann, *Army Exploration*, p. 151.
[35] Cullum, *Biographical Register*, I, pp. 452–53.

Lieutenant Franklin had a long successful career in military and private life. He joined the faculty at the Military Academy as an assistant professor in natural and experimental philosophy (1848–1851). After a year's leave of absence, he made surveys of Roanoke inlet (1852–1853), inspected lighthouse construction (1853–1856), supervised construction of a customs house and a marine hospital in Portland, Maine (1855–1857). He served another tour with lighthouse construction (1857–1859), and participated in engineering studies for the construction of a bridge over the Mississippi at Rock Island, Illinois (1859). He later supervised construction of the new dome of the Capitol in Washington, work on the Post Office Building, and an extension to the Treasury Department building (1859–1861). During the Civil War Franklin rose to the rank of major general of volunteers and saw action at Bull Run, Malvern Hill, Antietam, Fredericksburg, and Sabine Crossroads. He resigned in 1865 and became vice president and general agent for Colt Firearms Company (1865–1888) and held several public positions. He died in 1903.[36]

After the war Lieutenant Sitgreaves also rotated between duties in the East and West. He worked on the Creek Indian Territory Boundary Survey (1849) and at the Topographical Bureau (1850), and accompanied a Department of New Mexico expedition down the Zuni and Colorado rivers in 1851. He then inspected lighthouse construction from 1852 to 1856. After several years' sick leave, Sitgreaves returned to active duty in 1861. He worked to improve temporary defenses in Kansas and Nebraska and harbors on Lake Michigan. He attained the rank of lieutenant colonel in the Corps of Engineers in 1864, but retired because of a disability in 1866. Sitgreaves died in Washington, D.C., in 1888.[37]

Lieutenant Bryan, who had been assigned artillery duties during the war, returned to topographical duties. He joined the Department of Texas after the war and made extensive surveys (1848–1852). Bryan then took charge of surveys and construction of military roads in Kansas and Nebraska (1855–1858), served in Utah (1858), and worked on the Western Rivers improvement projects (1858–1859). He resigned his commission in 1861 and did not see service during the Civil War. He lived most of the remainder of his long life in St. Louis and died there in 1918.[38]

---

[36] Cullum, *Biographical Register*, II, pp. 152–54; *DAB*, III, pp. 601–02.

[37] Cullum, *Biographical Register*, I, pp. 518–19; *Appleton's Cyclopaedia*, V, p. 543.

[38] Cullum, *Biographical Register*, II, p. 261; Forty-Ninth Annual Report of the Association Graduates of the United States Military Academy at West Point, New York, June 11th, 1918 (Saginaw, Mich.: Seemann & Peters, 1918), pp. 65–67.

Lieutenant John Pope continued to serve a long career in the Army. After the war he participated in surveys of Minnesota (1849–1850) and the Department of New Mexico (1851–1853). Pope had an irrepressible personality even after receiving a reprimand from Colonel Abert, who at times noted Pope's misconduct, inefficiency, and even plagiarism of other Topographical Engineers' reports. After the Mexican War the Army gave him the responsibility to survey one of the proposed railroad routes to the Pacific along the 32d degree latitude. He also experimented, somewhat unsuccessfully, with artesian wells in west Texas and New Mexico (1855–1859). Pope constructed lighthouses (1859–1861), and during the Civil War rose to the rank of major general of volunteers. During the war he exuded his usual confidence and bravado by leading the Army of the Potomac to disaster from his "headquarters in the saddle" at Second Manassas. After the Civil War he held an important post as commander of the Department of Missouri (1880–1883). Pope retired as a major general in 1886 and died in 1892.[39]

For all purposes the campaign in northern Mexico had come to a stop. Except for some guerrilla warfare and maintaining a defensive posture, the American force served as an occupation army. Although the campaign in this theater of war did not result in any decisive action ending the war, it did provide several notable triumphs in battle, thus raising the spirit of the American public and the forces involved. The crucial test of arms remained. The strategic decision had been made to shift the bulk of American forces for the landing at Vera Cruz and the march on Mexico City. Perhaps this approach would force the Mexican government to sue for peace. The other topogs—Emory, Meade, and Hughes—moved on to new assignments, this time with General Scott's command.

---

[39] Cullum, *Biographical Register*, II, pp. 126–27; *DAB*, VIII, pp. 76–77; *Appleton's Cyclopaedia*, V, pp. 68–69; *National Cyclopaedia of American Biography*, IV (New York: James T. White, 1898–1969), pp. 282–83, 392. Goetzmann notes several of Pope's problems: Colonel Abert reprimanded him for disparaging Fremont's earlier work; Pope's 1849 report on Minnesota boldly plagiarized Nicollet's work; and his three years of artesian well experiments resulted in a dry hole; Goetzmann, *Army Exploration*, pp. 67, 74, 247, 365–68. Pope's explorations in New Mexico and his railroad survey are outlined on pages 246–48, 277–78, and 291–92.

Brevet Major General John E. Wool. (Library of Congress)

Young Robert E. Lee, 1838. (National Archives)

Major General Winfield Scott. (Library of Congress)

The landing at Vera Cruz. (Library of Congress)

Joseph E. Johnston during the Civil War. (National Archives)

Lieutenant George H. Derby. (National Archives)

Drawing the "Ass-sault" by Derby under the pseudonym John Phoenix. (U.S. Army Corps of Engineers); *below,* View of Cerro Gordo when Twiggs' division stormed the main heights. (Library of Congress)

Scott's Army taking detour around Lake Chalco. (James Walker painting)

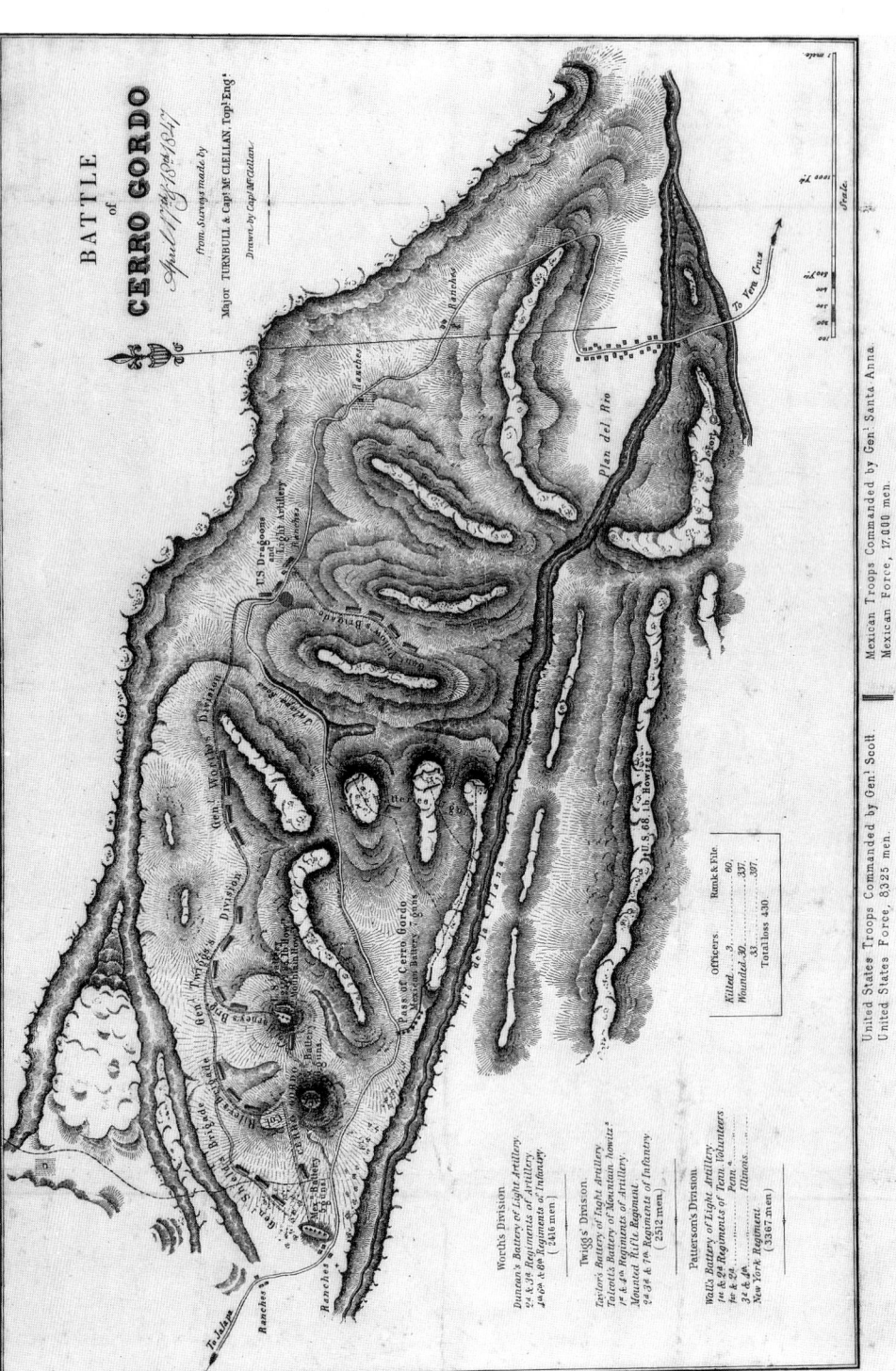

Map of Cerro Gordo by Major Turnbull and Captain McClellan. (National Archives)

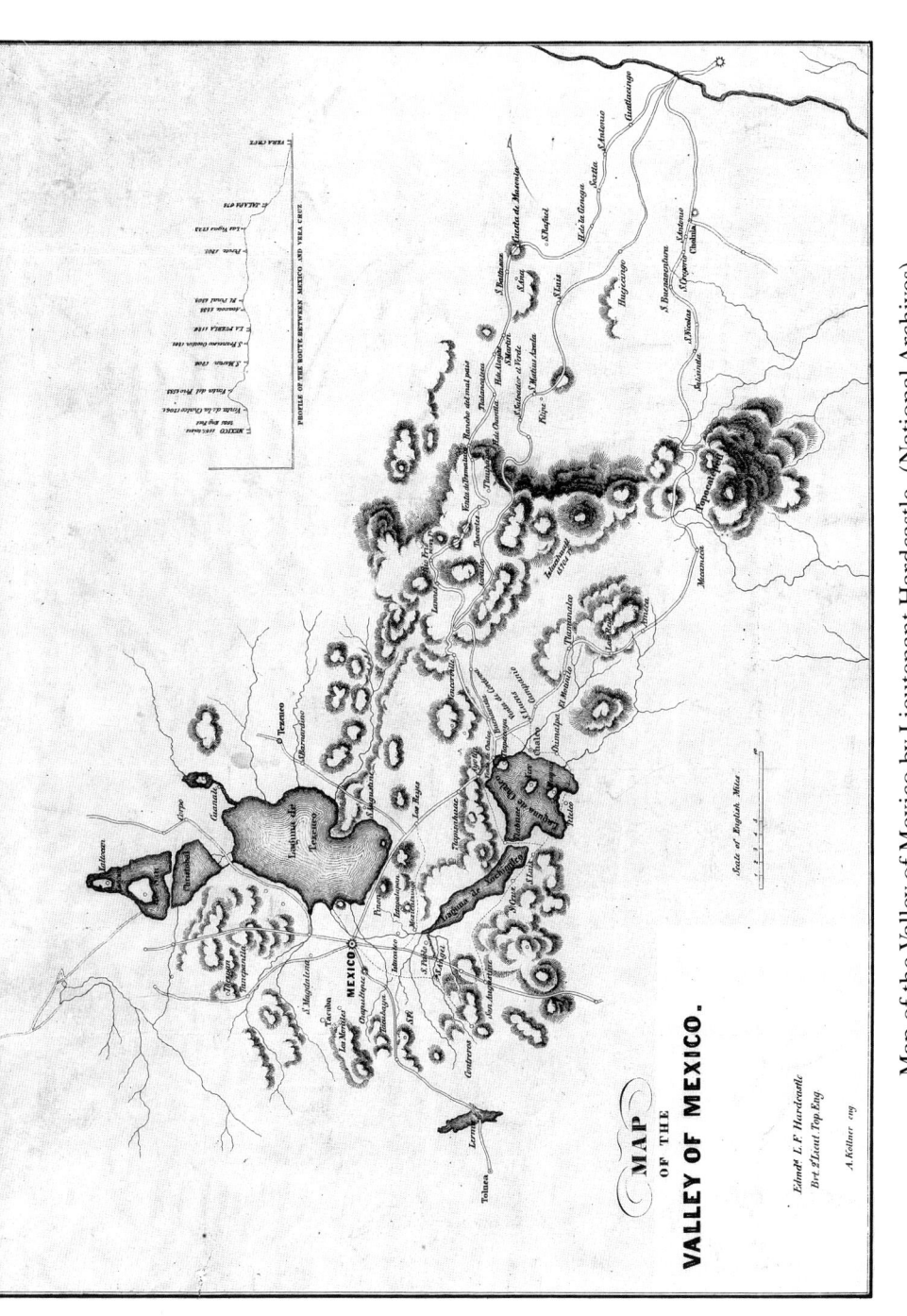

Map of the Valley of Mexico by Lieutenant Hardcastle. (National Archives)

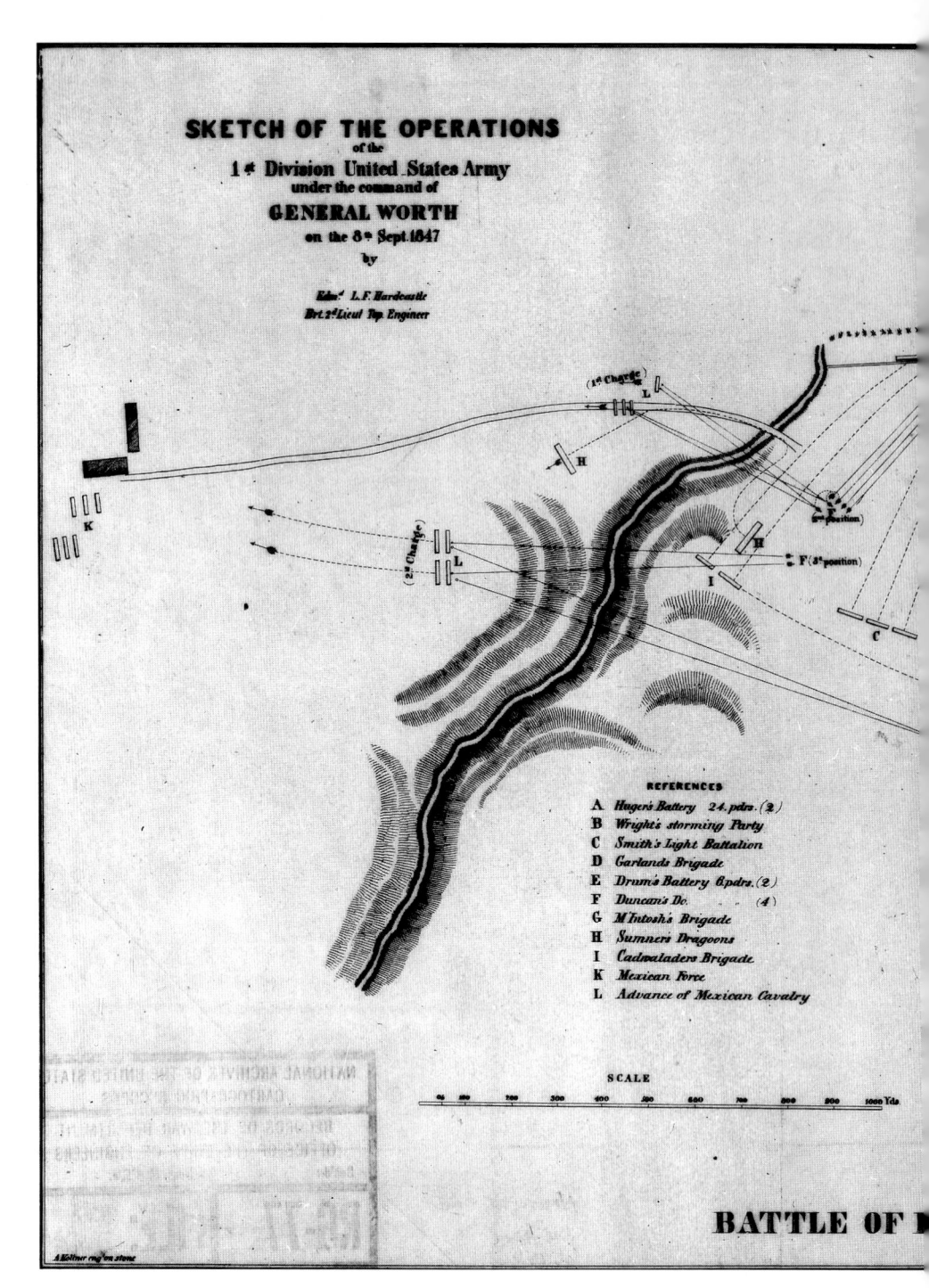

Map of Battle of Molino del Rey by Lieutenant Hardcastle. (National Archives)

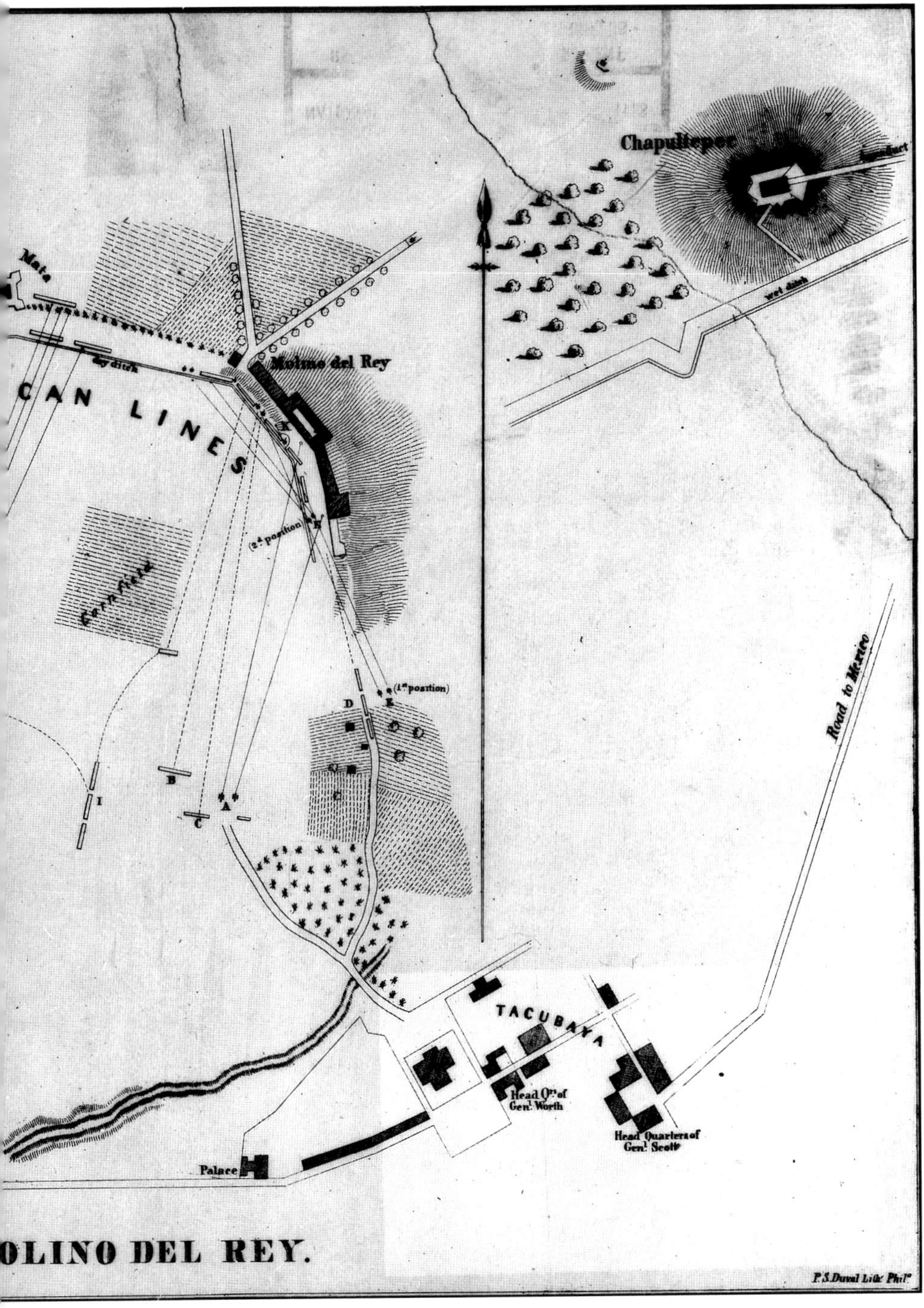
Mata
CAN LINES
Molino del Rey
Chapultepec
Cornfield
(2d position)
(1st position)
D
E
B
A
C
I
TACUBAYA
Head Qrs of Genl Worth
Head Quarters of Genl Scott
Palace
Road to Mexico
OLINO DEL REY.
P. S. Duval Lith. Phila.

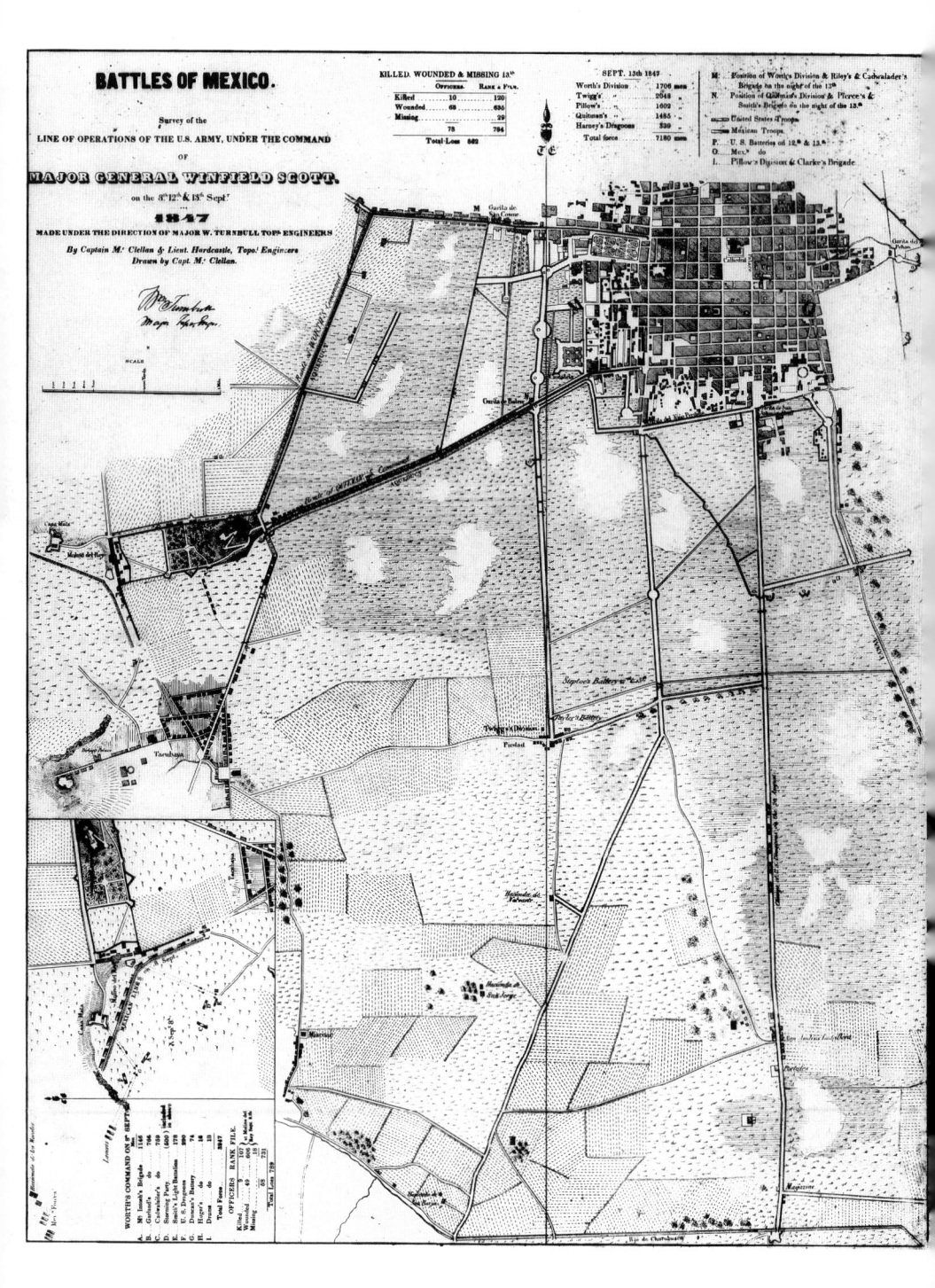

Map prepared by topographical engineers of battles for Mexico City. (National Archives)

Scott's entry into Mexico City. (Library of Congress)

Capture of the *tete de pont* at Churubusco. (National Archives)

CHAPTER 7

To Mexico City With Scott

By 1847 American strategy had shifted from northern Mexico in favor of landing an army at Vera Cruz and from there marching on to Mexico City. The conquest of the American Southwest had gone according to plan. American forces had secured the boundary of Texas, and General Taylor's army had successfully penetrated and occupied northern Mexico. Still the Mexican government, despite considerable internal turmoil, would not come to terms with the United States. In Washington Maj. Gen. Winfield Scott's earlier proposal and persistence for the landing at Vera Cruz finally received approval from President Polk. Scott, although the Commanding General of the U.S. Army, had decided that he himself would take to the field to command the expeditionary force.

To carry out these plans Scott worked out a joint operation with the U.S. Navy. The Navy had carried out blockade operations along Mexico's two coasts and occupied several key port towns. Now it came time for the Navy to provide the necessary mobility by transporting an army to the battlefield. Having done that the sea service would then concentrate on operating the transportation and logistical links to the United States.[1]

General Scott, nicknamed "Old Fuss and Feathers" for his insistence on military spit-and-polish, set about carrying out his meticulous plans for the first major amphibious operation in American history. He requested the construction of special surfboats for the landing and then left Washington for Mexico to meet with Taylor and assemble his army at a staging area on the sandy coral harbor of Lobos Island, some sixty-five miles to the southeast of Tampico. There forces deploying from the United States and most of Zachary Taylor's regulars were to gather for the forthcoming invasion.[2]

---

[1] Bauer, *The Mexican War*, pp. 232–37.
[2] Ibid., pp. 236–37; Eisenhower, *So Far From God*, pp. 255–57.

Scott's Topogs Assemble

Scott assembled a very capable staff of topographical engineers. In all, twelve topogs served in various capacities under Old Fuss and Feathers during the campaign and in the postwar occupation period. They included Major William Turnbull, his chief topog; Captains George W. Hughes, Joseph E. Johnston, and John McClellan; 1st Lts. William H. Emory (now a brevet major), Charles N. Hagner, and Eliakim P. Scammon; and 2d Lts. George W. Derby, Edmund L. F. Hardcastle, George G. Meade (a brevet first lieutenant), Martin L. Smith, and George Thom. Hughes and Emory served as leaders of a volunteer regiment, an indication of their unusual versatility; Johnston switched over to the command of an elite infantry regiment; and Scammon would serve as one of General Scott's aides-de-camp.

Not all the topogs served throughout Scott's campaign and occupation period. Meade, Scammon, and Derby returned to the United States early, Hughes returned later, and other topogs arrived well after the march inland commenced. By the time Scott reached the outskirts of Mexico City only Turnbull, McClellan, Thom, and Hardcastle remained on his staff. Smith and Hagner arrived in the war zone later.

Major Turnbull already had a distinguished service career before reporting as Scott's chief topographer. He received his West Point commission as an artillery officer but ended up detailed to the Topographical Bureau and later joined the Corps. In 1831 and 1832 he surveyed railroad lines in Mississippi, and from 1832 to 1843 he designed and supervised the construction of an aqueduct spanning the Potomac River in Washington. The Aqueduct Bridge at Georgetown, built to carry canal traffic over the river to join another canal, had the distinction of being among the earliest important engineering accomplishments in the United States. Over the next two years Turnbull supervised the repair of the Potomac River bridge, and in 1844 moved on to supervise harbor improvements on Lake Ontario. On 7 December 1846, he received his orders to report to General Scott at Point Isabel.[3]

---

[3] *DAB*, X, p. 57; Cullum, *Biographical Register*, I, pp. 211–12; *Appleton's Cyclopaedia*, V, pp. 184–85; Abert to Turnbull, 7 Dec 1846, LS 519, TE 77.

Captain Joseph E. Johnston, who like Robert E. Lee later became a Confederate general in the Civil War, received his commission from the Military Academy as an artillery officer. He resigned in 1837 to take up a private civil engineering practice and worked for the Topographical Bureau in Florida surveying depot and fortification sites, where he was attacked by Indians and received the first of his numerous wounds in combat. Johnston joined the Topographical Engineers in 1838 as a first lieutenant, and initially worked as a member of the United States and Texas Boundary Survey. His following assignments included Lake Erie harbor improvement work, a tour at the bureau, another tour in Florida (1841–1843), the Northern Boundary Survey (1843–1844), and the Coast Survey (1844–1846).[4]

Another former artillery officer Lieutenant Eliakim P. Scammon also transferred to the Topographical Engineers in 1838, one year after receiving his commission at West Point. He served his first year on active duty as an assistant professor of mathematics at the Military Academy before moving on to Florida as an assistant topographer. Scammon returned to the Topographical Bureau in 1840 for one year, then returned to West Point as an assistant professor of history, geography, and ethics. In 1846 he took over duties as the supervising engineer on the survey of New Bedford harbor, serving in that capacity until joining Scott's army.[5]

A recent Academy graduate, Lieutenant George W. Derby, immediately transferred from the Ordnance Corps to the Topographical Engineers. The top three or four graduates usually went into the Corps of Engineers, the next two to the Topographical Engineers, with the Ordnance Corps receiving the third ranking group of new officers. The mission of the Topographical Engineers especially appealed to Derby, which may have accounted for his high class standing, seventh in a class of fifty-nine. His high standing belied his nature, and he did not move on to high rank like many of his contemporaries. Instead, he would be remembered in later years for his boisterous "western" style of humor. Derby already had earned a

---

[4] Gilbert Govan and James W. Livingood, *A Different Valor: The Story of General Joseph E. Johnston. C.S.A.* (New York: Bobbs-Merrill Co., 1946), pp. 15–17; *DAB*, V, pp. 144–46; *Appleton's Cyclopaedia*, III, pp. 458–60; *National Cyclopaedia of American Biography*, V, pp. 328–29; Cullum, *Biographical Register*, I, pp. 428–29.

[5] *Appleton's Cyclopaedia*, V, p. 413; *National Cyclopaedia of American Biography*, VII, pp. 527–28; Cullum, *Biographical Register*, I, pp. 668–69.

reputation at the Military Academy as a notorious practical joker, and it did not take long for him to become the topog's humorist. Before arriving in Mexico, he worked on the New Bedford harbor survey.[6]

Lieutenant Edmund L. F. Hardcastle received his commission directly into the Topographical Engineers. A classmate of Derby's, Hardcastle ranked fifth in the class of 1846. He served for a short time with the Coast Survey before receiving his orders for Mexico. Hardcastle joined up with the irrepressible Derby for the long trip to their new assignment. The route they took, like Meade earlier, illustrates how several officers traveled to the war zone. They proceeded along the Ohio River by river boat, stopping long enough at Louisville to purchase a pair of fine Kentucky bluegrass horses, and continued down the Ohio and Mississippi to New Orleans. From there they went by steamer to Scott's temporary headquarters at Brazos Island. According to Derby, the two horses eventually ended up as food for the vultures in Mexico.[7]

By late December 1846 Scott had arrived in Mexico and detached most of Taylor's army. Almost all Taylor's regulars and an equal number of volunteers, about 8,000 in all, received instructions to assemble at Tampico and at the mouth of the Brazos River in Texas. From there they proceeded to the rendezvous at Lobos Island, the jumping off point for the amphibious operation at Vera Cruz. By February Captain John McClellan and Lieutenant George G. Meade, both veterans of Taylor's army, reported to Tampico to serve on General Patterson's staff. They reached Lobos Island the following month in time to board the ships heading toward Vera Cruz. Derby, who joined the general's staff at Brazos Island, recorded his impressions of camp life. After meeting General Scott he remarked, "The Major General is quite affable and frequently invites his staff to a dinner or a glass of wine, which they accept with astonishing readiness." Despite the severe living conditions and the changeable weather, Derby retained a positive outlook: "With a clear conscience, a strong man, a sharp saber, three pistols and a good horse I am good for a long leave of life even among the yellow bellies."[8]

---

[6] George R. Stewart, *John Phoenix, Esq. The Veritable Squibob, A Life of Captain George H. Derby, USA* (New York: Da Capo Press, 1937), pp. 33–45; *DAB*, III, pp. 251–52; Cullum, *Biographical Register*, II, pp. 261–62.

[7] Cullum, *Biographical Register*, II, p. 260; Stewart, *John Phoenix, Esq.*, p. 45.

[8] Quote from Stewart, *John Phoenix, Esq.*, pp. 46–47; Bauer, *The Mexican War*, pp. 239–40; *National Cyclopaedia of American Biography*, XXI, p. 443; Meade, *Letters*, I, pp. 184–87.

The Landing at Vera Cruz

By early March 1847 Scott had gathered his army of nearly 14,000 men for the invasion. He organized his expeditionary force into two divisions of regulars commanded by Brig. Gens. William J. Worth and David E. Twiggs, and a volunteer division under Maj. Gen. Robert Patterson. Scott then resolved his transport difficulties as best he could. Concluding that his army and supplies were as complete as they ever would be, Scott boarded his army for the voyage to Vera Cruz.[9]

On the 6th, at a point southeast of Vera Cruz and near the island of Anton Lizardo, Scott's transport flotilla rendezvoused with Commodore David Conner's naval squadron. Scott, Conner, and their staffs boarded the *Patricio,* a captured Mexican steamer pressed into American service, to reconnoiter the landing area. The reconnaissance proceeded quietly until the party approached the coast to take a closer look at the town and its defenses. According to Meade the vessel came to within 1.25 miles of the city's castle when the Mexicans suddenly opened fire. Fortunately for the Americans the defenders missed the ship. Meade, on board at the time, surmised that only the Mexicans' poor aiming precluded a near disaster for the American leadership. "This operation," he later wrote, "I consider very foolish; for, having on board all the general officers of the army, one shot, hitting the vessel and disabling it, would have left us a floating target to the enemy, and might have been the means of breaking up the expedition." Such a shot would indeed have left the U.S. forces lying off shore virtually leaderless. Aboard the *Patricio* were Scott's three division commanders (Twiggs, Worth, and Patterson), one of his brigade commanders (Gideon J. Pillow), the U.S. Army's Chief of Engineers and Scott's chief engineer (Colonel Joseph G. Totten), two of Totten's engineer staff (Robert E. Lee and Pierre G. T. Beauregard), and three topogs (Turnbull, Johnston, and Meade).[10]

Three days later the army, under the protection of the U.S. Navy's Home Squadron, came ashore in surfboats. The defenders

---

[9] Bauer, *The Mexican War,* pp. 240–41; Matloff, *American Military History,* p. 174; Eisenhower, *So Far From God,* p. 257.

[10] Meade, *Letters,* I, p. 187. See also Dufour, *Mexican War; A Compact History,* pp. 202–03; Bauer, *The Mexican War,* p. 241; Eisenhower, *So Far From God,* pp. 258–59.

did not oppose the landings which took place three miles to the southeast of Vera Cruz. Within a week siege lines encircled the strongly fortified city. In order to keep his casualties to a minimum, Scott decided to resort to a heavy bombardment rather than a direct assault, thereby persuading the Mexican garrison to surrender. He asked the Navy to bring ashore their heavier guns manned by sailors. The combined artillery of ship and shore batteries then proceeded to bombard the city from sea and land. Old Fuss and Feathers also called upon the services of his two engineering staffs to reconnoiter the Mexican defenses, supervise the construction of the siege lines, and site artillery locations.[11]

The Two Engineering Corps Roles at Vera Cruz

Colonel Totten made sure his corps dominated the engineering support during the campaign to Mexico City. With outstanding young officers in the Corps of Engineers such as Lee, Beauregard, and George B. McClellan, the Chief of Engineers' goal of ensuring a brilliant accomplishment by his corps in the campaign became even more attainable. His recommendations carried significant weight, for not only was he a full colonel, thereby outranking Turnbull, but also chief of the Corps of Engineers. Neither did he overlook the former subordinate role of the Topographical Engineers. Totten did call for topographic help, but he made certain that the role of his own engineers predominated the scene.[12]

The slights became quite evident to the topogs, particularly Meade who wrote disgustedly, "For my individual part I have been pretty much a spectator for a week, the Corps of Engineers having performed all the engineering that has been done. This is attributable to the presence of Colonel Totten, who wishes to make as much capital for his own corps, and give us as little as possible." Now more than ever, the young lieutenant regretted his separation from Taylor's command. Scott did make considerable use of his "indefatigable engineers," and the Corps of Engineers officers received a

---

[11] Kenneth J. Deacon, "Combat Engineers 34: Siege of Vera Cruz, 1847," *Military Engineer*, 57 (July 1965): 258; Bauer, *The Mexican War*, pp. 246–47; Eisenhower, *So Far From God*, pp. 260–62.

[12] Freeman, *Robert E. Lee*, I, pp. 226–27; Robert M. Hughes, *Great Commanders, General Johnston* (New York: D. Appleton Co., 1897), pp. 24–25; Irving Crump, *Our Army Engineers* (New York: Dodd Mead and Co., 1954), pp. 94–111.

considerable amount of praise in the general's official dispatches. Old Fuss and Feathers, however, did not overlook his topogs, and they obtained due recognition throughout the campaign.[13]

Totten's corps also employed the only engineer troop organization during the Mexican War. Company A, Corps of Engineers, organized at West Point and composed of sappers, miners, and pontoniers (the forerunner of the Corps' combat engineers), deployed to northern Mexico in October 1846. The following month the unit, equipped with a unique rubber floating bridge, received orders to join Scott's army. During the siege of Vera Cruz the company's officers and enlisted men reconnoitered positions, laid out and supervised the construction of gun emplacements and trenches, and cut off the water supply to the city. Lieutenant George B. McClellan, one of the company's officers, would rise to flag rank during the Civil War and command a Union army. Company A engineers marched with Scott's army to Mexico City and participated in the series of battles leading to the capital. By contrast, the Corps of Topographical Engineers remained an officer-only corps without units of any kind.[14]

Meanwhile, the young and eager junior topogs also began their own record of commendable service at Vera Cruz. By the 28th Major Turnbull reported that Captains Hughes and Johnston had joined Worth's command manning the right flank of the siege lines; Captain McClellan and Lieutenant Meade had moved to the center with Patterson; and Turnbull himself had joined Twiggs on the left. Lieutenants Hardcastle and Derby, who had arrived on the 17th, began a survey of the besieging line of investment. During their work both lieutenants volunteered for duty with the artillery, for which they received due recognition. Colonel James Bankhead, the chief of artillery during the siege, reported: "I should not omit to mention two young officers of the corps of topographical engi-

---

[13] Meade, *Letters,* I, pp. 192–93.
[14] G. A. Youngblood, "History of Engineer Troops in the United States Army, 1775–1901," *Occasional Papers of the Engineer School, No. 37* (Washington, D.C.: Press of the Engineer School, 1910), pp. 34–37. See also William H. Robinson, "The Engineer Soldiers in the Mexican War," *Military Engineer,* 24 (Jan 1932): 1–8; Gustaves W. Smith, "Company A Engineers in Mexico, 1846–1847," *Military Engineer,* 51 (Sep 1964): 336–40; *History and Traditions of the Corps of Engineers,* Engineer School Special Text, ST 25-1 (Fort Belvoir: Engineer School, 1953), pp. 18–24.

neers, Lieutenants Derby and Hardcastle, volunteered to serve in the trenches, and did serve well and gallantly for 24 hours."[15]

Official reports, however, sometimes tended to overplay actual deeds. When an artillery officer approached Bankhead to add his name to the report, another artillery officer reacted strongly and wrote,

> I would cut my tongue out before I would allow it to commit so great an act of indelicacy. Colonel Bankhead will not, I hope, do it. He has already been induced to insert the names of two Topographical Engineers who were at one of the Batteries, mentioned because they volunteered, not because they did as much or more than others. The fact is, that at the Batteries there was but little room for individual distinction.[16]

Regardless of inflated battle reports, members of both engineering corps played important and dangerous roles during the siege, thereby contributing immeasurably to the fortified city's surrender. Using the time-honored procedures outlined 150 years earlier by Marshal Sebastien Le Prestre de Vauban, the French master of siege warfare, the engineers located positions and supervised the construction of the system of trench lines and fortified field artillery positions. The siege lines moved ever closer to the walls of the city and its defensive fire. In doing so the trench lines cut off and brought the enemy positions under close fire. In the end Scott's application of siegecraft and firepower brought swift victory and few casualties to the Americans, and by 27 March the defenders capitulated.[17]

The first Americans to enter the city were engineers. Sent in to arrange terms of surrender, Lee of the Corps of Engineers and Johnston of the Topographical Engineers marked the start of two promising careers. Lee in particular had played a prominent role in the engineers' contribution to the victory at Vera Cruz, the first

---

[15] Report of the Secretary of War, 1847, Sen. Exec. Doc. 1, p. 244; Turnbull to Abert, 28 Mar 1847, LR 216, TE 77.

[16] Robert Anderson, *An Artillery Officer in the Mexican War, 1846–7* (New York: G.P. Putnam's Sons, 1911), p. 124.

[17] Deacon, "Siege of Vera Cruz," p. 258. Appropriately, the Corps of Engineers insignia is a castle depicting its role in fortifications. America traditionally looked to France for military expertise particularly in military engineering. The precepts of building and capturing fortifications as practiced by Vauban was carried forth in France by other engineers such as Simon Bernard, who during the Napoleonic era became one of Europe's recognized experts on fortifications. In 1816 the United States employed the knowledgeable Bernard, and he served as a key member of the Board of Engineers for Fortifications. See Moore, *The Fortifications Board 1816–1828*.

TO MEXICO CITY WITH SCOTT

of his many incredible feats in this campaign. One eyewitness recorded the entry of the two engineers into the city:

> They were then distinguished young officers, intimate friends to each other, and their martial appearance as they rode, superbly mounted, to meet the Mexican officers, gave a general feeling of satisfaction to our army, that such representatives of the "North Americas" had been chosen for such an occasion.[18]

Meade Departs

Although official reports cited the Topographical Engineers for meritorious service in the siege of Vera Cruz, there appeared to be more topogs present than believed necessary. Lieutenant Meade became a candidate for early release from the war zone. One consideration included his length of service, and Scott also believed that the young topog did not legitimately belong to his command. After conferring with Major Turnbull in late March, Old Fuss and Feathers ordered Meade's return to Washington.[19]

By April Meade reached New Orleans where he continued his outpouring of letters to his wife. In one letter he outlined the reasons for his return: "Major Turnbull said that I was unexpectedly with him, that I did not belong to his detail, and consequently he had officers enough without me." He added, "Again, I found myself at Vera Cruz a perfect cipher, the major, three captains, and one lieutenant I had over my head depriving me of any opportunity I might otherwise have of distinction."[20]

Meade felt that he departed the war zone with honorable service, but he still faced other concerns. Family finances particularly bothered him. This he noted, "has been a source of mortification to me greater than I can describe." Meade did seek advice from senior officers whether he should stay in Mexico, and they advised him to leave. Not sure whether leaving Mexico now meant he could be reunited with his family, the topog concluded:

> The above were reasons influencing me; but I had nevertheless to struggle against my own personal inclination, which, I frankly confess, was to

---

[18] Quote from Dabney H. Maury in Bradley T. Johnson (ed.), *A Memoir of the Life and Public Service of Joseph E. Johnston* (Baltimore: R.H. Woodward and Co., 1891), p. 291; Freeman, *Robert E. Lee*, I, pp. 226–27; Hughes, *General Johnston*, pp. 24–25.

[19] Report of the Secretary of War, 1847, Sen. Exec. Doc. 1, pp. 240, 248, 256.

[20] Meade, *Letters*, I, p. 194.

remain, and against the fear that, when I report to Colonel Abert, he may either send me right back to General Taylor, or else send me to some out-of-the-way place, where my separation will be almost as complete from you, without all the advantages of being with an army in the field.[21]

Meade did not return to Mexico, and he did go on to conclude a successful military career. Upon his return to Philadelphia, the citizenry received him cordially and presented the topog with a beautiful and costly sword for his service in Mexico. He then served under Major Bache who had charge of constructing the Brandywine lighthouse in Delaware Bay. Meade went on to compile surveys of the Florida reefs for the Topographical Bureau. In 1849 he received orders to report to Florida to survey fortification sites during renewed hostilities with the Seminole Indians. He returned the same year to continue his work under Major Bache. In 1851 he again reported to Florida to supervise lighthouse construction in the keys. A captain by 1856, Meade moved on the following year to take over the Great Lakes survey, which he directed with extreme efficiency until 1861. Soon after the first guns sounded in the Civil War he received an appointment as brigadier general of volunteers. Within a few years he found himself in command of Union forces at Gettysburg. His observations of field operations during the Mexican War, his appraisal of generals such as Taylor, and his preparation of battlefield maps undoubtedly undergirded the decisions he would make during one of the nation's most fateful battles.[22]

Cerro Gordo

After capturing Vera Cruz and establishing the port city as his base of supply, Scott quickly moved inland toward Mexico City. He also grew concerned over the impending approach of the dreaded yellow fever season. Especially prevalent along the lowlands of the coast, the disease could do more harm to his army than the enemy.

---

[21] Ibid., pp. 194–95.
[22] Ibid., pp. 199–218; *DAB*, VI, pp. 474–76; *Appleton's Cyclopaedia*, IV, pp. 279–81; *National Cyclopaedia of American Biography*, IV, pp. 66–68; Cullum, *Biographical Register*, I, pp. 601–08. Biographies of Meade also include Freeman Cleaves, *Meade at Gettysburg* (Norman: University of Oklahoma Press, 1960); Isaac R. Pennypacker, *Great Commanders, General Meade* (New York: D. Appleton and Co., 1901); Richard Meade Bache, *Life of General George Gordon Meade* (Philadelphia: Henry T. Coates and Co., 1898).

This spurred Old Fuss and Feathers to reach the more healthful higher altitude as soon as possible, thereby ensuring better prospects for the health of his men. Jalapa, a city in the highlands some seventy-four miles inland along the National Highway, became the next objective. Santa Anna, however, had raised another army and on 5 April reached the city first.[23]

Santa Anna decided to make a stand at Cerro Gordo, a rocky defile twenty-four miles to the east. Convinced that the Americans, with their artillery and wagon train, could only advance along the National Highway, the Mexican leader began to dig in his force of 12,000 men. They sited their cannons on the summits of a mountain called El Telegrafo and along the neighboring hills. Advised by his own engineers, the wily Santa Anna made most of the excellent natural defense positions afforded by the rocky terrain overlooking the road.[24]

By this time Scott had begun to move his army into the Sierra Madre Mountains. Twiggs led the march to Jalapa, and by 11 April his division encamped near the Plan del Rio, not far from Cerro Gordo. The following morning an advance party of his dragoons drew fire and the two armies prepared to do battle. Old Fuss and Feathers pitched his camp on the 14th and immediately ordered a careful reconnaissance of the Mexican positions. He soon realized that a frontal assault would be suicidal, and directed his engineers under Captain Robert E. Lee to check out the Mexican left flank.[25]

Lee did find a way to outflank the defenders, and Scott executed the first of several flanking movements in his march to Mexico City to decisively defeat his foe. After going out on several dangerous reconnaissance patrols, Lee found a way to traverse the rough terrain to the right of El Telegrafo. This enabled the Americans to bypass the main defensive positions and strike the Mexican rear. Troops improved the path, other soldiers manhandled artillery pieces up and down slopes, and an assault force seized an adjacent summit. On the morning of the 18th the Americans took El Telegrafo after a sharp fight. Just as the defenders there began to fall back to Cerro Gordo, the flanking force struck. The Mexi-

---

[23] Bauer, *The Mexican War*, pp. 260–61.
[24] Bauer, *The Mexican War*, pp. 263–64; Eisenhower, *So Far From God*, pp. 272–74.
[25] Dufour, *Mexican War; A Compact History*, pp. 211–15; Bauer, *The Mexican War*, p. 264; Eisenhower, *So Far From God*, pp. 274–77.

cans were completely routed, losing 1,000 killed or wounded and 3,000 prisoners. Scott lost only 64 killed and 353 wounded. An impressive quantity of guns and small arms fell into American hands—to say nothing of Santa Anna's spare wooden leg. The fleeing Mexican army virtually ceased to exist.[26]

Lee received due recognition after the battle, and several topogs also received credit for gallantry. Now serving with the regiment of voltigeurs (an elite mobile cavalry-like force consisting of dragoons, infantry, and artillery), Joseph E. Johnston began his combat duties with distinction. The voltigeurs wore a distinctive grey instead of the customary blue uniform, received training as expert skirmishers, and operated forward of the main force. Considered an honor regardless of the dangers, service with the voltigeurs became popular, and many soldiers volunteered to join. Johnston usually placed himself out in front during the attack, and his audacity in combat made him a magnet for bullets. The wounds he received at Cerro Gordo were the first of many to follow in the Mexican War campaign. A friend later recalled the topog's eagerness to gain information about the Mexican defenses:

> We had been halted in the timber, just out of sight of the enemy, some twenty minutes, when we heard the rattle of musketry, and a few minutes later the order came "fall back to the right and left of the road" to let the bearers of Captain Johnston pass by. He had received two severe wounds while making a daring Reconnaissance, and was borne back to Plan Del Rio.[27]

Although Johnston now served with the voltigeurs, he continued to accomplish topographical duties on a voluntary basis. On this occasion he brought back important information revealing Mexican capability to sweep the road with artillery fire. Already holding the rank of lieutenant colonel of the Voltigeur Regiment, Johnston first gained a brevet promotion to major and then to colonel for gallant and meritorious conduct and for wounds received in his reconnaissance.[28]

---

[26] Dufour, *Mexican War; A Compact History*, p. 216; Bauer, *The Mexican War*, pp. 264–68; Eisenhower, *So Far From God*, pp. 277–80. For accounts of Lee's reconnaissance see Freeman, *Robert E. Lee*, I, pp. 237–48; Kenneth J. Deacon, "Combat Engineers 25, Cerro Gordo, 1847," *Military Engineer*, 56 (July 1965): 258.

[27] Quoted in Johnson (ed.), *Johnston Memoir*, p. 292; Govan and Livingood, *Johnston*, p. 19; Hughes, *General Johnston*, p. 25; *Niles [Ohio] National Register*, 72 (15 May 1847): 161.

[28] Hughes, *General Johnston*, p. 25; Lloyd Lewis, *Captain Sam Grant* (Boston: Little, Brown and Co., 1950), p. 206; Cullum, *Biographical Register*, I, pp. 428–29; Heitman, *Historical Register*, I, p. 143.

While Lee and other engineers reconnoitered the Mexican left flank on the 15th, Lieutenant Derby accomplished the same mission along the right flank. Accompanied by a single escort, the topog pushed through the chaparral and cactus for 4.5 miles until reaching a good vantage point to observe the enemy positions. He calculated the number of troops and artillery and mapped the locations of the Mexican forces and the terrain. The following morning Inspector General Ethan Allen Hitchcock wrote, "Just returned to my tent from a long conference at the General's hut. Reconnoitering parties all present. Lee, Derby, and others have made the boldest examinations and have given a great deal of information. Enemy very strong on main road." Thus, along with Lee, Derby provided Scott with valuable information.[29]

The following day Derby received orders from Major Turnbull to accompany Twiggs' division to outflank the Mexican defenders. Lee oversaw the initial construction of a path for Twiggs' column and then guided the flanking forces while Derby stayed with the pioneers. "Suddenly," Derby later recalled, "we were surprised by a rapid fire from the first hill, which from a slight sprinkle became a perfect hail storm." Colonel William S. Harney's brigade then attacked up the hill (Atalaya), and Derby joined in the assault. Derby continued his account:

About half way up, my horse was shot and fell under me with a ball through his hind leg and I had to tie him up to a tree and foot it up the rest of the way which was far preferable as the hill was so steep it was impossible to ride. We drove the Mexicans from the 1st to the 2nd hill, racing after them and yelling like wild Indians, which last scared them as much as the firing. . . . I shot one fellow with a pistol who was about firing. He fell and begged for his life. I told him to lay still and nobody would touch him and went on. But when I came back after the fight to help him I found somebody had killed him. He was some sort of an officer and I took his sword and I got it [sic] somewhere now. . . . We occupied this hill that night and lay on our blankets. The Mexicans firing grape shot and canister over us occasionally but with very little effect.[30]

Derby also participated in the attack up El Telegrafo on the 18th. While the indefatigable Lee guided Scott's flanking forces farther around Santa Anna's defenses, Harney's brigade shouted a

---

[29] Quoted from Hitchcock, *Fifty Years in Camp and Field*, p. 250; Stewart, *John Phoenix, Esq.*, pp. 48–49.

[30] Quoted from Stewart, *John Phoenix, Esq.*, pp. 50–51.

great hurrah and charged down the Atalaya, across the hollow, and then up El Telegrafo. Derby accompanied the charge and later described the assault:

> Down we went through the whistling balls and crashing grape, men dropping here and there, the wounded groaning, but nobody scared, and with a tremendous yell we gained the ravine and commenced the ascent of Sierra Guardia [Cerro Gordo]. A fire, close, heavy and continued, from 1800 muskets was opened on us, but the ascent was so extremely precipitous that it afforded us protection, for most of the balls passed over our heads. The whistling was terrific, the air seemed alive with balls, but we went on cheering and returning the fire now and then, when we stopped for an instant to rest. At last we came to the highest crest within ten rods of their first breastwork. We gave one fire, then Colonel Harney shouted. . . . Away we went. The Mexicans saw us coming. Nothing could withstand such a charge, they gave one fire and ran. We followed, clambered up over the breastwork, chased them from the tower, over the hill, turned their own pieces on them, and the Sierra Guardia was ours. Up went the American flag and down came the Mexican.[31]

Derby also gave an account of his wound and a somewhat humorous and probably apocryphal encounter with Old Fuss and Feathers. The topog had been directing fire on the retreating Mexicans when suddenly a bullet struck him in the left hip. General Scott, later riding by the battlefield, saw the wounded topog and supposedly exclaimed, "My God Darby, you're wounded!" Derby then replied using a similar English pronunciation, "Yes, General Scatt." The general bristled, "My name is Scott, not Scatt!" The wounded lieutenant retorted, "And my name is Derby, not Darby." Derby, however, wrote of the general's visits to him in the hospital, when Scott expressed his sympathy and his pride in the young topographical engineer. The official dispatches mentioned the topog's deeds at Cerro Gordo, and he subsequently received a promotion to brevet first lieutenant.[32]

Because of his wound the irrepressible Derby returned to the United States, but not until he had an unusual encounter with Johnston. Another patient in the temporary hospital recalled Johnston's apparent lack of appreciation for Derby's antics:

> The partitions of the rooms were of reeds, wattled together, so that conversations could be heard from one room to the other. John Phoenix

---

[31] Ibid., pp. 51–52.
[32] Ibid., pp. 3–4, 52–54; Report of the Secretary of War, 1847, Sen. Exec. Doc. 1, p. 263.

TO MEXICO CITY WITH SCOTT 191

Derby was an incessant talker and uttered a stream of coarse wit, to the great disgust of Joe Johnston, who endured it in silence, till one day he heard Derby order his servant to capture a kid out of a flock of goats passing on down, when he broke out, "If you dare to do that, I'll have you court martialed and cashiered or shot."[33]

Fewer Topogs After Cerro Gordo

After Cerro Gordo, Major Turnbull dutifully reported the details of the battle and the latest activities of his shrunken staff to Colonel Abert. By then Meade had departed, Johnston had joined the voltigeurs, Derby had returned home wounded, and Hughes and Scammon (Scammon served as Scott's aide until May) had returned to the States because of illness. Suddenly the large and apparently overstrength topog staff had dwindled down to Turnbull, John McClellan, and Hardcastle. Appraised of this situation, Colonel Abert issued instructions for Lieutenants Hagner, Martin L. Smith, and Thom to report to Scott's command.[34]

The wounded Derby returned to the United States, and the rest of his life turned out to be a mixture of humor and tragedy. He served for awhile at the Topographical Bureau. Some truth exists of the tale that Colonel Abert transferred him later to a California mapping and exploration project in order to remove the lieutenant from the proximity of his daughter. The wounded war hero who dressed in an unusually bright uniform, handsome, young, and robust, undoubtedly appealed to Abert's young, marriageable daughter.[35]

The transfer to California turned out to be a pivotal point in Derby's life. There he launched a literary career under the name John Phoenix. He satirized the Army, American culture, and even the Pacific railroad surveys, all while remaining a dedicated Topographical Engineer. Between 1848 and 1854 he served in Minnesota, Texas, and twice in California. In 1850 to 1851 he conducted a notable reconnaissance on the lower Colorado River. In 1855 he moved up to Oregon and Washington to build roads; a year later he worked with the Coast Survey; and, between 1857 to 1859 he con-

---

[33] Dabney H. Maury, *Recollections of a Virginian in the Mexican, Indian, and Civil Wars* (New York: Charles Scribner's Sons, 1894), p. 39.

[34] Turnbull to Abert, 24 Apr 1847, LR 308, TE 77; Abert to Turnbull, 18 Oct 1847, LS 245, TE 77.

[35] Stewart, *John Phoenix, Esq.*, pp. 56–58.

structed lighthouses in the Southeast. After fourteen years' service he reached his highest rank as a captain. Because of the effects of sunstroke and failing eyesight, he was placed on sick leave. He died on 15 May 1861, having made material contributions to the work of the Topographical Engineers.[36]

Lieutenant George Thom reported to Mexico that summer, but he like Scammon ended up as an aide de camp. Commissioned directly at West Point into the Topographical Engineers in 1839, Thom started out as an assistant on the surveys on the northern boundary. The following year he worked on the Delaware harbor improvements project for a short period before returning to the boundary survey. There he received orders to report to Scott in Mexico. After his arrival Thom served his tour as Brig. Gen. Franklin Pierce's aide and saw some action in skirmishes between 1 July and 6 August 1847. By late October he became ill and returned to the United States where he continued to serve as a topog and later in the Corps of Engineers. He concluded his military career as a colonel after forty-four years of uninterrupted service.[37]

On to Puebla

After Cerro Gordo the way now appeared open to Mexico City, some 170 miles to the west. Worth's division took the lead, and without any difficulty his troops took Perote on 22 April and Puebla in mid-May. By then Scott had decided to release some 3,700 men—the bulk of his volunteer force—before their enlistments came to an end. (Only a handful agreed to reenlist for the duration of the war.) Always thinking of the welfare of his men, Old Fuss and Feathers wanted to minimize the danger that they might catch yellow fever as they moved back through Vera Cruz. He also realized that his twelve-month enlistees caused disciplinary problems and might mistreat the Mexican population. Guerrilla

---

[36] Ibid., pp. 59–92; *DAB*, III, pp. 251–52; Cullum, *Biographical Register*, II, pp. 261–62; Goetzmann, *Army Exploration*, pp. 250–51, 253–61. Derby's published works were *Phoenixiana, or Sketches and Burlesques* (New York, 1856) and *Squibob Papers* (New York, 1865). He went under the pseudonym of John Phoenix. See also George H. Derby, *Derby's Report on Opening the Colorado, 1850–1851*, Odie B. Faulk (ed.) (Albuquerque: University of New Mexico Press, 1969).

[37] Cullum, *Biographical Register*, I, pp. 741–43; *Appleton's Cyclopaedia*, VI, p. 76; Turnbull to Abert, 26 Oct 1847, LR 689, TE 77.

activity had increased along his supply route, and he wanted to maintain good relations with the civilian population. By now he depended almost totally on the local populace to supply his army.[38]

Scott then moved on with the bulk of his force to join Worth at Puebla. Arriving in late May, he pulled in the garrisons from Jalapa and Perote. At the risk of cutting off his connection with the coast along his supply route, Scott instead chose to reinforce his small command. He decided that his command must take its chances and, in the midst of a hostile nation, live off the land. The departure of the volunteers, however, in early June left him with only a little more than 7,000 men. Figuring the army still too small to move on to Mexico City, Old Fuss and Feathers elected to await reinforcements and developments in peace negotiations before resuming the march.[39]

During their three-month stay in Puebla, Scott's engineers collected and studied all the available maps of the approaches to Mexico City. Turnbull and Lee gathered information from natives and travelers and then penciled their findings on a map. Later, when they verified the entries, Turnbull and Lee inked over their penciled marks. Scott examined their map almost daily.[40]

Reconnoitering the Approaches to Mexico City

By 7 August 1847 Scott, his force now slightly under 11,000 healthy and sick soldiers, renewed the march to Mexico City. Twiggs' division led the way, with divisions commanded by Worth, Quitman, and Pillow following at one day intervals. Leaving only a small garrison behind at Puebla to protect his sick, Scott's columns moved farther inland.[41]

In the meantime, Santa Anna miraculously gathered together still another army—this time 30,000 men—for the defense of his capital city. A showdown outside the capital appeared imminent. As Scott's army approached the city, Santa Anna offered little resistance. Instead, he preferred to fortify the approaches to the city.

---

[38] Bauer, *The Mexican War*, pp. 268–71; Eisenhower, *So Far From God*, pp. 295–96. Scott tried to instill firmer discipline on his volunteers than did Taylor. Also see Johannsen, *To the Halls of the Montezumas*, p. 35.
[39] Bauer, *The Mexican War*, pp. 270–72; Eisenhower, *So Far From God*, p. 298.
[40] Freeman, *Robert E. Lee*, I, p. 250.
[41] Bauer, *The Mexican War*, pp. 273–74; Eisenhower, *So Far From God*, p. 310.

These defenses took advantage of several natural obstacles around Mexico City, particularly the swamps on either side of the roads and causeways leading into the city.[42]

By the 11th Twiggs' division reached Ayolta, some fifteen miles from Mexico City, and Scott himself arrived later that day to plan his next move. While Twiggs' troops encamped and the other divisions moved up into supporting positions, the engineers helped by the topogs reconnoitered the approaches toward the city. Besides the indefatigable Lee, other Corps of Engineers officers included Captain James L. Mason; 1st Lts. Beauregard, Zealous B. Tower, and Isaac I. Stevens; and 2d Lts. George B. McClellan, Gustavus W. Smith, and John G. Foster. Turnbull and Hardcastle accompanied their colleagues as necessary and prepared maps.[43]

These reconnaissance patrols provided considerable invaluable information which helped Scott to formulate a plan to outmaneuver Santa Anna's strong defenses. On the 12th Lee, Mason, and Stevens reported the presence of strongly fortified positions to the northwest at the El Penon heights overlooking the National Highway. This information, coupled with other reconnaissance reports, persuaded Scott to find another route and to outflank the Mexican stronghold. On the 13th Lieutenants Beauregard and McClellan made a reconnaissance to Mexicalcingo, just a few miles to the south of Mexico City. There they met Lee and Tower, who moved along separate routes farther south. Lee and Beauregard then relayed information that a rough road farther south around Lake Chalco could carry the artillery and wagon train toward San Augustin. By following this route an American force could outflank the Mexican positions at both El Penon and Mexicalcingo. A later reconnaissance by Colonel James Duncan, Worth's artillery chief, confirmed Scott's decision to move in that direction.[44]

On 15 August Scott issued orders to move south around the lake, thereby striking the capital directly from the south. Worth's

---

[42] Bauer, *The Mexican War*, pp. 274, 287–88; Eisenhower, *So Far From God*, pp. 308–10.

[43] Turnbull to Abert, 22 May 1847, LR 354, TE 77; Dufour, *Mexican War; A Compact History*, pp. 236–37.

[44] Bauer, *The Mexican War*, pp. 288–90; Eisenhower, *So Far From God*, pp. 312–13; Dufour, *Mexican War; A Compact History*, pp. 237–40; Williams (ed.), *With Beauregard in Mexico*, pp. 41–46. A copy of Duncan's report is inclosed in Ripley, *War With Mexico*, 2:648.

force set out while Twiggs, remaining at Ayolta, began operations to conduct a secondary attack to deceive the enemy. Worth occupied San Augustin on the 18th, only nine miles directly south of Mexico City. Three miles to the north near the hacienda of San Antonio, an engineer reconnaissance party, which included Turnbull and Hardcastle and their escort, drew a hail of Mexican fire. A direct assault toward strongly defended San Antonio appeared to be ruled out. Here too the terrain appeared to create an almost impossible barrier for even a flanking movement. A bog to the right and the Pedregal, an extensive lava field interwoven with deep cuts, fissures, and ridges, presented a unique natural barrier to the Americans' left.[45]

While Old Fuss and Feathers considered his next move, Santa Anna shifted the bulk of his forces between Contreras and Churubusco. Scott considered attacking west of San Antonio via the San Angel road, but on the 18th Lee and Beauregard brought back information suggesting the feasibility for a route through the Pedregal. While the engineers searched the western portion of the lava bed for a crossing, their escort clashed with Mexican pickets. This implied the existence of a path. The American scouting party also found a road that dwindled into a mule path and then disappeared amidst a jagged sea of lava. From this point, however, Lee could see the San Angel road only a mile and a half to the west. With this news Scott decided to open a road across the Pedregal. Such a passage would make possible the deployment of an artillery train to an enfilading position overlooking the San Antonio defenses. Lee then proceeded to supervise a 500-man work party drawn from Pillow's division to carve a passage through the lava.[46]

The Battles of Contreras and Churubusco

On the 19th the Mexicans detected the American road-building operation, and a clash lead to the bitter two-day Battle of Contreras (which really took place at Padierna). Without Scott's knowl-

---

[45] Report of the Secretary of War, 1847, Sen. Exec. Doc. 1, p. 349; Dufour, *Mexican War; A Compact History*, pp. 240–41; Bauer, *The Mexican War*, pp. 290–91; Eisenhower, *So Far From God*, p. 316.

[46] Williams (ed.), *With Beauregard in Mexico*, pp. 47–48; Freeman, *Robert E. Lee*, I, pp. 249–58; Dufour, *Mexican War; A Compact History*, pp. 241–44; Bauer, *The Mexican War*, pp. 291–92; Eisenhower, *So Far From God*, pp. 318–19.

edge or approval his subordinate commanders launched an attack which drew more Mexican forces into the battle. Fortunately for the Americans, Santa Anna's commander on the scene ignored an opportunity to crush a large part of Scott's force between two appreciably larger forces. Evening brought a heavy, cold rain. Again, thanks to Lieutenant Tower, the engineers found a way around the Mexicans' rear. That evening Lee, moving through the rugged lava fields and guided only by intermittent lightning flashes, carried word back to Scott of a new plan to encircle the enemy. Although exhausted, Lee guided additional troops to the battle in the early hours of the following day, thus allowing the flanking forces to rout the defenders. Ulysses S. Grant, then a lieutenant in the infantry, recalled, "This affair, like that of Cerro Gordo, was an engagement in which the officers of the Engineer Corps won special distinction. In fact, in both cases, tasks which seemed difficult at first sight were made easier for the troops that had to execute them than they would have been on a ordinary field." [47]

As the Mexican troops fell back in disorder, Scott directed an immediate thrust from his positions at Padierna and San Augustin toward Churubusco. Lee, moving with the advance element of Twiggs' division, guided an attacking force north of the town to Portales. To the south Mason, helped by Hardcastle, guided a brigade of Worth's division through the eastern fringe of the Pedregal around the defenses of San Antonio. Another Engineer, Stevens, relayed information from the west, and Scott ordered Twiggs' to attack the partially fortified San Mateo Convent Church just to the west of Churubusco. For a while inspired Mexican forces stopped the American advance at the convent. Just south of town at a fortified bridge the defenders also halted Worth's division coming up from the south. Repeated attacks by Worth's soldiers took the bridge in hand-to-hand fighting, and the convent's defenders surrendered under heavy bombardment. By the afternoon of the 20th both of Scott's forces met on the road north of town. The battle turned into a pursuit as the dispirited Mexican

---

[47] Quote from Ulysses S. Grant, *Personal Memoirs of U.S. Grant* (New York: Century Co., 1917), pp. 110–11; Bauer, *The Mexican War,* pp. 293–94; Eisenhower, *So Far From God,* pp. 319–24; Williams (ed.), *With Beauregard in Mexico,* pp. 48–59; Freeman, *Robert E. Lee,* I, pp. 259–72; Dufour, *Mexican War; A Compact History,* pp. 245–50; Report of the Secretary of War, 1847, Sen. Exec. Doc. 1, pp. 306–08.

soldiers fled northward to Mexico City. That evening Santa Anna sent word to Scott to discuss armistice terms.[48]

A Short-Lived Armistice and Molino del Rey

Scott could have continued the pursuit into the city, but he decided to pause, much to the consternation of his officers and men. Old Fuss and Feathers preferred to rest and regain control of his troops, hoping that the Mexicans might take the opportunity to accept surrender terms. In only two days his army had fought two hard battles. Several defensive works remained outside the city, and he believed taking the capital too formidable a task for a quick and easy success. American casualties in the two battles were also a point of concern—nearly 1,000 men killed or wounded out of a force of 8,500. Although he had conducted a brilliant campaign, the American commander remained well aware of his small army's vulnerability in the midst of the enemy's country.[49]

Under these circumstances Scott decided to accept the Mexican leader's armistice proposal on 24 August. Although Santa Anna lost almost a third of his force, roughly 10,000 men, in the two recent actions (more men than Scott had in his army), he could still call upon a willing pool of manpower. The respite restored Santa Anna's confidence, and he prepared to resume fighting. "During the armistice," Beauregard wrote, "no reconnaissance was permitted by the Commander-in-Chief, although it was a notorious fact that the enemy was violating it day and night." Seeing that the Mexicans were rapidly strengthening their remaining defenses and that negotiations were not accomplishing anything, Scott called off the armistice on 6 September. Two days later the Americans resumed the attack.[50]

By the 7th Scott's engineers resumed reconnaissance operations. The general's attention now turned toward El Molino del Rey, a mass of heavy stone buildings housing a mill and a foundry just to

---

[48] Report of the Secretary of War, 1847, Sen. Exec. Doc. 1, pp. 310, 315, 321, 323; Dufour, *Mexican War; A Compact History*, pp. 251–58; Bauer, *The Mexican War*, pp. 297–300; Eisenhower, *So Far From God*, pp. 324–26.

[49] Bauer, *The Mexican War*, pp. 300–301, 306; Eisenhower, *So Far From God*, pp. 327–31.

[50] Quote from Williams (ed.), *With Beauregard in Mexico*, p. 60; Bauer, *The Mexican War*, pp. 300, 307–08; Eisenhower, *So Far From God*, pp. 331–32.

the west of the fortress of Chapultepec. About 500 meters farther west Mexican engineers constructed bastioned earthworks around another massive building, the Casa de Mata. Captain Mason helped by Hardcastle hastily reconnoitered the Mexican defenses. Scott, who also heard that cannon were being made at the foundry, ordered Worth's division to conduct a night raid on the suspected factory. Worth, however, elected to hold off the attack until morning, and the raid turned into one of the bloodiest battles of the war. Fighting raged from dawn to dusk. Persistent assaults seized the buildings and the nearby Casa de Mata only after the attacking American troops suffered some of the heaviest casualties of the war. During the battle Turnbull and Hardcastle and their engineer counterparts continued their scouting duties and carried dispatches.[51]

The Storming of Chapultepec and Into Mexico City

Scott turned to his next objective, the rocky and fortified hill of Chapultepec towering over two main causeways leading into the city. By now Scott's command had dwindled to about 8,000 men opposing some 15,000 less experienced troops under Santa Anna. During the short pause, the engineers continued to go about their assigned tasks. They reconnoitered enemy defenses, supervised the construction of artillery positions, and advised Old Fuss and Feathers. On the 12th a heavy artillery bombardment began to rain down throughout the day on the steep hill and its old castle and the buildings of the Mexican Military Academy.[52]

The barrage resumed at dawn the following day, and the assault by Scott's four divisions got under way. While Twiggs' division conducted a diversionary attack on the city's southern causeways, the other three divisions participated in the main attack from the west. At 0800 the bombardment momentarily ceased. The regulars of Pillow's division with some help from Worth stormed up the slope from the west, while Quitman's division of volunteers and a small force of U.S. Marines advanced up a causeway south of the

---

[51] Report of the Secretary of War, 1847, Sen. Exec. Doc. 1, pp. 367, 426; Dufour, *Mexican War; A Compact History*, pp. 260–65; Bauer, *The Mexican War*, pp. 308–11; Eisenhower, *So Far From God*, pp. 334–36; Turnbull to Abert, 26 Sep 1847, LR 623, TE 77.

[52] Bauer, *The Mexican War*, pp. 310–13; Matloff, *American Military History*, p. 177.

hill. Despite some mistakes, including a lack of scaling ladders, the Americans seized the castle after a brief and bitter struggle.[53]

Without pausing the Americans moved on into the city. Quitman's troops, sensing total victory, immediately pursued the retreating enemy along the paved causeway to the Belem Gate. At the same time Worth's men moved northeast to the San Cosme Gate. The causeways canalized the advancing soldiers, and the Mexican defenders poured down fire on the densely packed columns. Most of the American losses that day—130 killed, 703 wounded, and 29 missing—took place along the causeways. The attackers, however, did not hesitate, and by nightfall both gates were in American hands.[54]

Before and during the battle the engineers continued to reconnoiter the southern and southwestern approaches to Mexico City. At a conference on the 11th Beauregard advised Scott that the attack on the capital should be from the west and that Chapultepec Hill should be seized before entering the city. To divert the Mexicans' attention, he also recommended a secondary attack south of Mexico City. This plan differed from recommendations submitted by other members of the general's staff. They advocated the main attack from the south. Earlier, however, Scott had considered a move similar to that recommended by Beauregard, and the general adopted that course of action.[55]

Recovered from his wounds at Cerro Gordo, former topog Lt. Col. Joseph E. Johnston led his voltigeurs in the assault on Chapultepec. As one of Pillow's three attacking columns, the elite infantry unit advanced along the southern walls of Molino del Rey to help seize the base of Chapultepec before the Mexicans could set off their land mines. They then pushed on up the slope to the base of the massive retaining wall of the fortress, where they had to wait for the ladders. When the ladders arrived, the voltigeurs scaled the walls and were among the first Americans to raise their regimental colors over Chapultepec. This time Johnston received several light wounds.[56]

Beauregard accompanied Johnston in the assault and later attested to the topog's personal bravery. Noting that, "there are, if

---

[53] Bauer, *The Mexican War*, pp. 316–18; Eisenhower, *So Far From God*, pp. 338–41.
[54] Bauer, *The Mexican War*, pp. 318–22.
[55] Bauer, *The Mexican War*, pp. 311–12; Dufour, *Mexican War; A Compact History*, p. 265; Eisenhower, *So Far From God*, pp. 337–38.
[56] Dufour, *Mexican War; A Compact History*, pp. 265–69; Bauer, *The Mexican War*, pp. 316–17.

any, few better or braver officers," Beauregard also recalled an exchange of words he had with Johnston during the assault on the Mexican fortification:

> I turned round and cried out to him as loud as I could, until I had drawn his attention (for the firing of the infantry and artillery, the hissing of the balls, etc. was perfectly deafening) and knowing the effect which such a demonstration under those would create in our favor, I said to him, holding at the time a loaded rifle in my hand, which I was about to fire, "Colonel, what will you bet on this shot?" He quickly replied, "A picayune, payable in the City of Mexico." (or he may have said: "Drinks in the City of Mexico," I cannot now recollect which), I then took deliberate aim, fired and cried to him, "you have lost, you will have to pay it." [57]

Scott's army cautiously entered the city the following morning. Exhausted and anticipating a bloody battle in the streets, the troops, much to their relief, discovered that Santa Anna had evacuated the city. Except for some intense guerrilla activity, and a 28-day siege of the Puebla garrison in September and October, the war had substantially ended. In the meantime, the United States pressed for peace negotiations, and the Mexicans tried to form a new government.

Scott Praises His Engineers

From Vera Cruz to Mexico City, General Scott and his senior commanders frequently cited the meritorious and gallant services of their two engineering corps. Publicity focused on the larger Corps of Engineers because of the exceptional and heroic acts its officers accomplished, especially the "gallant and indefatigable Lee." Only in such exceptional cases, however, were any details of specific accomplishments provided. General Patterson simply commended Captain McClellan and Lieutenant Meade for their services at Vera Cruz. General Scott mentioned Johnston and Derby for their gallant conduct at Cerro Gordo, but provided no other details. Scott's report referred to the contributions of Turnbull, McClellan, and Hardcastle after Contreras and Churubusco, and Worth underscored Hardcastle's "zeal, intelligence, and gallantry, in his particular department, as also in combat." Twiggs mentioned McClellan in his report. After Molino del Rey, Worth again

---

[57] Williams (ed.), *With Beauregard in Mexico*, pp. 80–81.

commended Hardcastle. Scott concluded his report on the seizure of Mexico City by noting the meritorious services of Turnbull and Hardcastle, and Twiggs again mentioned McClellan. General Pillow in his report cited Johnston and his voltigeurs for their part in taking Chapultepec.[58]

During this campaign, the Topographical Engineers also received several brevet promotions. Turnbull became brevet lieutenant colonel and later received a promotion to brevet colonel for gallant and meritorious service at Contreras, Churubusco, and Chapultepec. Johnston ended his tour in Mexico as a brevet colonel, and McClellan departed as a brevet lieutenant colonel. Hardcastle received brevet promotions to first lieutenant and captain after the campaigns around Mexico City. A latecomer, 2d Lt. Martin L. Smith received a brevet promotion to first lieutenant for meritorious service after the occupation of Mexico City.[59]

Hughes and Emory Take on New Roles in Mexico

Meanwhile, Hughes and Emory had returned to Mexico as members of a volunteer infantry regiment. After serving with General Wool's army during the march into northern Mexico, Hughes returned to Washington in the spring of 1847. By late June President Polk promoted him to a lieutenant colonel of volunteers with orders to assume command of a volunteer regiment with troops recruited from Maryland and the District of Columbia. On 23 July Hughes directed the advance element under Major John R. Kenly to proceed to Vera Cruz.[60]

By September the regiment had arrived in Vera Cruz and began its march inland. Hughes joined his command on 1 September, and by the 6th the volunteer unit moved out along the National Highway with the mission to reopen the road to Jalapa. Although Scott had arrived at the gates of Mexico City, portions of his line of communication to Vera Cruz had undergone continuous harassment and interdiction by Mexican guerrillas and bandits. In order to clear his assigned section of the road, Hughes had

---

[58] Report of the Secretary of War, 1847, Sen. Exec. Doc. 1, pp. 248, 256, 263, 306, 310–15, 321, 323, 367, 385, 400, 403.

[59] Cullum, *Biographical Register*, I, pp. 126, 211–12, 260, 367, 428–29,

[60] John R. Kenly, *Memoirs of a Maryland Volunteer in the Years 1846–7–8* (Philadelphia: J. B. Lippincott and Co., 1873), pp. 278–79.

been put in command of a large task force. Besides the five companies of his regiment, he also took charge of two companies of infantry from other regiments, two squadrons of Louisiana mounted troops, and an artillery battery.[61]

It did not take long for Hughes to see action. Not far from Jalapa the volunteers ran into guerrilla forces, and by the 9th the column routed the Mexicans from a strongly fortified position blocking the highway. Kenly later wrote, "great praise is due for the admirable manner in which he [Hughes] had succeeded in the attack and capture of the National Bridge, which during the whole war had been a thorn in our flanks, and had never before been held by an American army."[62]

For the next two months Hughes' regiment accomplished its security mission along its assigned section of the road. Despite Scott's capture of the capital, Mexican irregulars continued to harass American traffic along the National Highway. The former topog arranged a meeting with guerrilla leaders and nearly came to an agreement, but he received orders to move inland to reinforce Scott. This left the commander of the relieving unit to conclude negotiations. On 5 November Hughes proceeded west and temporarily encamped his regiment near Jalapa, but on the 22d he received orders to move his regiment back to Jalapa and to garrison the town. There he received an appointment as military governor of the province.[63]

Hughes accomplished his duties as military governor with tact and diplomacy, maintaining cordial relations with the Mexicans. When necessary, however, he kept order by employing stern measures. As usual most of the problems resulted from improper behavior on the part of American soldiers. To placate the local populace, Hughes issued a proclamation of general amnesty on 30 November. In general, the Americans and Mexicans mixed freely in Jalapa, and the military governor developed cordial relations with the leading clergymen in the community, especially the Franciscans. His friendship with the priests, however, resulted in some

---

[61] Ibid., pp. 291, 300; *Niles [Ohio] National Register,* 72 (14 Aug 1847): 372.
[62] Kenly, *Memoirs of a Maryland Volunteer,* p. 308.
[63] Ibid., pp. 328–65; Bauer, *The Mexican War,* p. 334.

resentment on the part of Mexican officials in the capital. Later these officials banished the head of the order from Mexico City.[64]

Hughes also had an interesting involvement with Santa Anna. In early 1848 Santa Anna received permission from the United States to depart the country. His aides then asked Hughes to provide an escort for Santa Anna's party to visit one of his estates in order to make final preparations for his departure. Hughes handled this sensitive affair with his usual tact. In a letter requesting General Twiggs' permission, Hughes concluded, "I think you will regard the matter as I do; that it is as fraught with the highest importance to our government in the present State of affairs as he is the great obstacle to the arrangement of a Peace." Hughes emphasized the importance of Santa Anna's safety and eagerly assumed responsibility to meet this request in order to get the ex-dictator out of Mexico.[65]

When Santa Anna reached Perote in late March Hughes entertained him and escorted the former Mexican leader and his entourage to the hacienda. Some tension occurred along the road when the Mexicans and their American escort had to pass through a regiment of Texas Rangers. The escort, however, surrounded Santa Anna and his party and pushed through the bitter Texans without incident. Santa Anna reciprocated Hughes' kindness by inviting the topog and several of his officers to visit the hacienda, where a rather pleasant gathering took place. A few days later Santa Anna safely departed the country.[66]

While Hughes was visiting Mexico City in April, Lt. Col. William H. Emory reported for duty with the regiment. After preparing his report and map of Kearny's expedition to California, the topog received an appointment to Hughes' volunteer regiment as second-in-command. Emory applied his usual thorough approach to this

---

[64] Kenly, *Memoirs of a Maryland Volunteer*, p. 377; Smith, *War With Mexico*, II, pp. 224, 230; Smith and Judah (eds.), *Chronicles of the Gringos*, p. 393. Hughes continued to provide information to the Topographical Bureau and transmitted a copy of his proclamation of general amnesty to the bureau; Hughes to Abert, 30 Nov 1847, LR 17, TE 77.

[65] Hughes to Twiggs, 15 Mar 1848, LR 200, TE 77; Bauer, *The Mexican War*, p. 385. Hughes provided the Topographical Bureau with several pieces of his correspondence regarding the departure of Santa Anna from Mexico.

[66] Kenly, *Memoirs of a Maryland Volunteer*, pp. 391–97; Bauer, *The Mexican War*, p. 385.

new and different job. Major Kenly aptly summarized the topog's contributions to the regiment:

> This gallant and accomplished officer gave to the regiment the benefit of his skill and experience by zealous efforts in its drill and instruction. He was successful in adding increased efficiency to the command and in winning the confidence and esteem of us all. From first to last, my relations with him, as they had been with Colonel Hughes, were intimate and friendly. He remained with the regiment until its final discharge at Pittsburgh, Pennsylvania.[67]

In submitting the Topographical Bureau's annual report to the Secretary of War, Colonel Abert praised Hughes' performance as a commander and military governor. The colonel wrote, "His march from Vera Cruz to Jalapa is spoken of as one of great merit and severe trial, in which he on several occasions encountered and beat the enemy." The chief topog concluded, "his highly judicious, energetic, prompt, and well judged measures, [were] mainly instrumental in keeping that extensive district quiet as well as the whole road from thence to Vera Cruz." On 16 June, following the ratification of the peace treaty between the two countries, the regiment departed Jalapa and marched to Vera Cruz. There the unit embarked on the 22d for the return voyage to the United States.[68]

Mapping the Valley of Mexico and Final Reports

During the march inland, the Topographical Engineers deferred any detailed reconnaissance patrols and mapping of the adjoining countryside because of operational concerns. The topogs also submitted more straightforward reports in comparison to the adventurous and interesting literary styles of Fremont, Emory, Abert, and to some degree even Hughes. Major Turnbull's reports were limited in scope, generally confining his remarks to the progress of the advancing army and the status of his officers.[69]

After the major fighting had subsided, however, several Topographical Engineers remained in Mexico to prepare maps and gather geographic data. From September 1847 to the summer of

---

[67] Kenly, *Memoirs of a Maryland Volunteer*, p. 431.
[68] Report of the Secretary of War, 1848, House Exec. Doc. 1, 30th Cong., 2d sess., 1 Dec 1848, p. 324; Kenly, *Memoirs of a Maryland Volunteer*, p. 468.
[69] Turnbull to Abert, 24 Apr 1847, LR 308; 22 May 1847, LR 354; 26 Sep 1847, LR 623, TE 77.

1848, when American forces withdrew, Turnbull's small staff mapped the region around Mexico City, reconnoitered the key roads, and prepared battle maps to accompany reports of the campaign. In October 1847 Turnbull reported to Colonel Abert that Lieutenants Hardcastle and Smith had set off to reconnoiter the area around Mexico City before preparing a map of the region. Lieutenant Charles N. Hagner traced the road between Mexico City and Taluca. He also forwarded copies of captured maps that included information on Acapulco, Vera Cruz, and various roads. McClellan helped to prepare the campaign maps of the battles around Mexico City before departing the command in December 1847. Turnbull returned to the United States in March 1848, and Lieutenants Hardcastle and Martin L. Smith remained to complete surveys for their map of the Mexico City region.[70]

One of the topogs' primary tasks required the preparation of detailed maps to accompany campaign and battle reports for submission to the War Department. In turn, the War Department prepared the maps and reports for publication in the *Congressional Series*. Turnbull and McClellan prepared the map of the Battle of Cerro Gordo, and Hardcastle did the same for reports submitted by General Worth. In August and September 1847 Turnbull, McClellan, and Hardcastle prepared the detailed maps depicting the battles for Mexico City. Considered the definitive depiction of terrain and unit dispositions, the maps later proved to be a valuable reference for historians researching the war.[71]

Hardcastle and Smith also prepared an excellent map of the Valley of Mexico. They accomplished their survey by triangulation and hand compasses, and the cartography accurately depicted the region as it appeared in 1848. The two lieutenants also recognized that they had the advantage of following in the earlier footsteps of Alexander von Humboldt, the noted German naturalist and explorer. Hardcastle and Smith noted a slight difference in mapping the lakes outside of Mexico City but believed that these lakes had changed over the years. Hardcastle also measured the distance between Mexico City and Vera Cruz by attaching an odometer to a

---

[70] Turnbull to Abert, 26 Oct 1847, LR 689; 7 Dec 1847; 2 Mar 1848, TE 77; Hagner to Abert, 16 Sep 1848, LR 460, TE 77; M.L. Smith to Abert, 7 Apr 1848, TE 77.
[71] These maps, many of which are large foldout types, may be found in Report of the Secretary of War, 1847, Sen. Exec. Doc. 1 and House Exec. Doc. 8.

wagon wheel. He found minor differences between his plottings and those of von Humbolt. After Turnbull prepared campaign maps to accompany battle reports, the two topogs incorporated his survey of the area south of the city into their map of the region. Congress later published the report and map. Unfortunately, the narrative report did not provide the interesting features commonly included in reports by Fremont, Emory, and Abert. Instead, it dealt primarily with details of military campaigns and included some geographic descriptions.[72]

Antiexpansionists in the Senate, however, viewed the map's publication solely from a negative political point of view. Much of the work accomplished by the Topographical Engineers in mapping regions of Mexico became suspect. Some members of Congress grew suspicious that securing such geographic information could be part of an administration plot to annex all Mexico.[73]

Later Careers of Scott's Topogs

The topogs serving in Scott's army continued to lead productive military and civilian careers. Upon returning to the United States, Hughes reverted from brevet lieutenant colonel back to a captain in the Topographical Engineers. He worked on a railroad survey across the Isthmus of Panama and planned to write a complete report of the operations of his volunteer regiment, but he resigned in 1851. As a civilian he entered the railroad business and later served in the House of Representatives as a delegate from Maryland. He also devoted himself to agricultural pursuits on his estate in Maryland, where he died in 1871.[74]

Emory also reverted to his regular rank of first lieutenant, but he remained in the Army to complete a successful military career. His topographic assignments included chief astronomer and later commissioner and astronomer for the United States Boundary

---

[72] Edmund L.F. Hardcastle and Martin L. Smith, "In Further Compliance with the Resolution of the Senate of August 3, 1848, Calling for a Map of the Valley of Mexico, by Lieutenants Smith and Hardcastle," Sen. Exec. Doc. 19, 30th Cong., 2d sess., 29 Jan 1849; Hardcastle to Abert, 2 Feb 1849, LR 67, TE 77. A copy of the report is reproduced in Appendix B.

[73] Goetzmann, *Army Exploration*, p. 152.

[74] Kenly, *Memoirs of a Maryland Volunteer*, pp. 484–85; *DAB*, V, pp. 348–49; *Appleton's Cyclopaedia*, III, p. 303; *National Cyclopaedia of American Biography*, IV, pp. 511–12.

Commission in the Southwest. In 1855 Emory transferred to the cavalry and rose to the rank of major general of volunteers in the Union Army during the Civil War. He retired in 1876 with a regular rank of brigadier general and died in 1877.[75]

Johnston, of course, became a prominent Confederate general during the Civil War. Like the other Mexican War veteran officers he reverted to his regular rank of captain. He resumed work as a topog in Texas and later worked on projects to improve western rivers. He transferred to the Cavalry in 1855 and rose to lieutenant colonel. At the outbreak of the Civil War, Johnston, by then a brigadier general, offered his services to Virginia and the Confederacy. He commanded troops at Bull Run in 1861, and later served in the Peninsula Campaign. Upon recovering from wounds suffered at Seven Pines, the former topog took charge of Confederate forces farther west and participated in the Vicksburg and Atlanta campaigns. Although Johnston never directly lost a battle in the war, his earlier tendency to take risks in battle ended after Seven Pines. After the war he went into business, and in 1878 served one term in Congress. He died in Washington in 1891.[76]

Turnbull remained with the topogs for almost the remainder of his life. He returned from the war to take over construction of the Customs House in New Orleans. In 1850 he assumed supervision of lighthouse construction, and two years later prepared engineer studies for bridging the Susquehanna River. The following year he completed studies to build a canal across the Falls of the Ohio River. Between 1853 to 1856 he supervised harbor improvements on the Great Lakes followed by similar work at Cape Fear, North Carolina. He died in 1857.[77]

John McClellan also spent his remaining years working for the Corps. He reverted to captain after the war, and between 1849 to 1851 served on the United States–Mexican boundary survey. In 1853 he began working on a project to improve the Tennessee River; however, he suddenly died the following year.[78]

Hardcastle stayed on in the Topographical Engineers for a few years before switching to a business and political career. After the

---

[75] Goetzmann, *Army Exploration*, pp. 182–87, 192–99; *DAB*, III, pp. 153–54; Cullum, *Biographical Register*, I, pp. 481–83.

[76] Cullum, *Biographical Register*, I, pp. 428–29; *DAB*, X, pp. 144–46.

[77] *DAB*, X, p. 57; *Appleton's Cyclopaedia*, VI, pp. 184–85; Cullum, *Biographical Register*, I, pp. 211–12.

[78] Cullum, *Biographical Register*, I, p. 367.

war he helped Emory on the United States–Mexican boundary survey until 1852. For the next four years he served on the Lighthouse Board, resigning his commission in 1856. By 1868 he became president of the Maryland and Delaware Railroad Company and also served in the Maryland House of Delegates between 1870 and 1878. He lived until 1899.[79]

Martin L. Smith stayed in the Army, and like Johnston served in the Confederate Army during the Civil War. After leaving the valley of Mexico City he surveyed roads in Texas and worked on the boundary survey. Between 1853 to 1854 Smith surveyed a ship canal across Florida. In 1857 he continued his topographical engineer work with the Coast Survey. At the outbreak of the Civil War he resigned his commission and rose to the rank of major general in the Confederate Army. He died in 1866.[80]

Throughout his campaign from Vera Cruz to Mexico City, General Scott increasingly relied on the services of his two engineering staffs. Their joint duties involved directing assault forces to key objectives and accomplishing dangerous reconnaissance missions. Under such circumstances, separating the actions of the two engineer corps in Scott's command became difficult. From the standpoint of publicity, the larger Corps of Engineers staff under Colonel Totten appeared to get credit for most of the engineering accomplishments. In any case, Old Fuss and Feathers effectively used both engineering corps to help him develop his strategy and tactics. In preparing for his march to Mexico City, Scott ordered his engineers to make a thorough reconnaissance of the enemy's positions and the surrounding terrain. The Commanding General began to rely so heavily upon his engineers that he hardly selected a route or issued an attack order without some form of reconnaissance. His engineers became experts at pointing out artillery batteries and vulnerable points in the enemy's lines. In one battle after another Scott executed brilliant flanking movements over terrain that the Mexicans had considered impossible for such maneuvers.[81]

---

[79] Cullum, *Biographical Register*, II, p. 260; Heitman, *Historical Register*, I, p. 499.

[80] *DAB*, IX, p. 319; *Appleton's Cyclopaedia*, V, p. 579; *National Cyclopaedia of American Biography*, V, p. 96; Cullum, *Biographical Register*, II, p. 126.

[81] Matloff, *American Military History*, p. 178; T. Harry Williams (ed.), *With Beauregard in Mexico: The Mexican War Reminiscences of P. G. T. Beauregard* (Baton Rouge: Louisiana State University Press, 1956), p. 10.

Working with the armies in the field and their indefatigable engineer colleagues, the topogs proved their mettle. Matthew F. Steele in his classic work, *American Campaigns,* noted that the only attack made without an engineer reconnaissance "was Worth's impetuous assault of the bridge-head at Churubusco. Truly did the Military Academy repay its cost to the Nation with the work of these young graduates in this single campaign."[82]

---

[82] Matthew F. Steele, *American Campaigns,* I (Washington, D.C.: U.S. Infantry Association, 1935), p. 122.

CHAPTER 8

So Much By So Few

While the topogs assigned to the war zone contributed directly to victory in the field, the Topographical Bureau also provided indirect support for the war effort. With more topog officers assigned to the Army field commanders, emphasis on civil works declined. Congress suspended appropriations for certain river and harbor improvements for the duration of the war and for a period thereafter. Officers who remained in the United States carried on with their work as best they could. Some continued their surveys of the Great Lakes and others worked on improving harbor defenses. Supervision of lighthouse construction proceeded, as did work on a few remaining civil works projects, but most of the corps' work was war related, including the supervision of the construction of steamboats for use in Mexico and continuing military reconnaissance patrols in Texas.

Topographical Corps Work in 1846

In 1846 the Corps of Topographical Engineers had forty-two officers, including six brevet second lieutenants. Two-thirds of the officers were working in the United States. Lt. Col. James Kearney, helped by six lieutenants, was in charge of the Great Lakes Survey; in the Gulf of Mexico islands of the Tortugas Major Hartman Bache and a team of two captains and two lieutenants oversaw surveys for the defense of the islands; and before their departure to Mexico in September, Lieutenants Derby and Scammon worked on a survey of the defenses of New Bedford harbor. Major Campbell Graham had recently completed a survey along the northern boundary; several of his assistants, including Emory and Pope, received orders to report to field commands. Before reporting to Scott's army gathering in Mexico, Major Turnbull, helped by two captains and one lieutenant, began to close his accounts on harbor improvements on Lakes Ontario and Erie. Brevet Lt. Col. Stephen Long remained at his Office of Improvements of Western Rivers in Louisville supervising the disposition of his equipment after the suspension of funds for improvements to the western rivers. There was a captain assigned to the Topographic Bureau as Colonel Abert's assistant and another on the sick rolls, one lieutenant at work on the Coast Survey, one assigned as an instructor at West Point, and three others assigned to the bureau to complete maps and calculations of the Northern Boundary Survey.[1]

Other officers were either in or near the war zone. By November 1846 Taylor's command had three Topographical Engineers and Wool and Kearny each had four. In addition, the corps had two lieutenants in Texas doing surveys. Major Graham, another topog, served as a courier to deliver the U.S. government's rejection of the armistice arranged by General Taylor after the capture of Monterrey. Three other officers, including Johnston and Hardcastle, had also received notification alerting them for duty in the war zone.[2]

Surveys for the defenses of the frontier and coastal regions proceeded in 1846. The coastal surveys involved surveying sites for fortifications and approaches to seaports from various points. Military reconnaissance expeditions of the coasts and inland frontier for the purpose of making maps were also part of this endeavor. Colonel Abert recommended the surveys of the Great Lakes be given high priority because they "are highly interesting to the military as well as the commercial interests of the country, and ought to be prosecuted with great vigor."[3]

The Corps of Topographical Engineers still did not have its own enlisted personnel. Abert continued to press the War Department to authorize the permanent attachment of soldiers to the Topographical Bureau, arguing that in a small army it was impractical to detail temporarily soldiers from other branches to serve with the Topographical Engineers and ineffective because these soldiers were unfamiliar with topographical functions. Said Abert:

---

[1] Report of the Secretary of War, House Exec. Doc. 4, 29th Cong., 2d sess., 11 Nov 1846, pp. 138–39.
[2] Ibid.
[3] Ibid., p. 140.

There can be no doubt that great economy would result from an enlisted body of about 200 men, including non-commissioned officers, as well as more efficiency to the service. Such a system would soon, by its economy, compensate for all its cost, on any of our surveys; but in operating in the field with an army, the necessity of it is very great. All the reasoning in its favor resolves in the simple axiom, that a man is better for a duty by knowing something about it.[4]

Congress did not agree. Despite the merit of Abert's proposal and its low cost (about $20,000), Congress would not assign enlisted personnel to the Topographical Engineers until 1861, when the Civil War broke out. In the field, the topog officers faced continual difficulties because of the lack of trained assistants. Because field commanders often were reluctant to provide enlisted men to help, the Topographical Engineers found it necessary to go to the expense and trouble of finding and hiring suitable civilian assistants.[5]

There were equipment and supply problems too. Abert needed special wagons "to transport the requisite instruments, maps, documents, and tools, and to preserve them from accidents." Damage to the delicate survey instruments remained a continuous problem, and repairing or replacing them proved very difficult when topogs accompanied an expedition to the field.[6]

Corps Projects in 1847

In 1847, the Corps of Topographical Engineers became even more war oriented. By November 1847 Abert reported twenty topogs, about half of the entire corps of forty-one officers, were serving in Mexico. Despite the drain of personnel assigned to the field commands, regular defense related and civil works projects made headway. Surveys for the defensive work construction in the Tortugas and New Bedford harbor reached completion, and new surveys in New York harbor commenced. Surveys for the defenses of San

---

[4] Ibid. In his annual reports of 1845 and 1848, Abert also recommended that enlisted soldiers be assigned to the corps. In March 1861 Congress did authorize a company of enlisted men, but the corps' recruiting efforts proved a dismal failure owing to the want of a suitable camp, the lack of officers to organize and train the recruits, and recruits preferred to join volunteer units. Ryan, *Topographical Bureau Administrative History*, pp. 324–28.

[5] Ibid.; Burr, "Historical Sketch," *Occasional Papers*, p. 43; Huston, *The Sinews of War*, p. 141.

[6] Report of the Secretary of War, House Exec. Doc. 4, p. 140.

Diego, Monterey, and the bay of San Francisco were under way in California, and there were followup surveys taking place in Texas.[7]

Though Congress had reduced funds for river and harbor improvements, a reduced number of topogs carried on with various civil engineering projects and surveys in the East. Three topogs worked on the Coast Survey; four remained at work on the Great Lakes Survey; and one supervised the paving of Pennsylvania Avenue in Washington, a project no doubt of high visibility in the capital. As the Topographical Engineers supervised lighthouse construction on an infrequent basis in the past, Congress in March 1847, transferred more lighthouse construction projects to the corps, an action that marked the real beginnings of the corps' involvement in this new field.[8]

Without funds for his Western Rivers' improvement work, Bvt. Lt. Col. Stephen Long turned to other projects. He took the opportunity to make necessary repairs on five of the corps' snag boats (named *Gopher, Dragon, Hercules, Sampson,* and *Sevier*) used to keep the rivers clear of obstacles. When the *Gopher* and *Dragon* were repaired in October 1846 they were turned over to the Quartermaster Corps for transports in the war zone. Long also supervised construction of a marine hospital, planned future river surveys, and supervised the construction of six steamers for the Quartermaster Corps. By February 1847, a contractor completed the first steamer, the *General Jessup,* in Louisville and readied it for service on the Rio Grande. It was followed by the *Colonel Hunt.* In Cincinnati a contractor finished building the *General Harner,* and in April readied it for service in the Gulf of Mexico. The fourth, the *Ann Chase,* was delivered from Cincinnati to New Orleans in June. The *General Butler* and *Colonel Clay* were under construction and expected to be ready by October 1847. In November 1846, Long also arranged for the construction of a steamer dredge for use in the Texas channels. Named the *Lavaca,* the dredge was

---

[7] Report of the Secretary of War, Sen. Exec. Doc. 1, pp. 656–57; Register of Letters Received by the Topographical Bureau, Mackay to Abert, 2 Oct 1846, 2 Nov 1846, 4 Jan 1847, 15 Apr 1847; M.L. Smith to Abert, 19 July 1847, 26 Aug 1847, TE 77.

[8] Report of the Secretary of War, Sen. Exec. Doc. 1, pp. 656–59; Ryan, *Topographical Bureau Administrative History,* p. 159.

ready by March 1847 for the tasks of deepening and widening the mouth of the Lavaca River.[9]

After Taylor and Wool marched their armies into northern Mexico, other topogs moved into Texas to continue survey and map work. In May 1847 Abert dispatched 2d Lt. Joseph D. Webster to Texas to continue the surveys started by Taylor's topographers. Webster had graduated from Dartmouth in 1832, entered the corps in 1838, and worked on road construction in Wisconsin and on the Great Lakes Survey. His orders entailed making an accurate survey of "the country embraced on the inclosed plan, upon the Texas side of the River, including both shores of the river, and East as far as the line from [Point] Isabel to Matamoros." His instructions included making road reconnaissance patrols and estimating material requirements for bridges between Brazos Santiago and the Rio Grande landing at Berrita. Since he did not have military assistants, Webster obtained authorization to hire a civilian assistant at three dollars a day.[10]

By January 1848 Webster reported that he had finished his survey and forwarded his completed map the following month. Besides adding more to the geographical knowledge of the lower Rio Grande, Webster suggested the advantages in constructing a railroad instead of a vehicular road. Abert did not respond to this suggestion, but now instructed the topog to cross over into Mexico to examine the river at Tampico. Following the ratification of the peace treaty between the two countries, Webster received orders to return to the United States to complete his map. Because he made his survey in Mexico near the end of the war, his map, like that of the Valley of Mexico, increased fear among opponents of the war in the United States that a plot existed to annex all Mexico. More likely the Topographical Bureau merely wanted to obtain as much information as possible in order to fill in the gaps of the more expedient surveys done by the topogs assigned to the field commands.[11]

---

[9] Report of the Secretary of War, Sen. Exec. Doc. 1, pp. 670–75; Richard G. Wood, *Stephen Harriman Long, 1784–1864, Army Engineer, Explorer, Inventor* (Glendale, CA: Arthur H. Clark Co., 1966), pp. 209–13.

[10] *DAB*, X, pp. 593–96; Heitman, *Historical Register*, p. 1013; Abert to Webster, 24 May 1847, LS 111, TE 77.

[11] Webster to Abert, 16 Feb 1848, LR 161, TE 77; Abert to Webster, 4 Apr 1848, LS 355; Abert to Webster, 24 July 1848, LS 432, TE 77.

In his annual report to the War Department in 1847, Abert proudly noted corps wartime achievements:

But one feeling seems to have animated them, to be efficient in any capacity which the wants of the service required. Always ready, always willing, and always capable, they have proved I hope the value of the corps, and its readiness to encounter any hazard which this country required, as their own gallant feelings would suggest. The war has shown them in the various capacities of engineers, commanders of detachments, in all of which they have proved their efficiency and usefulness, and the admirable results of the military school of which they are graduates.[12]

Colonel Abert's Overview of the Corps, 1848

In his annual report the next year, Colonel Abert supplemented his praise for the accomplishments of his corps with new project recommendations. The senior topog first pointed out that two-thirds of the officers of the corps served actively in the field during the Mexican War, that two Topographical Engineers died as a result of wounds (Blake and Williams), that several had returned from Mexico either with wounds or sick from fatigue and exposure. The reports of the commanding generals, he proudly noted, often complimented the Topographical Engineers for their services. Abert particularly cited four members of his branch—Joseph E. Johnston, George W. Hughes, William H. Emory, and William H. Warner. No mention, however, was made of John C. Fremont. In praising Johnston for his leadership of troops, Abert wrote, "in that capacity [Johnston] acquired great reputation for the skill he displayed in the drill and discipline of the regiment, and for his gallantry in command on several important occasions."[13]

The report also lauded the other three officers. Hughes was cited for his services as commander and military governor; Emory, for his heroic duty with Kearny and also for providing important geographical knowledge; and Warner, for his service with Kearny and his many important surveys in California. "I have named these four officers," Abert added,

because they were so fortunate as to obtain positions and exercise commands independent of and separate from their proper corps' function,

---

[12] Report of the Secretary of War, Sen. Exec. Doc. 1, pp. 666–67.
[13] Report of the Secretary of War, House Exec. Doc. 1, pp. 324–25. A copy of this report is reproduced in Appendix C.

exhibiting the versatility of talent in the corps, and its ability to fulfill any military duties which it may be found necessary or proper to assign to it.[14]

Abert then moved briefly to the important geographical contributions made by the Topographical Engineers in the field during the war. He pointed out that the observations and reconnaissances made by the corps while operating with the armies in Mexico were being compiled in a map. Emory's report, a map of Kearny's march from the Missouri to the Pacific, maps of engagements, and Lieutenant Abert's report and map of New Mexico were also in progress. These two reports, Abert noted, added much to the geographical knowledge of that region of the world and furnished civil, military, and commercial information for future use.[15]

Abert pointed out that the lack of adequate geographic and topographic information had posed special problems for the Army at the beginning of the war, and he argued that it was best to collect this type of information in peacetime. He stressed that accurate geographical and topographical knowledge of a country were particularly essential to military operations. "They are the eyes of the commanding general," the chief topographer wrote, and "With these he can see the country, and can know how to direct and combine all his movements or marches, whether offensive or defensive, and without them he is literally groping in the dark, incapable of plans for his own operations, or of anticipating those of an enemy." Some of the most important movements and operations, he added, were governed by reconnaissances, usually well out in front of the advancing army. Abert went on to state that the Topographical Engineers were charged with collecting geographic and topographic information, and that could be best done in time of peace.[16]

Abert concluded with a list of recommended projects. The period of the Mexican War reconnaissances led to a significant number of explorations; these he suggested should lead to the undertaking of civil and military construction projects in the West. He considered further exploration of the Red River very important to opening that river to navigation. A necessary measure, he suggested, entailed building a series of forts along the river in order to provide an artery through Comanche country. In order to facili-

[14] Ibid., p. 325.
[15] Ibid.
[16] Ibid., pp. 325–26.

tate the defense of the New Mexico frontier, he further pointed out the need to tie in a military road to the navigable waters of the Red River. As a result a transportation link could be established to the Rio Grande. Exploitation of the region's agricultural and mineral resources would follow. The colonel did not hesitate to add that "These distant military posts and military roads are the pioneers of civilization and wealth."[17]

Epilogue

The Treaty of Guadalupe Hidalgo was signed on 2 February 1848. The treaty provided for Mexican recognition of the Rio Grande border with Texas, the cession of California and New Mexico, American payment of $15 million to Mexico, and the American government's assumption of claims made by its citizens against Mexico. The United States acquired 529,017 square miles of territory. Polk concurred and the Senate ratified the treaty on 10 March. Despite more problems among the Mexican leadership, the two governments exchanged ratifications on 30 May. On 12 June American occupation troops departed Mexico City, and on 1 August the last American soldiers boarded their transport in the harbor of Vera Cruz to sail home.[18]

In 1848 the War Department established military departments in the newly acquired western lands. During the years between the Mexican War and the Civil War, the Topographical Engineers became a principal arm of the federal government in exploring and developing the West, in addition to its usual civil works roles improving rivers and harbors, building roads, and constructing lighthouses.[19]

The topogs also adjusted to peacetime routines. After the ratification of the peace treaty and the troops returned to the United States, the Army went through the usual reductions in personnel and funds. By the end of 1848 the Army had reverted to a peacetime strength smaller than the 10,000 authorized in 1815, with

---

[17] Ibid., p. 327.
[18] Bauer, *The Mexican War*, pp. 384–85, 388, 396.
[19] Beers, "History of the Topographical Engineers," pp. 349–51. For accounts of the explorations performed by Topographical Engineers after the Mexican War, see Goetzmann, *Army Exploration*.

units also returning to peace strength. Although the Army retained a higher proportion of officers to enlisted men than in the prewar years, the officers breveted to captains, majors, and colonels during the war reverted to their prewar grades. Active duty promotions in the Army, and particularly the small Corps of Topographical Engineers (the authorized strength remained unchanged at 36 officers between 1838 and 1861), returned to its usual agonizingly slow pace with officers advancing in grade based on a system of seniority. Promotions were limited to vacancies created by death, retirement, resignation, disability, or incompetency. Officers joining the corps as a second lieutenant could look forward to at least two promotions within 14 years, hardly a dazzling prospect to the ambitious. None of the six field grade officers appointed in 1838 (Abert, Kearney, Long, Bache, Turnbull, and James Graham) resigned, retired, transferred, or received a promotion before the summer of 1861. One officer's promotion to the vacancy created by Major Turnbull's death in 1857 represented the only change to this small but key group in over twenty-three years.[20]

Such grim promotion prospects or other personal matters caused several topogs to leave the Army or transfer to other branches. Between 1848 and 1856 seven members of the corps resigned from the Army and two transferred to another branch. After his resignation in 1851, Hughes entered the railroad business. The loss of Johnston and Emory, who went to the two new cavalry regiments in 1855, deprived Abert of two of his most able captains at a critical time in the corps' history. Significantly, several of these resignations and transfers left gaps in the ranks of the Topographical Engineers that were never really filled, another symptom of the decline of the bureau and the corps during that decade. It is also interesting to note that five of the resignations occurred during Jefferson Davis' four year tenure as the Secretary of War (1853–1857). His rigid attitude on granting leaves of absence, which allowed officers time off for up to eighteen months to han-

---

[20] Brevet rank was nearly always honorary, being effective only when the officer holding a brevet served on a court-martial or detached to another corps. Ryan, *Topographical Bureau Administrative History*, pp. 207–10.

dle urgent private business or important personal affairs, most likely prompted Hardcastle and Peck to resign.[21]

Those who stayed on as topogs endured low pay, hard and dangerous work, and family separations. By the end of 1856 there were thirty-five topogs still on the rolls, and the number grew to forty-five in 1861. These trained and talented engineers could have easily switched over to the more lucrative engineering opportunities in civilian fields. A strong esprit de corps and a preference to be a member of a small elite branch appears to explain the unusually high retention rate of topogs returning from Mexican War service. George Derby, despite his reputation as a humorist poking fun at the military, perhaps best summed up the major reasons for the topogs to stay in the Army:

> ... the faithful discharge of these [topographical] duties required the utmost familiarity with the higher and more abstruse branches of science, and the ... officer engaged in them has the satisfaction of knowing that he is doing something useful for his country, and that his exertions are appreciated by his countrymen.[22]

The work of a corps of fewer than forty officers between the Mexican and Civil Wars now appears impressive. These scientist-soldiers achieved the outpouring of accurate and professional maps, the exact delineation of international boundaries, the construction of civil and military works, and a vast accumulation of additional scientific knowledge. The railroad surveys in the 1850s showed the feasibility of spanning the continent nearly a decade before actual construction began.

These achievements were matched by remarkable individual careers. Fremont, of course, resigned, although he did lead a private expedition to the West in 1848, developed interests in California, ran unsuccessfully as the first Republican candidate for the presidency in 1856, and returned to the Army as a major general

---

[21] Those who resigned included Fremont (1848), Swift (1849), Hughes (1851), Webster (1854), Peck (1855), Hardcastle (1856), and George W. Ross (entered 1852 and resigned 1856); Scammon was dismissed in 1856. Ryan, *Topographical Bureau Administrative History*, pp. 214, 219–20; Official Army Register for 1856, Adj. Gen. Off., Washington, 1856, p. 9; Beers, "History of the Topographical Engineers," p. 291.

[22] George W. Derby, "Topographical Engineers," *The Squibob Papers* (New York: 1865), p. 229, quoted in Ryan, *Topographical Bureau Administrative History*, p. 221; also see Ryan, pp. 220–21; Official Army Register for 1856, p. 9; Official Army Register for 1861, Adj. Gen. Off., Washington, 1861, p. 10.

during the Civil War. Because the promotion outlook appeared poor, both Emory and Johnston transferred to the Cavalry in 1855 because of better opportunities for advancement. Topogs like Hughes, Hardcastle, Abert, and Peck went into business or academic life. Illnesses caused the deaths of a few more including Derby and John McClellan. The massacre of two topogs by Indians underscored the dangers of the frontier. Pit River Indians attacked and killed Captain William H. Warner near Goose Lake in northeastern California in 1849. Four years later Ute Indians killed Lieutenant John W. Gunnison near the Sevier River in Utah.[23]

During the 1830s and 1840s the Secretaries of War allowed Abert considerable leeway in running his bureau as he chose. His influence reached its peak during President John Tyler's administration (1841–1845), and his suggestions to the Secretaries of War were often treated like commands. During the Polk administration, however, these close and friendly relations lessened. Abert's difficulties with Polk and Secretary of War Marcy essentially stemmed from politics. The President and the Secretary of War harbored suspicions that several bureau chiefs, including Abert, were politically opposed to the administration. The President resented the chief topographer's opposition to his views regarding a rivers and harbors bill in 1846. Polk also omitted Abert's name from a long list of nominees for brevets for Mexican War service.[24]

By the 1850s the existence of a separate military engineering corps became tenuous. Although the topogs remained active, the Topographical Bureau began to decline after 1852. Relations between Colonel Abert and Secretary of War Charles Conrad (1850–1853) took a turn for the worse in 1852, when Conrad accused Abert of violating his orders by revealing the identity of the person who was to head the Office of Tennessee River Improvements to a congressman who had a vital interest. Later Conrad accepted Abert's apology, but this and other disputes left relations between the two men permanently strained. When Jefferson Davis took over the War Department the following year, he increasingly questioned the exis-

---

[23] Nine brevet second lieutenants entered the corps in 1861. Official Army Register for 1861, p. 10; Beers, "History of the Topographical Engineers," pp. 349–51. For more on the Warner and Gunnison expeditions see Goetzmann, *Army Exploration,* pp. 253, 285.

[24] Ryan, *Topographical Bureau Administrative History,* pp. 299–302.

tence of a separate corps and administrative bureau and did not see the need to retain a separate engineering corps.[25]

Control over duties the Topographical Bureau had done in the past began to slip away. Other science-oriented federal agencies were being established, and they began to assume some of the duties of the Corps of Topographical Engineers. The existence of the Smithsonian Institution, the Naval Observatory, the Office of the U.S. Coast Survey, and the establishment of the Pacific Wagon Road Office in the Department of the Interior reduced the services of the topogs from the levels called for in the previous two decades. Historian William H. Goetzmann notes that the prestige of the corps began to wane by 1855, in part because of the removal of proper functions from the corps plus some suspicion of sectional bias associated with the corps' evaluation of the Pacific Railroad Survey. Even though topogs carried out the famous Pacific railroad surveys and many other western explorations, control of these operations were later vested in an Office of Exploration and Survey under the direct control of the Secretary of War. The Corps of Engineers also began again to take over responsibilities for a portion of the river and harbor improvements work.[26]

As Colonel Abert's leadership abilities declined with age and failing health, so did the fortunes of the Corps of Topographical Engineers. In 1861, just three days before the firing on Fort Sumter, the old colonel retired because of physical disability. Major Hartman Bache and Colonel Stephen Long served as heads of the corps until 1863. The 45 topogs on the rolls in 1861 dropped to 32 a year later: 8 resigned from the Army to join the Confederacy, 4 including Abert retired, and one (Derby) died. Of the 32 remaining officers of the corps, 10 were on detached duty with U.S. Volunteer units. Not only did the bureau experience a shortage of officers, but the War Department gradually assigned more topogs to other organizations. With its civil works generally suspended, with only a small civilian work force, with most of its officers on duty elsewhere, and with no enlisted men at all, the Topographical Bureau spent most of its wartime duties running its office and waiting for its demise. On 3 March 1863, Congress approved "An Act to promote the efficiency of the Corps of Engineers," which abolished the

---

[25] Ibid., pp. 301–04, 342–43
[26] Ibid., pp. 342–43; Goetzmann, *Army Exploration*, pp. 341–42.

Corps of Topographical Engineers as a distinct branch of the Army and merged it with the Corps of Engineers. Its functions have remained a responsibility of the Corps of Engineers ever since.[27]

The Corps of Topographical Engineers remained a separate branch of the Army until 1863, primarily because of the ability of its chief, Colonel John Abert. He proved a good soldier, an able engineer, and an excellent administrator. Strictly military duties took up little of the Topographical Engineers' time or energy, with the result the corps served as a major scientific agency of the federal government for nearly twenty years. If the functions of this scientific corps did not appear all that essential to the War Department, the topogs certainly proved their worth to a young nation desperately short of trained engineers but anxious for results that only skilled engineers could provide.[28]

Was there then a need for a separate Corps of Topographical Engineers? The answer may be found in the years between 1815 and 1850 when the Corps of Engineers concentrated considerable effort on the construction of a system of coastal fortifications and continued to work on this system until 1861. Had the Topographical Engineers returned to the Corps of Engineers in 1838, building these fortifications most likely would have remained a primary function of topographical officers. That, however, did not happen. Colonel Abert was given an opportunity to take full advantage of the unique functions and skills of a small specialized corps. During the period of the Mexican War, he effectively guided his officers in their attempts to glean vast amounts of new geographic information.[29]

As noted, the officers who returned from the Mexican War went on to greater accomplishments in western exploration and in their respective military careers. Most significantly, several of these officers played a major role in the outcome of the Civil War. The

---

[27] Beers, "History of the Topographical Engineers," p. 352; Goetzmann, *Army Exploration*, pp. 432–33; Burr, "Historical Sketch," *Occasional Papers*, p. 43. Colonel Abert died in 1863; his military service spanned a fifty-year period. *Appleton's Cyclopaedia*, I, p. 8; *National Cyclopaedia of American Biography*, IV, p. 383; *DAB*, XI, pp. 2–3. For a more detailed account of the Topographical Corps' last two years see Ryan, *Topographical Bureau Administrative History*, pp. 317–38.

[28] Ryan, *Topographical Bureau Administrative History*, pp. 341–42.

[29] Ryan, *Topographical Bureau Administrative History*, pp. 342–44. For additional information on the fortification program see Moore, *The Fortifications Board 1816–1828*.

TABLE 2—TOPOGRAPHICAL ENGINEERS APPOINTED GENERALS
(U.S.A., VOLUNTEERS, BREVETS) IN THE CIVIL WAR

Ranks and Names January 1861	Highest Civil War and Lifetime Rank
Majors	
Hartman Bache	Brig. Gen. (brevet, 1865)
Captains	
Thomas J. Cram [1]	Maj. Gen. (brevets, 1866)
William B. Franklin [1]	Maj. Gen. (brevet, 1865)
Andrew A. Humphreys	Maj. Gen. (Vols, 1862; brevets, 1865; Brig. Gen. Chief of Engineers, 1866)
George G. Meade [1]	Maj. Gen. (Brig. Gen. Vols, 1861; Maj. Gen. Vols, 1862; Brig. Gen. U.S.A., 1863; Maj. Gen. U.S.A., 1864)
John Pope [1]	Maj. Gen. (Vols, 1862; Brig. Gen. U.S.A., 1862; brevet Maj. Gen., 1865)
William F. Raynolds	Brig. Gen. (brevet, 1865)
Martin L. Smith [1]	Maj. Gen., C.S.A.
William F. Smith	Maj. Gen. (brevets, 1865)
George Thom [1]	Brig. Gen. (brevet, 1865)
Amiel W. Whipple	Maj. Gen. (brevets, 1863; died, 1863)
Israel C. Woodruff	Brig. Gen. (brevet, 1865)
First Lieutenants	
Henry L. Abbot	Maj. Gen. (brevet Brig. Gen. Vols, 1864; brevet Brig. Gen., 1865; brevet Maj. Gen. Vols, 1865)
Nathaniel Michler	Brig. Gen. (brevet, 1865)
John G. Parke	Maj. Gen. (Brig. Gen. Vols, 1862; brevet Maj. Gen., 1865)
Orlando F. Poe	Brig. Gen. (Vols, 1862; brevet, 1865)
Gouverneur K. Warren	Maj. Gen. (Maj. Gen. Vols, 1863; brevet Maj. Gen., 1865)
Brevet Second Lieutenants	
James H. Wilson	Maj. Gen. (brevets, 1865)
Former Topographical Engineers	
William H. Emory [1]	Maj. Gen. (Brig. Gen. Vols, 1862; Maj. Gen. Vols, 1865; brevets, 1865)
John C. Fremont [1]	Maj. Gen. (Maj. Gen., 1861)
Joseph E. Johnston [1]	Gen., C.S.A.
Eliakim P. Scammon [1]	Brig. Gen. (Vols, 1862)
Joseph D. Webster [1]	Brig. Gen. (Vols, 1862)
Thomas J. Wood [1]	Maj. Gen. (Brig. Gen. Vols, 1861; Maj. Gen. Vols, 1865; brevets, 1865)

[1] Mexican War service.

Sources: George T. Ness, Jr., "Army Engineers in the Civil War," *Military Engineer* 57 (Jan–Feb 1965): 40; Thomas H. S. Hamersly, *Complete Army and Navy Register of the United States of America, From 1776 to 1887* (New York: T. H. S. Hamersly, 1888), pp. 249, 271–72, 379–80, 428, 446, 528, 630, 636, 677–78, 695, 697, 712, 771–72, 803–04, 840–41, 853–54, 868, 874–75, 876; Volunteer Services section, pp. 94, 114.

SO MUCH BY SO FEW   225

list of those who achieved the rank of general (Regular Army, Volunteers, and brevet promotions) is impressive: George G. Meade, John Pope, Joseph E. Johnston, William B. Franklin, William H. Emory, John C. Fremont, Martin L. Smith, Thomas J. Wood, Eliakim P. Scammon, George Thom, Thomas J. Cram, and Joseph D. Webster. These twelve officers represented approximately 25 percent of the total strength of the Corps of Topographical Engineers during the Mexican War. During the war a total of twenty-four officers who had served at one time or another in the Topographical Engineers were promoted to generals, an impressive number considering that the corps had forty-five officers in 1861.[30]

The traditions of the Corps of Topographical Engineers are maintained today in the U.S. Army Corps of Engineers. The corps continues to pioneer technological advances in map making through its Army Engineer Topographic Laboratory, and some Engineer topographers currently carry on their mapping responsibilities as part of the Department of Defense Mapping Agency. Army topographic battalions, separate companies, and other specialized detachments directly support field commands in the United States and overseas.

In World War I the Army produced more than nine million copies of maps. In World War II, the Army Map Service, a direct descendent of the old Topographical Bureau, produced over 500 million copies of 40,000 different maps. Large numbers of maps and other topographic services were provided during the Korean and Vietnam wars. Army topographers have cooperated with the U.S. Geological Survey, the federal agency responsible for preparing detailed topographic and geologic maps of the United States and its territories.[31]

Following treaty agreements, the Corps of Engineers' topographers have assisted foreign governments' map making efforts. Taking to the field and operating under conditions not unlike the Topographical Engineers a century earlier, Army topographers have

---

[30] Goetzmann, *Army Exploration,* p. 433. Listings of the Topographical Engineers who served in the Mexican War, their brevets received during that war, and ranks of those who served in the Civil War may be found in Burr, "Historical Sketch," pp. 41–43; Cadmus Wilcox, *History of the Mexican War* (Washington, D.C.: Church News Publishing Co., 1892), p. 615.

[31] Pamphlet, Army Map Service (Washington, D.C.: Government Printing Office, 1968), p. 22.

participated in the Inter-Americas Geodetic Survey in mapping Latin America. Other Army topographers mapped countries under the most grueling conditions. Reminiscent of Emory's reconnaissance of the Southwest, Army topographers of the 64th Engineer Battalion (Base Topographic) in the 1960s surveyed such diverse areas as Libya, Ethiopia, and Iran and the tropical jungles of Liberia.

The topogs who served during and following the Mexican War left a remarkable legacy. They aided in winning the war. They made useful up-to-date maps and reports which helped to accelerate the movement of people to the West. They improved young America's navigation and transportation system, thereby opening markets and raising the output of goods and services. What is amazing is that all of these remarkable achievements were done by an organization which by the end of 1847 consisted of only forty-three officers.

APPENDIXES

APPENDIX A

Report of Captain Hughes of Wool's March Into Mexico

INTRODUCTION

Immediately after the breaking out of hostilities with the republic of Mexico, the government of the United States, for the purpose of bringing the war to a speedy conclusion by "conquering a peace" from the enemy, determined to invade her adjacent territories in several directions; and, simultaneously with the movement of General Taylor into Tamaulipas and New Leon from the lower Rio Grande, and of General Kearny into New Mexico and California, General Wool was directed to organize an expedition against the State of Chihuahua.

These conjoined movements were well devised, if it were the intention simply to reduce and to occupy the northern portion of Mexico from the Rio Grande to the Sierra Madre until a peace, on reasonable terms, could be secured; but if the ultimate object was to penetrate to the enemy's capital by the divisions of Taylor and Wool, it was extremely ill-advised; as, first, the forces were too widely separated for mutual support, and too weak for each to advance far as an independent corps. Second, the bases were too remote from the supplies, and the lines of operation much too long. The distance from San Antonio to the city of Mexico, by the way of Chihuahua, over any known route practicable for an army carrying with it artillery and munitions of war, cannot be less than two thousand miles, and from Camarago, on the Rio Grande, about eight hundred miles, being considerably longer than Napoleon's line of operation from his depots to Moscow. Beside this, the country to be traversed presented difficulties of no ordinary nature to an invading army, being for long distances destitute of water and subsistence—in fact, mere desert wastes. In both cases the communications must have been abandoned, thus violating one of the first principles of war, unless forced to it by a stern necessity.

It is fair, however, to presume that it was not the policy of government to attack the city of Mexico from the Rio Grande, although, at the time, it seemed to be contemplated in public opinion. Be this as it may, the occupation of the northern provinces was most fortunate, and exercised an important influence, in every respect, upon the glorious campaign which, commencing with the reduction of Vera Cruz, terminated with the capture of the Mexican capital and the restoration of peace.

The division under General Wool was concentrated at San Antonio de Bexar, in Texas, and consisted of one battery of field artillery of six guns, to which were added two small pieces captured from the Mexicans by the Texans, and manned with volunteers;* one squadron of first and one squadron of second dragoons; one regiment of Arkansas horse; three companies of sixth infantry, with which was incorporated one independent company of Kentucky foot and two regiments of Illinois infantry; making in all about three thousand four hundred men. To this corps was also attached the usual allowance of officers of the general staff and of the staff corps. The battery had marched from Carlisle barracks, Pennsylvania, nearly the whole distance by land; the first dragoons, Arkansas mounted men, and sixth infantry, from posts in Arkansas; and the Illinois volunteers from Lavaca, Texas, by land. These different commands reach San Antonio in excellent condition in the month of August, 1846. the squadron of second dragoons has been stationed for some months in the vicinity of the town.

It is due to General Wool to say, that with great industry, and that administrative capacity for which he is justly distinguished, he soon organized this almost chaotic mass into an efficient and well-drilled army, and had made preparations, within a few months, for supplying it with all the necessaries for a long campaign, in a country but little understood. The efforts to effect this were almost herculean, (requiring infinite labor and knowledge of a peculiar character, not always attendant upon eminent military or tactical ability,) and can be fully appreciated only by those familiar with the subject, and with the difficulties encountered; especially when a long interval of peace had left us nearly destitute of many of the essential materials of war. It is true that in these exertions the commanding general was ably seconded by intelligent, energetic, and experienced officers of the general staff, and of the quartermaster's and subsistence departments, and great credit was reflected upon all for the sagacity with which our wants were anticipated, and the promptitude with which they were supplied; and probably no better appointed army ever took the field.

As has been already intimated, the region of country to be traversed was almost entirely unknown. The jealousy of the Spaniards, and indolence of the Mexicans, has prevented the publication of maps based upon reliable authority, and, owing to the excursions of the savage tribes, the

---

*Those guns were lost at Buena Vista and retaken at Contreras.

APPENDIX A

present race of Mexicans were but imperfectly acquainted with it, and therefore but little information could be procured from them, except in relation to the ordinary routes between their villages; in consequence of which, we were almost literally compelled to grope our way, and, like a ship at sea, to determine our positions by astronomical observations, and topographical parties were usually kept in advance to ascertain the lengths of the daily marches, the most advantageous places for encampments and supplies of water, fuel and forage. In this way we have been able to collect a vast amount of geographical information, which may prove useful and interesting.

Some years before, a Mr. Connolly conveyed a wagon train, on a trading expedition, from red river to Chihuahua, passing considerably to the north of San Antonio, and crossing the Puerco* river not far from the mouth of the Conchos, above the first cañon of the Rio Grande; but no connection had ever been established with that trail from San Antonio, and it was doubtful whether a pass for that purpose could be found through the mountains.

Captain (afterwards General) Z. M. Pike stated in his narrative that a road formerly existed between Chihuahua and San Antonio *via* Presidio de Rio Grande, and that M. St. Croix, viceroy of Peru, took this road (through the Bolson Mappimi) in 1778, on his way from Chihuahua, Coquilla, Allares and Texas. This route has long since been abandoned on account of the excursions of the Indians, and no one could be found who had ever passed over it, or who even possessed any traditionary knowledge of it. Its practicability, therefore, for an army with artillery, infantry and wagons, was extremely problematical. Soon after reaching San Antonio I proposed (see appendix) to reconnoitre the different routes; but the want of sufficient escorts, and the exigencies of the service, I suppose, prevented it.

On arriving at Presidio Rio Grande it was pretty satisfactorily ascertained, from all that we could learn, that Santa Rosa, at the foot of a range of the Sierra Madre, was necessarily a point in our march, the direct San Fernando route, through the Bolson Mappimi, having been abandoned as surrounded with too many uncertainties. From thence it was said there were three practicable routes, either of which might be selected, viz: by the headwaters of the Sabinas river, through San Carlos and Alamo, by Cuatro Cinegas, Santa Catarina and Santa Rosalia; or by Monclova and Parras. It was discovered, on further investigation, that the first route, being simply a rough mule track, for long distances absolutely destitute of both water and subsistence, would not answer the purpose. Whether the second was more favorable could not be determined, except by information to be obtained at Monclova and by actual reconnaissance,

---

*Properly the Pecos river: it is called both on the maps. It has its rise beyond Santa Fe.

and during the protracted halt at that place (induced by the Monterey armistice) General Wool instructed me to make the examinations necessary to solve the question, which resulted in the strong conviction of its impracticability. (See memoir of a reconnaissance to Cuatro Cienegas.)

These various explorations strengthened the previous impression that to reach Chihuahua it would be necessary to march by Parras, situated on the main road from Saltillo to that city. Parras was a strategic point of some importance, and fortunately, as it regarded future operations, General Wool determined to take it in his route. From that position he would be able easily to reach his original destination—to move on Durango or Zacatecas, or to form a junction with the army under General Taylor, as policy or necessity might dictate.

It was satisfactorily ascertained, on reaching Parras, that no further physical difficulties, except those merely of distance, remained to be surmounted, but that the large portion of the enemy's force, which had assembled for the defense of the threatened province, had been withdrawn for the purpose of strengthening the main army at San Luis Potosi, and that, therefore, the necessity of marching the whole division further in that direction no longer existed, leaving it free to act as circumstances might require. In the mean while news was received that Santa Anna, in the hope, by the rapidity of his movement, of overwhelming General Worth, who with a single brigade was occupying Saltillo, before he could be reinforced, had suddenly put his whole army in motion. In consequence of this information General Wool marched for Saltillo, and succeeded in uniting with General Butler (who had hastened up from Monterey) and with General Worth. And thus terminated the expedition destined for Chihuahua—the division being subsequently merged into the main army of occupation.

Santa Anna finding that he could not deceive the vigilance of General Worth, and that the American troops thus concentrated were to strong for him to attack with any prospect of success, returned to San Luis Potosi to bide his time. On the withdrawal, soon afterwards, of a considerable portion of the "army of occupation" for the expedition to Vera Cruz, he again moved on Saltillo, *but did not reach it.* The fatal pass of Buena Vista intervened, and in the bloody and glorious battle well did the "army of Chihuahua" perform its duty.*

---

*This movement has sometimes been sneeringly called "Worth's stampede," and I think it but an act of justice to that distinguished soldier, and to the truth of history, to say that, in a long and free conversation with General Santa Anna, at his hacienda of Encero, near Jalapa, in reply to a question from me, he said that it had not only been his intention to attack Saltillo at that time, but that a large portion of his army had left San Luis Potosi for that purpose, and was only recalled when it was ascertained that General Worth had made himself acquainted with the movement, and by his rapidity of action had procured a concentration of force to an extent beyond his (Santa Anna's) anticipation. He further stated that, knowing

APPENDIX A

The following memoir, descriptive of the march of the column under General Wool from San Antonio to Saltillo, was written from time to time as leisure or circumstances would permit, in the midst of arduous duties and the difficulties incident to an active campaign; for even when the army was at a halt, the topographical engineers were busily engaged in reconnoitering the country for considerable distances, sometimes eighty miles from the camp. Very few changes in, or additions to, the original papers, have been made, which as fast as written were laid before the commanding general, and copies transmitted to the Topographical Bureau.

The reconnaissances during the march were principally made by Lieutenant Sitgreaves and myself, and the astronomical observations by Lieutenant Franklin. Lieutenant Bryan was for a short time attached to the personal staff of the commanding general, and was subsequently assigned to the command of a volunteer section of artillery connected with Captain Washington's battery.

Mr. Josiah Gregg, the author of "The Commerce of the Prairies," well known for his scientific attainments, accompanied the Arkansas cavalry, and frequently observed in company with Lieutenant Franklin. At my request, he furnished me with an interesting description of the march of the command to which he was attached from its rendezvous, on Red river, to San Antonio, which is appended to the following memoir.

The instructions from the Topographical Bureau, under which I acted, were not only general, but very minute in their character, requiring me, independently of such duties as might be assigned by the commanding general, to collect information in reference to the habits and disposition of the people, the geography, natural history, resources, military strength, statistics, and political history of the countries through which we might march; and I only regret that these important duties have not been more satisfactorily performed.

---

his own force was but badly provided, and would be greatly exhausted by the long desert which intervened between him and Saltillo, he did not think it safe to encounter the veteran troops of the United States army; and that he would not subsequently have attacked General Taylor, as he was aware that he fought to great disadvantage, but for the fact that his (Taylor's) division was composed mainly of new levies, who, he supposed, would scarcely stand his first demonstration.

General Santa Anna explained his policy to me, and said that from the fact of a reconnaissance having been made from Parras in the direction of Durango and Zacatecas, by order of General Wool, he was led to suppose that that general would move on Zacatecas as the advance of the American army, and that he had been informed General Wool was actually on his march in that direction; and therefore his calculation was to defeat us in detail—first crushing Worth, then beating Butler, when Wool, with his small column, would be completely cut off. This well-devised scheme, however, was fortunately frustrated by the vigilance of General Worth, who kept himself well informed of the movements of his skilful antagonist.

MEMOIR

TOPOGRAPHICAL BUREAU,
Washington, January 20, 1849.

To Colonel J. J. ABERT,
Chief of Topographical Engineers:

SIR: In compliance with a resolution of the Senate of the 8th August, 1848, I have the honor to submit the following descriptive memoir of the march of a division of the United States army under the command of Brigadier General John E. Wool, accompanied by the astronomical determinations of latitude and longitude of the most important points on the line of march.

On the 29th of August, 1846, the United States steamer transport John L. Day, on board of which the topographical party under my command were passengers, entered the bay of Matagorda (after a stormy voyage of four days from New Orleans) by the pass Cavallo, in which we found eight feet water,* and the next morning at high tide reached the town of Lavaca, in Texas, which has been selected as the depot of supplies for General Wool's division, destined for the invasion of Chihuahua.

The next day (the 31st) I left, accompanied by First Lieutenant L. Sitgreaves, topographical engineers, for San Antonio, by the Goliad road, on the San Antonio river, (1) the two other officers of the corps, Lieutenants Franklin and Bryan, having remained behind for the purpose of making astronomical observations, with directions, after that duty was completed, to proceed to San Antonio, *via* the Gonzales road, on the left bank of the Rio Guadalupe, sketching in the topographical features of the country, and determining the position of the most important points on the route. From the want of adequate transportation for the delicate astronomical instruments, a portion of these instructions were not executed.

We reached San Antonio on the 6th September, and there found the headquarters established, and nearly all the troops belonging to the expedition concentrated in the vicinity of that healthy and beautiful town. In a few days afterwards we were joined by Lieutenants Franklin and Bryan.

(For a description of the two roads leading from Port Lavaca to San Antonio de Bexar see appendix, A and B.)

The town of San Antonio is supposed to contain about two thousand inhabitants, mostly Mexicans; the greater part of the males are agriculturists and herdsmen, so far as they have any occupation. It has no manufactures, and but few mechanics—such as carpenters, masons, tailors, shoemakers, and blacksmiths.

---

*According to a survey since made by Captain Mackay, topographical engineers, there are nine feet water on the bar at extreme low water: the tide rises only six inches.

APPENDIX A

The town (see special map) is built on both sides of the river of the same name, and is bounded on the west by the San Pedro: the principal part of the town, however, lies in a horse-shoe bend on the west bank of the river, and its streets are washed by its waters running rapidly through them. It is about five miles from the source of the river, in latitude 29°26'* and longitude 98°50' west of Greenwich. (The longitude has not yet been precisely determined, and we are waiting, for this purpose, to make further observations on the satellites of Jupiter, which we hope to accomplish to-night.)

The buildings belonging to the government in the town might be conveniently converted into hospitals and barracks for a considerable force. The Alamo, on the left bank of the river, if placed in a suitable state of repair, would accommodate a regiment, and might at the same time be rendered a strong defensive work, well supplied with water.

As a frontier post, it may be regarded as one of some importance. About one mile east of the Alamo is a strong tower, twenty-one feet square at base, thirty feet high, sixteen feet square at top, three stories high, with a look-out on top. It is built of stone, the walls three feet thick, with three loop-holes on each side. It is not arched. The entrance is from the east. Within a short distance of it stands another building, eighteen feet square at base, twelve feet high, and with a groined arch; the walls are three feet thick—the entrance from the west: it was obviously a magazine. The two buildings are defended on the southeast angle by a bastion with two long curtains enclosing the buildings on two sides. The advance works are of earth, and consist of a deep ditch and parapet. Between these works and the building was a well, now partially closed with rubbish.

Most of the land in the vicinity of San Antonio was formerly, and much of it still is, irrigated from the river an the San Pedro. It may, however, well be questioned whether this operation is not injurious rather than beneficial to the lands, for the soil being highly calcareous, and the water being nearly saturated with the same substance, too much carbonate of lime must, in the course of years, be deposited in the fields. The remedy for this excess may be found in deep ploughing, following in the rotation of crops. The country bears evidence of having been at one period in a high state of cultivation and fertility, supporting a large and concentrated population, who in time of danger sought refuge in the town and in the missions of the *Alamo, Concepcion, San Juan Espada,* and *San José* monastic fortresses, whose stately and melancholy ruins attest their former magnificence and grandeur.

It is stated, on the authority of the surveyor of Bexar county, that within the limits of our map nearly two thousand acres of land are now in corn,

---

*The position of our camp is latitude 29°26'53".

yielding on an average about thirty bushels to the acre—sixty thousand bushels; but this is probably an over-estimate. Corn usually sells at 50 cents per bushel: it is now bringing $1.25, or rather more. For a great distance around San Antonio the grazing is excellent, and herds of cattle abundant. In ordinary times a good, well-broken ox is worth $25; for beef, about $9; or a cow and calf, about $13; at present the prices are much higher. The cattle are of the old Spanish breed—the oxen large, with immense horns; rapid walkers, and strong. They are fed exclusively or herbage and fodder: they keep easily, and made good beef. The cows are bad milkers, but might be easily improved by a cross on the Durham or Devon.

The county of Bexar contains about four thousand inhabitants, including Castroville. Its territorial limits extend to the Rio Grande.

According to the authority before mentioned, there are this year nearly eight hundred acres of corn growing on the Leona creek, averaging about thirty-five bushels per acre—twenty-eight thousand bushels. While the lands are rich in this region, the demand heretofore for agricultural productions has been so limited that there has been but little inducement to grow more grain than would suffice for the wants of the permanent population.

The San Antonio river has its source in a large spring, five miles north of the town, and, as far as our map extends, flows nearly due south. It becomes almost at once, in gushing from the rocks, a noble river, clear, full, and rapid in its course. For the first ten miles it rarely exceeds one hundred feet in width, and from three to six feet in depth. The principal fords below the infantry camp are at the town of San Antonio and at a short distance below the mission of Conception. The former is good and practicable for artillery: the later is not so good, the water being not less than four feet deep, with a very rapid current. There are, however, many points where fords might be made accessible by cutting down the banks. The river in its upper waters varies but little in its level, and is not greatly affected by the heaviest rains. At San Antonio there is a trestle-bridge over the river, near the Alamo, recently repaired, or rather rebuilt, by the quartermaster's department for military purposes.

One source of the San Pedro is on the Nacogdoches road, about two miles above the town. It is a small but beautiful stream, flowing to the rear of the town, and debouching into the river about two and a half miles below. I am inclined to regard the San Pedro as an off-shoot from the San Antonio, as it presents (on the Nacogdoches road, where it is first visible) more the appearance of a subterranean stream than a spring.

The rainy season usually commences about the autumnal equinox, and generally terminates with the vernal. I do not, however, understand that the rain is often excessive so as to break up the roads, but that there

APPENDIX A

are generally slight showers daily during the period, and that scarcely any water falls during the dry season or summer.

As soon as the rainy season sets in the temperature falls, and the atmosphere, which is remarkably pure, becomes very agreeable. The vicinity of San Antonio is said to be very healthy, and there is apparently no cause for disease. Fresh meat rarely putrifies, but is gradually dried up by the action of the air. The sickness amongst the troops and teamsters is probably owing to their exposure while marching here, to their imprudence, and to the (merely temporary) effects of the water.

The temperature of the water is about 76° Fahrenheit in the morning. The thermometer the last week has ranged to 98° in the shade.

Comparison of Mexican and English measure.

Mexican.	English.
1 foot.	= 11 1/9 inches.
1 vara	= 33 1/3 inches.
10 varas.	= 100 yards.
1,000 varas.	= 925 yards.
1,000 varas, sq.	= 176 3/4 acres.
1 labor.	= 17,725 2/3 rods.
1 litro	= 4,428 402/1000 rods.
1 league = 5,000 varas .	= 2 2/3 miles (nearly.)
1,900 8/10 varas.	= 1 mile.

In compliance with the direction of the commanding general, I left San Antonio, with the topographical staff, to precede the march of the army, on the 23d of September, at 5 o'clock p.m., having previously sent the wagons in advance. We found the party encamped on the west side of the Little Leona, seven miles from San Antonio, a tributary to the river of the same name, and uniting with it not far below the town. One of our two wagons having taken a wrong direction, did not join us till next morning. Our ride, on a course nearly due west, was over an open prairie, with occasional patches of musquette chaparral.*

The Leona is a small and lovely stream of pure water, with high banks, discharging in the rainy season a large volume of water. It was, when we crossed it, about thirty feet wide and one foot deep. There are several thriving settlements on this creek, and a good deal of corn is grown.

The topographical party consisted of the following persons, viz:

George W. Hughes, captain topographical engineers;

L. Sitgreaves, 1st lieutenant topographical engineers;

---

*The term chaparral is applied to a close thorny thicket.

W. B. Franklin, 2d lieutenant topographical engineers;

F. T. Bryan, brevet 2d lieutenant topographical engineers (temporarily detached;)

Dan Drake Henrie, interpreter;

James Dunn, hunter and guide, (left three days afterwards, ill;)

Two wagoners, four laborers, and two private servants.

We were furnished by the ordnance department with six rifles and a keg of ammunition.

September 24.—Left camp at 10 o'clock a.m., having waited until that time for the missing wagon to come up. The country immediately west of the creek is high and broken, and the road for more than a mile quite precipitous, when it suddenly changes to a beautiful open and rolling prairie, covered with a luxuriant growth of sweet and nutritious grasses. We saw plenty of game. The only bushes on our route were stinted musquette—a species of acacia, which, even in a green state, make excellent fuel. Stopped to noon on a little stream of good water, near a remarkable landmark called *Padre Monté*. We crossed during the day three small streams of pure water, and at 8 o'clock in the evening, after a march of eighteen miles, reached the Medina river, and encamped on its left bank a mile below the village of Castroville.

September 25.—The preceding day had been excessively hot, and the whole country seemed parched for the want of rain, the ground being cracked into large fissures. At 2 o'clock this morning the weather suddenly changed, the thermometer falling from 98° to 52° Fahrenheit, and a severe norther set in, accompanied with lightning, thunder, and rain, which fell in torrents. The greater portion of Texas and the adjacent Mexican provinces are subject to these sudden and extreme transitions of climate; which often prove deleterious to animal life. It cleared at 11 o'clock in the morning, when Lieutenant Sitgreaves was sent to examine the ford below the camp, on the old Presidio road, and to measure the width and depth of the ford at Castroville, while Lieutenant Franklin and myself made a reconnaissance of the country for several miles around on both side of the river.

The Medina is a truly lovely stream, with high banks, the ground on the west side rising into abrupt hills some 300 feet in altitude. At the ford, which is over a rocky ledge at the foot of a considerable fall, it is about 100 feet wide and two feet deep. Directly opposite is situated the flourishing village of Castroville, on an extensive and rich plain formed by the receding of the highlands. The German settlement at this place, made under the auspices of Mr. Castro, a French gentleman, who obtained a large and valuable concession of territory from the republic of Texas, consists of about 700 inhabitants, who have brought with them to this wilderness the habits of industry, sobriety, and economy of their father-land.

APPENDIX A

There are two fords above the town—one called the canon, two and a half miles distant, and is pretty good; rocky bottom, somewhat worn into holes, and rather dangerous for horses; the banks precipitous and rather marshy. It was here that the Mexican General Woll,* in 1842, in his descent on San Antonio, crossed his artillery and infantry, and in his subsequent rapid retreat, passed over his entire army. Woll's ford, where the infantry crossed, is three miles beyond, but is now impracticable, owing to the mud since deposited several feet deep. There is said to be no other ford for thirty miles above. The ford below the village is passable, but not very good, the bottom being rather muddy.

September 26.—Temperature of water at 7 o'clock a.m., 62° Fahrenheit. Left at 9 o'clock, and crossed the Castroville ford. A mile beyond is a very bad and rocky hill, down which it is necessary to lock the wagon wheels: after which the country is open and level until the road intersects the cañon trail, when turning suddenly to the left, (more to the west,) it gradually ascends to a considerable height, covered with a beautiful growth of live oaks, interspersed with musquette and bushes of the same species. Herds of deer were continually crossing our path, and we occasionally disturbed a wild turkey, or a zapolota (the Mexican vulture,) from his loathsome meal, who, lazily flapping his wings, circled around us and croakingly complained of the intrusion.

There is no water between the Medina and Quihé, a distance of ten miles. Being informed by our guide that there was no water for several miles ahead, we here encamped on the east side of the creek, in a very pretty, live oak grove. The water was good, and the grazing excellent. The country in the vicinity of the brook was well timbered with willow, live oak, and pecan. There is a small German settlement at this place, a branch of the Castroville immigration, which we found in a most wretched condition, the people having suffered greatly from sickness, caused probably by two small lakes of stagnant water in the vicinity. They may, however, be easily drained, and as they have considerable fall at this outlet, might be made available for water-power. This stream is a tributary to the Hondo, flowing into the Frio, which finally discharges into the Nueces. Temperature of water at 9 o'clock p.m., 71°.

September 27.—At 6½ a.m., temperature of water 65°. Left camp at 7 o'clock a.m. Our route, for several miles, was through a beautiful, wide, and fertile bottom. The road to Lucky's creek is good. We found the creek,

---

*On this expedition General Woll exhibited strategic talent of a high order. The Texans having learned that a force had assembled at Presidio for the invasion of their territory, despatched their most trusty spies to watch the enemy; but such was the secrecy of his movements, that he completely eluded their vigilance, crossed the Rio Grande almost in their presence, opened a new road 164 miles long, and entered San Antonio almost simultaneously with the scouts who had returned to report that there was no Mexican force east of the Rio Grande.

contrary to expectation, full of good water, two feet deep, and flowing clearly and rapidly. On the west bank is a lovely grove of large live oak, and a rich valley, almost boundless to the eye, of excellent grazing. An army of 10,000 cavalry might encamp here for a week, and not exhaust its luxuriance. The Lucky is usually dry; but, like most of the streams of western Texas, does not, apparently, depend for its supply of water on recent rains; for the geological formation, consisting mostly of cavernous limestone, affords many subterranean discharges, which at times leave large rivers nearly dry, and swell small brooks (often dry) into respectable rivers, without any obviously adequate cause. Hence, to some extent, the uncertainty of finding water at particular localities, except after very recent examinations. The distance from the Quihé is four miles. To the Hondo, four miles, the road is rough, and the descent bad, bottom not good, and ascent to the west bank pebbly. Seven miles brought us to a small stream of good water, not noticed in any of the maps; banks low, bottom rocky, water eighteen inches deep, (presumed to be generally dry), grazing good—one and a half mile, over a level plain, to the Saco. This creek resembles the Hondo or Sycamore, (for it is known by both names,) but the crossing is not so bad, and it contains rather more water, which in the latter river stands in pools; but it is represented to be, a few miles above the crossing, a flowing stream as large as the Medina; it has probably a subterranean discharge. We encamped on the west bank of the Saco: the grazing was not very good. The day was excessively hot, and the night very cold. The scenery in the neighborhood is eminently grand and picturesque, exhibiting on the river banks high mural escarpments, which assume many striking and interesting imitative forms and fantastic shapes.

September 28.—Left at 7 o'clock 25 minutes. For about four miles the road is rough, and the country much broken with abrupt ridges and two very steep ascents in that distance. The timber mainly live oak, in extensive groves. We then entered upon a level prairie of great extent, and covered with a coarse sedge; grazing bad. At nine miles, reached the Ranchero creek; no running water here, but that which is standing in pools is good; the descent and ascent bad, and the bottom covered with large and loose stones. To the Cañon or Sabinal the country is rather barren, and but few live oaks to be seen. The timber principally musquette. This stream is also called the Cypress, and many trees of that species grow on its banks; best camping ground on west side; distance four miles. To Little or Indian creek five miles; no water except in pools, but that good; timber musquette; grazing but tolerable; best camping ground on west side, where we stopped for the night; very cold after midnight.

September 29.—Left at 7 o'clock 10 minutes; day hot; saw no game; passed over a barren and uninteresting country; very few live oaks, and but little wood of any description. Arrived on the Frio at 12 o'clock, dis-

APPENDIX A   241

tance nineteen miles, and encamped on the west bank; a deep and beautiful stream, the water pure and cold; several large live oaks on the banks; bad grazing on east bank, good on west; encamped on west bank.

September 30.—Temperatures of air 58°—of water 57°; eight miles to Leona; for some distance good grazing; for four miles further the road is rough and rocky; for one mile before reaching the Leona, the ground is covered with a thick growth of musquette, different varieties of oak, among which the live oak, pecan, &c., mostly young. The Leona is a beautiful stream, about fifty feet wide, and the valley wide and extremely rich. It is at all times full of water, and preserves a nearly uniform level; its banks are low, and the passing bad; the bottom firm, but banks muddy; water good, and about three feet eight inches deep. We encamped on the west side, in a pleasant grove of live oaks and pecans; grazing good.

October 1.—Accompanied by Lieutenant Franklin, made a reconnaissance of the river for seven miles above the camp on the east bank, searching for another ford, which proved unsuccessful. For the whole of that distance, and apparently for a much greater distance, the valley is wide, well timbered, and extremely rich, the sweet grasses growing with great luxuriance. Returning, we ascended with great labor the "Pilot's Knob," a remarkable and steep basaltic hill about five hundred feet high, from which we (probably the first white men who looked out from its summit) enjoyed a most extensive and magnificent view for many miles around, and could trace the graceful and meandering course of the river by its fringe of woods far up to its mountain source—its naciamento, or birth, as it is called in the poetical language of the Mexicans—thus correcting the erroneous statements, made upon respectable authority, that it took its rise in a large spring near the base of the Pilot's Knob. Such a spring—and a noble one it is—does exist at this place, and is the fountain-head of a considerable affluent to the Leona, but is certainly not deserving of the credit it has received of being the parent of that lovely water nymph. A short distance below our camp is a fine water-fall, which will doubtless not long be left to waste its beauties on the desert wilds, but will be turned to some useful purpose subservient to the wants of civilized man.

Returning to camp found myself quite ill from an attack of fever and dysentery, induced by alternate exposure to the hot sun, heavy dews, and low temperature of the nights: for, having discovered that a large band of Camanches were on our trail, we have been compelled for the last few nights to keep our small party constantly on watch and patrol, selecting strong positions for encampments; their object was probably to steal our horses.

October 2.—The engineers came in with the pontoon train early; the general and staff and advance of the army arrived in the afternoon, where they remained for the rest of the day.

October 3.—Still ill. The advance moved on, about 9 o'clock a.m., towards Rio Nueces, which was about twelve miles off; encamped on the east side of the river with the staff, artillery, and squadron of the 1st dragoons; pasturage pretty good; the river is about three hundred feet wide, crossing good; water excellent; and about two feet deep.

October 4.—Left at 6 o'clock a.m.; ground low, and in wet weather difficult for wagons. To Arrest creek nine miles, and thence to Dry creek, six miles further, when the country more dry, elevated, and broken to La Chapperosa, seven miles, where we encamped, making our march to-day twenty-two miles. The water, which was muddy and bad, stands in pools; grazing pretty good. The latter portion of the road to-day was sandy; the ground covered with musquette thicket.

October 5.—Still ill, and travelling in a wagon. Last night Lieutenant Franklin was sent forward to look for water and grazing, with an escort of the 1st dragoons; sent back his report early in the morning. Five miles to the Saladino, a very pretty, small stream of pure water, which has been always represented as being brackish. The natural crossing was deep and boggy; but a bridge erected by Colonel Harney having been repaired by the engineers, we were enabled to cross without difficulty, after a short delay. The grass on the west side of the stream was good. To Fish creek seven miles, then eight miles to our encampment, making twenty miles march; water standing in pools, but palatable; grazing also good, but fuel scarce.

October 6.—Left a 6 a. m., and marched ten miles to the Cuevas; scarcely any drinkable water on the route. At our encampment the water stood in pools, covered with a thick scum, and not very palatable; grazing good and fuel scarce.

October 7.—Remained this day on the Cuevas.

October 8.—Moved on to the Rio Grande, eleven miles, and encamped on the west bank of the river, where we found abundance of food, water, and grass, but very small supplies of fuel.

General Wool left San Antonio on the 28th of September with the advance and main body of the army, consisting of nineteen hundred and fifty-four men, and reached the Rio Grande after a march, including stoppages, of eleven days. The rear-guard, under Inspector General Churchill, remained some days longer in San Antonio, for the purpose of bringing the additional supplies, some of which had not yet come up from Lavaca.*

---

*General Wool followed what is called "Woll's road," it having been opened by that general, as stated in another place. Although longer than the other roads, it is more frequently travelled in consequence of its crossing the water-courses near their sources, and being, therefore, more easily forded. There are three roads from San Antonio to Presidio, but the lower road is rarely used. There is a road diverging from our route near and west of the Nueces river to San Fernando, crossing the Rio Grande about twenty-five miles above the Presidio ford.

APPENDIX A

On arriving, after a toilsome march, at the extreme southwestern limits of our wide-spread republic, and looking out upon the noble river whose swift currents washed the conterminous boundaries of the two countries, the greatest enthusiasm prevailed; and as the glorious flag of the stars and stripes was for the first time displayed in that far-off wilderness, many an eye glistened with patriotic emotion, and many a pulse beat high with the hope of future expectation. Alas! how many of that gallant band repose peacefully in the bosom of that country upon which they then gazed with mingled feelings of deep intent and of dark uncertainty.

Resumé of distances on our line of march from San Antonio de Bexar to the Rio Grande.

To the Leone	7 miles.	
Medio	5 "	
San Lucas Spring	4 "	
Taos creek	4 "	
Medina river	5 "	. . 25 miles from Bexar.
Quihé creek	10 "	
Lucky's creek	4 "	
Hondo	6 "	
Small creek	6½ "	} Not mentioned in any of the maps; water good and abundant.
Saco river	1½ "	
Ranchero	9 "	
Sabinal	4 "	
To the Little Sabinal	5 miles.	
Rio Frio	9 "	. . 80 miles from Bexar.
Leona	8 "	
Nueces	12 "	. . 100 miles from Bexar.
Arrest creek	9 "	
Dry creek	6 "	
Chapperosa	7 "	
Saladino	5 "	
Fish creek	7 "	
Creek	8 "	
Cuevas	10 "	
Rio Grande	12 "	

164 miles from San Antonio to west bank of the Rio Grande.

Observations for the determination of longitude and latitude have been made as often as practicable; but as they have not all been reduced, I have thought it best not to give an imperfect list of them, but to have them designated on the topographical map which Mr. Sitgreaves is preparing.

October 10.—Crossed the river with several officers of the staff under orders from the commanding general, for the purpose of selecting a camp beyond the Presidio. The Rio Grande del Norte as this place is truly a noble river, with high banks, never overflown, well deserving of its name—the "*Great River of the North.*" At the ford it is eight hundred and sixteen feet wide, water nearly uniformly three and a half feet deep, bottom hard gravel, and current rapid. Several wagons crossed to-day, but with considerable difficulty. The party was escorted by a squadron of 2d dragoons, under the command of Colonel Harney, which encamped at a very pretty position, near a hacienda, about two miles beyond Presidio.

Presidio del Rio Grande is about five miles from the river, the general course of the road being south 52° west. It is a town of about twelve hundred inhabitants, pleasantly situated on a small creek, furnishing abundant water for irrigation, flowing into the river a few miles below the ford. There is a good deal of corn, cotton, sweet potatoes, beans, and sugarcane grown in the vicinity, and fruits are plentiful. The town, built of adobes, or unburnt bricks, is in a dilapidated condition. It was created, by an edict of the king of Spain, in 1772, a military post, and prison for army convicts. About one mile in the direction of the ford are the ruins of an old monastery, erected as a mission by the Jesuits. Its walls are thick, and built of stone, and are still in a tolerable state of preservation, and might at little expense be rendered a strong defensible position. Within the town is a stone tower, built for and formerly occupied as a guard-house. The inhabitants are said to be extremely hostile to us, but did not manifest it by any offensive acts, but, on the contrary, were kind and civil in their deportment.

At night returned to camp on the east bank of the river.

October 11.—Lieutenants Sitgreaves and Bryan were sent to examine Woll's ford, or rather ferry, where Woll crossed with his whole army on his expedition to San Antonio, about one and a half mile above the camp. At this point the river is some six hundred feet wide, very rapid, and not fordable. Opposite to it, on the right bank, there are several large plantations of sugar-cane, corn, and cotton. In the afternoon examinations were made below the ford, but no good crossing place could be found. About three miles below the camp the river is broken into several cascades, over which boats can safely pass only in floods. To-day a flying-bridge was put in operation by Captain Fraser, of the engineers, who had built pontoons in San Antonio for the purpose, which were transported to this place in wagons. For the purpose of protecting it, and to keep open the communication with San Antonio, where Colonel Churchill still was with the rear-guard and a portion of the supplies, the engineers were directed to construct defensive works on both banks, and two companies of volunteers were left behind as a guard. Lieutenant Franklin was occupied with the astronomical calculations

October 12.—To-day the whole army, wagons, &c., crossed the river, the infantry passing over the flying-bridge, and marched through Presidio, encamping about four miles south of the town. The grazing here was good, but the water bad, being hard, saline, sulphurous, and unhealthy, in consequence of which we were compelled to dispense with the soldier's favorite dish, bean-soup.

October 13.—Went into Presidio by order of the commanding general, for the purpose of obtaining information in relation to the routes to Santa Rosa. Met General Shields on his way to camp from Camargo. He gave me the first authentic intelligence of the details of the battle of Monterey, and of the capitulation. Yesterday, as General Wool reached the right bank of the Rio Grande, a Mexican officer, with an escort of lancers, presented himself to him with a communication from the political chief of the State of Coahuila, enclosing a copy of the articles of capitulation, and complaining that General Wool's march was in direct contravention of its provisions.

This, however, was not the General's construction of that convention; and he returned for answer, that he should continue his forward movement. The information procured in the town was not very satisfactory. We learned that there was a direct road over the mountains to Monclova, but that it was probably not practical for artillery and wagons; that there was a direct road to Santa Rosa by the way of Peyoté, but the same objection existed to it as in the first case. The conclusion was, that, all things considered, it would be more certain to take the more circuitous way through San Fernando de Rosas.

October 14.—Yesterday and to-day, Lieutenant Bryan was occupied in surveying the roads in the vicinity of Presidio.

I received orders to proceed to-morrow morning, escorted by a squadron of dragoons, under the command of Lieutenant Colonel Roane, of the Arkansas mounted men, on the way to Santa Rosa; and on reaching that town, to wait for the advance of the army, or for further instructions. The object was to reconnoitre the country, especially in reference to supplies, water, and encampments, with directions to communicate the information thus obtained daily to the commanding general.

October 15.—Left the Presidio camp at 7½ o'clock in the morning, accompanied by Lieutenant Franklin, with Pike's and Preston's companies of mounted men. There was no water to be found until we arrived within two miles of the town of San Juan de Nava, although the whole country was obviously once irrigated and in a high state of cultivation, as we noticed everywhere dry ditches, once filled with water, and frequently passed houses in ruins. As far as the eye could reach on both sides, we saw nothing but a wide-spread champaign country, bearing evidence of former prosperity. It is now nothing but a desert waste, abandoned to the dreaded Camanches, or the not less terrible Mescaleros and Apaches, who have driven the timid inhabitants from their rural dwellings, and cooped them up within the precincts of the villages, converting this once smiling garden into a howling wilderness.

As we approached Nava, it presented a most beautiful and attractive appearance. The fields were cultivated, with fresh pure water running in every direction; large trees surrounded it, and the white dome of the village church glittered in the sun through their foliage; but alas! "'twas distance lent enchantment to the view;" for, on entering it, we found it filthy and miserable. It numbers in population abut 1,000 souls. The alcalde, a half-naked Indian, and the padre, called on us, and through their intervention we procured an abundance of supplies, and ascertained that a sufficiency of beef, corn, and fodder could be obtained for the army, at reasonable prices, as many of those articles had been brought from the neighboring settlements in anticipation of our visit.

We marched through the town; but not finding a convenient camping ground, as the whole country was intersected with irrigating ditches, we returned to the east side, and there pitched our tents. Wood was very scarce, and we could with difficulty find enough to cook our food. I directed the alcalde to have a large supply furnished the next day for the army; which was fortunate, as a severe norther set in the next night, soon after the arrival of the troops.

The length of march to-day was about twenty-five miles.

October 16.—Resumed our march at 7 o'clock a.m. For some two miles the country was cultivated; after which, all again was desolate, until we reached San Fernando de Rosas, a distance of eleven miles. About four miles this side of town, a road branches off to the villages of Morales and San Juan, and is in fact the direct route to Santa Rosa; and was afterwards followed by Colonel Churchill. It is some eight or ten miles shorter than the road by San Fernando.

San Fernando de Rosas (of the roses) is pleasantly situated on the left bank of the Escandido,* a beautiful and limpid stream of pure cool water, which, rising about fifteen miles to the southwest, winds gracefully around two sides of the town, and discharges into the Rio Grande, thirty miles above the Presidio ford. It is extensively used for purposes of irrigation; and the valley of San Fernando is broad, rich, and productive. The town contains about 2,000 inhabitants, and two plazas, around which are built the better class of houses, which are large, neat, and comfortable. On the main plaza is the parochial church, a building of some architectural pretension. The whole town, surrounded as it is with a belt of large

---

*"Concealed brook."

APPENDIX A 247

trees, wears a pleasing aspect, in striking contrast with Presidio and Nava; and the people are well dressed, presenting an agreeable appearance. A great deal of corn and numerous herds of cattle are produced in the vicinity, and near the neighboring villages of Morales and San Juan; the former containing about 900, and the latter about 700 souls.

The escort, after halting a short time for refreshments, passed through the town, re-crossed the stream, and encamped about six miles beyond, having changed our course considerably to the south after leaving the town. There are several ranchos near the camp, from which we procured an abundant supply of corn, fodder, and other necessities. We found the water and grazing good, and fortunately plenty of fuel, as a violent norther set in about 12 o'clock at night, accompanied with a cold drifting rain. An encampment for the army was selected some four miles this side of San Fernando, on a plain affording good grazing, with running water on both sides, and plenty of wood convenient.

October 17.—Broke up our camp at 8 o'clock, the most of the men being stiff and uncomfortable from the effects of last night's norther, and from the sudden change from excessive heat to cold. The wind was chilly, raw, and penetrating. A march of eleven miles over a barren and uncultivated country brought us to the celebrated *Santa Rita* springs, the sources of the water which supplies the villages of San Juan, Morales, and Nava, and which formerly was conducted as far as our Presidio camp, irrigating the whole intermediate country, a distance of forty miles, through which it was carried in artificial channels. The surplus water is now wasted after passing Nava, near which it has formed an extensive and pestilential marsh.

The numerous springs at this locality unite in several small, deep, and picturesque lakes, much frequented by several kinds of water fowl. We encamped near them in a fine grove of live oak. There is considerable growth of wood and timber in the vicinity, but the grazing is not good. The ground is moist, and the grass, although luxuriant, is coarse and sedgy. This position was recommended to General Wool as his camping ground. Several Mexican carts had followed us to-day laden with corn, and after supplying our own horses, they were directed to wait the arrival of the main army; the last corn, as we were informed, that could be obtained this side of Santa Rosa. Our march to-day was short, in conseqence of representations made to us that no water could be found for a distance of more than thirty miles ahead. It was also a convenient day's march for the army. Several Mexicans came in during the night for protection against the Indians, who were prowling about in small parties.

October 18.—Left camp at 7 o'clock in the morning. For about three miles our road passed over an undulating country, well wooded, with a luxuriant growth of sweet grasses. Another mile brought us to the intersection of the San Juan and Morales road. The ground soon afterwards became very broken, and we began gradually to ascend by a tortuous course the Sierra de San José, a range of hills which we observed to our left from the time of leaving the Presidio camp. They trend nearly northeast and southwest, and the Rio Grande bursts through them about ten miles below the town of Presidio. It is over these highlands that the Peyoté and Monclova roads pass. Our road was good, and reached the summit of the hills with easy grades. They are covered with a thin growth of grass; and many varieties of the cactus, the *sotol* (from which the Mexican mescal is distilled,) and an occasional maguey, (*agave Americana,*) the palmetto, and yucca folia, make their appearance, the first that I have noticed on our march. The rocks are of fossiliferous limestone, and it is said that mines of copper and silver were formerly worked in these mountains. We passed the summit of this range about eight miles from yesterday's camp, and then commenced descending, by a road similar to that by which we had ascended, to the Llano de San José, a wide and extensive, but sterile plain. From the top of these hills we caught the first sight of the Sierra Gordo, sometimes called the Sierra Santa Rosa, a spur of the great Sierra Madre, or Mother Mountain. As the mist which rested like a veil on its lofty peaks was gently lifted by the sun, the view was most grand and imposing. We overlooked the great plain before us, which was limited in that direction only by a wall of serrated mountains rising to the height of 4,000 feet, and stretching to the north and south as far as the eye could reach, and apparently presenting an impassable barrier to our further progress. We could also recognise the course of the two large rivers which flow through the plain, by the woods which fringe the banks. From the same point we looked back upon the lovely valley of San Fernando.

At a distance of sixteen miles from Santa Rita, we found a pool of clear, fresh looking water that the advance-guard had passed, under the assurance of the Mexicans, who were with us, that it was brackish, nauseous, and poisonous, not fit even for the horses. We had received uniformly the same accounts of it from all quarters, but it looked so cool and tempting, and our thirsty animals showed such a positive desire to drink it, that I determined to try it, and to my surprise found it as pleasant to the taste as it was inviting to the eye. What had given rise to the notion of its bad qualities I could never ascertain; but that it was unfit for use and poisonous to animals, was certainly entertained by the people of the country; and no Mexican could be induced to drink it or permit his horse to use it, but preferred to ride fourteen miles further to the Rio Alamos without water. The pasturage here was good, but fuel very scarce. Sent back a man to General Wool recommending this place as a suitable encampment for the army. The pool occupied the bed of a large creek with steep banks, discharging a large quantity of water in the rainy season, at which time it must be impassable. It drains into the Alamos. The sierra of

APPENDIX A

San José divides the drainage of the valley of San Fernando from that of Santa Rosa, both of which, however, discharge into the Rio Grande.

From the pool it was fourteen miles to the Rio Alamos (or cotton wood river,) the first ten miles of which was over a level prairie of good grass; the next four was a pretty rapid descent to the river, where we encamped. The Peyoté road comes in at the ford about one mile back. We found the banks of the river covered with a thick growth of trees, principally cotton wood—a species of poplar. There is also in this valley a fine growth of nutritious grasses.

October 19.—The Alamos is about 100 feet wide, four feet deep, hard pebbly bottom, and the current a perfect torrent. Last night and this morning we examined the river for several miles above and below, but could find no other ford. It was generally deeper in other places, although the current was less and the bed of the stream soft. With great exertions we succeeded in getting over; the small wagon, containing the instruments, having been secured with ropes to prevent its being carried off. From all previous Mexican accounts we were induced to believe that we should not be able to cross at all. As it was, we narrowly escaped losing one mule, and two men who were forced from their horses by the current, and were rescued with great difficulty.

After crossing the river, the road turns suddenly to the left; and half a mile further on, the roads diverge, the left one leading to the ferry over the Sabinos river, just above the junction with the Alamos, being the most direct route to Monclova; and the right hand one to the Sabinos ford, being the Santa Rosa road. At the ferry the river is not fordable. Four miles from the Alamos we came to the *Rio Sabinos*, or Cypress river, which takes its designation from the numerous and large cypress trees growing on its banks—a stream neither as wide, deep, nor as swift as the former, although from their confluence it gives its name to their united waters until they discharge into the Salado, which is an affluent to the Rio Grande at Guerrera. This river at times overflows its banks to a great distance, showing that in the rainy season it discharges an immense volume of water, when, from its depth and the velocity of the current, it must be utterly impassable even with boats. For this reason neither of the two rivers could be permanently bridged without incurring an enormous expense. When Santa Anna took this direction in his celebrated invasion of Texas in 1834, which terminated so disastrously at San Jacinto, he impressed all the people of the surrounding country, and compelled them to build temporary bridges (which were swept off by the next flood) over both rivers, for the passage of his troops. The army not being provided with a pontoon train, which had been left at Presidio for the use of the rear guard, experienced great difficulty in crossing these rivers; but, by making a bridge of the loaded wagons, which were sufficiently heavy to stem the torrents, the infantry were passed over without loss; several mules and horses, however, were drowned.

A short distance from the right bank we found an excellent camping ground, with plenty of fuel and grass. The water in both streams is excellent. A march of four miles brought us to the "three ranchos," a good camping ground on a cool and beautiful mountain brook; and four miles still further on is another good encampment on the same water-course; and one and a half mile further, about half a mile from the town of Santa Rosa, we encamped on the left bank of the above mentioned stream, in a broad and lovely plain, verdant with grass, and with waving fields of corn and the sugar cane, almost at the foot of a magnificent volcanic mountain range, whose jagged peaks rose to an elevation of some 4,000 feet above the level of the plain.

These mountains were visible from the banks of the Sabinos, and indeed we caught a glimpse of them from the summit of the Sierra San José; and as we approached them, all were exhilarated by the contrast between this beautiful spectacle and the dull monotony of the level prairies which we had traversed so long as to deem them almost interminable.

Soon after leaving the Sabinos we were met by a courier from the civil authorities of Santa Rosa, who announced to us that the municipality would meet us in the road and tender to us the formal rendition of the town. After encamping, the principal officers of the command and a small escort entered the town with the alcalde, and it was agreed that to-morrow we should take possession; accordingly, on the 20th of October, the squadron marched into town with flags flying and sabres drawn, and we accepted the surrender of Santa Rosa, which had been freely and officially tendered by the civil authorities. A few invalid soldiers under the command of a superannuated colonel, who had been left behind by Colonel Castaneira, were disarmed, and the guns placed in charge of the alcalde. The arms were of British manufacture, and bore the Tower proofmark.

There is a difficult mule track from Santa Rosa to Santa Catarina through the mountains, but nothing which can be called a road. Its general direction is south. Presidio de Bavia (an old military post) is N. 60 W., (about) 80 miles distant, on a pretty good road: from thence to Chihuahua there is a mule track. By the way of San Fernando and Bavia is the shortest route Chihuahua; but whether practicable for an army, is a doubtful matter.

Resumé of distances from the Rio Grande to Santa Rosa.

To Presidio Rio Grande .... 5 miles.
    Our camp .... 4 "
    Nava .... 24 "

APPENDIX A   251

    San Fernando .... 11 miles.
    Camp .... 6 "
    Santa Rita springs .... 11 "
    Waterpool .... 16 "
    Rio Alamos .... 14 "
    Rio Sabinos .... 4 "
    Santa Rosa .... 10 "
                                                                105
                                                               104
                                                                209 miles.

from San Antonio to Santa Rosa.

Santa Rosa is agreeably situated, at the very foot of a lofty range of mountains called Monté Rosa, elevated by igneous action. The outliers are of volcanic origin, and are formed of basalt and lavas. The high peaks consist of limestone, overlaying a schistose slate, in which the silver ore is found. It is of a very dark blue color. The lodes of different metals, particularly lead and silver, are said to be numerous, and their yield extremely rich. There has been, since the expulsion of the Spaniards, no systematic or intelligent working of the mines in this district, and the veins are usually abandoned as soon as the water fills the shafts. The workings I have seen, it appeared to me, could be easily drained by adits for many years to come, without incurring the expense of pumping. The principal ores are silver and lead, and I am inclined to believe that this is one of the richest mining regions in Mexico. The usual process of separation of the metals consists in first pulverizing the ores and washing out the dust and light matter with water; the remaining portion is put into an elbow furnace, heat applied, the scoria raked out on one side, and the metallic silver left behind in a kind of retort. The amalgamation process has never been introduced here.

Santa Rosa is said to contain three thousand inhabitants, but I doubt if its population exceeds two thousand. It is well watered from mountain streams; its climate is agreeable and salubrious, and a good deal of corn and sugar are produced here; but still the town wears that appearance of decay so common in Mexico. Its former prosperity depended on its mining operations, which have been nearly entirely suspended for many years by the depredations of the Indians. The old laws of Spain, "the laws of the Indies," in relation to mining and mining interests, are still in existence, and are said to be very judiciously framed. The fee simple of the mines belongs to the government, and leases, with certain privileges, are granted to individuals at very moderate rates. Any person discovering a new mine, or one that has been abandoned, may *declare* it; that is, may take a lease of it, on application to the proper authorities, and by complying with certain prerequisites, amongst which he is to work the mine a certain number of days each year on penalty of forfeiture. The inhabitants of Santa Rosa are generally federalists, and friendly to the United States. Our camp was continually crowded with men, women, and children, from early in the morning until retreat, and we were freely supplied "with all the delicacies of the season." Baskets of nice cakes, confectionery, and fruits were sent in as presents to the officers; and when our men visited that town, the people were watching at the doors to invite them into their houses to partake of their hospitality. It was quite amusing to see how soon they *fraternized*, and it was evident that the population hailed us a protectors and deliverers; and, in fact, more than one proposition was made to me to encourage a *pronunciamiento* against the Mexican government.

A very large and rich mine was formerly worked within two miles of the town by a company, at the head of which was the Spanish governor of the province, who held his court in Santa Rosa with much splendor. The mine was worked very skillfully, if we may judge by the large adits and mills, the ruins of which we saw. The mining was in successful operation (yielding vast quantities of silver, according to the popular account) when the revolution commenced, which soon drove the proprietors from the country, and with them all safety and enterprise. During the Spanish domination, despotic as it was, Mexico must have presented a prosperous and interesting appearance, for everywhere are seen the monuments of former greatness. At that time, too, the security of life and property (except for offences against the State) was perfect, and the revolution was the result rather of social than of political causes, in which, by-the-by, most revolutions of separation find their origin.

CAMP NEAR MONCLOVA, MEXICO,
November 18, 1846.

SIR: In compliance with your instructions, I have the honor to submit the following journal of the route from Santa Rosa to this place.

The army marched from Santa Rosa to-day (Sunday, October 25.) The road runs along the foot of level plateaus of table land, extending from the base of the Santa Rosa mountains, in nearly an easterly direction, for eight and a half miles, when it turns southeasterly, through an opening in the plateaus, four miles to the "Arroyo Alamo," a shallow stream, with broad pebbly bed and low banks, upon which the army encamped. For the first eight miles the country is pretty well covered with the usual chaparral growth of musquette, Spanish bayonet, &c. We crossed also in this distance two small rivulets; one about three, and the other six miles from camp, and one or two dry beds of mountain streams—neither difficult for wagons. The rest of the road was across open rolling prairie.

APPENDIX A

Monday, October 26.—Our course to-day was S. 40° E. 7½ miles to the Carrecitos (little caves,) and one mile further to the Sans, both small beds, with the water standing in pools; the country open and rolling. From the Sans the road deflects gradually towards the mountains, to a course about S. 5° W. 8½ miles to the Ahuza, (buzzard,) a fine running stream, two hundred and fifty feet across the bed, the stream being divided into several rivulets, by stony islands, the whole bed stony, and the banks low and firm.

Tuesday, 27*th.*—Three miles to the Guachapina, and four more to the Piletes—both small prairie streams. Five miles beyond crossed the Lampasos, a considerable stream, but the water is sulphurous, and is said to be poisonous for cattle. The country rolling and covered with small bushes, Spanish bayonets, and varieties of cacti. The maguey (agave Americana) begins here to make its appearance in considerable numbers. A short distance east of the Piletes a road turns off to the right towards a pass in the mountains. It had the appearance of having been recently travelled by wagons. Thirteen miles further on, we came to the "hacienda de Nuestra Senora de Guadalupe de los Hermanas," about a mile beyond which, upon a small stream, whose source is a hot spring with a temperature of 111° F., we encamped. This spring is walled in, and is a place of considerable resort by the fashionable of Monclova. This hacienda numbers one hundred and sixty peons, and has a large extent of ground, say one thousand acres, in cultivation. It is situated by three small knolls, called "Los Hermanas," (the sisters, from which it derives its name,) lying between the Guachapinas and the northern extremity of the Lampasos mountains—the two ranges being here not more than three miles apart. The latter range is said to extend to Monterey. A cold, drizzling rain set in about four o'clock, as we commenced pitching our tents. The rear-guard and train did not arrive till after dark.

Wednesday, 28*th.*—Remained in camp.

Thursday, 29*th.*—Two miles to the Nadadores, or Arroyo de Carmil, which we crossed by a bridge. It contains brackish water, running between steep clay banks. Between the Nadadores and the Monclova river, half a mile further on, is an old hacienda (del Tapado) occupied only by peons, but with considerable cultivation in its vicinity. The road from here continues along the left bank of the Monclova, five and a half miles to the hacienda de los Ajuntas, a village of some five hundred souls, near which the army encamped.

Friday, 30*th.*—Marched fourteen miles, and encamped near Estancia de Arriba, a small hamlet of some twenty houses. Passed several ranchos, and a good deal of corn and cotton. The road continues near the Monclova to near Estancia, where it makes a bend to the east about a mile or two from the road, which it meets again at Monclova.

The vicinity of the road, where not in cultivation, is covered with bushes, cacti, &c. General course from "Los Hermanas" to Monclova S. 20° W.

Saturday, 31st, and November 1 and 2.—In camp.

Tuesday, November 3.—Marched to Monclova, four miles, all the way through cultivated fields, and encamped on the east side of the river, opposite to the Alameda.

Very respectfully, your obedient servant,

L. SITGREAVES,
1st Lieut. Topographical Engineers.

To Captain GEORGE W. HUGHES,
Chief Topographical Engineers,
Centre Division, Army of Mexico.

The main army, under the immediate command of General Wool, reached the vicinity of the town of Monclova on the 30th of October, and on the 3d of November the camp was moved to a position opposite the Alameda, on the east side of the river, and close to the town, where it remained, in consequence of the Monterey armistice, until the 23d of November, having in the mean time been joined by the troops left behind to guard the passage of the Rio Grande, and to escort the wagon train. During this long halt the topographical engineers were engaged in making surveys of the surrounding country, and astronomical observations, reconnaissances for long distances from the camp in different directions, drawing maps, and reducing the previous observations.

Advantage was taken of this detention to improve the discipline and drill of the troops, to collect supplies from the surrounding country, and to establish depôts and a hospital in Monclova. The commanding general, looking to the long line of communications with San Antonio and Lavaca, had determined to abandon that line of communication, and to form a new base of operation resting on Monclova, which is the heart and centre of a wide and fertile region, abounding with all necessary supplies. When the army moved, Major Warren, a gallant and efficient officer of the 1st Illinois regiment, with four companies of volunteers, were left behind to guard the magazines and to control the population, which was known to be extremely hostile, and on our approach to the city to have organized a force of 2,500 to oppose us. They were, however, disbanded by Colonel Blanco before our arrival. This same force was afterwards led by Colonel Blanco to the gorges of the mountains in the rear of Saltillo during the battle of Buena Vista, to complete the anticipated victory by the indiscriminate massacre of our men after they had been defeated by Santa Anna.

On the 21st of November, Lieutenant Franklin was sent to Monterey and Saltillo to communicate with General Taylor. He was instructed to reconnoitre the roads over which he passed in going and returning. He re-

APPENDIX A

joined us at the camp of Benedito on the 27th. His report will be found in the appendix.

Monclova, a city of about 8,000 inhabitants, and under the Spanish domination, the capital of the province of Coahuila, is pleasantly situated on the Rio Monclova, a small and beautiful stream of pure water rising about ten miles to the south of the town, near the hamlet of Castana. The city of Monclova is a fine and rather cleanly town. The houses are well built, (the better class of stone,) and the principal church is a very large and imposing structure. There is here also an extensive and once comfortable hospital (now abandoned to the bats) erected by the Spanish government, and large quarters for troops. The introduction of running water through all of the streets, and its numerous alamedas, (skirted with long avenues of trees,) and its numerous well irrigated gardens, impart to Monclova, particularly to persons who have recently traversed the dry and uncultivated plains of Coahuila, a most agreeable and charming aspect. It wears, nevertheless, the melancholy appearance of decay and of premature old age so common to Mexican towns.

The Rio Monclova is a tributary to the Salado,* and its valley is extremely well cultivated for nearly its whole extent, especially in the vicinity of the town, where it expands to a width of five or six miles. Immediately above the city are large reservoirs of water, and extensive waterpower, an inconsiderable portion of which is expended on three grist mills. The principal productions of this district are corn, cotton, sugar, beans, and figs—the first greatly predominating, and constituting the main staple. Very little wheat is grown, and the larger portion of flour consumed is brought from Cienegas. Although this region is well adapted to manufactures, from its mild climate, its vast water-power, the cheapness of subsistence, common labor, and wool, and the peculiar capability of the surrounding country for the production of cotton, it furnishes nothing but a few domestic fabrics of the simplest character, and but few mechanics of any description, the most skilful of whom are foreigners.

Monclova is not defensible, inasmuch as it is commanded from several directions by high hills, the possession of which by a considerable force would determine the fate of the town.

General Wool having decided to march on Parras, an important strategic point from which he might move either on Chihuahua or Durango, concentrate with General Taylor on either San Luis Potosi or Zacatecas, or, if necessary, unite with General Worth at Saltillo, I was directed to leave the camp (on the right bank of the Monclova river) near the town, and select a position for the army in the vicinity of the small hamlet of Castana. Under this order, on the 23d of November I chose a

---

*Wide memoirs of a reconnaissance from Monclova to Quatro Cinegas.

camp on the Saltillo road, about one mile south of the village, near the headwaters of the river—the Arkansas cavalry and Beall's squadron of 2d dragoons having already occupied adjacent ground.

The distance from Monclova to our new camp was 10 miles, the road good, and confined to a narrow valley between mountain ranges, some of whose jagged peaks rise to the height of nearly 4,000 feet. The formation is volcanic, intersected wtih *trap dikes,* in which *loadstones* or *natural magnets* are found. There is neither water nor cultivation in this march, and the country is almost destitute of vegetation.

Castāna is a collection of mean ranchos built of the *adobe* or unburnt brick, the common building material of the country: wood is too scarce, stone too expensive, and bricks cannot be burnt, owing to the calcareous nature of the soil. The adobe takes mortar well, and when plastered with *stucco,* (and there is none better than the Mexican,) will last a very long time, resisting the heaviest rains; but when not so protected, they are washed away in a few years. Nearly all the houses in Coahuila are constructed with flat roofs, and are almost universally one story high. The roofs of the better kind are formed by placing on the walls, which are thick and high, joists about eighteen inches apart, over which are arranged diagonally a covering of shingles, and over all is deposited a thick coating of dirt and cement. The houses have often extensive court yards, in which flowers are planted; and they are provided with large reservoirs, kept full of running water, sometimes spouting into jets high in the air. Fireplaces and chimneys are rarely seen in Mexico.

At Castana the valley opens to a width of nearly eight miles, and is well irrigated and cultivated, its principal productions being corn and cattle. All the land in this district of country belongs to few wealthy proprietors; and nearly the whole laboring population are *serfs,* called *peons,* (slaves sold for debt,) who are transferred with the estates like so many "villiens of the glebe." No portion of northern Mexico can be cultivated except where running water is at command for purposes of irrigation; so that the arable land is very limited in proportion to that which may be regarded as absolutely sterile.

Taking Monclova as a centre, the district described by a radius of twenty miles probably produces annually about three hundred thousand bushels of maize, a good deal of sugar and cotton, and large herds of cattle, sheep, and goats, for the rearing of which two latter classes of animals the whole country would be admirably adapted but for the ravages of the Indians, who render even the suburbs of the towns unsafe.

From Castana there is a mule-track to Cinegas, through the mountain passes, by the way of Pozuelos, mentioned in another memoir.

On the 24th, the whole army encamped on the ground which had been previously selected for that purpose. It was well supplied with those

APPENDIX A

essentials to an army—abundance of good water, grass, and fuel; which latter article was soon wanted, as a *severe norther* set in soon after the tents had been pitched. The weather changed suddenly from extreme heat to a temperature below the freezing point, and the wind blew a perfect gale, covering the camp with a cloud of dust, through which it was almost impossible to distinguish a single object. The whole surface of the soil appeared to be in motion; and it was, indeed, but one heap of sand, there having been no rain for nearly four months. Early in the morning of the 23d the thermometer stood at 24° Fahrenheit, and before 4 o'clock of the same day rose to 95°. This statement will convey a pretty good idea of the vicissitudes of this changeful climate.

I left the camp at Castana before 6 a. m. on the morning of the 25th, in advance of the army, which soon followed. It consisted of one squadron of 1st dragoons, one squadron of 2d dragoons, one battery of eight guns, field artillery, the Arkansas regiment of mounted men, a battalion of 6th infantry, including one company of Kentucky volunteers, and the 1st and 2d Illinois volunteers—a detachment of one squadron of Arkansas and four companies of Illinois volunteers having been left as a garrison at Monclova. The command numbered about two thousand healthy and able-bodied men, inured to the climate, and familiar with privation, well appointed, and anxious to meet the enemy.

It may be proper here to remark, (for the purpose of avoiding repetitions) that in addition to my other duties, I was charged with the service of selecting and laying out encampments, and of assigning the troops to their ground. It therefore became necessary for me to precede the advance-guard of the army in every march, by several hours. On the evening of the 25th, the army encamped at a reservoir called *Bajan*, having marched twenty miles. We here found good water, plenty of fuel, and tolerable grazing. The road was good, passing over a wild and uncultivated country, with high mountains on either side. Our course was southwesterly. As we approached Bajan the ground became *marly*, the dust from which was very distressing to the men, who presented the appearance of having been sprinkled with dirty flour. As far as Bajan the roads to Monterey and Saltillo are common, but at this point they diverge. At Bajan is a large stone reservoir, filled with sweet water from a copious spring, and was formerly supplied with large stone troughs, for the accommodation of the muleteers; now in ruins.

On the 26th, the camp was broken up before day light, the army following the Saltillo road, which generally passes over an uncultivated and uninviting country, similar to that of yesterday's march. The men still complain of the effects of the calcareous marl, which injures their feet and eyes. We encamped at *La Joya*, or *Agua Nueva*, a fine large spring, where we also found a sufficiency of wood and grazing; the weather was oppressively hot. The direction of our march to-day was WSW.—distance fourteen miles.

On the 27th we reached the *Venadito,* and encamped on one of its numerous branches, after a most fatiguing march of thirty miles over a dusty road, and exposed to the intolerable heat of the sun. For the whole of this distance there is not a single drop of water, except a little in the Tanque San Fillipe, which was so putrescent that even the mules refused it. The infantry suffered greatly in this march, and came up in small squads. At the Tanque, about fifteen miles from the last camp, we left the main road, and changed our course more to the west, through an easy mountain pass. We were now fairly on the road to Parras.

The *Venadito* is a small stream rising near Patos, (see the map,) falls into the San Juan,* which, flowing past Monterey, discharges into the Rio Grande at Camargo.

There are several plantations near our camp, on which large quantities of maize are grown. The country also produces numerous herds of goats and cattle.

Between Castana and the Benedito, a distance of 66 miles, there is no settlement; we saw a few ruined ranchos, which had been destroyed by the Indians.

November 28.—Owing to the sufferings yesterday of the men and beasts, the general determined to remain on the Venedito, where we are comfortably encamped, with an abundant supply of water, fuel, forage, and grass.

It was observed quite early in the day that the stream was rapidly and mysteriously diminishing, and by noon there was scarcely any of it remaining. The General directed me to ascertain, if possible, the cause of this sudden disappearance. After consulting with several Mexicans at the hacienda, who all protested that they knew nothing about the matter, and suggested that the water had probably been drawn off, some 16 miles up the river, for the purpose of irrigating the wheat-fields. I proceeded up the stream about 2½ miles, when I discovered that the supply branch on which we were encamped had been dammed up, and a breach cut by which the water was diverted into another channel. I immediately destroyed the temporary dam, partially stopped the breach, and turned the stream back into its former bed, and then directed a gang of peons to complete the work; a guard was afterwards posted to prevent a recurrence of the mischief. There can be no doubt, judging from all the circumstances of the case, that the act was done with a malicious design.

---

*The drainage of the San Juan is very extensive; and its sources being high up in the Sierra Madre, the downfall-water is discharged into it from the mountain sheds with great rapidity, in consequence of which it often overflows its banks near the Rio Grande, inundating the town of Camargo in the rainy season. The country from Bajan, twenty miles beyond Parras, from Castanuela, Patos, and Agua Nueva, drains into the San Juan.

APPENDIX A

About four miles south of Bajan, a road diverges from the main road, and again unites with it near the hacienda of Benedito, passing though the "Boca de los Treize Rios," and is about 15 miles shorter than our line march, but is represented to be very rough and rocky.

November 29.—Left Benedito at daybreak, and marched to *Sanceda*, a distance of 16 miles. After leaving the hacienda Venedito (two miles beyond our camp) the country is poor, barren, and sandy, till we reach the hacienda of Sanceda, on the right bank of the river, which here takes the name of "Rio los Angelos," where the valley is broad, rich, and well cultivated, abounding in corn, cotton, and cattle. We encamped on the left bank of the stream near the intersection of the Parras road and a by-way to the hacienda near the mountain of "Los Angelos," between which and our camp there is a road from Monterey to Chihuahua. Our course to-day was south and southwest, the road being bounded on both sides by high mountains.

November 30.—Broke up our camp before sunrise; the general direction of the route was south 28° west. A march of six miles brought us to the forks of the road; the one leading to *San Antonio de Jarrol*, the other to *Tulia*, which is said to be the better one, but having an uncertain supply of water, in consequence of which we selected the San Antonio road. For some distance this route is a mere mule track, exhibiting no signs of having been recently traversed with wagons; it was in places very rough, and intersected with arroyos. At a distance of 13 miles we came, to the hacienda *Jarrol*, and three miles further brought us to *San Antonio de Jarrol*, both situated on the same stream with our two preceding encampments; it is here called the "Arroyo de San Antonio." We again encamped on the same stream, after a march of 16 miles.

The hacienda San Antonio de Jarrol is a very large corn plantation, which also produces some cotton and cattle. The Venedito valley is long, broad, fertile, and highly cultivated, but the road was confined to the high and arid country, covered with a growth of *cacti*—of which there is an infinite variety, many of them of great beauty—*artemisia*, equiseta, the *sortal* (from the large bulbous root of which an intoxicating liquor is distilled,) the maguey or agave Americana, from which the pulque and muscal (favorite Mexican drinks) are obtained; the *Spanish bayonet*, which is a large tree often twenty-eight feet high and three feet in diameter; the *yucca aloefolia* and the *lecheugillo*, a kind of dwarf bayonet, growing about eighteen inches high, and its leaves dentated like the sortal or saw-grass, and their extremities pointed like the Spanish bayonet. This plant furnishes the raw material for the mats, ropes, and gunny bags of the country. It is prepared by *rotting*, which destroys all of the leaf but the fibre, which is extremely strong.

The hacienda Florida is within sight, some eight miles off. To Patos is eighteen miles. The march to-day was nearly due south, but at this point the road turns nearly due west.

December 1.—Left camp at daybreak with the headquarters; but was soon sent ahead to look for an encampment, which we found at *La Pastora*, an "*estancia*" or cattle rancho, supplied with good water from a well about twenty feet deep within its enclosure. The camp was pitched about a mile from the estancia, partly on a running stream and partly on a reservoir, into which the water of the stream was collected for the use of cattle. The grazing was indifferent and fuel scant. The labores* here are exclusively devoted to the growth of wheat. The road from Tulio comes in at this point, passing through our camp. We marched to-day sixteen miles, over a dry and uncultivated country similar to that passed over yesterday, which may in fact be said of every day's march. The fuel generally consists of a small growth of *musquette*, of *huasaché*, (a true acacia,) and a species of *pseudo acacia*. On our march from Monclova we have occasionally seen the black-tailed deer; a large kind of hare, (the same I believe as that described by Townsend;) the prairie wolf, and a large black or dark-colored wolf; the American mocking bird, the paisano (described by Major McCall,) the quail (of the U.S.,) and a beautiful tufted dove-colored partridge. The cattle are of the same character as those mentioned in the memoir on San Antonio de Bexar; they make excellent draught oxen and good beeves. They have also an excellent breed of hogs in northern Mexico, which attain an immense size; they fatten easily, and their meat is remarkably sweet and nutritious. I think they resemble the China hog; their color is commonly a darkish blue.

December 2.—The march to-day was only eight miles, and the camp was pitched on both banks of the *Rio Tenago*, a beautiful full stream flowing rapidly over a pebbly bottom, after bursting its way through a rocky ledge, over which it falls in numerous cascades. It rises near Castanenala, where its waters are of a deep red, but the coloring matter is all deposited before reaching this place, and they become perfectly pelucid. At this point a small portion of the stream is drawn off to La Pastora, and the remainder is all absorbed by the labores.

In the rainy season it flows into the Venadito, (called also the San Antonio and the Los Angelos,) a tributary to the San Juan, the deep, *dry* bed of which we crossed on the 30th of November, about six miles south of Sauceda. When full it would be impassable for an army without bridging or boats.

At Tenago we found mournful evidence of the insecurity of life and property in this unhappy and distracted country. A few ruined ranchos showed that there had once been a settlement in this beautiful and secluded valley; but a few years since, as we were informed by a Mexican, a

---

*The word *labore*, in Mexico, means either a definite measure of land or a cultivated field.

band of Camanches made a descent on its peaceful and unoffending inhabitants, and slaughtered 120 in one single building, where they had huddled together like a flock of sheep scared by hungry and ferocious wolves. There is scarcely a mile of our march through Mexico that is not marked by the wooden cross and a pile of stones—sad memento, that on that spot some poor creature had met his fate at the hands of ruthless savages, or of his own countrymen, quite as merciless as the dreaded Camanches. On more than one occasion, when our small advance had been mistaken, in the distance, for a party of Indians—for such was the rapidity and silence of our progress that our presence was often a surprise—it was touching to see the women flee to the place where, perhaps, a father, a mother, or a husband had perished, and, clasping the cross in their arms, quietly await that martyrdom which sad experience had taught them to regard as inevitable.

On the 3d of December the army arrived early, after a march of twenty miles, at *Cienega* Grande, and encamped—Bonneville's battalion, the advance, having started at 2 o'clock in the morning to avoid the excessive heat of the sun. The road was very rough and difficult for wagons and artillery.

Cienega Grande is situated on the main road from the Rio Grande, via Camargo, Monterey, Saltillo, and Parras, to Chihuahua and Durango. It is a large and valuable estate, producing wheat, corn cotton, horses and cattle; which has been reclaimed, as its name (*Big Marsh*) implies, from an extensive swamp or shallow lake.

The next day we marched eighteen miles and encamped on low ground, with good water and grass convenient, near the hacienda of San Lorenzo de Obaja. This is the most magnificent and lordly establishment we have yet seen. It is picturesquely situated on a lovely stream of water, surrounded by its alamedas or pleasure grounds, through which the water has been diverted, with long avenues of trees leading up to it from different directions. It is quadrangular in shape, about 500 feet by 300 feet deep, divided by a cross building into two large courts. The exterior aspect is very imposing, with its white surface and turrets on each angle, loop-holed for defence, which lend to it quite a castellated appearance. Its interior arrangements and decorations are very rich, in keeping with the exterior. The floors are formed of cement brought to a perfectly smooth surface, polished and colored, and the walls are painted in fresco. The population of this hacienda, including the surrounding houses, is about 800, the most of whom are peons. The intelligent and hospitable proprietors of this vast establishment were educated at Bardstown, in Kentucky, and appear to entertain most lively and agreeable recollections of the country in which they passed their boyish days. They have imported machinery from the United States for their mills, cotton gins, and prizes; and in no part of the world have I seen better farming arrangements—everything is convenient, sightly, comfortable, and efficient. This estate is of immense extent, but of course much of it is not arable, and is valuable only for the rearing of stock. The cultivated land is devoted to the growth of corn, wheat, cotton, and fruits, and to the production of wine and brandy from the grape, and is justly regarded as one of the most celebrated vineyards in Mexico. The wines are of three kinds—the *carlone,* the *vino blanco,* and the *dulce*: the first is a kind of *claret Burgundy,* very delicate and palatable; the second is a species of *Malaga Madeira*; and the third resembles the *muscadel.* They are all pure juice of the grape, and the better kinds, which, when old, give an agreeable aroma, are formed from the natural expression of juice without the application of artificial force. The ordinary kinds are trodden out by naked men in vats. The brandy, "aqua de vide," resulting from the distillation of the wine, is also a very pure liquor; and if the art of rectification or separating the essential oils was well understood, would no doubt rival the best French brandies. This region of the country, the soil of which appears to be calcareous, intermixed with the debris of the slates, may truly be called the land of "corn, of the olive, and the vine." Its climate is salubrious, mild, and equable, and is exempt from the visitation of the northers; and is by far the most agreeable and attractive portion of Mexico that we have yet seen. I regret that my short and interrupted visit to it did not permit me to institute those minute statistical, geographical, and economical researches which I had proposed to myself; but the commanding general will readily understand the reasons to which I allude. Corn sells $2 50 the fanega, (not quite three bushels;) flour $9 the cargo, (of 300 pounds;) beef four cents the pound; wine $1 the gallon, and brandy seventy-five cents.

The Messrs. Yvarras have attempted, but without success, to substitute our agricultural implements for the crude and primitive implements in use. The peons cannot or will not employ them, and, with their characteristic tenacity and aversion to change of habits, obstinately, adhere to the rude cart, whose clumsy wheels are formed of segments of hard wood fastened together with trenails and bound with thongs of cow-hide, to which the oxen are harnessed, drawing by the horns; and a plough made of a crooked piece of wood, iron pointed, which simply scratches over the surface of the ground.

From San Lorenzo to Parras is about five miles. On the 5th December we occupied a position half way between the hacienda and the town. The camp was pitched on a charming plain, watered by numerous springs, facing the town, with the high and magnificent peaks of the Sierra Madre towering in our front, at the very base of which, and occupying the first acclivity of its slopes, is built the lovely town of Parras—a collection of haciendas, perhaps it may be termed, rather than a city, for the vineyards and gardens separate the houses from each other, except on the principal streets. The water, gathered from the recesses of the mountains, and stored on its terraces in large stone reservoirs, is, after irrigating the vineyards, permitted to descend in cascades and numerous brooks to the lower town, all of whose streets it washes.

APPENDIX A 263

Parras and its dependencies are said to contain a population of fifteen thousand souls, but I regard this as an exaggerated estimate. Its inhabitants are industrious, sober, thrifty, intelligent, and unfriendly to the present form of their government. From them we experienced nothing but kindness and hospitality. The great mass of the people, including the better class, uniformly exhibited towards us the most amiable deportment, and carefully guarded and attended on our sick, who were necessarily left behind when the army left, protected only by a single company, which was ordered off in a few days afterward. Our camp was constantly crowded with the beauty and fashion of the town, who visited the tents of the officers without hesitation or restraint, and the most cordial feelings and intercourse were established between us. This was the pleasant result of the good conduct of the troops, the largest portion of which were volunteers, and shows what may be made of them by a proper course of discipline, stringent but kind. The town, in a military point of view, may be regarded as a large and strong fortress, easily defended against an assault, and capable of sustaining a protracted siege. But for the friendly disposition of the inhabitants, it might have given us some trouble.

Resumé of distances form Monclova to Parras, Mexico.

From Monclova to Castaña	10 miles.	
" Castaña to Bajan	20 "	
" Bajan to La Joya	14 "	(Agua Nueva.)
" La Joya to Venadito	32 "	
" Venadito to Sauceda	22 "	
" Sauceda to San Antonio	16 "	(De Jarral.)
" San Antonio to La Pastora	16 "	
" La Pastora to Tenajo	8 "	
" Tenajo to Cienega Grande	20 "	
" Cienega Grande to San Lorenzo	18 "	(De Abajo.)
" San Lorenzo to Parras	5 "	
Total	181 miles in eleven marches.	

The division of the army under the command of General Wool has thus marched, taking La Vaca as the starting point, more than seven hundred miles, transporting its supplies, medical stores, and munitions of war, with a celerity and success almost unexampled in the history of modern warfare; and the day after its arrival at Parras, it was, *in every respect*, in a condition to have resumed its line of march for an equal or still greater distance.*

---

*The 6th infantry, 1st dragoons, artillery and Arkansas cavalry, taking their respective points of departure, had marched, up to Parras, nearly two thousand miles.

Although it may seem foreign to the subject of my duties, I cannot refrain in this connexion from paying what I believe to be a well-merited tribute of respect to our quartermaster's and commissary's departments. Certainly no army in the field was ever better served, the evidence of which is seen in what I have just written. I may also, I trust, be permitted here to say, in the last official communication which I may address to you,† that in the discharge of the arduous and multifarious duties I have experienced from the commanding general nothing but kindness and liberality. Almost every suggestion, in the line of my duty, which I had the honor to make to him, was promptly met, and every possible facility extended for its successful execution. And besides this, I may venture to add that I was a daily witness of the zeal with which he exerted himself for the comfort of this army and the service of his country. It may not be inappropriate here to remark that all the inhabitants on our line of march remained quietly at their homes, in the undisturbed possession of their property: not a house, that I am aware of, was deserted, nor was there an outrage, to my knowledge, perpetrated on any of the people. Everything that was procured from the country, either for the use of the army or for the individual use of officers, was most liberally paid for, and persons and property on all occasions respected.

As I was absent on a reconnaissance towards Durango‡ when the army suddenly moved on Saltillo, I must refer to Lieutenant Sitgreaves, topographical engineers, for a descriptive memoir of that march. I rejoined headquarters at San Juan de la Vaqueria on the third day after the army left Parras, having found my way through the mountain passes.§

In closing this communication, there are many reflections in relation to the social, religious, commercial, and political conditions of the Mexican people, the government, and the character of the country we have recently traversed, which naturally force themselves on the mind; but want of present leisure prevents me from giving expression to them now. I write hurriedly, on board of a steamboat, with scarcely time to read what I have written, and I have therefore done but little more than to give you an almost literal transcript of my journal.

---

† Captain Hughes at this time had been detached, and ordered to proceed with General Worth to Vera Cruz.
‡ See memoir in relation to this exploration.
§ I struck the main road to Saltillo at Castañuela; but such had been the admirable manner in which the division has moved, that until I approached within three miles of the infantry camp under Colonel Churchill, there was no sign of troops having marched in that direction, with the exception of the camping grounds—not a broken wagon, or a dead animal, or a straggler was to be seen; and yet the infantry averaged for two days nearly forty miles a day.

APPENDIX A 265

MOUTH OF THE RIO GRANDE,
February 1, 1847.

SIR: Being detained at this place for the want of transports to convey us to our destination, I do not know that I can better employ my time than by attempting to supply, to some extent, the omissions and deficiencies of my previous memoir; but whether I shall accomplish it or not will depend on circumstances over which I can exercise no control.

It seems to me clearly the policy of the government to establish a line of military posts on "Woll's road," from San Antonio de Bexar to the ford on the Rio Grande, near Presidio, for the purpose of extending protection to the settlers and traders against robbers and the predatory Indian tribes. To carry out this plan effectually would require a regiment of mounted men, with its headquarters at San Antonio de Bexar, a post on the Quihé; another on the Leona, and the third on the Rio Grande, at the ford. These posts, with the exception of the one on the Rio Grande, might be withdrawn in a few years, as there can be no question that the protection which they would afford would be the means of rapidly settling the country with a population that would soon be able to defend itself. Beside this consideration, it must be obvious to even the most superficial observer that hostilities with the Comanches and Lipans, the most warlike of the native tribes, are neither remote nor contingent. I regard it as inevitable, and believe that we shall never establish cordial relations with them until they have been severely punished—an affair, by-the-by, not easy of accomplishment. A defeat in a contest with the United States would result in their precipitation upon the northern provinces of Mexico, which they would assuredly desolate—a consequence which we may deplore, but cannot avert.

A reference to my memoir, and accompanying maps, in relation to the march of General Wool's army from San Antonio to Santa Rosa, will show how well Western Texas is watered, and may convey some faint idea of the richness and beauty of the country embraced between the Rio San Antonio and the Nueces; beyond which latter river, until we approach the Rio Grande, it would be no great exaggeration to say that "'tis all barren." It is true that there are occasional narrow strips of rich land, but for the whole of that distance (64 miles) we crossed but one stream of running water.

All the rivers between San Antonio and the Nueces may be characterized as beautiful and noble streams of clear and excellent water, and many of them would afford an almost unlimited amount of water-power; I particularly refer to the San Antonio, the Medina, the Quihé, (perhaps below the settlement,) and the Leona, (nearly equal to the San Antonio.) The others are objectionable on account of their periodical floods. I know of no country better adapted to manufactures than western Texas, and there is perhaps no region of the world where wool can be grown at so low a rate, or where the necessaries of life may be produced so cheaply. The heat of the climate, it might be supposed, would deteriorate the quality of the fleece; but such I am told is not the case. The soil is calcareous, with small angular fragments of flinty pebbles scattered over it, the drift from the mountains deposited by a current flowing from south to north, the traces of which we saw at almost every step from the Guadalupe up to San Antonio; and no doubt they may be found beyond it, leading to their mountain sources. The country may be described as a rolling prairie, pretty well wooded, and, after leaving the Medina, eminently beautiful and picturesque, covered at most seasons of the year with a luxuriant growth of grass, and abounding with game. At almost every rod we started up herds of deer, and flocks of partridges and wild turkeys. The reverse of the picture is, that it abounds with venomous reptiles, snakes, scorpions, centipedes, and tarantulas. The latter are much dreaded, and regarded with more horror than any of the tribe. They are provided with fangs nearly as large as those of the rattlesnake, while they possess none of his magnanimity, or rather indolence of habit. The principal annoyances to travelers consist of innumerable crowds of *ticks* and *red bugs,* who fasten and prey upon him with instinctive avidity.

It is melancholy, in traversing this rich and beautiful country, so eminently fitted for the support of human life, to find it but one vast solitude, undisturbed save by some wary travellers or trader, who pursues his stealthy course at night, with the hope (often vain) of eluding the crafty savage, who looks out from his mountain home like an eagle from its eyrie, watching for his victim. But it requires only a slight effort of the imagination to fancy it peopled with an industrious and teeming population, its heights crowned with human habitations, its fertile valleys in cultivation, and its plains covered with bleating flocks and lowing herds. It remains but for the government to *will it,* and this picture will be realized. It involves simply the establishment of the line of posts which I have indicated to produce these beneficient results, for the natural advantages of the country could not fail to attract the attention of foreign immigrants, and of our own roving and adventurous countrymen.

The formation of the country is calcareous; the rocks, often rising, near the rivers, in high bluffs and isolated hills, intersected by *trap dikes.* This we particularly noticed on the Rio Frio. Near the Leona* I observed numerous small holes in the rocks, about one foot in diameter, and perfectly smooth and circular in shape. They were probably formed by the action of water. The country beyond the Rio Grande, between it and the Sabinos, is similar to that already described, but is neither so well wooded nor watered: it is nevertheless well calculated for the rearing of stock, for

---

*I can scarcely allow myself to speak of the beautiful river, and its rich and lovely valley, for the language of truth, when applied to it, must necessarily assume the appearance of fiction.

APPENDIX A

where the natural flow of water is deficient it may be supplied by wells; and there are large quantities of arable land abandoned for the want of labor, and in consequence of the insecurity of life and property. As we approach Santa Rosa, some ten miles beyond the Sabinos, a change is observed in the geological formation, and we are obviously entering upon a country of igneous origin. The rocks first seen are conglomerate, composed of angular fragmentary limestone, united with a calcareous cement; the whole being probably due to watery discharges from the now extinct volcanic craters.

At Santa Rosa we reach for the first time the *Sierra Gorda*—a subordinate chain of the great "Sierra Madre," or Mother Mountain. This range seems to be a continuation of that through which the Rio Grande bursts its way at the cañon below the mouth of the Rio Conchos, and which, sweeping in a curvelinear direction northeasterly, passing to the west of Santa Rosa, Monclova, Monterey, and Victoria, terminates near the mouth of Limon river, between Tampico and Vera Cruz, on the Gulf of Mexico. At Las Hermanas an inferior range diverges from it in the direction of Candela, and again unites with it near Monterey. It is very difficult, and indeed almost impossible, at present, accurately to define this great mountain chain;* but when our *ensemble* maps are compiled, we may be able to do so with considerable precision. We skirted its entire base from Santa Rosa to Monclova, at which point our examinations gave us a transverse line of more than one hundred miles through the mountain passes; and we actually crossed it in our march to Parras. Besides this, we have two lines of reconnaissance from Monclova to Monterey, one from Monterey to Saltillo, two from Saltillo to our line of march from Monclova to Parras, two between Parras and Saltillo, and two from Parras to Alamo de Parras. These, in addition to the explorations of topographical engineers with General Taylor's army, of the Rio Grande from its mouth to Camargo, and then to Monterey, from Monterey to Victoria, and thence to Tampico, and perhaps from Matamoras to Victoria, with General Patterson's command, will give us the means of satisfactorily determining the principal geographical features of northern Mexico. I also understand that examinations have recently been made of the Rio Grande from Camargo to a point some thirty miles above Presidio, which encourage the hope that this noble river may become navigable, with slight improvements, at certain seasons of the year, nearly as high up as the Conchos, and render it not improbable that steamboats may at no distant day ascend even to Chihuahua, to Paso del Norte, and to the vicinity

---

*The published maps of this portion of Mexico are absolutely *worse than useless*; and we were compelled to guess our way, step by step, as we could obtain no reliable information except by personal observation. Arista's manuscript map (captured at Resaca de la Palma) is tolerably accurate; but we did not obtain a sight of it till after our arrival at Saltillo.

of Santa Fe. This, however, is venturing on the field of speculation. The mountain at Santa Rosa is one unbroken chain for many leagues in extent, without one single pass or defile leading over it. The highest peaks rise to an altitude of nearly four thousand feet above the level of the plain, and it must at one time have been covered by the sea, and subsequently been elevated by some internal force. Dr. Long, an intelligent American, who has resided many years in this country, and has pretty thoroughly explored the mountains, informed me that he had found marine shells on the highest points. I regret that my engagements prevented me from examining any considerable portion of this interesting region. Along the base of the mountain, and rising directly from it, may be seen a range of conical hills about five hundred feet high, of a nearly uniform shape and size. It is in these hills that the silver lodes mentioned in a previous memoir are found. Running out nearly perpendicularly from the main range are a series of tubular hills, varying from one hundred to three hundred feet in elevation, presenting to the eye the appearance of a perfect level on the top, with regular sides and truncated extremities. They are constituted generally of basaltic rocks, and are covered with a luxuriant growth of grass; but some less regular in figure are composed of lavas and volcanic ashes. We lose sight of these peculiarities near Hermanas, and the mountains assume the form of vast buttresses separated by narrow defiles, leading high up into and often through them—such as are described in the memoir.

Beyond Monclova the mountains are composed of a mass of white marly altered limestone, showing the action of heat upon it under pressure. The same formation was observed at Monterey and Saltillo. Where the mountain sides have been abraded by the rains, they exhibit the appearance of white stripes from top to bottom. I regret that it is not in my power to communicate more satisfactory information in relation to the geology of this unexplored and almost unknown country; but my official duties greatly interfere with such researches.

The finest agricultural region in Coahuila is in the vicinity of Santa Rosa; but owing to the want of laborers, and to the depredations of the Indians, a very large proportion of the arable land is left uncultivated, and for the same reason the rich silver mines—the most valuable, probably, in Mexico—abandoned. While much of the surface of this State is sterile, and large quantities of it unfit for cultivation, owing to the want of water for purposes of irrigation, (for, in consequence of the long droughts, no land can be tilled without it,) there are extensive tracts of arable soil still in its primitive and virgin condition, which, under a better and more paternal government—one capable and willing to protect life and property—might be rendered highly productive, for in few parts of the world does nature more liberally reward labor judiciously applied.

APPENDIX A

Nothing can be imagined, in a country pretending to be civilized, so inefficient, despotic, capricious, and oppressive as the government of the (so called) Mexican republic. It matters not who is in power, the result is the same. It not only extends no protection to its citizens, but it absolutely forbids them the use of arms for their own defence, and deprives them of them by unceremonious domiciliary visits; they are forbidden to possess them without a special license; exactions are imposed on them in every form that human ingenuity can invent; and, in one word, the government is known only by its malign influence, and felt only by its oppression. When the inhabitants of Alamo de Parras invoked the interposition, against the depredations of the Indians, of General Raez, who commanded a large force at San Miguel, he returned them the pious answer, that "he hoped God would protect and bless them, but that he could not move from San Miguel"—a benediction (which if not a coldblooded mockery) more becoming a bishop than a soldier. It is a fact that the only security which the people of Coahuila had felt for many months was after our arrival, and in the presence of our troops; and it was only during our march and occupation of the country that they could venture to travel a few miles from their own homes with the assurance that the next chaparral did not conceal the lurking savage or the merciless bandit—both alike seeking his life and property.

The system of *peonage,* or domestic slavery, keeps in bondage at least *four-fifths* of northern Mexico. No system of slavery can be more harsh and degrading, for it carries with it none of those kindly sympathies and early associations which so often alleviate it in the United States. Peons are persons sold for debt, and it rarely happens that one is ever redeemed from bondage till old age renders him useless to his owner, who then charitably permits him to beg for the remnant of his life. The only appearance of liberty which he enjoys, is that of selecting a master who may choose to buy him from his owner by paying the claim against him, which, when tendered, (with the consent of the slave,) he is compelled by law to accept as a discharge of the obligation. The poor peon lives in a miserable mud hovel or reed hut, (sometimes built of cornstalks, thatched with grass.) He is allowed a peck of corn a week for his subsistence, and a small monthly pay for his clothes; but as all his purchases are made from his master, each year generally finds him still deeper in debt, for the payment of which he at last pledges all he possesses—*his children!* and they are bound for the parent till they are legally capable of incurring debts of their own, and become eligible to a state of slavery on their own account. And yet Mexico calls herself a free country!

The State of Coahuila is bounded on the east by Tamaulipas and the Rio Grande, on the north by the Rio Grande and Chihuahua, on the west by Chihuahua, and on the south by Chihuahua, Durango, and New Leon.

It contains about 193,000 square miles, with a population of only 125,000, or not quite one and a half to the square mile. Two-thirds of its surface is a level plain, and the remainder consists of mountains and warm, fertile valleys. Its principal rivers are the Rio Grande, the Alamo, the Sabinos, the Salado, and the San Juan, of which the first is alone navigable for any considerable distance. Its chief towns are Santa Rosa, Monclova, Parras, and Saltillo—the latter being the seat of government. It is situated in latitude 25° 25' 30" north, and longitude 101° 1' 45" west of Greenwich, on one of the numerous tributaries to the San Juan. It contains about 11,000 inhabitants, is a cleanly, well-built, well-paved, and well-watered town, and is the ecclesiastical as well as political capital. The cathedral, facing the main plaza, is a large and imposing stone structure, of a mixed order of architecture, the Arabesque predominating, with a richly ornate facade of cut stone, *painted* with various colors. The plaza is extensive, and the buildings on it generally two stories high, with balconies or porticoes. I think I can recognise in the domestic architecture of the cities an intimate blending of the Mexican, the Moorish, and the Flemish—the two last having been imported by the Spaniards, and engrafted on the original Aztec style. Directly fronting the cathedral is a beautiful and copious fountain, at which the female peons, in their picturesque costumes, may be seen at all hours of the day drawing water, and chatting with the characteristic volubility of the country; for most Mexicans, unlike the Spaniards, are inveterate talkers. Saltillo is a place of considerable trade, and is the seat of the only manufactories of which Coahuila can boast. These establishments are represented to be in a very flourishing condition, paying high wages to the employes, and large dividends to the stockholders. The city is not defensible, being situated in a valley which is commanded on three sides. The true battle field for its defence in front is just beyond the hacienda of San Juan de Buena Vista, about four miles beyond the town. On this approach is a narrow defile occupied by the road, on the right hand of which rises a high bluff hill, and on the left is a wide, deep, and almost impassable arroyo. This pass may be completely swept by a converging fire of artillery, and can be turned only by light infantry on the one hand, while on the other side of the ravine, (in which is a running stream of water,) no troops can pass without exposing their flank to the artillery within point blank range. To occupy the whole valley would demand about 4,000 men of all arms, with powerful batteries of field artillery, and it would probably require some 1,500 more to hold the town, protect the depôts and guard the passes. These forces could defend Saltillo in that direction from overwhelming numbers and superior guns. The true position for the defence of the city in the rear, from the direction of Monterey, is at *Los Muertos,* thirty miles distant, one of the strongest mountain gorges I have ever seen. It is in fact the portal to the whole interior country. The Mexicans seem to have contemplated making a stand at this place after the termination of the armistice, and had half constructed several strong works which were calculated to command all the approaches within the reach of their guns. Why they should have abandoned this apparently impregnable post is still "a marvel and a mystery," unless we may venture to suppose that the known presence of a large column at Monclova, which might have taken them in reverse, impressed them with the idea that the forward movement of that division would render their position untenable, and jeopard the safety of their army.

More than half of the whole State of Coahuila belongs to the two brothers *Sanchez*, who also own some thirty thousand peons. Several of their vast estates are managed by stewards, while the remainder are rented. Their principal town residence is in Saltillo, but their favorite country seat is the magnificent hacienda of Patos. This powerful family, together with their relations, the Blancos, the Yvarros, and the Zualagos, own nearly the entire State and *its population*. They have taken no open or active part in the present war, and have preserved friendly and even kindly relations with many of our officers; but the Blancos and Sanchezes are understood to be prepared, under more promising circumstances, to uphold the Mexican government with their wealth and influence.* Nearly all our expenditures for supplies have found their way directly or indirectly into the coffers of these princely nabobs.

Except for the education of the clergy, there are no seminaries of learning deserving of the name in Coahuila; but there is an ecclesiastical college in Saltillo of some reputation, but the course of instruction sedulously excludes everything approaching to science, and is confined to the classics and to the reading of the Fathers. The consequence of this state of things is, that by far the greater portion of the population are plunged into the most profound ignorance, and can neither read nor write. Many of the better class were formerly sent to the United States to be educated, but for some years this plan has been abandoned, and they are now sent for that purpose to France and to the city of Mexico.

Four-fifths of the population of northern Mexico are of the aboriginal race, (pure, or mixed in different degrees with Spanish blood), the lineal descendants of the once powerful Aztec monarchy. In habits, costumes, mode of life, wants, and civilization, they have probably changed but little, with the exception of the abandonment of their barbarous sacrificial rites, since the conquest, and they retain even much of their original language. They are a good-looking people, and while one seldom sees a very large man amongst them, they are certainly a well-made, agile, and mus-

---

*This they have since done. One of the Sanchezes was with Miñon at the capture of Major Gaines, at Encarnacion, and gave him information of that movement. Colonel Blanco raised a large Mexican force of rancheros, and threw himself in the rear of Saltillo to cut off our retreat.

cular race, (which we have been in the custom of underrating) of abstemious habits, and of great powers of endurance, on foot or on horseback. They are scarcely equalled as couriers, and are unsurpassed in marching. It may seem a paradox to say that they possess much *boldness* and little *courage*; they would venture where other men would hesitate, and yet would offer but faint resistance when danger is upon them. Hence it is that they so often fall victims to the Indians.

Fancy to yourself a rather light-colored Indian, dressed in a pair of leather unmentionables, without suspenders, buttoning from the knee downwards, which are usually left open in warm weather for comfort, and to exhibit the white drawers underneath; a common cotton shirt, often wanting; a red sash tied tightly around the waist; a pair of sandals on his feet, and enormous iron spurs on heel; with a heavy conical felt hat (that would almost resist a sabre cut) on head, and a long iron-pointed aspen goad in hand, and you have a perfect picture of the ranchero, or rather vachero. Mounted on a spirited pony, with a lasso at his saddle-bow, and he is no mean adversary for a single man to encounter. He rides well and fearlessly, and throws the lasso with unerring aim. It is a beautiful sight to see him with his red blanket (worn as a poncho in cold weather) streaming in the wind, his head bent eagerly forward, and lasso whirling in circles high in air, riding down some refractory animal that he seldom fails to catch, at the first throw, by the neck or hind foot, bringing him violently to the ground. The animal thus caught feels that the contest is ended, and quietly submits to its captor. It is amusing to see the young urchins following the example of their elders, and practising on little pigs and tender kids, who by no means appear to enjoy the fun. It verifies the old fable of the "boys and frogs." It may be sport to the one party, but is often death to the other. Every Mexican, whatever his condition may be, is expert with the lasso, and the throwing of it may be regarded as a national amusement. One of our men became intoxicated at the hacienda of Lorenzo, near Parras, and was in the act of raising his carbine to shoot Don Manuel, its amiable and accomplished proprietor, who, quick as thought, threw the noose over him and pinioned him by the arms, when our stalwart Arkansas cavalier became as meek and quiet as a lamb.

The wealthier classes dress very much in the same style, but of richer fabrics, their buttons being usually of silver, and they are particularly ostentatious in their saddles and housings, which are often overloaded with heavy silver ornaments. They are also very curious in the color and patterns of their blankets and the materials of their cloaks.

The women are rather under what we regard as the medium size, slight in figure, well-formed, and graceful; and while few are beautiful, many of them, while young, are good-looking and agreeable; their hands and feet are small, with well turned ankles; they have generally white

APPENDIX A 273

teeth, good mouths, magnificent black eyes, and glossy black hair, in the dressing of which they daily bestow much pains. They appear to be amiable and kind-hearted, and are said to make good wives and mothers. They are cleanly in their habits; for, most of the towns and haciendas being situated on running streams, they have every advantage for bathing, of which they avail themselves most liberally, without encumbering themselves with much superfluous clothing. Their usual dress consists of thin slippers, without stockings, a cloth petticoat, usually red, and a chemise which exposes more of the person than is in most countries considered to be consistent with a due regard to modesty; but this is the custom of the country, and I am not disposed to criticise it; with a rosary around the neck, and gold ear-rings, and you have the female costume complete. When they go abroad the reboso is generally worn either over the head, concealing the greater portion of the face, or over the shoulders, like a shawl. It is worn by all Mexican women; its quality depending on the condition of the wearer. To their ordinary domestic duties they add the weaving of rebosos and blankets; the latter are worn by the men as an outer covering, and is literally "a bed by night, a garment all the day." Many of them are of fine texture, and of great beauty of figure and color. Their prices vary from $3 to $75, and even to $100. Many of the better class of females are well-educated and accomplished ladies, who would grace the saloons of the most polished capital. The town of Mier is celebrated all over the republic for the beauty of its blankets.

Mexican cookery is, to my taste, *detestable*; but many Americans, less fastidious perhaps, affect to like it. Everything is rendered as hot as fire by *red pepper*, which enters in enormous quantities into each dish as an essential ingredient. The favorite dish in Mexico is the frijoles (friholes,) which is universally brought on the table as a *bonne bouche*. It consists of small, brown, black-eyed beans, boiled for six or eight hours in soft water, and then mixed with melted lard and salt. It is, when thus cooked, a very agreeable vegetable. Another article of food, and almost as great a favorite, is the tortilla. It is prepared by boiling maize in a pretty strong ley (of ashes,) which separates the husk. It is afterwards washed in clean cold water till all the impurities are removed, and it is then mashed (for I know not how better to express it) on a short stone table, placed in an inclined position, with a stone *rolling-pin*, till it is ground into a soft, plastic paste. A woman then, wetting her hands, (it is to be hoped that they have been previously well washed,) takes up a small portion of the dough, and by dexterously shifting it from one hand to the other, patting it at the same time, (and producing a loud noise,) soon brings it to the required consistency, shape, and size. It is then baked on a griddle, and taken hot to the table, where it serves the triple purposes of bread, forks, and spoons. With butter, it would no doubt make a palatable bread; but in

Mexico no butter can be found, except in the houses of foreigners. It is even extremely difficult to procure *cow's* milk, notwithstanding their numerous herds, and goat's milk is generally used; but that cannot be always obtained, and is not fit for use till it has been boiled. We succeeded occasionally in obtaining *curds* at some of the haciendas. In no portion of the world have I seen better wheat bread, cakes, or confectionary. The Mexicans are peculiarly skilful in the preparation of fruits and confectionary.

The wealthier classes live in a style of great luxury, and I have seldom partaken of more elegant and sumptuous entertainments than at their hospitable boards. The services of china and silver are beautiful and rich, while the courses follow each other in rapid succession; and the tables groan with a profusion of meats, fruits, confectionary, and wines, piled upon them. A gentleman, whose curiosity once induced him to count the courses at a dinner, assured me that they exceeded twenty in number.

During my short stay at Saltillo, I had an opportunity of witnessing their burial rites. A young lady of great beauty, whose loss was deeply deplored, had recently died, and an immense concourse of people attended the funeral solemnities. The deceased was dressed in white, with white satin slippers on her feet, her head decked with garlands, her raven locks gracefully disposed over her shoulders, her hands crossed in front, and holding a large bouquet of flowers: thus adorned, "like a bride awaiting her bridegroom," she was placed on a white couch, also trimmed with flowers, and surmounted with a canopy of satin, roses, and feathers. On this bier the mortal remains of the poor young girl, beautiful even in death, were paraded, feet foremost, through the principal streets of the city, and around the main plaza, exposed to the wondering stare of curious strangers. The procession was headed by three priests, dressed in the rich vestments of their order, chanting prayers for the deceased, the chanting being accompanied by three violins; others carried banners and crosses; incense was burnt; four men in clerical costume bore the bier on their shoulders, and then followed the mourners, friends, and relations of the deceased; the whole being preceded by a band of music, while the bells of the Cathedral tolled mournfully. The ceremonies within the church were not different from those of the Roman Catholic religion in other countries.

The Mexicans have been often represented as a subtle, treacherous, and cruel race, in whom no reliance can be placed with safety. This may be so; but if I should speak of them from personal observation alone, I should say that they are naturally hospitable, kind-hearted, and amiable. In their manners they are extremely courteous, and the most civil people I have ever known. My duties generally carried me in advance of the army—sometimes several days ahead, and often to considerable distances with small escorts. On one occasion, being unwell, I remained over night in a town of 1,400 inhabitants, without a soldier within eight miles of me;

APPENDIX A 275

and another time, I was fifty miles distant from the camp, with only three dragoons as a guard; and yet at no time did I feel the slightest apprehension for my safety, nor have I any reason to suspect that my confidence was misplaced. Wherever I went, whether to the princely hacienda or the humble rancho, I was treated with kindness and hospitality; and I must confess that the impression made upon me was greatly in their favor. With a better and wiser form of government—one able and willing to destroy their miserable system of *peonage*, to insure the liberty of the press, educate and liberalize the people, and develop the resources of the country—cannot doubt that they would rise high in the scale of civilization. It is true, that while they possess many of the virtues, they exhibit also many of the vices of an ignorant and half-barbarous people. We have recently often heard of deeds of extreme cruelty perpetrated by them on the Rio Grande; but it remains to be seen how far they were acts of retaliation, provoked (but not justified) by the outrages they have endured. From Saltillo to Mier, with the exception of the large towns, all is a desert, and there is scarcely a solitary house (if there be one) inhabited. The smiling villages which welcomed our troops on their upward march are now black and smouldering ruins, the gardens and orange groves destroyed, and the inhabitants, who administered to their necessities, have sought refuge in the mountains. The march of Attila was not more withering and destructive. It is but an act of justice to General Taylor to say that he did everything in his power to prevent these excesses, and that they were principally committed by some of the quartermaster's men, who, until they were taught to the contrary by the strong arm of power, did not consider themselves as being amenable to martial or any other law; and by desperate adventurers, called by the army "outsiders," who followed the army for plunder, and frequently organized themselves into bands to carry on their depredations, not being very particular as to whether they robbed Mexicans or their own countrymen. They emphatically "made war on their own hook." Many of these miscreants were sent home by General Taylor, and every possible precaution was taken to prevent their entrance into Mexico. Many of their misdeeds came under my personal observation, but the difficulty was to identify the individual. In general, the troops behaved with great forbearance and humanity.

In the northern provinces of Mexico there is a strong feeling in favor of a federal, and in decided opposition to a central form of government. This is the instinctive result of a sense of self-preservation, for these people are not prone to indulge in abstract speculations. As there may be said to be no government many miles beyond the city of Mexico, they feel that, while they bear more than a just proportion of the burdens of the state, they receive none of its fostering care or paternal protection. The Federalists are called the American, and the Centralists the Mexican party. The former have been in favor either of becoming an integral portion of our Union, or an independent republic, under our protection and guarantee. How far this would *now* be practicable or desirable, is a question for the politician to settle: the trade of which the joint right of navigating the Rio Grande would give us almost the exclusive advantage, and the introduction of American machinery, to be paid for in the precious metals, might be a matter of some consequence. With the slightest encouragement during the last summer, the whole State of Coahuila would have pronounced against the existing government of Mexico.

Very truly, your obedient servant,

GEO. W. HUGHES.

To Colonel J. J. ABERT,
Chief Topographical Engineers,

CAMP NEAR MONCLOVA,
Mexico, November 14, 1846.

SIR: Having completed the reconnaissance of the country from Monclova to Quatro Cienegas, (and its vicinity,) on the route to Chihuahua, I have now the honor to submit to the commanding general, in addition to my short communication of the 12th instant, the following descriptive memoir, and accompanying topographical map, of the country embraced in the general's instructions of the 6th instant.

Owing to circumstances not necessary to mention, our first day's march (the 7th of November) terminated at the hacienda of Pozuelos. We left the plaza of Monclova by the main road to Monterey and Saltillo, but soon after quitting the city turned suddenly to the right, skirting the base of a high mountain range to our south, and leaving a series of hills of variable heights to the north. Our course was nearly due west, over a wild and barren region, for several miles, when we entered upon a wide and pretty valley, which, at a distance of nine miles from the city, brought us to the hacienda de Pozuelos, or the *hot well,* an artificial excavation some forty feet deep, which discharges a large volume of hot water, very palatable when it has been allowed to cool. This well irrigates two large plantations, which nearly exhaust the supply—the surplus being lost in the swamps near Nadadores.

A mule track to Saltillo diverges from this well, as is shown on the map. Our first encampment was at the base of a high chain of mountains, which apparently blocked our further progress in that direction; but by pursuing a circuitous course bearing from NW. to SW. through the highlands, we reached, at a distance of eleven miles by a good road, the San Pedro spring, the source of a large creek flowing in a northwesterly direction down the valley of the Sacramento, which we followed for about three miles to La Villa Nueva, a small and modern town of four hundred

APPENDIX A

and fifty inhabitants. In this quiet and secluded valley we saw the first appearance of improvement since our entrance upon Mexican soil. Within a few miles of each other, two new and respectable looking towns have recently sprung into existence, and many acres of rich but waste lands have been brought into successful cultivation. Here there are no wealthy proprietors nor lordly haciendas to please the eye with their immense proportions, but, what was more gratifying to an American, small, neat tenements, occupied by the owners and tillers of the soil. This valley was covered for miles with fields of maize and cotton, but it is so difficult to obtain authentic statistical information, that I am unable to state the amount of their production.

From Villa Nueva, a course of N. 85 W. brought us, over a distance of eight miles across the valley, to a remarkable mountain pass called el Puerto del Sacramento. It is about three hundred yards wide, the mountain rising almost vertically to an altitude of nearly 2,000 feet, and a huge rock directly in the pass gives it the appearance of a gigantic propylon of some vast temple. The road follows up this gorge, (through which flows a large and rapid stream, called the San Juan, that rises west of Cienegas,) for about six miles, where the mountains widen out, leaving between them a broad an most lovely valley, at the lower end of which is built the hacienda of San Juan. There is not a mile of this pass that does not offer a strong position for defence; but the most formidable is at the upper outlet of the gorge, where it is scarcely two hundred and fifty yards wide, with huge and inaccessible mountains rising almost perpendicularly from its two extremities, while the ground slopes down the pass as evenly as a glacis. As far as I could ascertain, it would be difficult to turn this position if occupied by an enemy.

To the south of the hacienda there are extensive salt ponds, which render the running water rather brackish, and probably impregnate them with sulphate of magnesia.

From the hacienda, a ride along the mountain on the north of the valley for twelve miles in a direction a little south of west brought us to the town of Quatro Cienegas, situated in the midst of this upland valley. For about eight miles the land, though rich and easily irrigated, is left uncultivated, and produces only a luxuriant growth of tall, wild grass.

The town of Cienegas contains, according to the last census, 1,428 inhabitants, or, including its dependencies (of St. Catarina, Rosarios, and Villa del Sacramento) subject to the jurisdiction of the alcalde, 2,682. The people of this district are distinguished for their industry, sobriety, and attachment to their religion. In politics, unlike the citizens of Monclova, they are mostly federalists, and unfriendly to the ruling powers of Mexico. We found them, as they had been represented, favorably inclined to our government and its institutions. To us, individually, they were unbounded in their kindness and hospitality. For miles around the town the land is cultivated like a garden, and produces the great staples of wheat and cotton in abundance. The grape vine is also reared successfully in large vineyards, and furnishes both a red and white wine of tolerable quality. The first is said to be good, but we saw it only in a dried state. It yields by distillation a pure, but not agreeably flavored brandy, called aguardiénte. The maguey, (*agave Americana,*) growing sometimes to the height of forty feet, is planted for its pulque. Peaches, figs, melons, and pecans find here a congenial soil and propitious climate.

Nothing can be more enchanting to the sight than this broad and lovely valley, intersected in every direction by streams of running water, surrounded on every side by lofty mountains, impassable except through a few narrow chasms just wide enough to admit the roads and the rushing brooks whose waters are gathered within their recesses. I looked down upon the scene from an eminence, and could but liken it to the Happy Valley of Rasselas.

There are two grist-mills near Cienegas, and two cotton-gins (of American manufacture,) all driven by water-power. The buildings are large, well proportioned, and imposing in appearance; but the machinery of the grist-mills is of the most simple and primitive construction. The shaft is vertical, with a tub-wheel attached to the lower extremity, and the upper millstone to the top. The nether-stone is fixed in the floor, above the pit, and the shaft revolves inside of it, carrying with it the upper stone. The wheat (which in Mexico is always washed and dried before grinding) is taken in sacks, and thrown into a hopper, from which it descends between the stones, and is ground into flour. These mills are unprovided with bolting apparatus, as the flour and bran are not separated for ordinary use. When white bread is baked, (and the best in the world is made in Mexico,) the flour is sifted by hand. The mechanic arts have made but little progress in Mexico, and labor-saving machinery, for ordinary purposes, is almost unknown. Their tools, carts, and agricultural implements are of the rudest description, and are obviously literal copies of their original models. The type of their mode of harnessing and driving oxen, and the form of their carts and ploughs, may be found in the Egyptian drawings and bas-relief. By changing their seed-grain, and introducing the best American system of agriculture, I have no doubt that, with their natural advantages of soil, climate, and means of irrigation, the crops in this portion of Mexico might be more than doubled. At present they never till the earth to a greater depth than three inches; and this has been their system from the beginning. The markets for this district are Monterey, Saltillo, San Luis Potosi, and Chihuahua. Clear cotton is worth here from $5 to $6 the cargo of 300 lbs., and flour $7. Very little maize is grown here; but in the Sacramento it sells for $1.50 to $2 the fanega—a

APPENDIX A

little short of three bushels. There are no mines in the vicinity, and no manufactures except those already mentioned.

The roads leading from Cienegas are, 1st, to Monclova, the route we travelled; 2d, to Saltillo, by a mule track, ninety miles; 3d, to Parras, one hundred and eighty miles, by a good cart road, but the deficiency of water for a long distance has caused it to be in a great measure abandoned; 4th, to Sta. Catarina, by a good wagon road, will watered.

St. Catarina, a small hamlet of four hundred and sixteen inhabitants, is situated at the foot of an elevated plateau called the Bolson de Mappimí, about 30 miles N. 80 W. of Cienegas. The road passes alternately through mountain defiles and narrow valleys.

In the mountains between Cienegas and Sta. Catarina there are very extensive forests of white pine and oaks of different kinds, growing to an immense size. The route to Chihuahua passes through St. Catarina; and it is here the real difficulties begin. For at least ninety miles there is no water, except in the rainy season; and several persons who have recently traversed the Bolson de Mapimi unite in saying that the present season is unusually dry, and that the water, which is sometimes to be found in holes, has entirely disappeared. There is only a mule track, and no wagon road, in this direction, after leaving St. Catarina. A Mexican cart has been driven over this line; but it was found necessary often to shift the load, and even to take the carts to pieces, owing to the abrupt and broken nature of the country.

From Agua Chile to Chihuahua the road is said to be excellent; but there is a deficiency of water to Sta. Rosalia, from whence there is an abundance of everything necessary for the subsistence of troops to Chihuahua. Supposing the representation to be true, (and I have no reason to doubt them,) the natural inference is, the route is impassable for artillery, infantry, and the wagon train. Dragoons mounted on mules, and taking with them pack-mules to carry water, could no doubt effect a passage by this route; but I should consider it to be a most hazardous undertaking to attempt it with any other arm of the service.

Having executed, as far as practicable, the instructions of the commanding general, I returned with the escort as far as the Puerto del Sacramento over our former route, and from thence diverged through the valley of Ranchos Nuevos to the outlet of the Sacramento, in a direction nearly N. 80 E., across the valley. At this point the San Pedro, the San Juan, and the Sacramento creeks unite, forming a large and rapid stream, called the Nadadores, flowing into the Rio Monclova near the Hacienda Las Hermanas, where the junction of the two produces the Rio Salado. This latter river soon afterwards unites with the Sabinos—retaining, however, its original name—and finally discharges its waters into the Rio Grande at Revilla, or Gueresa, as it is sometimes called on the maps.

The pass above mentioned is similar to those already described, the road and the creek occupying nearly the whole of the defile, while the mountain rises suddenly to the height of probably fifteen hundred feet. There are several large caves in the rocks, from which saltpetre is obtained. This defile is about six miles long, and terminates at the rancho Leco. We had now left the mountains, and descended into the plains of Monclova. The road from the rancho soon brought us to a large and new hacienda belonging to Señor Gonzales; and six miles farther, in a nearly straight road, to the town of Nadadores, containing about eight hundred inhabitants. Before reaching this town we passed over a low but very rich country, much of which has been recently drained and cultivated. The position of the village is flat and unhealthy. San Juan Buenaventura lies about three miles off to the north. There is a great deal of corn, cotton, and wheat growing in the neighborhood of this town. Near San Juan is a grist-mill and cotton-gin, driven by water-power; and there is another grist-mill on a stream called the Sta. Gertrudes, about four and a half miles from San Juan.

From Nadadores to Monclova is about sixteen miles in a southeasterly direction; the road is good, and much of the land in a high state of cultivation. The inhabitants of this village are not very favorably disposed towards us; but many gentlemen of wealth and intelligence are bitterly averse to their present form of government. One of them, who had been in the United States, said to me with great emphasis: "Sir, we have a glorious country, and a good population; but our government is the worst in the world. I would rather be under the dominion of a Comanche chief." The great scourge of this country, which I have attempted to describe in these papers, after its government, is to be found in the sudden irruptions of the Indian tribes—the Lipans, the Mescaleros, and the Comanches—the most treacherous and ruthless of our nomadic races. On our return we found the country in alarm. Couriers had been sent to all the small villages to say that a party of three hundred warriors had passed through the mountains near Santa Rosa, and was descending upon the upland villages, by the way of Santa Catarina. We saw nothing of the Indians, but heard of their being on our trail. So bold are they, or so little do they respect their Mexican neighbors, that a few of them will not hesitate to ride into towns of the size of Cienegas, and lay them under contribution.

I was escorted on this tour of duty by Captain Porter's company of Arkansas cavalry; and it is but an act of justice to the officers and men to say that I have no complaints to make of their conduct, buy everything to commend.

The distance to Cienegas, *via* Pozuelos, is about fifty miles; *via* Nadadores, (by a smoother road,) it is some six miles farther. For the *dry* season, this is the preferable route.

I was accompanied in this expedition by Captain Howard, commissary of subsistence, who succeeded in purchasing a large quantity of wheat flour.

Very respectfully, &c., &c., &c.,

GEO. W. HUGHES,
Captain Topographical Engineers.

Captain J. H. PRENTISS,
Assistant Adjutant General, Centre Division, &c., &c., &c.

A.

August 31.—From La Vaca, eight miles, to the Placedores, a small rivulet, course nearly west across level prairie; very muddy prairie—very muddy from recent rains; thence four miles further in the same direction to the house of ———, a Frenchman, on the right bank of a small muddy stream, with banks eight to ten feet high.

September 1.—After crossing this the road continues about WNW. over the same kind of prairie, six miles, to another stream of the same character as the last, up the right bank of which it runs some two miles; and thence a little more northerly to a belt of timbers, two miles from Victoria. Whole distance thirty miles.

September 2.—At Victoria crossed the Guadalupe, some 200 feet wide, by ferry; thence about two miles, through a thickly timbered bottom, to an open rolling prairie, dry and hard, except at the crossing of two gulleys and a rivulet, twelve miles to the Coleto, a small clear stream, with hard sand and rock bottom. Thence in the same general direction, a little N. of W., thirteen miles to the Manahuila, the crossing of which was muddy and difficult, and six miles further to Goliad, passing another stream of similar character.

September 4.—From Goliad seven miles to the Cabeza, and thence NNW. six miles to a pond in the prairie, near which we encamped.

September 5.—Twelve miles to a grassy stream, with bad water; thence two miles to another small stream of good water, having a pretty grove upon its banks. Five miles further crossed a fine stream, with high steep banks. Thence sixteen miles to a rancho, on the right bank of the Cibolo, a considerable stream, with hard stony bottom; the whole distance over rolling prairie, dry and sandy, and covered with muskeet (mezquite?) grass; the timber becoming more abundant. Course about NW., a little N. From the Cibolo six miles to a small stream, and six miles further to a rancho, which is some distance off the road to the left, and on the banks of the San Antonio river. The San Antonio is here some 100 feet wide, with very high, steep banks. Nine miles hence, through pretty well timbered land, to Canteen's rancho, on a fine stream, with steep banks at its crossing. From Canteen's rancho twelve miles across open prairie to the Salado, and nine miles thence to San Antonio, which we reached on the 6th of September.

Respectfully, you obedient servant,

L. SITGREAVES,
Brevet Captain Corps Topographical Engineers.

B.

MEMOIR.

There are two roads leading from La Vaca, Texas, to San Antonio de Bexar. One of these, the shorter of the two, diverges from the other at Victoria, thirty miles from La Vaca. This passes through Goliad, and is the road which was used by General Wool for the transportation of his supplies. There other passes through Gonzales and Seguin.

I was ordered by you to proceed by the latter route from Victoria to San Antonio, and incidentally to make a reconnaissance of the country passed over by it.

There were no supplies furnished by the quartermaster's department on this road; consequently I was obliged to leave my instruments at Victoria, to be sent by the shorter route, and to set out with no other instrument than a pocket compass. As it was mid-summer, to save our horses we left Victoria just at dusk. During the day the flies are so numerous that the horses are set nearly frantic, and humanity as well as his own comfort will dictate to the traveler in this part of Texas that he must lie by during the day and travel at night. In consequence of this night travelling, my notes have been very imperfect.

The road continues along the left bank of the river Guadalupe, varying in its distances from the river from a quarter of a mile to a mile and a half.

For the first twelve miles the road goes over a wet prairie, which had been washed by the water into holes, which gives the euphonious name of "hog-wallow" to the prairie. The road is miserable even in dry weather, and in wet weather is said to be impassable. From the soft nature of the soil, the slightest fall of rain makes it bad; and a long continued rain, one can easily imagine, would render the prairie fitter for navigation in boats than for travelling in wagons.

After crossing the prairie the country in the vicinity of the road is found to be thinly timbered with a growth of what is commonly called the post-oak. The road itself is good, being sandy, and the face of the country is level. This timber does not grow regularly, as in the woods of the north,

APPENDIX A

but is scattered in clumps. The height of the tree seldom exceeds twenty feet. The road generally winds through parts where there is no timber. The soil seems to be fertile, but the country is very thinly settled. The distance from Victoria to Gonzales is sixty-three miles, and from the point at which timber commences, fifty-one miles from Gonzales. I noticed in the whole distance but one place where the timber was not post-oak. This was at a small creek eight miles from Gonzales, called McCoy's creek, the banks of which were well timbered with sycamore, oak &c.

The country becomes more hilly as the road approaches Gonzales, but in no other respect did I notice a change.

Gonzales is a small place of but little interest, containing about 300 inhabitants. It is situated near the junction of the St. Mark's and Guadalupe rivers. The former is crossed by a ferry, the road still continuing along the left bank of the Guadalupe. In the vicinity of Gonzales the country is more thickly settled than I had yet found it.

After leaving Gonzales the soil became visibly more sandy. The hills increased in height, were stony, and the whole face of the country was unprepossessing. This appearance continues as far as a short distance from Seguin, in the vicinity of which place the country visibly improved, and the settlers became much more numerous.

Seguin is thirty-four miles from Gonzales. It is a small place, but little larger than Gonzales. Here, as well as along the whole route, the houses are built of logs. They are divided into three parts. The centre is merely a shed, the roof of the house being all that protects it from the weather. The other two parts are on each side of the centre shed, and are the kitchens, bedrooms, &c., of the establishment. They are rude but very comfortable dwellings, particularly so for so new a country.

About two miles from Seguin the road crosses the Guadalupe, by means of a wooden bridge. The banks of the river are here well timbered with a fine growth of oaks, of various kinds, sycamores, &c.

After leaving the Guadalupe, the road runs nearly west to San Antonio, a distance of thirty-two miles. The muskeet (a variety of the acacia) covers the whole face of the surrounding country. Here it is first seen on the route west, and it continues with little intermission as far as the centre division marched. A succession of parallel ridges, running nearly north and south, intersect the road, giving to the journey something which at first appears to be variety, but which soon proves to be an interminable sameness. The traveller looks forward to see San Antonio in the distance when he has arrived at the top of one of these hills, but he is disappointed again and again, until he gives up in despair, and, without looking to the right or left, rides sluggishly on until the gray walls of the Alamo, immediately in front of him, give him the pleasing assurance that his journey is ended.

Halfway between the Guadalupe and San Antonio the road crosses the Cibolo, a fine, clear stream, about thirty feet in width, very shallow, but with a fine gravelly bottom. Several smaller streams are crossed at intermediate distances, so that this part of the route is as well watered as the first part.

On the whole, this route from Victoria to San Antonio may be said to be a good natural road. With the exception of the first twelve miles the road is good in all weathers, and in all seasons of the year. The greatest obstacle is the St. Mark's river. At present the only means of crossing it is by a ferry, but in a few years the more thickly settled state of the country will render a bridge indispensable; and when this is constructed, there will be an uninterrupted communication from La Vaca to San Antonio.

There will never be any difficulty about supplies on this route, for as the country grows older the farming population will continually increase.

Respectfully submitted:

W.B. FRANKLIN,
Brevet 1st Lieut., U. S. Topographical Engineer.

To Major GEORGE W. HUGHES,
U. S. Topographical Engineer,
Chief of the Topographical Staff, Centre Division.

Captain GEORGE W. HUGHES, *Corps of Topographical Engineers,* will find, in the following memoranda, a hasty and imperfect account of the march of the Arkansas regiment of mounted volunteers to the general rendezvous, at San Antonio de Bexar, which I submit in obedience to his request, accompanied by a rough map of the route taken by the same. This notice must necessarily be very unsatisfactory, not only because I was absent from the command during a considerable portion of the march, but, as I now greatly regret, I took my notes with too little care during that part of our expedition. I then supposed (yet, I have since had reason to believe, very erroneously) that, as the interior of Texas had been so often traversed by tourists, we could find in print reliable and satisfactory information as to the geography of the country, &c. And as there are already extant some two or three maps, compiled, professedly, from *actual surveys,* any topographical notes, with the idea of correcting the current maps, seemed equally supererogatory; yet experience has convinced me that the latter are likewise remarkably imperfect. I should note, with regard to the map, that though I endeavored to keep an approximate estimate of distances, I paid very little attention to courses; and, what I still more regret, I was able to determine but very few latitudes, owing, in part, to ill-health, but more to a series of cloudy weather—excessive rains, in fact—during a large portion of the trip. I happen to have with me the

APPENDIX A   285

diary of a tour through the interior of Texas in the year 1841; but my notes of courses and distances were kept in a separate memorandum-book, which I unfortunately left behind; yet as each day's journey (assisted by my memory) affords an approximation to the distances. I have marked this route, also, with plain dotted lines, however, while that of the Arkansas regiment is colored. The most important points in the intervals are filled up from published maps, or other information, to show their relations; yet I profess to be responsible for none, except those on the routes I have travelled. But, soliciting indulgence for this explanatory digression, I will proceed to the expedition.

The Arkansas regiment rendezvoused at the town of Washington, Hempstead county, Arkansas, in the last of June, and elected their "field officers" early in July. It certainly speaks well for the patriotism of this new State to know that about thirty companies of volunteers offered their services to the governor, and many others would have presented themselves had they not discovered they would be too late.

It seems that the route originally chalked out for this regiment (as well, indeed, as for most of this column) was to cross Red river at Fulton, Arkansas, and proceed thence southwestward, *via* Trinity colony and Austin city, to San Antonio; but on account of receiving supplies at Robbins's Ferry (Trinity river) it became necessary to turn the route in that direction. However, as the arms, equipage, &c., of the regiment, failed to reach Fulton, as was expected, Colonel Yell considered it expedient to come by Shreveport, Louisiana, hoping to meet his supplies there; in which, however, he failed.

I arrived early in July, from Missouri, at the rendezvous, and found the regiment preparing to march. I proceeded, soon after, to Shreveport, for the purpose (besides other business) of having some temporary tents, &c., provided—the troops being almost wholly without. On the 18th July the regiment marched from Washington, and on the seventh day reached Shreveport—a distance of about one hundred and ten miles. It should be noted, in justice to the energy and expedition with which the officers executed their duties, that on the 24th the regiment marched fifteen miles, and ferried Red river by ten o'clock the same evening—about eight hundred men and horses, with a train of forty wagons—in two or three very inferior boats. In fact, I may here remark, once for all, that the Sabine, Trinity, Brazos, Colorado and Guadalupe rivers were severally crossed, in addition to making a fair day's march, in one day.

On the 26th day of July the regiment marched from Shreveport, and encamped near the village of Greenwood, (about four miles east of the Texas line,) making about sixteen miles over a gently undulating, but rather level country. Remaining behind, on business, I did not overtake the regiment till ten o'clock on the night of October 4th. I found it encamped about three miles east of Crockett, a village in Texas, about one hundred and fifty miles from Shreveport. The road throughout this distance is generally good; country alternately level and undulating; sometimes hilly, but by no means mountainous.

This region may generally be regarded as of rather thin soil; yet much of it of fertile character, producing Indian corn and most vegetables reasonably well, and cotton very finely. This latter should be regarded as the great staple of those regions. The timber is mostly post-oak, black-jack, black hickory, and in some places short-leaf pitch-pine. We also find sweet-gum, chinquopin, and many other growth, with great abundance of sassafras. I may here remark, that I observed no sassafras west of the waters of Trinity river. As yet, we find no prairies on this route, except an occasional insignificant, timberless glade.

August 5th.—At Crockett the regiment was divided, one-half taking the road to a ferry three miles below Robbins's, while the balance kept the direct route to Robbins's ferry. I came with the latter division; made some fourteen miles; road tolerably good.

Thursday, 6th.—About twelve miles to Trinity river; ferried it, and pitched camp two or three miles to the west. The other division (under Colonel Roane) crossed at the lower ferry and reached same camp tonight.

The regiment had necessarily to remain here two or three days, to receive a lot of supplies which had been transported to Robbins's ferry on steamboats; but owing to bad weather, the delay was longer than had been contemplated. During our stay here it rained almost incessantly; in fact, it had been remarkably—very unusually—rainy for the last month or six weeks, where *I* have travelled. I think I might safely say, that in forty days I had at least thirty rains upon me.

Monday, 10th.—Marched from the Trinity camp to-day. Owing to the excessive rains, the roads had become not only very muddy, but miry; so that, though the horsemen made near fifteen miles, most of the "train" only came about ten—the wagons frequently bogging down, even on the high grounds, to the very axletrees. I should have noted that Major Bonneville's command of infantry and dragoons reached Trinity on Sunday last.

Tuesday, 11th.—Last night's camp was on a creek, called Cany, (a branch of the Bidais,) which the rains had swelled to swimming; therefore it was found necessary, this morning, to bridge it, which was completed before midday, and at one o'clock we marched, making about eight miles—crossing another branch or two of the Bidais—still leaving a portion of the train behind. Before this was got up, several hard showers of rain that intervened so flooded the brooks on the way, that it was necessary to bridge a couple more of them, wherefore all the train did not reach this camp till the 13th.

APPENDIX A

Friday, 14th.—Marched about twenty miles; camped nearly two miles to northeast of a little village known as Fanthorp's. Some handsome and fertile-looking upland prairies, interspersed with groves of black-jack, post-oak, &c. Water scarce during dry weather.

Saturday, 15th.—Some eighteen miles; country somewhat similar, yet fewer prairies, and consequently less rich land; for it may be observed that, in all this region, the prairies are the most fertile lands, except river bottoms, that are to be found. Camp at the edge of the Brazos bottom.

Sunday, 16th.—Four miles through the very boggy bottoms of Brazos river; ferried the river at Washington, immediately below the mouth of Navasoto river.

Monday, 17th.—Marched about twenty miles, and camped four or five miles west of the village of Independence. West of the Brazos river the country assumes a richer and more agreeable appearance. Though from a few miles beyond Trinity river we have had frequent detached prairies, yet they are neither so extensive nor so beautiful as those west of the Brazos. But these are not of the character of the broad, monotonous, and almost interminable plains found between our western frontier and the Rocky mountains; they are high and rolling, beautifully interspersed with groves of live oak, hackberry, and occasionally pecan, romantically bespeckled almost everywhere with chance isolated trees of the same, the whole bordered by dense forests of post-oak, black-jack, black hickory, &c., with cedar, cottonwood, sycamore, &c., on the streams. These prairies are generally as fertile-looking as they are beautiful, producing all the vegetables exceedingly well, especially yams and sweet potatoes; while we were assured that the great staples of cotton, sugar, and even wheat, might be cultivated to great advantage, although here, at least on the road, we met with nothing but Indian corn on the farms. The crops of this showed quite fair for the climate, though not equal to those of the north.

Tuesday, 18th.—Made about twelve miles over a country quite similar to that of yesterday. Though in these regions we perceive little local indications of bilious disease, still I was informed that the inhabitants suffered from fever and ague to no small degree, especially in autumn. Speaking of the forest growth, I should have noted that live oak timber, though of a scrubby character, now became quite abundant in the highlands. An occasional scrubby *mezquite* tree also made its appearance; though, as yet, I had seen but one or two. I might here remark, also, that prior to this time, at least as far as the Brazos, the bottoms of the rivers and larger creeks were generally thickly set with that species of *cane* which so abounds in the lower Mississippi valley; yet, from this forward I observed no more of it. No sassafras nor pine west of Trinity waters on this route; yet the latter is quite abundant higher up on the Colorado.

Wednesday, 19th.—About sixteen miles; country similar to that of yesterday.

Thursday, 20th.—Six or seven miles to the village of Rutersville; contains scarcely over one hundred souls. Thence five or six miles to La Grange, a town of two or three hundred inhabitants, near the east bank of the Colorado river. I should have remarked that Major Bonneville's command passed us at Fanthorp's, beyond the Brazos, and was now a day ahead. Crossed the Colorado half a mile below La Grange without difficulty, and pitched a romantic camp on the bordering high bluff; a good spring hard by. This was my first convenient opportunity to take latitude; found the camp in 29° 53' north.

Friday, 21st.—Marched some twelve miles, and camped on a high and romantically beautiful ridge, sparsely covered with live oak and pecan trees; broad prairie spreads out to southward, but country mostly timbered to the north and west. The timber about our camp resembled, for all the world, an old waste orchard of large apple trees. The route today led through a country variegated with handsome prairies and groves of live oak, pecan, post-oak, black-jack, black hickory, &c. The two first indicate the richest lands, growing generally most abundant about the prairies. Latitude of this camp 29° 46½'.

Saturday, 22d.—About fourteen miles to-day, and camped on a small stream, said to be the headmost branch of La Vaca river.

Sunday, 23d.—I left the regiment this morning in company with Major Borland and escort for San Antonio. Though yesterday's march was over a country similar to that of day before, that from here to Gonzales is of a poorer character, and mostly timbered with black jack, post oak, and some black hickory, also occasional live oak, &c. About sixteen miles to Beach creek. Large *mezquite* timber now began to make its appearance. Ten miles further to the village of Gonzales, near northeast bank of Guadalupe river. Much complaint of bilious disease about here. Gonzales contains scarcely one hundred souls. Two miles, and ferried the San Marco river; only about fifty feet wide, but deep and sluggish. Six miles further, and bivouacked at King's. Old King afforded one of the most perfect samples of a "Texan Hoosier" that I had met with; emphatically "a jolly old soul," with no lack of "breath to blow his own trumpet of fame." He came to Texas, he said, thirty-four years ago; had reared a large family there—sons and daughters and sons-in-law settled all around him. Taking his own story for it, he had been in all the battles with every enemy, whether savage or Mexican, that had invaded the country, and had had a thousand "hair-breadth 'scapes." In the sequel, to prove his patriotism, he charged us double price for everything he furnished us.

Monday, 24th.—About twenty-five miles, and stayed to-night at the little village of Seguin—cutting our day's journey short on account of there being no settlement in reach ahead; in fact, none between this place and San Antonio. The truth is, this route is mostly very sparsely settled, espe-

APPENDIX A

cially west of the Colorado. The village of Seguin, though now containing less than one hundred souls, may yet become a flourishing town, as it is a healthy-looking site, near the northwestern bank of the Guadalupe river, and beautifully watered by several fine springs. It might become a manufacturing town, as two falls of the Guadalupe—one immediately below, the other above town—afford extensive water-power. It is also believed that the Guadalupe river may be made navigable to this vicinity, for small steamboats, during more than half the year. Likewise all the other important streams of Texas crossed by us afford flattering prospects of navigation for half the year. The Sabine has already been ascended to a considerable distance; the Trinity far above Robbins's ferry; the Brazos, also, above Washington, and the Colorado to La Grange. But the navigation of both Colorado and Brazos is considerably interrupted by rapids. On the latter, just below the crossing of the "old San Antonio road," near the mouth of Little Brazos, I saw a fall of at least five or six feet perpendicular in the distance of fifty yards. The Trinity, though a narrow stream, affords the best navigation, perhaps, of any river in Texas. As far as the Guadalupe river the *long gray moss* of the south is found particularly abundant in the low grounds, and frequently even in the highlands; but west of the Guadalupe bottoms I saw none at all, except about the head of the San Antonio river.*

Tuesday, 25th.—Crossed Guadalupe river this morning about a mile from Seguin; river here some thirty or forty yards wide—clear, deep, and sluggish. From Seguin to Cibolo creek about fifteen miles, thence to Salado creek fifteen miles, and five miles further to San Antonio de Bexar. The last two streams are of beautiful, clear water—nearly equal, being of small mill-power size. The country, after crossing Guadalupe river, assumes decidedly a new character—level, dry-looking plains, fertile-looking soil, being a dark vegetable loam; timber scarce, but no perfectly bare prairies, being sparsely set everywhere with scrubby *mezquite*, and occasional pecan, hackberry, live-oak, &c., altogether very similar to the lower plains about San Antonio.

The Arkansas regiment followed the same route, and arrival at San Antonio (or Camp Crockett) on the 28th of same month.

Captain Hughes desired some account of the history of San Antonio de Bexar. In this brief notice I shall aim to insert nothing that was apparent to every observer, as I could not have the presumption to relate what Captain Hughes was more capable of seeing for himself.

---

*I should have remarked, that up the course of the Guadalupe river there are some fine lands—in fact, some of the most fascinating farm sites I ever saw; literally "hills and dales" delightfully connected. On the one side we could have a rich, high prairie bottom of one thousand acres, or more; and on the other, gently elevated hills, beautifully shaded with live oak, &c., for residence sites. The alternation of prairie and timbered land still continued.

Tradition says that the present site of the town was originally a *Pueblo* of Indians, called the *Texas,* whence the name of the province. Judge Morgan (of San Antonio) informed me that according to the archives, a presidio, or garrison, was established there in 1715, and that a colony of families immigrated to the place from the Canary Islands in 1732. Nevertheless, it will be perceived from the following passage in "Los Tres Siglos de Mexico," p. 78 of vol. 2, that attempts at least were made at a much earlier period. After speaking of the settlement of Monclova, the author relates that in the year 1691, "in the neighboring province of *Asinais,* or, as called by the Spaniards, *Texas,* (perhaps the most pacifically-inclined nation on the continent,) the governor of Coahuila was ordered to select a site for a *presidio*; and it was provided that fourteen *padres Franciscans* should labor in that ministry. The *presidio* and missions were actually located during this period; yet a long drought having supervened after the lapse of two or three years, which caused the death of the cattle that had been taken there, the loss of the crops, and the ill will of the Indians towards the Spaniards on account of the vexations occasioned them by the latter, nearly all the missions were abandoned.

Yet, by the two following passages from the same history, pp. 113 and 130, we will perceive that Judge Morgan's information was virtually correct, or nearly so: "1715. At the close of this year the *presidio* of Texas was already established, and the *padres Franciscans* employed themselves in reducing those savages and forming *pueblos.*" "1731. In this year the Marquis de Casafuerte sent a colony of Canarians, who settled in the town which he caused to be built, the plan of which was laid off by Don Antonio de Villaseñor."

According to tradition, the original *presidio* was located west of San Pedro creek, two or three hundreds yards from the *Plaza Militar.* But upon the immigration of the Canarians (or Isleños, Islanders, as more frequently termed by the people,) the Indians, I suppose, having been pretty well rooted out, the former located themselves just east of the present church, forming what is still termed the *Plaza de los Islenos.* The church is said to have been founded about 1740, and the *Plaza Militar,* immediately back of the church, was doubtless established between this period and the immigration of the Canarians.

Of those old missions in the vicinity of San Antonio I need only say a word concerning their foundation. The most important are said to have been built under the direction of a famous monk called Padre Margil. The mission of La Concepcion, as tradition says, is the oldest, which is confirmed by the date, over the door, of 1754; while that of the Alamo is 1758. I could find no date about either of the other ruins except on the steeple of San José, which I think is not to be depended upon, being 1781.

APPENDIX A   291

I can now think of nothing else that would be likely to interest Captain Hughes, of which he might not have obtained information himself more satisfactory that I could presume to give him. I will merely add that, by various observations, I determined the latitude of the public square of San Antonio to be 29° 25' 30"; longitude, by eclipses of Jupiter's satellites, about 98° 52' west from Greenwich.

Owing to the very hasty manner in which the foregoing paragarahs were written, I find, upon glancing over them, so much monotony, repetition—indeed, confusion, and ambiguity, I fear—that I could not offer them to Captain Hughes in their present condition, had I time to re-write them; but I must trust to his indulgence for an apology.

Very respectfully,

JOSIAH GREGG.

PARRAS, *December* 7, 1846.

Memoir of a reconnassiance of a route from Monclova, Mexico, to Monterey, Mexico, made in November, 1846.

SIR: On the 14th of November, 1846, I left Monclova, under orders from Brigadier General Wool, to proceed to Monterey with all possible despatch, and to report to Major General Taylor for despatches. Incidentally I was made a reconnaissance of the route between the two places, but the first object was speed. An escort of six men of the Arkansas regiment, commanded by Lieutenant Desha of that regiment, accompanied me, as did also Captain Webb of the Illinois volunteers, and Mr. Dannoy of New Orleans, a commissary agent. Both of the latter were on their way to the United States.

Having no guide, I was obliged to depend for my knowledge of the road on such information as I could pick up about it in Monclova on the morning of the start.

I left the town about 7 a.m., and after travelling for about two hours in a direction east of south, arrived at a small village called Castaña. Here was a fine stream of good water, and a very good camping ground. The village is small, not containing more than two or three hundred inhabitants. They are supported by the cultivation of the land in the vicinity, which produces fine crops of corn. Twenty-three miles farther in Bajan. This is a deserted rancho, and the ground in the vicinity gives evidence of having once been in a high state of cultivation. There is a small stream of good water here, and a pool formed by an enbankment. In the immediate vicinity of the pool the ground is marshy, and there is a fine growth of grass upon it. Here I encamped for the night. At Castaña I was joined by a

Mexican, who, finding out that I was going to Monterey, requested permission to travel with me. As he said he had been over the road frequently, I was very glad to grant him the permission, and found him very serviceable as a guide throughout the whole route.

From Monclova to Bajan the road is nearly straight. Between Monclova and Castaña it is rough, but from the latter place to Bajan it runs over a plain, and is very smooth. The only vegetation along this part of the route is the muskeet and prickly pear. At intervals, some coarse dry grass appeared, but it was so covered with the dust, which was very thick, that it was almost useless as food for the horses.

The road runs along a valley, bounded on both sides by high mountains, the tops of which are about ten miles apart.

As far as Bajan the roads to Monterey and Parras from Monclova coincide. At that point they separate—that to Monterey striking to the east, and the Parras road keeping to the west.

The Monterey road for twenty miles is good, running over a soil that appeared to require only water to make it fertile. As it is, nothing but muskeet and cactus grow, solely owing, I imagine, to the absence of rain. The direction of the road varies a little north of east, bending gradually to the south. About twenty miles from Bajan is a miserable rancho, where we found a large flock of goats. These subsist on the scanty herbage in the vicinity, and water is obtained for them from a large well. The water was pretty good, but would not have been sufficient for General Wool's command without a large supply of vessels to contain it, for constant drawing for twenty-four hours would have been required for the large quantity of animals with the army.

From this point the road becomes more rough, and approaches nearer to the mountains to the east of it. The direction is still southeast. About seven miles from the rancho it crosses a small stream, on which was a fine growth of grass. The water of this was so bitter than we could not drink it. Eight miles farther is another rancho, the family at which appeared to be engaged in making muscal. Nothing but the maguey and muskeet grows in the vicinity, and the master of the place told me that he obtained his corn at a hacienda to the northeast, which was not in sight. Probably this rancho is a dependency of the hacienda spoken of. The only water was contained in a tanque, was nearly putrid, and there was very little of it. We arrived here at 4 p. m., and after feeding our horses, and resting for an hour, set out again. About 12 p. m. we encamped in a large growth of muskeet, with some good grass. The night was very dark, so that, from the last rancho to camp I know nothing of the road, except that it was very rough, and once we made a considerable ascent and descent, which, with the partial view of the mountains near us, led me to believe we were going through some mountain pass. The whole distance travelled to-day was fifty miles.

APPENDIX A

As there was no water at or near the camp, we started about 4 o'clock a. m., and, after travelling twenty miles over a road a good deal cut up by rain channels, arrived at a place named, according to the guide, Cañas.

This we found to be a hacienda, with a large extent of ground in a high state of cultivation. Sugar-cane was the principal crop. There was some corn growing, but not more than enough for food for the inhabitants of the place. We rested here during the heat of the day, and about 3 p. m. started again, and after travelling twelve miles, encamped two miles south of a place called by the guide Pueblito. The vicinity of the road during this day's march, until we arrived at Cañas, presented almost identically the same appearance that it had previously. It was entirely barren, producing nothing but muskeet and maguey, and was hemmed in by high mountains, apparently ten miles apart. At Cañas all this changed. The maguey disappeared, the Spanish bayonet taking its place; the soil produced some grass, and we appeared to be getting into a country susceptible of some cultivation. Four miles south of Cañas we crossed a stream about thirty yards in width and two feet in depth, which flowed eastwardly through a gap in the mountains to the west, and which had worn for itself, in the soft soil, a deep and broad bed. The road was crossed at intervals of two or three miles by small streams flowing from the mountains, and the banks of these were well settled by small farmers, who produced an abundance of corn.

On the 18th, making an early start, we arrived at a village about five miles from Pueblito, called Abasolo. It contained about five hundred inhabitants, and is beautifully situated on both sides of the river above mentioned.* Here we obtained corn for our horses. Two miles farther, is a small village called Chipinque; three miles from this, another of the same size named Topo Grande; and six miles farther, another called Topito. The river leaves the road at Chipinque, flowing off towards the east. At Topito another small stream crosses the road, flowing northeast. It is doubtless a branch of the first stream. Thirteen miles farther is Monterey.

Along the whole of this day's march (twenty-four miles) the country was well settled, well watered, and the soil was fertile—the whole face of the country presenting a more cheerful appearance than anything I had yet seen in Mexico.

The great scarcity of water on the part of the road midway between Monclova and Monterey presents an obstacle to the march of an army almost insuperable. In the whole distance from Castaña to Cañas there is but one running stream, and the water of that is so impregnated with salts that it is impossible to drink it. My guide told me that it affected horses so much

---

*This stream is doubtless a branch of the San Juan.

that they never were allowed to taste it. The supplies of water at the two ranchos are so limited that they would not go far towards remedying the evil.

The road is but little travelled by Mexicans; for the Camanches, in making their marauding excursions into the west, cross the road in several places, so that a small party is in great danger along the whole route. I was informed Bajan had been deserted on account of the depredations of the Indians, and that now it is a favorite camping-ground for them on their way to and from the scenes of the depredations.

Respectfully submitted:

W. B. FRANKLIN,
Brevet First Lieutenant United States Top. Engineers.

To Major G. W. HUGHES,
Corps Topographical Engineers, United States army.

From Monterey to Saltillo.

Not finding General Taylor at Monterey, I left that place on the 20th of November for Saltillo, where he then was. As the road between these two places has been often described by reconnoitring officers who have gone over it, I shall merely state that it is a good wagon road, well watered, and with an abundant supply of forage throughout the whole distance, which is between fifty-five and sixty miles.

About half way between the two places is a hacienda called La Rinconada. This was the usual camping-ground for our mounted troops in their marches from one place to the other, as they generally made the trip in two days. Infantry made the march in three days—on the first day encamping at a village named Santa Catarina, about eight miles west of Monterey; on the second at a rancho, about twenty-one miles from Saltillo, named, from a warm spring near it, Ojo Caliente; and the third day marching into or near to Saltillo.

On the 21st of November 1 met General Taylor and his staff, on their return from Saltillo to Monterey. After delivering my despatches, I was ordered by him to proceed to Saltillo, and await further orders from him there. I arrived at Saltillo that evening, and two days afterwards received despatches from him, with orders to proceed from that place to Monclova by the shortest route.

From Saltillo towards Monclova.

On the 25th of November I left Saltillo for Monclova. By the kindness of Major General Worth, then in command at Saltillo, I had been furnished with a guide; and Lieutenants Armstead and Buckner, 6th in-

APPENDIX A 295

fantry, started with me to join their regiment, part of which was with General Wool's column. These gentlemen, (the escort which came with me from Monclova,) the guide, and myself, formed the party.

For the first nine miles from Saltillo the road to Monclova is excellent, being perfectly straight and smooth, and nearly level. The direction for this distance is nearly north. The country in the vicinity is in a good state of cultivation, and the principal crops were corn and wheat.

Capillania is a small village on the road, nine miles from Saltillo. It contains about five hundred inhabitants, and is pleasantly situated on the stream that flows by Saltillo. Here the road begins to run along the stream and becomes rough. Seven miles farther is a rancho called San Diego, where we encamped for the night.

Next morning, after marching four miles in a direction north of west, we crossed the river; and about a mile farther the road enters the mountains, winding about in every direction. It is so very rough that it would be extremely difficult, indeed almost impossible, to bring a wagon-train through it. Where it is possible, it is kept along the banks of the river, which it crosses and recrosses several times. This rough road continues about ten miles, when it emerges from the mountains on to a smooth plain, on which it ran for the remainder of the day's march.

Twenty-five miles from San Diego is a large hacienda called Mesillas. There was a large number of cattle here, and a great extent of ground in cultivation, on which corn and wheat were the only crops. Where the road leaves the mountains were a few huts, in the vicinity of which a little corn was raised. Two miles in front of Mesillas we crossed the river, leaving it flowing to the east, and saw nothing more of it. Five miles north of Mesillas is another large hacienda, called Perros Bravos, where we spent the night.

Leaving Perros Bravos, after marching four miles we crossed a road which ran to Parras; and two miles farther, a stream called by the guide the Salinos. Its course was nearly east and west. It was about twenty yards wide, and eighteen inches deep. It flowed to the east, and is probably the same stream I crossed before at Cañas. Nine miles from Perros Bravos is Anelo. This is a very large hacienda, beautifully situated on a small rivulet, near the Salinos. There was, in addition to the corn and wheat, some sugar-cane raised here. Fifteen miles northwest of Anelo is the Estanque of San Felipe. This, as its name implies, is an artificial reservoir of water, and was made, I imagine, for the use of the cattle of Anelo, which are allowed to wander in the vicinity. Between Anelo and this place the road is perfectly level, hemmed in on both sides by mountains, and the ground in the vicinity is covered with a growth of grass and muskeet.

When we were about five miles from the tanque, our attention was attracted by a long line of dust to our left and front. Not knowing what it could be, we consulted the guide, who informed us that it must be caused by Indians. We were obliged to rest satisfied with this information, but were undeceived when we arrived at the tanque. There we met some volunteers who were engaged in repairing a wagon. They informed us that General Wool's division had passed there that day on their march to Parras, and that they were encamped about fifteen miles farther on the road to our left. Following their directions, we reached the General's camp about 8 o'clock in the evening. Had it not been for the fortunate accident of the breaking down of this wagon, we would probably have gone on to Monclova, as the road was so dusty that every trace of the march of the army was effaced almost as soon as it was made.

It would be almost impossible to march an army from San Felipe to Saltillo by the route through Anelo and Mesillas, on account of the roughness of the road through the mountains north of San Diego. With this exception the road is very good, and the supplies both of forage and water are abundant. The whole distance from Saltillo to the estanque of San Felipe is seventy miles.

Respectfully submitted:

W. B. FRANKLIN,
Brevet First Lieutenant Topographical Engineers.

To Major G. W. HUGHES,
Topographical Engineers, United States army.

On the 17th of December, 1946, General Wool received intelligence from General Worth, which led him to believe that the presence of his division of the army would be highly necessary in the vicinity of Saltillo.

On the same day the whole division was put *en route*, though they had but two hours' notice. The force under the command of General Wool consisted of the following troops: one company of field artillery, four companies of dragoons, and three companies of infantry—all regulars. Of volunteers, there were one regiment of cavalry, two regiments of infantry, and one independent company of infantry incorporated in the battalion of the three companies of regular infantry. The whole amounted to about three thousand men.

There are two wagon roads from Parras to Saltillo. The more direct of these is good for fifteen miles from Parras, where it crosses a line of mountains called Los Infiernos. The road is so rough and dangerous in these mountains, that without very thorough repairs, made with the expenditure of much time and labor, it is impassable for a train. This consideration induced the general to take the more circuitous route, which passes through Cienega Grande, making the distance about fifteen miles longer. This route joins the other road near Castañuela, about thirty miles from Parras.

APPENDIX A

With the single exception of the passage through Los Infiernos mentioned above, the route from Saltillo to Parras is excellent, and by the road that General Wool marched there is not a single obstruction. It runs through a valley from beginning to end, so that it is nearly level; is intersected by numerous small streams flowing towards the north, so that there is no scarcity of water, and the few haciendas scattered along afford plenty of forage—the only supply needed by General Wool's division.

One company of the regular infantry was left as Parras as a guard of the sick, and one squadron of the volunteer cavalry was absent with Captain Hughes, topographical engineers, on an expedition towards Durango. The remainder of the division, with the exception of three companies of volunteer infantry which had been left at Monclova, was put *en route* on the 17th of December, 1846. On the afternoon of that day of dragoons and artillery encamped about ten miles from Parras, in a gorge of the mountains, and the infantry and volunteer cavalry about three miles from Parras.

On the 18th the artillery and dragoons encamped at a rancho near Castañuela, and the infantry at a small rancho called Misteña, fifteen miles behind.

On the 19th both columns marched to Patos, a large hacienda, the residence of the Sanchez family.

On the 20th the division reached San Juan de la Vaqueria, and on the 21st encamped at Agua Nueva, a rancho about seventeen miles south of Saltillo.

The original intention of the general had been to encamp at La Encentada, seven or eight miles nearer Saltillo, but on arriving there he changed his mind, and marched back to Agua Nueva.

The distance from Parras to Agua Nueva, by the route marched by General Wool, was a little more than one hundred miles, so that in the space of four days of division had marched that distance, being on an average more than twenty-five miles a day.

This is probably the best march that was made during the war; and it is to be remembered, too, that the men were in excellent health and spirits after its completion.

W. B. FRANKLIN,
Brevet 1st Lieutenant U. S. Topographical Engineers.

SAN ANTONIO DE BEXAR, *September* 9, 1846.

SIR: I have been assigned, by orders from the Topographical Bureau of the 6th August, 1946, as chief of the topographical staff of the army under the command of Brigadier General Wool, and, by the same orders, the following officers have been designated as my assistants, viz: 1st Lieutenant L. Sitgreaves, 2d Lieutenant W. B. Franklin, 2d Lieutenant F. T. Bryan.

And I now have the honor to report that I am prepared to execute any duty to which I may be assigned by the commanding general.

Lieutenant Sitgreaves is present with me, Lieutenants Franklin and Bryan having been left at La Vaca to make astronomical observations for the determination of latitude and longitude. They have also been directed to reconnoitre the Gonzales road to this place. The road by the way of Goliad has been carefully examined by Lieutenant Sitgreaves on our way up.

I would respectfully suggest that, as soon as it suits the convenience of the general-in-chief, a strong body of mounted men should be thrown forward to the Rio Grande for the purpose of affording protection to the topographical parties. Such force would probably be better and more cheaply subsisted near San Fernando than here. I propose to accompany the advance guard of the army, with the view of reconnoitring the country between the Rio Grande and the city of Chihuahua, through the mountains, as I am persuaded of the existence of a road in the direction; but whether practicable for artillery and wagon trains, I have no means of ascertaining. According to Captain (afterwards General) Z. M. Pike, "M. St. Croix, afterwards viceroy of Peru, took this road (that is, over the mountains) in 1778 on his way from Chihuahua, Coquilla, Allases, and Texas." With a regiment at Presidio de Rio Grande, or at San Fernando, as a point d'appui, I will undertake, with two companies of mounted men, to penetrate through the mountains.

It has also been suggested that a route practicable for artillery may be found through the highlands on the east of the Rio Grande, intersecting to the Puerco river about seventy-five miles above its mouth, and crossing the Rio Grande at the confluence of the Conchos. If it should meet with the approbation of the general, I also propose to examine the country in that direction; it will at least contribute to our geographical information of a portion of our territory but imperfectly known.*

In the mean time I propose to examine the country in the vicinity of San Antonio, and to correct the map of Texas by information to be obtained from the various commands which have entered the State in different directions, concentrating on this point. Lieutenant Brent, of Captain Washington's company, has taken copious notes of their line of march, of which I shall, with his permission, avail myself.

It is also my desire, as soon as a corps of topographical rangers can be organized, (under the authority of a recent regulation of the War Department,) to at once enter upon a reconnaissance of the country between

---

*This is the route recently examined by Colonel Hays, and pronounced to be practicable for wagons. It will open a direct communication between our post in Texas and those in New Mexico.

APPENDIX A 299

this place and the Nueces, with the object of being able to designate the most convenient positions for the encampments of the different corps on their march, (a duty devolved on the topographical staff by paragraph 880, general regulations of the army,) for which I propose leaving at least one officer of my command at headquarters with the main body of the army. Having referred to the extended and exposed nature of our duties, it seems to me that the topographical rangers should consist of at least two companies, who would constitute generally a portion of the advanced guard of the army en route, and would be occupied at other times in detachments for the protection of the reconnoitring parties.

Very respectfully, sir, your obedient servant,
GEORGE W. HUGHES,
Captain Topographical Engineers.

Lieutenant J. McDowell,
A. A. Adjt. General of the army of Chihuahua.

The topographical party is provided with the necessary instruments for the determination of geographical positions by latitude and longitude.

SAN ANTONIO, *December* 13, 1948.

SIR: It may be of interest and importance to yourself, and the department you direct, to receive some additional information to that which you doubtless already possess of the country lying between this place and the State of Chihuahua, in Mexico. The citizens of San Antonio have for many years been anxious to establish a trade with that portion of Mexico by opening a direct communication with it; but numerous difficulties and obstacles prevented the accomplishment of this object. In August last the citizens of San Antonio fitted out an expedition to explore a route practicable for wagons to Presidio del Norte, and Paso del Norte, which I had the honor to conduct. We set out on the 27th August, and returned the 12th December, having succeeded in discovering a way perfectly practicable for wagons at all seasons of the year. The road will run from this place east of north to the head of either the San Saba or Conchos rivers, both tributaries of the Colorado, and which rise within a few miles of each other, distant abut one hundred and fifty miles; from thence, in an almost southwest direction, to the Rio Pecos or Puercos, fifty miles; thence up the Puercos about fifty, and from thence, in a southwest course, to Presidio del Norte, one hundred and fifty or one hundred and sixty miles; making in all a distance of about four hundred miles, either by the way of Presidio del Norte, ascending the Rio Grande, or by going fifty miles higher on the Rio Pecos than the Presidio road will go, and then passing over to the Rio Grande and ascending it. We did not examine the whole distance to the Paso del Norte, but have learned from information upon which we fully rely, that there will be no difficulty whatever in going from one town to the other. The distance from Presidio del Norte to Paso del Norte is about one hundred and fifty miles. For seventy-five miles of the way from this place (San Antonio) to the head of the San Saba there is a good wagon road now is use, and from that point the country is generally level, with but few hills, and they are small. From the San Saba to the Pecos the country is almost perfectly level, covered with muskeet trees, and bearing an abundance of grass and but little water. I have little doubt, however, that at most seasons of the year water can be found at intervals of ten to twelve miles. We were four days in passing this plain, and found water at every encampment. A further examination of this country will no doubt show more water. At the point where the road will strike the Pecos the hills begin to recede from the river, and the valley, in a few miles, open into a wide plain, which continues nearly the whole length of the river. There is abundance of grass and fuel on this plain, but no trees; the wood used for burning, and almost the only growth, is the small muskeet. From the Pecos to the Rio Grande the country is for more than half the distance level; the remainder of it is down a valley, where the points of some hills are necessary to be crossed, but offering at no place any considerable obstruction. Fifteen miles above the Presidio del Norte, on the Rio Grande, there is large timber in abundance, and the distance to Paso del Norte is generally level. The average distance from the Rio Pecos to the Rio Grande is, from about forty miles above their junction, nearly one hundred and twenty-five miles. Ten or fifteen miles below Presidio del Norte, high broken hills, set in close to the river, so as to render approach to it difficult, or even almost impossible, except at a few points. These hills continue below the mouth of the Pecos about forty or fifty miles. From the mouth of the Pecos up to within a few miles of where the road will probably cross it, the same character of hills, rugged and broken, renders travelling very near the river next to impossible. About seventy-five miles southeast of Presidio del Norte, we passed through a country giving every indication of great mineral wealth; and we were informed by the residents of a rancho below Presidio, that a silver mine in that neighborhood had formerly been worked by the Mexicans, which was reported to have been very rich, but the working of it to any great extent was prevented by the Indians. Rich specimens of gold and silver were shown us from mines in the vicinity.

From Matagorda bay to Presidio del Norte will not much exceed five hundred and forty miles, or seven hundred miles to Paso del Norte; and nearly the whole distance is level, with an abundance of grass, fuel, and water. The Rio Pecos may not be found fordable at all times; but it is a narrow stream, and easy ordinarily to cross. If I might venture to suggest the most favorable time for the movement of troops from this part of the

APPENDIX A

country to Paso del Norte, I would say the latter part of March, at which season of the year the grass is good and abundant, and the weather is mild and pleasant. In the winter months, soldiers would suffer considerably on the plains from the cold north winds.

Respectfully,

JOHN C. HAYS.

Hon. W. L. MARCY,
    Secretary of War.

Recapitulation of latitudes observed in Texas and Mexico, 1846–'47.

La Vaca, Texas	28° 37' 00"	north.
Victoria, "	28 46 57	"
One mile north of San Antonio, Texas	29 26 53.4	"
Left bank Medina river, near Castroville, Texas	29 20 15.3	"
Right bank Seco river, Texas	29 20 56.95	"
" Little Sabinos, Texas	29 15 52.7	"
" Rio Frio, Texas	29 17 32	"
" Leona, Texas	29 08 00	"
Left bank Nueces, Texas	28 59 13.8	"
Reynoso creek, Texas	28 39 38.9	"
Las Cuevas, Texas	28 30 53.7	"
Left bank Rio Grande, Texas	28 22 43.4	"
Four miles from Presidio del Rio Grande, Mexico	28 20 48.5	"
Near Nava, Mexico	28 24 43	"
Five miles from San Fernando de Rosa, Mexico	28 24 39.5	"
At Santa Rita river, Mexico	28 16 52.3	"
Rio Alamos, Mexico	27 58 20.5	"
1½ mile ESE. of Santa Rosa, Mexico	27 52 02.7	"
Arroyo del Ahura, (right bank,) Mexico	27 33 20.0	"
4 miles north of Monclova, Mexico	26 57 46	"
½ mile NE. of Monclova, Mexico	26 54 44.26	"
Castaña, Mexico*	26 47 00	"
Bajan, Mexico*	26 34 30	"
La Joya, Mexico*	26 23 15	"
Near hacienda Venadito, Mexico	26 02 11	"
Three miles from hacienda Sauceda, Mexico	25 45 17.4	"
San Antonio, (de Jarral,) Mexico	25 33 55.7	"
Pastora, Mexico	25 38 46.3	"
Cienega Grande, Mexico	25 33 40.7	"

---

*Observed by Mr. J. Gregg.

1¾ mile north of Parras, Mexico	25	26	48	"
Parras, Mexico	25	25	00	"
Hacienda Casañuela, Mexico, (probably)	25	25	24	north.
Hacienda Los Muchachos, Mexico	25	17	58.5	"
Saltillo, Mexico	25	26	22	"
Hacienda Patos, Mexico	25	22	31	"
Agua Nueva, Mexico	25	11	43.6	"
Monterey, Mexico	25	40	13	"

The above latitudes were determined by observations with the sextant upon the north star, (Polaris.)

Corpus Christi, (according to Captain Cram,) Texas	27°	47'	17".87	north.
North end of Padre island, Texas	27	37	00	"
Brasos Santiago, Texas	26	06	00	"
Baca del Rio Grande, Texas	25	58	00	"

Recapitulation of longitudes observed and calculated.

	In arc.	Time.
San Antonio, Texas	98° 52' 30"	6h. 42m. 4.8s.
Presidio del Rio Grande	100 31 12	
Right bank Sabinos river	101 33 00	(Observed by J. Gregg.)
Monclova	101 39 18	6h. 46m. 37.2s.
Saltillo	101 01 45	6h. 44m. 7s.
Monterey	100 25 36	6h. 41m. 42s.
Corpus Christi, (according to Captain Cram,)	97 27 02.5	west of Greenwich, according to Captain Cram.
Brasos Santiago	97 12 00	

These longitudes were all determined by observations on the eclipses of Jupiter's satellites, except that of Saltillo, which was determined by the method of lunar distances.

[The above determinations are the result of 350 observations, besides the independent ones by Mr. Gregg, of which he kindly permitted us to avail ourselves, and are filed in the Topographical Bureau for future use.—GEO. W. HUGHES.]

NOTE.—The river San Antonio flows into the Guadalupe not far from the debouche of the latter on the bay of Esperitu Santo, and both are represented as being navigable for steamboats, the San Antonio to Goliad, (and in the rainy season for a much greater distance,) and the Guadalupe some twenty miles above Victoria. A short railroad has been projected from Indian Point, at the mouth of La Vaca river, in Matagorda bay, to the mouth of the San Antonio. When this work is completed it will open an

APPENDIX A

excellent communication through San Antonio do Bexar for the Chihuahua and Santa Fe trade, taking the route recently discovered by Colonel Hays to the mouth of the Conchos river, an affluent of the Rio Grande, from which point there are excellent roads to Chihuahua and to Paso del Norte. The trade to the upper and interior portion of Coahuila would also naturally take this direction to San Antonio, which would thus become an important commercial entrepot.

APPENDIX B

Report of the Survey of the Valley of Mexico

WASHINGTON, *November* 30, 1848.

SIR: In submitting to your consideration the map of the valley of Mexico, made on such a scale as will, I trust, delineate clearly its great natural features as well as peculiar form, I find myself obliged, to a proper understanding of the same, to give some account of the movement of our troops from their descent into the valley at Cordova until the capture of the city. Not having found, among the numerous maps and charts taken with the city, any one of the valley deserving confidence, I am inclined to believe that this is the first survey of it, by triangulation, ever made. Baron Humboldt's map of the same is, perhaps, as correct as any yet published; but it will be seen, by a comparison of the accompanying map with his, that the southern part of the valley is entirely changed in form. Lakes Chalco and Xochimilco, being given in position and extent, are also very different, together with a corresponding change in the position of places and distances between them. There are various other corrections which it may not be necessary to indicate more particularly than by the map itself.

This remarkable interior basin, as is generally known, is absolutely closed on every side by a mountain barrier varying in height at different points from two hundred to over ten thousand feet above its bottom. Its appearance in descending into it is remarkable, presenting amost every variety of scenery, and that, too, of unsurpassed beauty and interest. First to attract notice are the six lakes—Chalco, Xochimilco, Tezcuco, San Christobal, Xaltocan and Zumpango—stretching across the valley in an almost continuous line from south to north, their shores bordered by extensive fields spread out on a nearly perfect level, reaching back to the mountains, and under the highest state of cultivation. These lakes are fresh, or may be called so, with the exception of Tezcuco, (which, by distinction, is called the salt lake,) and are respectively spread over a surface of about 39, 29, 96, 6, 21 and 8 square miles, occupying about one-fifth of the valley proper. Nine populous towns, independent of the city of Mexico, are located in different parts, each surrounded by neat and smiling villages, whose inhabitants, although poor, are nevertheless temperate, laborious and industrious. Ten old, extinct volcanoes, distinctly presenting their craters, rear their conical shapes in the southern part of the valley; and it needs but a casual observation to impress the opinion that the entire basin was at one time in a state of the most intense ignition.

Now their sides are seen covered with luxuriant crops—the volcanoes resembling huge artificial mounds, whose slopes are smoothed and cultivated with the utmost precision and care. In a particular instance, after ascending to the jagged circular crest of one whose top had fallen in, on looking down into it you perceive, some one hundred feet below, two beautiful fields of twelve or fifteen acres each, and separated by a low wall of lava, the existence of which could not have been suspected. Glancing over the range of mountains which limit the valley, to the south is seen Ajusco, its scarred and blackened peak elevated more than 11,000 feet above the sea, speaking plainly to every beholder of the internal heat to which it was once a vent; to the east and southeast are seen Iztaccihuatl and Popocatepetl, the latter even now silently emitting a column of smoke, both with a perpetual covering of snow, towering in impressive grandeur far above the plains below, glittering in the rays of the sun, their outlines and inequalities so distinctly and sharply defined as to make them seem almost within reach, yet looking so cold, while everything else seems scorching under that tropical sun, that one turns towards them involuntarily, again and again, to see if he is not laboring under some optical illusion. The basin is of a general circular form, the diameter of the edge or crust of the rim being about fifty miles.

The quantity of arable land in the valley may be estimated at about 830 square miles, and most of this is under a very high state of cultivation. The principal productions are corn, barley, and wheat, although almost any known vegetable is grown there. The soil is unusually rich, and where the inhabitants can resort to artificial irrigation, extremely productive. Horses, cattle, and sheep are numerous.

The lakes of the valley seem to have remained very nearly of the same extent as at the time of the conquest, with the exception of Tezcuco, which has receded some two miles; the land formerly covered gradually becoming fertile, under the freshening influences of rains.

The recession is doubtless due to two causes, first, that one of the largest rivers of the valley, the Guatitlan, has been turned from its course, and made to flow along an artificial cut through the mountains bordering the basin to the northwest, into the Tula river, which empties into the Gulf of Tampico; secondly, to the actual decrease of the various streams emptying into it, caused by the clearing up of the mountain sides.

Chalco is the deepest of these lakes, averaging from four to five feet; Tezcuco, the largest and lowest, is extremely shallow, in no place being more than from six to eight feet deep, and generally not more than one or two. This lake would probably yearly disappear were it not that lake Chalco, by means of the Royal canal connecting them, is emptying into it more than 130 cubic feet of water per second.

But the object of greatest interest and attraction is the city of Mexico itself, whose origin is so remarkable, and whose singular beauty and wealth have been so much spoken of. Originally surrounded by Lake Tezcuco, the lands have now become somewhat dry, so that seen from a distance it has the appearance of standing in the midst of a beautiful and fertile plain, easy of access from any quarter. This is by no means the case; the ground, low on all sides, is intersected in every direction by ditches both wide and deep, which, from the superior elevation of lakes Chalco and Xochimilco, are always filled with water, and the city now stands as dependent upon its causeways for communication with the surrounding country, and as strong by position as when the Spaniards first arrived there.

It was on the 11th of August, 1847, that General Scott descended into this basin from Cordova, and in the following order: General Twiggs, with his division, led and encamped at Ayotla; next followed General Quittnan, and took up a position a short distance in his area; General Worth came third, occupying the town of Chalco, and last came General Pillow, bringing up the rear, and encamped near General Worth. From this position of the army there are four routes leading to the capital, either in themselves practicable for the movement of troops, but differing in distance, and in their capabilities for defence. The shortest and most direct is the main road which passes Pinon Viego, and enters the city by the San Lazera garita. General Santa Anna, with a large part of his force, had taken up a position on this road, the formidable character of which will probably be understood from what follows. On leaving Ayotla, the road bends around the base of an old volcano for five miles, then leads over a causeway built across an arm of Tezcuco for two miles more, passes Pinon Viego, and is causewayed for seven miles more on to the city. At the termination of this first causeway rises Pinon, a mount of an oblong shape, shooting up abruptly four hundred and fifty feet above the level of the lake, its summit accessible from the sides of Ayotla only at one point, and is surrounded on all sides by water, except that nearest the city. To render this naturally strong position still stronger, there were three lines of works thrown up, the first at the base, the next at the brow, the third at the extreme summit of the hill. The works at the base ran entirely round Pinon, and consisted of a ditch fifteen feet wide, four and a half feet deep, and of a parapet fifteen feet thick, the superior slope of it being about eight and a half feet above the bottom of the ditch. The causeway was also cut, and

APPENDIX B

defended by a battery of two guns. The various works of this position mounted about sixty pieces of artillery, nearly one half of which could be brought to bear upon this narrow causeway, sweeping its entire length. The second and third lines consisted of strong breastworks only. Here the Mexican leader made his first stand after the battle of Cerro Gordo, and the position was undoubtedly well selected.

The next most direct route is by Mexicalzingo, which, leaving the lake and Pinon on the right, was unobstructed until within range of the batteries at the town just mentioned. This route, just before reaching Mexicalzingo, also leads over a causeway three-quarters of a mile long, bordered on one side by an extensive marsh formed by Lake Xochimilco, and on the other by very low grounds partially flooded, and intersected in every direction by ditches filled with water, and impassable from their width and depth. Extensive field works also guarded this approach to the city, rendering it about as formidable to an attacking force as the one first described. The third route which presents itself is by the populous town of Tezcuco, and leads through the richest part of the valley. Branching off the right from the main road, just below the hacienda Buena Vista, its general direction is north, running nearly midway between lake Tezcuco and the mountains, until it has passed the town of Tezcuco, when turning to the west it crosses the celebrated stone dike of San Christobal, then skirts the back of Guadaloupe, and enters the capital by the beautiful causeway connecting this last town with the city. The road is remarkably fine the entire distance, the country on either hand thickly populated, level and under the finest state of cultivation, and there are no obstacles to be encountered either natural or artificial, until within two miles of Guadaloupe. At the time General Scott entered the basin, General Valencia, with the troops afterwards conquered at *Contreras*, occupied the town of Tezcuco, fulfilling the triple object of a corps of observation, a decoy to induce pursuit by the *American army*, until entangled among the works defending the city from that side, or in case of defeat before Pinon or Mexicalzingo, to come in the rear of our troops and intercept their retreat. It is evident from an examination of the Mexican works, that failing to take either of the two first mentioned routes, General Scott was confidently expected to approach Mexico by this. The formidable works thrown up at Santiago Sacualco, guarding the entire space between the lake and the mountains, as well as the road which turns it to the north, also the works thrown up on the Queretaro road, at the mountain pass, north of Tenepantlas, and the strong line of defence near the city, demonstrate the determined resistance they expected to make there. The fourth route is to the south of Lake Chalco, and winding along the base of the mountains which bound the valley to the south, strikes the main road leading south from Mexico into the *terra caliente* at San Augustine. The presence of the enemy on the three first mentioned approaches only showed the fourth to be unguarded, and although in itself the least favorable for the passage of troops and trains, and most easily defended, proved to be the one most favorable under existing circumstances. It has been supposed by many, and stated by some, that the Mexican commander, considering this last route wholly impracticable, had failed in taking measures for its defence. This does not clearly seem to have been the case.

From an examination of the accompanying map, it will be seen, that when an enemy is in front of Pinon the communication between it and troops on the other routes is only by way of the city of Mexico itself; in other words, our troops being at Ayotla, General Santa Anna's forces at Pinon were one day's march distant from those at Mexicalzingo, three from those under General Valencia, and would have been about four days' march distant from troops thrown forward on the Chalco route. Fords on these different routes were by no means within supporting distances of each other. Holding the position that General Scott did then, it would have required, of an equal enemy, four times his own force to have opposed successfully his further advance. The Mexican forces were not numerically equal to this, and they were accordingly concentrated at the threatened point.

It is evident that as long as the American troops were in front of Pinon, the enemy necessarily held to their position. In moving off, the former could gain one day the start. This brought the only difficult parts of the Chalco route actually nearer General Scott than the Mexican chief. If to this we add the delay necessary in moving heavy artillery, and breaking up from a fortified position, it would seem that instead of oversight it was rather impossible for General Santa Anna to meet our forces sooner than he did.

This view seems confirmed by observing the works thrown up at *San Antonio* and vicinity, which could have had reference only to the route in question.

The United States troops being situated, as before mentioned, at the point commanding the four approaches to the capital, reconnaissances made during the 12th, 13th and 14th of August determined, first, that Penon was too strong to be attacked, unless absolutely necessary; next, that the route around the lakes was practicable for our trains and artillery, and preferable to attacking by Mexicalzingo. This movement was finally determined upon and commenced the 15th of August, the order of march being the reverse of that by which the army had entered the valley, with this exception. General Worth's division passing that of General Pillow was in the advance, General Twiggs's division now bringing up the rear. The movement was completed, comparatively speaking, without opposition, as the few Mexican troops that showed themselves upon our flanks near Santa Cruz fled at the first approach of our light troops and the third day, after breaking up from before Pinon, the advance of the army entered San Augustine, and the next day the rear division came up. The army was not on the great southern road, leading to Cuernavaca, and if the enemy were taken by surprise, they could advance along it unmolested towards the city, as far at least as where the Mexicalzingo road unites with it.

A strong party sent forward to ascertain what was in front, at a sudden turn of the road, were met by a discharge of grape, which killed Captain Thornton of the dragoons, and caused the reconnoitring officers to recoil in surprise from before the strong position of San Antonio and the line of works which stretch off to the left into the marshy ground of Lake Xochimilco.

From these works, it would seem that the enemy had anticipated the possibility of this movement of the army. Certain it is, they were prepared, as before, to resist a nearer approach to the capital. The entire Mexican force had left the positions first occupied, the eastern approach being no longer threatened, and were ready to make that obstinate defence that shortly ensued. The army having reached this point, it was for the commander-in-chief now to decide whether, after having avoided Pinon to spare life, he would rush his forces against San Antonio, or, threading his way across the Pedrigal to the San Angel road, avoid this strong position, and, at the same time, gain the high grounds, where his movements would for a time be unimpeded by marshes and ditches.

The latter course was decided upon, and, on the 19th, General Pillow's division advanced to open the road. As the movement commenced, it was ascertained that General Valencia, with the troops which had been at *Tezcuco*, was in front, ready to dispute the possession of the San Angel road. After advancing about three miles the progress of the division was arrested, it having come within reach of Valencia's guns.

The only route across the Pedrigal is a rocky path, considered practicable for mules and persons on foot only, although a horseman can pick his way along it. It was at the point where this path struck the road, just referred to, that General Valencia had chosen his position, fortified it with breastworks, within which there were above 20 pieces of artillery sweeping the path and main road. Avoiding the enemy's artillery, by deviating from this path to the right, our light troops succeeded in making the way over the field of rock without much loss, and gained the road in question at a point between Valencia's position and that of Santa Anna, at San Angel. The successful attack on the rear of the entrenched camp by our troops, under General Persifor F. Smith, and the brilliant victory of Padierna or Contreras, on the 20th, are well known.

Immediately after this success, and during the same morning, General Worth, whose position had been in front of San Antonio, succeeded in turning this strong work, and at the same time that General Pillow's and Twiggs's divisions were pursuing the Mexicans through San Angel and onward, he was pressing their retreat along the San Antonio road towards the city, capturing men and artillery. This double pursuit brought the three divisions about the same time to the river Churubusco, and, very unexpectedly to all, upon the formidable works defending its passage.

These works consisted, first, of a church and adjoining building, with a high stone wall enclosure, all strongly fortified, defended by about 2,000 men, and mounting 7 guns; second, of a *tete du pont*, mounting three heavy pieces, and swarming with troops, as well as the river banks to the right and left; also, the road to the rear leading to the city. It will be seen from the accompanying map, that the fortified church naturally fell to General Twiggs's and Pillow's divisions to take, commanding the road leading from San Angel to this point, by which they were advancing, and that the *tete du pont* effectually arrested the progress of General Worth until carried. Almost simultaneously with the attack on these two works, carried after a prolonged and most obstinate defence, a movement was ordered under General Shields to turn the enemy's right flank. This command found the enemy in overpowering force: the number of wounded and slain, however, attest the bravery and determination with which they struggled on to accomplish the object; but it was not until General Worth, having carried the *tete du pont,* came dashing along the road, that the Mexican force was driven from its position, and precipitated headlong towards the city.

After gaining the battle of Churubusco, General Scott was in possession of every thing except the last line of works encircling the city; and for the first time since his entrance into the basin, could, in reality, select his point of attack, and fight on something like an equality.

The armistice following immediately after this battle, the army, during its continuance, occupied the towns of San Augustine, San Angel, Coyacan, Miscoac and Tacubaya.

From this disposition of the forces, they threatened at once both the southern and western approaches to the city, and could, with almost equal facility, attack along either. In looking at the capability for defence of the roads leading from these two directions, it can scarcely be doubted but that the army entered the city from its strongest side. This fact affords but another proof of the foresight and skill of the general commanding, who could so deceive his enemy in reference to the real point of danger, as to make him dismantle his works on the side at last attacked, and leave them in a measure defenceless.

After the armistice was broken, the battle of *Molino del Rey*, the storming of Chapultepec, and taking the city followed in rapid succession. Of these I shall only remark in reference to the battle of *Molino del Rey*.

It has been frequently asserted that this battle was fought unnecessarily, that the American loss was great without any corresponding advantages, and that it had little or no bearing upon the subsequent capture of Chapultepec.

That our loss was greater than it would have been could the force and position of the enemy have been more accurately known, is doubtless

APPENDIX B

true. True also that greater advantages than those resulting from that battle were gained in the course of the war, and with far less loss; but this by no means shows that the results of the battle of Molino were not of the greatest importance in the after successes. The *Molino del Rey*, or *Mill of the King*, from its position stands in the relation of a very strong outwork to the castle of Chapultepec, which is situated on a small rocky isolated mount 150 feet high, and a half mile nearer the city. As the mill is commanded and defended by the castle, so it reciprocally commands and defends the only good approach to the latter.

The consequences of the battle to the enemy were, that in addition to the loss of an important outwork and the weakening the main work necessarily resulting from it, also, the usual results in killed, wounded, dispersed, and taking prisoners, they were driven from a commanding position into the low grounds at the base of Chapultepec, these grounds being completely commanded from the Molino, and were powerless in preventing the siege pieces from taking up the most favorable position for battering the castle. In the final attack upon the castle, one of the two assaulting columns (General Pillow's) started from this very mill, and from what has been remarked should have been the successful one, as was the case, for it started from within the enemy's work and found itself on an equality with him up to the very moment of scaling his walls at the crest of the mount, whereas the other assaulting column (General Quitman's) taking the only remaining approach to the castle, a causewayed road leading from Tacubaya, was successfully held at bay by the outworks defending this road at the base of the hill, until after the castle was taken; and the opposing force was taken in rear by troops passing through and around Chapultepec.

The victory of Molino also had, as it could not well fail to have, the effect of completely demoralizing the enemy, destroying his confidence to hold any position.

In glancing over the operations in the valley, one cannot but be astonished at the uninterrupted success which attended every movement; neither can one fail to admire the unshaken resolution and steady confidence in himself and troops exhibited by the commander-in-chief, under circumstances when one reverse would probably have been followed by utter annihilation.

It would have been fortunate, in view of the number of lives lost, had the force led into the valley been greater. Could General Scott, at the time of moving around Lake Chalco, have left a strong force at Ayotla, Mexico would have fallen, comparatively speaking, an easy prey; for had Valencia left his position and gone to defend the southern part of the city, the northern would have been left defenceless. Had General Santa Anna left his position at the Penon and Mexicalzingo for those of Churubusco and San Antonio, the eastern approach to the city would have been unprotected, or he would have been taken in rear by the Mexicalzingo road; or had both generals remained as at first, the troops moving round the lakes would have met with no opposition in entering Mexico by the south; again, had their troops been so distributed as to guard every approach, their line of defence would have been weak at all points from its great extent.

For more particular information respecting the route around Lake Chalco, and the connected movement of the troops thereon, I have the honor to refer the colonel of the corps to the accompanying memoir of Lieutenant (now brevet Captain) Hardcastle.

I remark, in conclusion, that all the main points on the map are determined by triangulation, the remainder being filled in from compass surveys.

That part of the map south of the city is taken from surveys made under Lieutenant Colonel Turnbull of the corps.

Having no instruments with me of sufficient delicacy and accuracy to determine the longitude and latitude as well even as they had previously been determined, no observations for that purpose were attempted. Having met in the national college with the instrument for determining the declination of the needle, used by Baron Humboldt in 1804, and afterwards presented to that institution by him, I take occasion to state that the declination recorded on the map was determined by it.

To Lieutenant (now brevet Captain) Hardcastle of the corps is due a full proportion of whatever merit the map may possess, having been with me from the commencement of the work to its completion.

I have the honor to be, with great respect, your obedient servant,

M. L. SMITH,
Lieutenant Topographical Engineers.

To Colonel J. J. ABERT,
Colonel Corps Topographical Engineers,
Washington City.

WASHINGTON, D. C., *January* 15, 1849.

SIR: I have the honor to submit the following memoir, as an accompaniment to the map of the valley of Mexico, explanatory of the route of the United States army marked upon it. It may be proper to remark that the substance of this memoir is taken from my journal of the march of the army, written out from day to day, as the events occurred.

APPENDIX B

The advance of the United States army, known as "the army of the south," under the command of Major General Winfield Scott, made its descent into the valley of Mexico on the afternoon of the 10th of August, 1847. This advance corps, composed of the second division of regulars, commanded by Brigadier General Twiggs, and the cavalry brigade, under Colonel Harney, was accompanied by the general-in-chief. For the night, position was taken at the Venta de Cordova, the Venta Nueva, and the hacienda of Buena Vista.

On moving from Puebla, the American army was divided into four divisions, which followed each other on successive days. The advance moved slowly and with ease, never exceeding twelve or fifteen miles in a day's march, so that none of these divisions were at any time separated by a greater distance from each other.

On the morning of the 11th, (August,) being within twenty miles of the enemy's capital, and having on the day previous discovered in our front a large body of their cavalry, both of which indicated our proximity to the enemy in large force, the forward movement of this advance corps was delayed until the next division, under Major General Quitman, was close at hand. By eleven o'clock, this command was seen coming down the mountain slope, and the advance moved forward to the town of Ayotla. The division composed of artillery and infantry occupied the town, and the brigade of cavalry advanced a mile and a half beyond, and took possession of the hacienda of San Isidro.

The town of Ayotla, situate upon the northern border of Lake Chalco, is, by the most direct route, fifteen miles distant from the city of Mexico. This place was selected by the general-in-chief as the point where he should await the arrival of the rear divisions of the army, and from which he could reconnoitre the enemy, and best deceive him as to the route by which he could approach the Mexican capital; for, by reference to the map, it will be seen that from near this point four different roads commence, by which the city of Mexico may be reached.

The first day (August 12) at this position was occupied in making examinations upon the national road, which was the most direct one leading to the city. Seven miles beyond Ayotla, at the Penon, the enemy were found to be strongly fortified and in large force. (At this point, already described, the road passes by the base of a high solitary hill, overlooking the plain for several miles in every direction. Entirely surrounded by water or impassable marshes, it was approachable only by the long narrow causeway of the high road. A position strong by nature, it was bristling with fifty pieces of cannon, arranged in batteries, well placed so as to sweep down the columns of an approaching foe. A long and double line of breastworks for infantry surrounded the base of the hill; and, in fact, every contrivance that art could lend to make this position impregnable seemed to have been bestowed upon it. The auxiliary means of fortification were so complete that this was evidently the stronghold of our enemy, and the spot where they were best prepared and most anxious to receive us.) On this day the first division of regulars, under the command of Brevet Major General Worth, came up, and took position at the town of Chalco.

During the second day (August 13) the examination of the route passing through Mexicalzingo was made; here, also, the enemy were found to be well fortified. (The approach to the town was a straight, narrow causeway, with a wet marsh on each side of it. One battery across the road and enfilading it, as well as a long line of works towards the north, completed the fortifications at this point. Between Mexicalzingo and Penon there extended a continuous marsh, intersected by deep ditches filled with flowing water, which rendered it impassable. The works at this point served, therefore, as a continuation of the same line at Penon.) During this day, the rear division, composed of the new regiments, under Major General Pillow, arrived, and took position near the town of Chalco.

August 14th—Our entire force, numbering about ten thousand rank and file, was now assembled in the valley of Mexico, and there remained to be examined two of the four routes leading to the capitol. It was known to us that General Valencia, with a large Mexican force at Tezcuco, was prepared to dispute our passage over the northern route. Of the southern route, along the margins of lakes Chalco and Xochimilco, very unsatisfactory reports had been brought back by the Mexican guides that had been secretly despatched to explore it. But on this day it was examined as far as Tuliagualco, a distance of 12 miles beyond Chalco, and found to be practicable for our operations. From information gathered from the unoffending and much frightened population, it was believed there were neither fortifications nor natural obstacles sufficient to prevent our passage over this route. The road was narrow, passing between the base of the mountains and the edge of the lakes, and, to all appearances, had never before been travelled by wheel carriages; but it was firm and practicable, and seemed to possess the great advantage over all the others that the enemy had not anticipated, and therefore not prepared for our approach by this route. The road being one seldom travelled, it was little known, and generally believed to be subject to overflow from the adjacent lakes.

On the 15th of August it was made known to the American army that the approach upon the Mexican capital would be by this route, along the southern border of the lakes. To this effect the orders of the general-in-chief were announced, and immediately carried into execution by the advance of Worth's division upon this line. The movement had now commenced by which the plan of operations of the American general was developed to the enemy, for up to this time they had been completely de-

APPENDIX B 315

ceived by the demonstration made upon the national road by occupying the town of Ayotla.

It was on the afternoon of the 17th of August that the advance under General Worth arrived at the town of Tlalpan, or San Augustin, where the lake route first intersects the great southern road, leading from the city of Mexico to Cuernavaca and Acapulco. The time occupied in accomplishing this distance might be considered great, as celerity in our movements was now of the first importance, without a strict examination of the operating causes. The route being untravelled and rough, was of itself difficult to pass over, and for a greater portion of the way contracted, on the one side by mountains, and on the other by the lakes; it was a long and narrow defile, where resistance might be expected at any point. To be prepared to resist an attack, either upon the centre, the front, or the rear, and to afford protection to the baggage train of our army, it was necessary to move with circumspection, and to keep our forces close together. From the town of San Gregorio, the enemy's light troops were continually in our front, harassing and retarding the advance by cutting ditches across the road, and rolling down rocks from the adjacent mountains, which, in many places, completely blocked up the way. All these things combined, necessarily delayed the passage over this route beyond the ordinary time for accomplishing such distance. But if a little more time were consumed by adopting due precaution, the wisdom and prudence of such a course is best illustrated by the fact of the successful accomplishment of the movement, for, with the loss of, perhaps, only a single man, the American army was now upon one of the high roads to the Mexican capitol, and but nine miles distant from it.

On the morning of the 18th, (August,) the division in advance moved up the main road and took position in front of the hacienda of San Antonio, where the enemy had thrown up fortifications. While the examination of this position was going on and the rear divisions were concentrating upon San Augustin, a reconnoissance was being made to the west of this town, to ascertain the practicability of reaching another road to the capital passing through the town of San Angel, and nearly parallel to the one we had already reached. For this road through San Angel was believed not to be so well prepared for defence as the great southern highway, along which the enemy would be likely to expect an invasive foe coming to besiege their capital.

On the 19th, (August,) the examination of the enemy's position at San Antonio was continued, and the reconnoissance towards the San Angel road, which yesterday had been interrupted by the presence of the enemy, was resumed. For the purpose of ensuring the latter, first Pillow's and afterwards Twiggs's division, were sent out in this direction. These were intended to force a passage, and, at the same time, to afford protection to the working parties in the construction of a road over the rugged and broken country that was here presented. After proceeding about three (3) miles in this westerly direction, the enemy's light troops were met, and a skirmish commenced about noon, which, before night, became a general action. Thus began the battle of Contreras, which terminated so gloriously for American arms on the following morning. The general route of our troops in turning the enemy's position at Padierna, by passing through the village of *San Jeronimo*, (improperly called *Contreras*,) is marked in red upon the map.

The Mexican forces, routed from their entrenched position at Padierna, early on the morning of August 20, were pursued by our victorious troops along the road through San Angel and Coyacan. While this pursuit was going on, a movement was made upon San Antonio, causing the enemy to abandon that position, and this second retreating force was hotly pursued by Worth's division down the road to Churubusco. At this point the American troops pursuing from Padierno and those from San Antonio met near about the same time; the former were arrested by the fortifications thrown up around a large convent, the latter by the *tete du pont* defending the bridge across the Churubusco river. The concentration of our forces under such circumstances, at this point, brought on the battle of Churubusco, which terminated late in the day to our complete success, adding another victory to the deeds of American arms on this day.

After the battles of August 20th, and as an immediate consequence of them, the armistice was entered into, by which active and hostile operations on our part ceased for a time. During this period our army was distributed at the towns of Tacubaya, Mixcoac, Coyacan, San Angel, and San Augustin, and each corps was quietly occupied in maintaining the discipline and providing for the comfort of its soldiers, besides giving attention to a large proportion of sick and wounded.

It was at 12 o'clock, meridian, on the 17th of September, that the armistice was mutually dissolved by the commanders of the two antagonistic armies. Reconnoissances of the enemy's lines were immediately commenced, and to the credit of the American general be it said, that he positively forbid any observations of this sort being made by our engineers during the armistice.

Early on the morning of September 8th was fought the battle of Molino del Rey, where the enemy were completely routed, and the preparations he had made for casting cannon, &c., at the Molino, were destroyed.

Strict examinations of the entire line of works from Chapultepec to the gate of San Antonio were carried on from day to day, until the point of attack was decided upon, by the general-in-chief, on the 11th of September. A large proportion of our forces had been concentrated at Piedad and the hacienda of Nalverte, and while, on the morning of September 12th, our

APPENDIX B

batteries opened a fire upon the castle of Chapultepec, (which was the real point of attack,) an active demonstration was made upon the enemy's line, near the gate of San Antonio. To carry out this plan successfully, troops were silently moved from Piedad to Tacubaya on the night of September 12th, and on the next morning the castle of Chapultepec was stormed. After the fall of this commanding work, our troops, under the command of Generals Worth and Quitman, advanced by the two roads leading from this point to the city; the former general approaching by the longer route through the gate of San Cosme; the latter by the shorter one, through the gate of Belen. Upon the map is marked the advance of these two corps, up to the time of the capitulation of the city of Mexico, on the night of September 13th, after the Mexican army had fled.

I am, sir, very respectfully, your obedient servant,

ED. L. F. HARDCASTLE,
Brevet Captain U. S. Topographical Engineers.

Lieut. M. L. SMITH,
U. S. Topographical Engineers.

APPENDIX C

Report of the Chief, Topographical Engineers, 1848

BUREAU OF TOPOGRAPHICAL ENGINEERS.
Washington, November 17, 1848.

SIR: In conformity with established usage, I have the honor to submit the following annual report of the operations of the corps since the last report, and an estimate for the duties for the ensuing year.

The peace with Mexico returned to the United States the large proportion of the officers of the corps which had been employed with the army in that country. The greater part of these were maimed with wounds, or sick from the fatigues and exposures which their duties required. Of their services in Mexico it is not necessary that I should speak. The reports of commanding officers pay frequent and brilliant compliments to their services, and the brevets which have been bestowed attest an accordance of the judgment of the Executive with these compliments. But, in addition to their regular corps duties, several of the corps occupied and exercised important military commands. Captain J. E. Johnston, of the corps, now brevet colonel in the army, in the exercise of his corps duties, until after the battle of Cerro Gordo, where he was severely wounded while reconnoitering the enemy's position, was afterwards made lieutenant colonel of the regiment of voltigeurs, and in that capacity acquired great reputation for the skill he displayed in the drill and discipline of the regiment, and for his gallantry in command on several important occasions. On the peace, he returned to his corps as a captain under a law of the last session and with the brevet of a colonel.

Captain G. W. Hughes, after important services in the duties of his corps with the army in North Mexico, and afterwards at Vera Cruz and Cerro Gordo, returned to the States emaciated and broken down by the climate, his fatigues and exposures. But rapidly recovering his health, he was placed at the head of a regiment of volunteers, and immediately went

APPENDIX C

back with his command to Mexico. His march from Vera Cruz to Jalapa is spoken of as one of great merit and severe trial, in which he on several occasions encountered and beat the enemy. He was then made military and civil governor of the department of Jalapa and Perote, and by his highly judicious, energetic, prompt, and well judged measures, was mainly instrumental in keeping that extensive district quiet as well as the whole road from thence to Vera Cruz. He continued in this command until termination of the war, when he returned to the United States, and has since resumed his duties in his corps, with the brevet of major.

First Lieutenant W. H. Emory. This officer accompanied General Kearny throughout his important and perilous march from the Missouri to the Pacific, as the chief of his engineer staff, executing also, towards the close of those operations, the duty of adjutant general to General Kearny's command. After the fighting in California had ceased, he was ordered back to the United States with despatches for the War Department. He was soon afterwards appointed the lieutenant colonel of Colonel Hughes's regiment of volunteers, (the Maryland and District of Columbia volunteers) and immediately joined him at Jalapa, with a part of that regiment which had not previously marched. He continued with Colonel Hughes until the end of the war, rendering important military services, after which he returned to the United States, and resumed duties in his corps, with brevets which gave him the rank of major.

First Lieutenant Wm. H. Warner. This officer was placed in charge of the ordnance train of General Kearny's command. He has also executed similar duties under Colonel Mason, in California, where he is at present, exercising the proper duties of his corps with the brevet rank of captain. He was severely wounded in the conflicts under General Kearny.

I have named these four officers because they were so fortunate as to obtain positions and exercise commands independent of and separate from their proper corps' functions, exhibiting the versatility of talent in the corps, and its ability to fulfil any military duties which it may be found necessary or proper to assign to it.

But there are other duties of the corps of less eclat, but not of less usefulness and importance, which shall now be reported.

All the interesting observations and reconnoitring made by the corps while operating with the armies in Mexico, are now being compiled in a map, under resolutions of the Senate, and will soon be completed, and be submitted to Congress. Of these examinations there has been already laid before Congress, Major Emory's report and map of General Kearny's march from the Missouri to the Pacific, and plans of the several engagements in which that command was involved; also Lieutenant Abert's map of New Mexico, and the report of his examinations of that country. These two reports add much to our geographical knowledge of that region of the world, and furnish great facilities to any future operations in that quarter, whether civil, military, or commercial.

Accurate geographical and topographical knowledge of a country are particularly essential to military operations. They are the eyes of the commanding general. With these he can see the country, and can know how to direct and combine all his movements or marches, whether offensive or defensive, and without them he is literally groping in the dark, incapable of devising plans for his own operations, or of anticipating those of an enemy. With this knowledge, war becomes a science, in which intellect will ever predomidate over numbers; without it, war becomes the mere exhibition of physical force: slow, expensive, and often disastrous, as numbers and courage can alone be relied upon. Unless a knowledge of the country through which an army has to move is possessed, the army can act only on the defensive, and if this knowledge has to be obtained in the presence of an enemy, it is always at great loss of time, necessarily imperfect, and at great hazard of the services and lives of invaluable officers. Some of the most important movements and operations of the late war were governed by previous reconnoissances, made generally in advance of the army, and in the presence of the enemy, who might by his vigilance have interrupted or defeated them. We see, therefore, in these, as well as in hundreds of other instances which could be cited, the importance of geographical and topographical knowledge in army operations. Now this knowledge, a duty of the corps of tographical engineers to collect, can be well obtained only in time of peace. Peace is, therefore, the period which best enables a people to acquire the information necessary for the defence of their own soil, or to attack that of an enemy. From these general and important considerations it is no doubt owing, that in General Order 49, of the 31st of last August, by "the President of the United States," that this bureau is required to furnish officers of the corps of the commands of Oregon, California, New Mexico, and Texas. These are frontier commands, but lately the seat of war, exposed and even now threatened with hostile depredations from numerous bands of warlike and discontented Indians, long accustomed to domineer over those parts of Mexico and Oregon, now the possession of the United States, and whose tastes for plunder have been lately so often gratified without adequate chastisement, even nearer to us than the limits lately acquired.

These commands will probably require about twenty-five officers of the corps, and these officers can be of but little use, or can render comparatively but unimportant and unsatisfactory services unless means of making the surveys which may be considered necessary are allowed. The army can furnish escorts and safeguards, but it cannot furnish the means necessary for making surveys. Even in addition to its escorts, if it were able, which it is not, also to detach the numbers required for surveys, in

APPENDIX C

the various capacities of mechanics, chain-men, axe-men, boatmen, guides, and laborers, which these duties require, it could not furnish the requisite instruments, boats, tools, pack-horses, wagons, & c., &c.; and the men which might be detached are rarely of the kind qualified for such duties, while such detachments are destructive of discipline and of usefulness in their proper corps. Economy of cost, and the well-being of these duties, do therefore most eminently call for some arrangement by which such duties can be performed, independent of calls upon the army, except for escorts and safeguards. In my long experience as an officer in the field, as well as at the head of this bureau, in which first capacity I have operated with men detached from the army, but two modes have suggested themselves as adequate to meet the difficulty.

One is that which the government has now for so many years adopted, namely, the making of small annual appropriations to meet the contingencies of a survey. The second is that of enlisting men specially adapted to these duties. Although this last is the practice of other countries, it has never been adopted by us. It is without doubt the better course, admitting, as it does, of the most economical, the most prompt, and the most intelligent execution of the duty, reducing the contingencies of a survey to those smaller items, independent of the pay and support of the class of mechanics and others as before enumerated, which have now to be employed temporarily, and at far greater cost, and whose experience and the facility and knowledge acquired in the duties are continually lost by frequent changes, which the temporary nature of their present employment involves.

But inasmuch as this latter course has not been adopted by the government, I can submit no estimate in reference to it, and shall on that account submit estimates in conformity with established usage.

As before remarked, the commands of Oregon, California, New Mexico, and Texas, have to be supplied with officers of the corps, and surveys have to be made in those commands.

I therefore respectfully submit for considerations—

For military surveys in Oregon.................................	$10,000
For military surveys in California..............................	10,000
For military surveys in New Mexico...........................	10,000
For military surveys in Texas, and from the navigable waters of the Red River to the Rio Grande	15,000

Our knowledge of the Red River above Nachitochez is more general than precise, but there is every reason to believe that its capacity for boat navigation extends far into the interior of Texas, even as high as old Fort Washita, to which point, and above it, it is represented that two feet of water can be carried throughout much of the year. These facts make that river a line of great military importance in reference to the defence of that frontier, and if correct, will enable the government to establish a series of military posts upon that river, and to be supplied from it in the very heart of the Camanche country. And if from the head navigable waters of this river a good military road can be traced to the Rio Grande, its facilities in the defence of that frontier will be invaluable, as well as in whatever relates to the defence of New Mexico by ready and easy access to that quarter, and by such means of more fully developing its agricultural and mineral resources.

These distant military posts and military roads are the pioneers of civilization and of wealth, by the protection they afford to remote settlements, the value they give to public lands, the encouragement to cultivation by the consumption of produce, and by the intelligence and good habits diffused by such a nucleus of well-informed and orderly persons of both sexes as generally constitute the population of our garrisions.

The usual surveys in reference to the military defences of the frontier, inland and Atlantic, have to be attended to. These are generally of positions to be fortified and of their approaches, upon a scale sufficiently large to plan the works required, and embracing all those details collected by no other surveys, necessary to determine upon the true position and probable cost of the contemplated work. For these objects a small amount of ten thousand dollars is only required, as there is an unexpended balance of a former appropriation.

The survey of the lakes has been pushed forward as rapidly as circumstances would admit. The large proportion of the corps required for the armies in Mexico, obliged a rather restricted employment upon this survey during the last season, but the whole of that intricate navigation at the western end of Lake Erie, between a line from Sandusky to Point Pelee, and thence west to the mouth of Detroit river, with its several islands and shoals, has been thoroughly surveyed, and the maps and charts are now being made.

The collection of lake surveys has become so numerous, under the various appropriations which have been made, that the office is now ready to issue an atlas of charts which would be of great aid to the commerce of the lakes. The cost of engraving a suitable edition would not exceed five thousand dollars, for which an estimate is respectfully submitted. The advantage of such a publication would be invaluable, and would give to the great and increasing commerce of the lakes those guides of which it now stands so much in need. No additional estimate for the survey of the lakes is submitted. The late period of the last session of Congress at which the existing appropriation was made and the restricted operations as before described, have left a sufficient balance for the operations of the next season, which, together with the desire of avoiding all demands which the well being of public service shall not make extremely necessary, have induced me to omit any additional estimate on this account for the ensuing season. It is contem-

APPENDIX C   323

plated, in the course of the ensuing season, to make a geographical connexion between the survey of the lakes and the Atlantic coast, by means of the magnetic telegraph, which now extends to Buffalo, Detroit and Chicago.

A law of the 3d March, 1847, assigned to this office the construction of several light-houses.

In the annual report of November 22, 1847, these are all referred to in so much detail, that it leaves but little now to be said in this report.

Light-house on the Whale's Back rock, Portsmouth, New Hampshire.

In the report of last year, the light-house on this position is minutely described, the plan of construction, and the defects in the plan. It is there stated that the repairs of this work would involve a cost about equal to that of a new iron pile structure, and would in the end be a patched structure, and would probably fail in meeting just expectations. It is also stated in the same report that as fears of "immediate danger to the present structure are not entertained, no work has been commenced." Other reasons induced a delay in the work at this place; these were to await the experience of erecting an iron pile light upon a much more exposed position, Minot's Rock, Boston harbor. Having now overcome the chief difficulties in the work on Minot's Rock, another careful examination of the Whale's Back Rock light will be made in the ensuing spring, when it will be decided whether the "rebuilding" directed should be farther postponed or be immediately commenced.

Light-house on Minot's Rock, Boston harbor.

This has been a work of extreme difficulty, and of no little danger, and the results are a singular exhibition of the triumphs of perseverance and mechanical ingenuity. The rock is exposed to the whole burst of the Atlantic wave. A small portion of it, involving a circular area, rarely exceeding 25 feet in diameter, is bare at low water and during very calm weather. But no part of this area is more than three feet above extreme low water, and during slight winds the sea breaks over the whole with great violence. Upon this small and extremely exposed position, a footing had to be obtained, and holes had to be drilled in the rock, in which were to be inseted the iron piles to sustain the structure. This short description will sufficiently apprise all those who have any knowledge of a sea shore of the serious and continued difficulties of working on such a place. It gives me great pleasure to add that no lives have yet been lost in the work, although there have been several accidents, and additional pleasure to say that all the piles to sustain the work have been established, as well as the skeleton iron frame of the top, intended to connect the piles and to sustain the keeper's house and lantern. All serious difficulties are therefore overcome.

The work has been under the superintendence of Captain Swift of the corps, and the resident agent and contractor was Mr. Benjamin Pomeroy, a person of the most extraordinary perseverance and inexhaustible ingenuity, and well acquainted with working in such positions. The report of Captain Swift is hereto added as an appendix. A small appropriation of 4,500 dollars is now required to procure and complete the illuminating apparatus for this lighthouse, which I believe will be found to be one of the most useful on that coast.

Brandywine Shoal light.

This structure is on a sand bar in the mouth of Delaware Bay. The lower tier of piles are all in place braced and connected, so that in reference to this work, it may also be said that its chief difficulties are overcome. The work will be left in this condition before the superstructure is put up, in order to see the effect of winter storms and of floating ice upon it. As the report and estimate of the superintending engineer, Major H. Bache, has not yet been received, I am necessarily obliged to delay any further notice of the work, or additional estimate to a future time.

Carys fort reef light-house.

This is also an extremely difficult position upon the Florida keys, and is to be made upon iron piles sunk into the rocky soil of the reef. The reef has been carefully examined, the structure is being prepared, and it is contemplated that during the month of December the materials and frame will be transported to the reef, and the erection of the building be commenced.

Sand Key light-house.

It was so late a period during the last session that the difficulty in the law in reference to this work was removed, but little more has been done than to survey the position. Moreover, it is extremely desirable to profit in the erection of this light-house by the experience which will be acquired in the erection of the one on Carys Fort reef.

Wangoshance Shoal light-house, straits of Michigan.

We have succeeded in establishing the pier work, essential to the protection and construction of this work, and also the concrete foundation within the piers, upon which the keeper's dwelling and light-house are to be erected.

All these structures are works of extreme difficulty, in much exposed positions, requiring great care, great energy, untiring perseverance, and more than common mechanical resources in the superintending engineer. The success which has attended our efforts, as already described, is proof that these qualifications have not been wanting, is the best compliment upon the plans which have been pursued, and justifies the anticipation that the whole of these works will in good time be completed, and will be permanently established.

The construction of the light-house at Monroe, Michigan, an assignment to this bureau, at the request of the Treasury Department, is nearly completed. The superintending engineer reports that it will be finished during the ensuing month of December.

Sea wall for the protection of Fairweather island, near Black Rock, Connecticut.

A part of the small balance of the appropriation of 1847 was expended in the construction of this wall early in last December, when it was inspected and received, and the rest of this small balance was expended in May, 1848, in repairing an old wall formerly put up at this place by the Treasury Department, for the protection of the light keeper's house.

The late period at which the appropriation of 1848 was made, necessarily run the work late in the season. 700 perches of the wall had been laid by the 1st of November, leaving about 1,200 more perches yet to be put down. Of these about 600 perches will probably be finished during the present month; the balance of the work will have to be suspended until after the ensuing spring.

In addition to these duties, an officer of the corps, Lieutenant Colonel Turnbull, on application from the Treasury Department, has been assigned to superintend the building of the custom-house at New Orleans. And, on application from the same department, this bureau has been authorized to superintend the construction of a marine hospital at Chicago, one at Paducah, and one at Natchez. The additional estimates which these works require will be submitted to the consideration of the Treasury Department, as the work, although now a duty of this bureau, is, from the wording of the law, under the superintendence of that department.

An officer of the corps, Major J. D. Graham, is occupied, under the State Department, in efforts to restore the maps of the northeastern boundary, which were destroyed by fire. He has three assistants from the corps temporarily assigned to him.

On an application from General Brooke, two officers of the corps were assigned to him for the purposes of making a military reconnoissance of the upper Mississippi, with a view of establishing certain frontier posts, and to make the surveys of the localities which should be selected. The duty will be completed during the present month.

There was a resolution of the House of Representatives, dated August 8, 1848, directing the Secretary of War to have a "survey and examination made of that part of the Potomac river between the Long bridge and Georgetown, with a view to ascertain the cause of the formation of land on the flats along the banks of the river, and that he cause also an estimate to be made of the cost of repairing the Long bridge; and also of constructing a bridge across the Potomac at the aqueduct of the canal at Georgetown, and also an estimate of the probable cost of keeping up a steamboat ferry in the place of the Potomac bridge, and that the report be made at as early a period in the next session as practicable."

The execution of this resolution will of necessity be very imperfect without making the survey as directed, and this survey, in order properly to elucidate the questions involved in the resolution, should extend as far below the bridge as Alexandria. But there is no appropriation out of which the expenses of the survey, directed to be made, can be met; and it does not appear to have been covered by any appropriation during the session in which the resolution was passed. Under these circumstances, I am not aware of any other course to be pursued than to submit to the consideration of the department an estimate for the survey directed to be made. Since the Long bridge was erected, the river has experienced very serious modifications in its shoals and channels, immediately adjacent to the bridge and below it, as well as above the bridge. All these changes should be minutely ascertained, and carefully delineated, before an intelligent and reliable report, under the resolution, can be made. But, inasmuch as the expenses incident to the resolution cannot be met without an appropriation, an item for three thousand dollars on that account is submitted.

Appropriations for various streets and avenues of the city.

As it was only those streets, or parts of streets, directed to be paved, which were placed under the War Department, it will be only of these upon which any report will be made from this office. It was late in the season when these appropriations were passed, and, in addition, it was directed that the work should be done by contract, after thirty days' notice to bidders in the cities of Washington, Baltimore, Philadelphia, and New York. This change in the system involved many serious and injurious delays: in the time necessary to prepare the advertisements, in the notice of thirty days required to be given, in the examination of the bids and the making of the contracts, and in the preparations for work, as no bidder could make the requisite preparations until after he was assured

APPENDIX C 327

that he would obtain the contract. These causes of delay absorbed so much time as to render it comparatively impossible to complete the work this season, as, from these causes, it could not be commenced before the 9th day of October. Without these delays, more than half of the work would have been completed by the day, when, owing to these delays, the work had to be commenced.

The system heretofore has not been to do such work by contract, except for materials and particular parts in which the contract system could be adopted to advantage, and I venture, without fear of error, to say that, in reference to economy of cost, energy of execution, and quality of both work and materials, that the paving heretofore done will compare advantageously with that of any part of the country.

The appropriation for completing the centre strip of the avenue is inadequate to the work, as it does not cover the low bid at which the contract is made. A small item, to meet this deficiency, and to cover charges for overseers and superintendents, is submitted, amounting to $1,200.

There is also additional work to that contemplated in the appropriation for fifteenth street, which will cost about $1,500, and also a sewer or drain under fifteenth street, which will cost about $2,160. This street is the drain of large bodies of water, requiring an underground sewer or drain sufficient capacity. To pave the street before constructing this drain would be an extravagant mode of proceeding, as much of the pavement will have to be taken up, and the ground re-excavated, in order to make the drain at any future period, at an increased expense, which will nearly double the cost at which the work can now be done; and, as I fear we will not be able to do the paving of fifteenth street this winter, an estimate for this drain, of $2,160, is respectfully submitted to your consideration.

In doing the pavement that has been ordered, the side walks are of necessity taken up to some extent, and seriously deranged in their slope. I allude now particularly to the side walks on the streets in front of the executive buildings. These side walks, badly bedded when first laid, are also much worn and broken. It is respectfully suggested that these should be relaid. The cost will be about $6,000.

Seventeenth street, the street west of the war office, is so intimately connected with the work now being done, under the laws of the last session, that the work will necessarily be imperfect and liable to serious changes hereafter, unless seventeenth street be included in the operation. This street, like fifteenth street, is the drain of vast bodies of water, and will require a large culvert, and the whole surface of the street to be modified to a different grade. The work should extend to the south of the present Navy Department lot, and will cost about $13,000.

An estimate, in accordance with the expositions of this report, will be submitted to your consideration.

Respectfully, sir, your obedient servant,

J. J. ABERT,
Colonel corps Topographical Engineers.

Hon. W. L. MARCY,
Secretary of War.

P.S. The estimate was made in conformity with this report, but was afterwards modified by direction of superior authority.

WASHINGTON, *November* 4, 1848.

SIR: I have the honor to make the following report upon the several works enumerated below, which, by the orders of the bureau, are entrusted to my superintendence:

1. *Light-house on Whale's Back, harbor of Portsmouth, N. H.*

The report which was made on the 2d April, 1847, contains the reasons which induced me to recommend that no steps might be taken towards the rebuilding of the light-house at the Whale's Back until the light at Minot's rock, in Boston harbor, should be in a state of forwardness.

I represented, in the report above referred to, that the old light was in no immediate danger; and I doubt not now that it may answer all the purposes of a new structure for some years to come; still, it would be proper to have another careful inspection of the building made in the ensuing spring, when it could be determined whether the rebuilding should be further postponed or not.

2. *Minot's Rock light-house, Boston harbor, Mass.*

At the date of the last annual report (October 15, 1847) the condition of the work at the Minots was stated, and some of the difficulties which attended the operations of that season were specified. As the frame or main structure may now be considered completed, a brief description of the work and some details connected with it during the progress of construction, may be regarded as not uninteresting.

Minot's Rocks, or, as they are generally designated, "the Minots," lie off the southeastern *chop* of Boston bay, about seventeen miles from the city, and something less than eight miles from the Boston light.

These rocks or ledges, with others in their immediate vicinity, are known as the "Cohasset Rocks," and have been the terror of mariners for

APPENDIX C

a long period of years; they have been, probably, the cause of a greater number of wrecks than any other reefs or ledges upon the coast, lying, as they do, at the very entrance to the second city of the United States, in point of tonnage, and, consequently, where vessels are continually passing and repassing. The Minots are sunken, and bare only at one quarter flood, and the trend of the coast in that direction from Boston bar being southeasterly, vessels bound in, with wind heavy at northeast, are liable, if they fall to leeward of Boston light, to be driven upon these rocks.

As evidence of the great necessity of a light at these dangerous rocks, I have in my possession, from a reliable source, a statement of the number of vessels, with their names and tonnage, which have struck upon the Cohasset rocks within the last thirty years, but mostly, as my informant remarks, within the last fifteen years, to wit: ships, 10; brigs, 14; schooners, 16; sloops, 3; total 43. Of these, 27 were a total loss. From all this, it may be clearly inferred that it became necessary that these hidden dangers should be pointed out to the seamen, and, instead of the fatal breaker to give him the first warning of his approach to danger, that there should be a friendly beacon erected upon the rock, to guide him in the storm, and enable him to avoid the horrors of shipwreck; and these, doubtless, were the considerations which led to the enactment of the law for building the light-house in question.

The rock selected for the site of the light-house is called the "Outer Minot," and lies farther seaward than others in the group known as the Cohasset rocks. At extreme low water, an area of about thirty feet in diameter is exposed, and the highest point in the rock is about three and a half feet above the line of low water. It is very rare, however, that a surface greater than twenty-five feet in diameter is left bare by the sea. The rock is granite, with vertical seams of trap rising through it.

From observations upon the tides, made at Boston light-house by the coast survey, from June 7th to October 27th, 1847, the following results were obtained; and, by the kind permission of the superintendent, communicated to me, together with a tracing of the coast from Boston light to Scituate light.

Rise of highest tide	14 feet 7 inches.
Mean rise and fall of tides	9 " 4 "
" " " spring tides	10 " 8 "
" " " neap "	8 " 3 "

The form of the light-house frame is an octagon, of 25 feet diameter at base. The structure is formed of eight heavy wrought iron piles, or shafts, placed at equal distances from each other, with one, also, at the centre. These piles were forged in two pieces each, and are connected together by very stout cast iron or gun metal sockets, the interior of which is bored, and the pile ends are turned and secured to the sockets by means of large steel keys passing through the piles and the sockets. Above and below the joints, or sockets, and connecting the middle pile with each outer pile, there extends a series of wrought iron braces; and the outer shafts are connected together to similar, extending from one to the other, and thus the whole structure is tied together. At each of the angular points in the octagan and at the centre a hole of twelve inches in diameter and five feet in depth is drilled in the rock, the outer holes with the inclination or batter given to the outer piles and the middle holes vertical.

The surface of the rock being irregular in shape, and the holes in each case five feet deep, it is evident that the piles must be of unusual lengths, the least length in the lower series is thirty-five and a quarter feet; the greatest is thirty-eight and three-quarters feet, and the others are of various lengths between them. The piles in the upper series are of uniform length, viz: twenty-five feet each, the inclination or batter of the piles towards the centre is such as to bring the heads of the upper piles within the periphery of a circle of fourteen feet diameter, and there, at an elevation of sixty feet above the base of the middle pile, or fifty-five feet above the highest point of the rock, the pile heads are secured to a heavy casting or cap, to the arms of which they are securely keyed and bolted. The middle shaft is eight inches in diameter at foot and six inches at top, and the outer shafts are eight inches at foot and four and a half inches at top. All of these are forged ten inches in diameter, at the point where they leave the surface of the rock and taper uniformly down to eight inches diameter in both directions, within a distance of five feet. The lower braces, placed nineteen feet above the rock, are three and a half inches in diameter; the second series, nineteen and a half feet above the first or thirty-eight and a half feet above the rock, are three inches diameter, and a third series, introduced eight and a quarter feet below the cast iron cap, to form the support of the floor of the store room, is made of two and half inch square iron.

The outer piles being inclined towards the centre, and the piles and the braces being inflexible, it is clear that, so long as the braces remain in place, the pile cannot be withdrawn from the hole, for the whole structure acts as an immense "luvis;" either the braces must be ruptured, or the rock itself must yield, before a pile can be displaced.

Upon the pile-heads are cast-iron sockets, furnished with arms three feet in length, pointing outwards. These sockets are keyed to the head of the piles, and are bolted to the arms of the cap or spider, flush with its upper surface; thus giving a diameter at top of 20 feet from out to out. The object of the arms is to afford support for a footway or gallery outside of the keeper's house, which is placed immediately on the cap, and there secured by bolts and keys.

The keeper's house is octagonal in shape, and 14 feet in diameter; the uprights or stanchions are of cast-iron, and rest upon the cap immedi-

APPENDIX C 331

ately over the pile-heads, where they are secured with bolts and keys; these uprights are cast with double flanches, between which two-inch plank, tongued and grooved, are to be fitted horizontally, and at right angles to these another series of plank is to be set on end or vertically, and, together, these form the side or frame of the house; upon this frame the roof will be placed, and, finally, upon this the lantern will be set up.

The drilling of the holes in the rock for the light-house occupied the better part of two seasons. The erection of the iron structure in place, it may be conceived, was comparatively a work of much less difficulty, and, with favorable weather, an undertaking requiring not much time. That some of the difficulties may be known of working down 9 holes of 12 inches diameter and 5 feet in depth, in a rock of granite traversed by veins of the most obstinate trap, in a situation exposed to the delays produced by every breeze which had *east* in it, I will enumerate briefly, from the journal of operations kept at the rock, some of the details, for future reference.

Early in April, 1847, I invited Mr. Benjamin Pomeroy, the contractor who had in 1843 erected for me the Black Rock beacon, in Long Island sound, (a structure built upon the same principle that the Minot Rock light is built upon,) to accompany me to Cohasset, with the view of inducing him to undertake the drilling of the holes by contract, and also to take the piles, braces, and cap at Messrs. Alger & Co., South Boston, where the work was to be executed, and to erect them in place at the Minot. After waiting eight days at Cohasset for a favorable opportunity to examine the rock, we effected a landing, and, with the advantages of a smooth sea and a very low tide, made sufficient measurements to determine the probable area of sound rock which might be relied upon for the base of the proposed light-house.

The proposition made by Mr. Pomeroy, to drill the holes in the rock for the reception of the piles for the light-house, I considered too high, and consequently I declined it and sought elsewhere for a competent individual to undertake the work; after advertising in the newspapers, I received proposals from Mr. James Savage, and entered into an agreement with him to drill the holes, but after some weeks' delay Mr. Savage abandoned the contract; I then recommended and was authorized to accept the proposals of Mr. Pomeroy, and he undertook the work at once, but by the failure of the first contractor the greater part of the best portion of the season, 1847, was lost, and it was not until July 22, that the new contractor, Mr. Pomeroy, actually commenced work upon the rock.

The mode of working the holes down had for some time occupied the thoughts of the contractor, and he became satisfied that holes of the magnitude required in that exposed situation, where the sea was so continually breaking over the rock, could be drilled by machinery only, and that it would be necessary to have that machinery elevated beyond the ordinary reach of the sea.

The drill used was of a peculiar form, with an edge in shape somewhat similar to the letter z, made of the best cast steel, and fitted to an iron shaft some 30 feet in length, and weighing, with the drill attached, about 600 pounds.

The machine for working the drill was a wheel and axle furnished with tooth and pinion, and a crank or windlass at each end; this was placed on a frame of stout oak, and it required the power of four men to work it effectively. A cam and a fly wheel were attached to the axle, and at every revolution the drill was raised about eight inches, and driven ordinarily at the rate of about fifty strokes per minute, the men being relieved every twenty minutes.

To support this machine, it was necessary to erect upon the rock a triangle or shears of very heavy spars, secured at their feet by means of pintles, and chained down to Lewis bolts inserted in the rock; upon the triangle was placed a platform, and upon this the machine was worked, the drill being kept at the proper degree of inclination for the hole by means of guides, through which the shaft moved up and down; the whole arrangement answered the purpose admirably well, and the holes were cut as truly and as perfectly as an auger hole could be cut in a piece of wood.

The triangle and drilling machine were swept from the rock twice by the sea during the first season's operations, and the men were frequently washed from the rock, but happily no lives have been lost. The work was suspended at the rock on the 25th October, 1847, and by reference to the journal of operations, noted carefully day by day, it will be seen how short a space of time can be reckoned upon for work in a situation so exposed.

In the report of the contractor of the 8th November, 1847, accompanying the journal of operations for that season, is the following remark:

"It will be seen by my journal, that from the 22d July to the 25th October, I was able to land on the rock, to do work, only 25 days, viz: 5 days in July, 13 in August, 7 in September and none in October. The whole number of hours we did actually work on the rock was only 120 hours, of which 53 were from the triangle when we could not stand on the rock to work."

The total number of men employed in 1847 by the contractor was 34, the average number about 21; in addition, a schooner of about 80 tons burthen was chartered by the contractor for himself and his hands to live on board of, and the vessel was kept moored near the rock at all times when she could lie there in safety, or when the weather would admit of it; by this arrangement every hour of time, in which work could be done at the rock, was rendered available.

All the necessary preparations for the work of the present season were made early in the spring; a new triangle was provided of heavy spars,

APPENDIX C   333

some forty-five feet in length, and strengthened by a number of very stout iron braces, and with bars of iron on each spar, extending over all that part of the triangle which was exposed to the shock of the sea; a vessel and hands were employed by the contractor, but no work upon the rock was effected until the 18th, 19th, and 20th May, and from that period until the 3d and 5th of June nothing was done, the weather and sea preventing even a landing. Between the 14th and 29th of June the sea generally was smoother, still there were several of the intervening days on which little or nothing could be done; from 29th June to 19th July, but three landings were made, and at these times the sea ran so high there was but little work accomplished.

On the 21st July, this remark is found in the journal: "To day and yesterday worth more for work on rock than last four weeks."

The holes were all finished on the 16th August; that is to say, 9 holes of 12 inches diameter, 5 feet deep each.

Some delay was produced in this stage of the work, by an alteration which I had decided some time earlier in the season to make, to wit: to increase both the size and the length of the lower series of piles, and this increase in dimensions produced some delay in the forging at the machine shop. The difference in size between piles of hammered iron 25 feet long and 8 inches diameter, as originally designed, and piles 35 feet long and increased to 10 inches diameter, the size ultimately adopted, involved some difficulties, and required a little more time in the fabrication than I had reckoned upon, so that it was not until the 2d September that 6 piles of the lower series were forged.

On the 4th and 5th September, these 6 piles were erected in place, and, by the 21st, the three remaining lower piles had been placed, and three of the braces belonging to that series placed also.

From the 21st September until the 7th October, no landing could be effected upon the rock. On that day the middle pile of the upper series was placed in its position; on the 10th October two more were put up; on the 12th five more, and on the 16th the last pile of the upper series was set in its place. On the 26th October, the cap, or spider, a casting to rest upon the heads of the piles to receive the dwelling house of the keeper and the lantern, consisting of eight arms and weighing some five tons, was hoisted partially towards its place, and on the 30th October this difficult undertaking was successfully completed, and the spider fixed in its proper position and secured there, at an elevation of fifty-five feet above the top of the rock.

The Boston light being a revolving light, and the Minot being the next in order upon the coast, should be a fixed light; accordingly the apparatus ordered is of that character, and is composed of fifteen brass lamps, with reflectors of 21 inches diameter in the clear, with very heavy plating of silver, and the best description of work.

The framing of the lantern is of wrought iron; and is a polygon of sixteen faces, diameter at the angles eleven feet six inches, height six feet six inches, furnished with cast-iron ventilator, the glass, French plate, forty-four inches by twenty-four inches, and three-eighths of an inch thick; the extent of the illumination will be two hundred and ten degees.

Thus it will be seen that the entire height of the structure from the surface of the rock to the top of the lantern will be about seventy feet, and upwards of fifty feet above the line of highest water.

The weight of iron work in the shafts, braces, couplings, collars, spider, or cap, and columns for keeper's house is nearly seventy tons; of this upwards of forty tons is wrought iron, and the residue of cast iron; the average weight of each complete shaft is about 8,200 pounds; that cast iron couplings for connecting the upper shafts with the lower are three feet long, and weigh nearly 800 pounds each; they are made of the best gun metal. The weight of the lantern and illuminating apparatus will be about four and a half tons. The lantern, lamps, reflectors, and other fixtures for the light-house will cost four thousand five hundred dollars, as will appear by the detailed estimates of same, rendered on the 24th ultimo.

Below the keeper's house, and enclosed within the pile heads, a species of cellar, or store room, of the size of the house, is to be built, to contain oil, fuel, provisions, &c. I had hoped last season that all this might have been accomplished before the boisterous weather of the present year came on, and the light brought into use this winter; but this has not been practicable, as the journals of operations will clearly prove.

On the other hand, it may be considered not unwise to allow the skeleton structure to stand through one winter exposed to the fury of the sea, before the light-house is fitted up with its illuminating apparatus, and before it is occupied by a keeper.

3. *Sea-wall for the protection of Fair Weather island, near Black Rock, Connecticut.*

The balance of the appropriation of 1847, except $108, was expended in the construction of the sea-wall before the 1st December last, and it was inspected and accepted by me on the 7th of that month, the work having been faithfully executed, according to contract, under the superintendence of Seth Perry, esq., the agent. In May, 1848, $105, remaining of the appropriation of 1847, was expended in repairing the wall heretofore built, under the direction of the Treasury Department, for the protection of the light keeper's house.

The late period at which the appropriation was made for the completion of this work, (12th August, 1848,) will prevent all the stone work, for the protection of the island, from being laid before the close of season.

On the 1st November instant, seven hundred perches had been laid, and there remains to be laid about 1,200 more; of this, perhaps one-half, or six hundred perches, will be finished during the month of November, and the residue must be suspended until the ensuing spring.

Very respectfully, sir, your obedient servant,

M. H. SWIFT,
Captain, Topographical Engineers.

Colonel J. J. ABERT,
Chief, Topographical Engineers.

Bibliography

Primary Sources

Manuscripts

National Archives. Record Group 77, Records of the Office of the Chief of Engineers. Letters Sent by the Topographical Bureau, 1829–1863.
———. Letters Received by the Topographical Bureau, 1824–1865.
———. Register of Letters Received by the Topographical Bureau of the War Department, 1824–1866.

Government Documents

Abert, James W. "Journal of Lieutenant James A. [sic] Abert, from Bent's Fort to St. Louis in 1845." *Sen. Exec. Doc. 438*, 29th Cong., 1st sess. Washington D.C., 1846
———. "Report of the Secretary of War, Communicating in Answer to a Resolution of the Senate, a Report and Map of the Examination of New Mexico, Made by Lieutenant J.W. Abert of the Topographical Corps." *Sen. Exec. Doc. 23*, 30th Cong., 1st sess. Washington, D.C., 1848.
Emory, William H. "Notes of a Military Reconnaissance [sic] from Fort Leavenworth, in Missouri to San Diego, in California Including Part of the Arkansas, Del Norte, and Gila Rivers." *House Exec. Doc. 41*, 30th Cong., 1st sess. Washington, D.C.: Wendell and Van Benthuysen, 1848.
Fremont, John C. "Geographic Memoir upon Upper California, in Illustration of his Map of Oregon and California: Addressed to the Senate of the United States, by John C. Fremont." *Sen. Misc. Doc. 148*, 30th Cong., 1st sess. Washington, D.C.: Wendell and Van Benthuysen, 1848.
Hardcastle, Edmund L.F. and Martin Luther Smith. "In Further Compliance with the Resolution of the Senate of August 3,

1848, Calling for a Map of the Valley of Mexico, by Lieutenants Smith and Hardcastle." *Sen. Exec. Doc. 19*, 30th Cong., 2d sess. Washington, D.C., 1849.

Hughes, George W. "Report of the Secretary of War, Communicating . . . a Map Showing the Operations of the Army of the United States in Texas and the Adjacent Mexican States on the Rio Grande; Accompanied by Astronomical Observations, and Descriptive and Military Memoirs of the Country," 1 Mar. 1849. *Sen. Exec. Doc. 32*, 31st Cong., 1st sess. Washington, D.C., 1850.

Kearny, Stephen Watts. "Report of a Summer Campaign to the Rocky Mountains . . . in 1845." *Sen. Exec. Doc. 1*, 29th Cong., 1st sess. Washington, D.C., 1846.

Kern, Edward M. "Journal of an Exploration of Mary's of Humboldt River, Carson Lake, and Owens River and Lakes in 1845." Appendix to James H. Simpson. *Report of Explorations across the Great Basin of the Territory of Utah . . . in 1859.* Washington, D.C.: Government Printing Office, 1876.

Report of the Secretary of War. *Sen. Doc. 1*, 28th Cong., 2d sess. Washington, D.C., 1844.

———. *Sen. Doc. 1*, 29th Cong., 1st sess. Washington, D.C., 1845.

———. *House Exec. Doc. 4*, 29th Cong., 2d sess. Washington, D.C., 1846.

———. *Sen. Exec. Doc. 1*, 30th Cong., 1st sess. Washington, D.C., 1847.

———. *House Exec. Doc. 1*, 30th Cong., 2d sess. Washington, D.C., 1848.

Warren, Gouverneur K. "Memoir to Accompany the Map of the Territory of the United States from the Mississippi River to the Pacific Ocean (1858) . . . Exploring Expeditions since AD 1800." War Department. *Reports of Explorations and Surveys to Ascertain the Most Practical and Economical Route for a Railroad from the Mississippi River to the Pacific Ocean 1853–6.* House Exec. Doc. 91, 33d Cong., 2d sess. Washington, D.C., 1861.

Autobiographies, Memoirs, and Reminiscences

Anderson, Robert. *An Artillery Officer in the Mexican War, 1846–7.* New York: G.P. Putnam's Sons, 1911.

Benton, Thomas Hart. *Thirty Years View.* 2 vols. New York: D. Appleton and Co., 1854.

Calvin, Ross (ed.). *Lieutenant Emory Reports: A Reprint of Lieutenant W.H. Emory's Notes of a Military Reconnoissance* [sic]. Albuquerque: University of New Mexico Press, 1951.

Carson, Kit. *Kit Carson's Autobiography.* Milo Milton Quaife (ed.). Lincoln: University of Nebraska Press, 1935.

Cooke, P. St. George. *The Conquest of New Mexico and California: An Historical and Personal Narrative.* New York: G.P. Putnam's Sons, 1878.

Derby, George H. *Derby's Report on Opening the Colorado, 1850–1851.* Odie B. Faulk (ed.). [Albuquerque]: University of New Mexico Press, 1969.

Fremont, John C. *Memoirs of My Life.* Chicago: Belford, Clark and Co., 1887.

———. *Narratives of Exploration and Adventure.* Allan Nevins (ed.). New York: Longmans, Green and Co., 1956.

Grant, Ulysses S. *Personal Memoirs of U.S. Grant.* New York: Century Co., 1917.

Henry, William S. *Campaign Sketches of the War With Mexico.* New York: Harper and Brothers, 1847.

Hine, Robert V., and Lottinville, Savoie (eds.). *Soldier of the West: Letters of Theodore Talbot During His Services in California, Mexico, and Oregon, 1845–53.* Norman: University of Oklahoma Press, 1972.

Hitchcock, Ethan Allen. *Fifty Years in Camp and Field: Diary of MG Ethan Allen Hitchcock, USA.* W.A. Croffut (ed.). New York: G.P. Putnam's Sons, 1909.

Jackson, Donald, and Spence, Mary Lee (eds.). *The Expeditions of John Charles Fremont.* 3 vols. Urbana: University of Illinois Press, 1970.

Kenly, John R. *Memoirs of a Maryland Volunteer in the Years 1846-7-8.* Philadelphia: J.B. Lippincott and Co., 1873.

Larkin, Thomas O. *The Larkin Papers.* 10 vols. Berkeley: University of California Press, 1951.

Maury, Dabney H. *Recollections of a Virginian in the Mexican, Indian and Civil Wars.* New York: Charles Scribner's Sons, 1894.

Meade, George (ed.). *The Life and Letters of George Gordon Meade.* 2 vols. New York: Charles Scribner's Sons, 1913.

Schubert, Frank N. (ed.). *March to South Pass: Lieutenant William B. Franklin's Journal of the Kearny Expedition of 1845.* No. 1. Engineer Studies Series. Washington, D.C.: U.S. Army Corps of Engineers, Government Printing Office, 1979.

Smith, George Winston, and Charles Judah (eds.). *Chronicles of the Gringos; The U.S. Army in the Mexican War, 1846: Accounts of Eyewit-*

nesses and Combatants. Albuquerque: University of New Mexico Press, 1968.
Smith, Gustavus W. *Company "A", Corps of Engineers, U.S.A., 1846–48 in the Mexican War.* n.p.: The Battalion Press, 1896.
Williams, T. Harry (ed.). *With Beauregard in Mexico: The Mexico War Reminiscences of P.G.T. Beauregard.* [Baton Rouge]: Louisiana State University Press, 1956.

Newspapers

Niles [Ohio] National Register, 31 Oct 1846 through 14 Aug 1847.
Washington *Union News*, 16 June 1846.

Secondary Sources

Books and Monographs

Bache, Richard Meade. *Life of General George Gordon Meade.* Philadelphia: Henry T. Coates and Co., 1898.
Bancroft, Hubert Howe. *A History of California.* 7 vols. San Francisco: A.L. Bancroft and Co., 1884–1890.
———. *History of Mexico.* 6 vols. San Francisco: A.L. Bancroft and Co., 1883–1888.
Bashford, Herbert and Wagner, Harr. *A Man Unafraid: The Story of John Charles Fremont.* San Francisco: Harr Wagner Publishing Co., 1927.
Bauer, K. Jack. *The Mexican War, 1846–1848.* New York: Macmillan Co., 1974.
Bigelow, John. *Memoir of the Life and Public Service of John Charles Fremont.* New York: Derby and Jackson, 1856.
Billington, Ray A. *The Far Western Frontier, 1830–1860.* New York: Harper and Row, 1950.
Brooks, Nathan C. *A Complete History of the Mexican War.* Chicago: Rio Grande Press, 1965.
Burr, Edward. "Historical Sketch of the Corps of Engineers, U.S. Army." *Occasional Papers of the Engineer School.* No. 71. Washington, D.C.: Government Printing Office, 1939.
Carleton, James Henry. *Battle of Buena Vista.* New York: Harper and Brothers, 1848.

Clarke, Dwight L. *Stephen Watts Kearny, Soldier of the West*. Norman: University of Oklahoma Press, 1961.

Cleaves, Freeman. *Meade of Gettysburg*. Norman: University of Oklahoma Press, 1960.

Cowdrey, Albert E. *A City for the Nation: The Army Engineers and the Building of Washington, D.C., 1790–1967*. Washington, D.C.: U.S. Army Corps of Engineers, Government Printing Office, 1979.

Crump, Irving. *Our Army Engineers*. New York: Dodd Mead and Co., 1954.

Cutts, James Madison. *The Conquest of California and New Mexico*. Philadelphia: Cary and Hart, 1847.

Dellenbaugh, Frederick S. *Fremont and '49*. New York: Knickerbocker Press, 1914.

De Voto, Bernard. *The Year of Decision, 1846*. Boston: Houghton Mifflin Co., 1943.

Dufour, Charles L. *The Mexican War; A Compact History, 1846–1848*. New York: Hawthorn Books, 1968.

Dyer, Brainerd. *Zachary Taylor*. Baton Rouge: Louisiana State University Press, 1946.

Eisenhower, John S.D. *So Far From God: The U.S. War With Mexico, 1846–1848*. New York: Random House, 1989.

Eyer, Alice. *The Famous Fremonts and Their America*. n.p.: Fine Arts Press, 1948.

Freeman, Douglas Southall. *Robert E. Lee, a Biography*. 4 vols. New York: Charles Scribner's Sons, 1933.

Frost, J. *The Mexican War and Its Warriors*. New Haven, CT: H. Mansfield, 1849.

Fry, Joseph Reese. *A Life of General Zachary Taylor*. Philadelphia: Grigg, Elliot and Co., 1847.

General Taylor and His Staff. Philadelphia: Grigg, Elliot and Co., 1848.

Goetzmann, William H. *Army Exploration in the American West, 1803–1863*. New Haven, CT: Yale University Press, 1959.

———. *Exploration and Empire*. New York: Alfred A. Knopf, 1966.

Goodwin, Cardinal. *John Charles Fremont: An Explanation of His Career*. Stanford, CA: Stanford University Press, 1930.

Govan, Gilbert, and Livingood, James W. *A Different Valor: The Story of General Joseph E. Johnston. C.S.A.* New York: Bobbs-Merrill Co., 1956.

Grivas, Theodore. *Military Governments in California, 1846–1850*. Glendale, CA: Arthur H. Clark Co., 1963.

Haferkorn, Henry E. *The War with Mexico, 1846–1848: A Select Bibliography.* New York: Argonaut Press, 1965.

Henry, Robert Selph. *The Story of the Mexican War.* New York and Indianapolis: Bobbs-Merrill Co., 1950.

Hill, Forest G. *Roads, Rails and Waterways: The Army Engineers and Early Transportation.* Norman: University of Oklahoma Press, 1957.

Hine, Robert V. *Edward Kern and American Expansion.* New Haven, CT: Yale University Press, 1962.

History and Traditions of the Corps of Engineers. Engineer School Special Text, ST 25–1. Fort Belvoir, VA: Engineer School, 1953.

Howard, Oliver Otis. *Great Commanders, General Taylor.* New York: D. Appleton and Co., 1897.

Hughes, Robert M. *Great Commanders, General Johnston.* New York D. Appleton and Co., 1897.

Huston, James A. *The Sinews of War: Army Logistics, 1775–1953.* Army Historical Series. Office of the Chief of Military History. Washington, D.C.: Government Printing Office, 1966.

Ide, Simeon. *A Biographical Sketch of the Life of William B. Ide.* Glorieta, NM: Rio Grande Press, 1967.

Jackson, W. Turrentine. *Wagon Roads West: A Study of Federal Road Surveys and Construction in the Trans-Mississippi West, 1846–1869.* New Haven, CT: Yale University Press, 1965.

Jenkins, John S. *History of the War Between the United States and Mexico.* Auburn: Derby and Miller, 1850.

Johannsen, Robert W. *To the Halls of the Montezumas: The Mexican War in the American Imagination.* New York and Oxford: Oxford Univ. Press, 1985.

Johnson, Bradley T. (ed.). *A Memoir of the Life and Public Service of Joseph E. Johnston.* Baltimore: R.H. Woodward and Co., 1891.

Lavender, David. *Climax at Buena Vista: The American Campaigns in Northeastern Mexico, 1846–47.* Philadelphia: J.B. Lippincott Co., 1966.

Lewis, Lloyd. *Captain Sam Grant.* Boston: Little, Brown and Co., 1950.

Mansfield, Edward D. *The Mexican War.* New York: A. S. Barnes and Co., 1850.

Marti, Werner H. *Messenger of Destiny: The California Adventures, 1846–1847, of Archibald H. Gillespie, U.S. Marine Corps.* San Francisco: John Howell Books, 1960.

Matloff, Maurice (ed.). *American Military History.* Washington, D.C.: Office of the Chief of Military History, 1969, rev. 1973.

Moore, Jamie W. *The Fortifications Board 1816–1828 And the Definition of National Security.* The Citadel: Monograph Series: Number XVI. Charleston: The Citadel, Jan 1981.

Nevin, David. *The Mexican War.* The Old West Series. Alexandria, VA: Time-Life Books, 1978.

Nevins, Allan. *Fremont, Pathmarker of the West.* New York: Longmans, Green and Co., 1955.

Nichols, Edward J. *Zach Taylor's Little Army.* New York: Doubleday, 1963.

Pennypacker, Isaac R. *Great Commanders, General Meade.* New York: D. Appleton and Co., 1901.

Ripley, R. S. *War With Mexico.* 2 vols. New York: Harper, 1849.

Rives, George L. *The United States and Mexico, 1821–48.* New York: Charles Scribner's Sons, 1913.

Royce, Josiah. *California from the Conquest in 1846 to the Second Vigilance Committee in San Francisco.* Boston and New York: Houghton Mifflin and Co., 1914.

Sabin, Edwin L. *Kit Carson Days, 1809–1868.* 2 vols. n.p.: Press of the Pioneers, Inc., 1935.

Schubert, Frank N. *Vanguard of Expansion: Army Engineers in the Trans-Mississippi West, 1819–1879.* Washington, D.C.: U.S. Army Corps of Engineers, Government Printing Office, 1980.

———. (ed.). *The Nation Builders: A Sesquicentennial History of the Corps of Topographical Engineers, 1838–1863.* Washington, D.C.: U.S. Army Corps of Engineers, 1988.

Singletary, Otis. *The Mexican War.* Chicago: University of Chicago Press, 1960.

Smith, Justin H. *The War with Mexico.* 2 vols. New York: Macmillan Co., 1919.

Steele, Matthew F. *American Campaigns.* 2 vols. Washington, D.C.: U.S. Infantry Association, 1935.

Stewart, George R. *John Phoenix, Esq. The Veritable Squibob, A Life of Captain George H. Derby, USA.* New York: Da Capa Press, 1969.

Taylor and His Generals, a Biography . . . Together with a Sketch of the Life of Major General Winfield Scott. Hartford, CT: Silas Andrews and Son, 1848.

Upham, Charles W. *Life, Explorations and Public Service of John Charles Fremont.* Boston: Ticknor and Fields, 1856.

Wallace, Edward S. *The Great Reconnaissance: Soldiers, Artists and the Scientists on the Frontier, 1848–1861.* Boston: Little, Brown and Co., 1955.

Weigley, Russell F. *History of the United States Army.* New York: Macmillan Co., 1967.

Wheat, Carl I. *Mapping the Trans-Mississippi West, 1540–1861.* 5 vols. San Francisco: The Institute of Historical Cartography, 1957–1963.

Wilcox, Cadmus. *History of the Mexican War.* Washington, D.C.: Church News Publishing Co., 1892.

Wood, Richard G. *Stephen Harriman Long, 1784–1864, Army Engineer, Explorer, Inventor.* Glendale, CA: Arthur H. Clark Co., 1966.

Youngblood, G.A. "History of Engineer Troops in the United States Army, 1775–1901." *Occasional Papers of the Engineer School.* No. 37. Washington, D.C.: Press of the Engineer School, 1910.

Articles

Beers, Henry P. "A History of the U.S. Topographical Engineers, 1813–1863." *Military Engineer*, 34 (June 1942), pp. 287–91, and (July 1942), pp. 348–52.

Burgess, Harry. "The Influences of Bridges on Campaigns." *Military Engineer*, 19 (Mar 1927), pp. 146–48.

Deacon, Kenneth J. "Combat Engineers 23; San Pasqual, 1846." *Military Engineer*, 55 (Sep 1963), p. 348.

———. "Combat Engineers 25; Cerro Gordo, 1847." *Military Engineer*, 56 (Jan 1964), p. 46.

———. "Combat Engineers 34; Siege of Vera Cruz, 1847." *Military Engineer.* 57 (July 1965), p. 258.

Fremont, John Charles. "The Conquest of California." *The Century Magazine*, 41 (April 1891), pp. 917–28.

Hart, Charles D. "Slavery Expansion to the Territories, 1850." *New Mexico Historical Quarterly*, 41 (Oct 1966), pp. 269–86.

McDonald, Archie P. "West Point Engineers." *Military Engineer*, 57 (May–June 1965), pp. 187–89.

Robinson William H. "The Corps of Topographical Engineers." *Military Engineer*, 23 (July 1931), pp. 303–06.

———. "The Engineer Soldiers in the Mexican War." *Military Engineer*, 24 (Jan 1932), pp. 1–8.

Shunk, Maj. William A. "Services Of Graduates in the War of 1812 and in the Mexican War." In *The Centennial of the United States*

Military Academy at West Point, New York, 1802–1902. vol I. New York: Greenwood Press, 1969, pp. 586–631.
Smith Gustavus W. "Company A Engineers in Mexico, 1846–1847." *Military Engineer*, 56 (Sep 1964), pp. 336–40.
Spencer, Ivor D. "Rubber Ponton Bridges—in 1846!" *Military Engineer*, 37 (Jan 1945), pp. 24–27.
Thornhoff, Robert H. "Taylor's Trail in Texas." *Southwestern Historical Quarterly*, 70 (July 1966), pp. 7–22.

Dictionaries and Encyclopedias

Appleton's Cyclopaedia of American Biography. I, III–VI. New York: D. Appleton and Co., 1888–1901.
Cullum, George W. *Biographical Register of the Offices and Graduates of the United States Military Academy*. I, II. Boston: Houghton Mifflin Co., 1891.
Dictionary of the American Biography. III, V, VI, VIII–XI, XIII. New York: Charles Scribner's Sons, 1964.
Heitman, Francis B. *Historical Register and Dictionary of the United States Army*. I. Washington, D.C.: Government Printing Office, 1903.
National Cyclopaedia of American Biography. IV, V, VII, XXI. New York: James T. White, 1898–1969.

Unpublished Dissertation

Ryan, Gary David. *War Department Topographical Bureau, 1831–1863: An Administrative History*. American University, 1968.

Index

Abert, Lt. James W.: 22, 27–28, 29, 30, 45–49, 66, 68, 71, 73, 74, 84, 87, 89–101, 150, 154, 217, 221
Abert, Col. John James: 9, 10, 14, 15, 16, 17, 22–23, 26, 27–28, 45, 46, 66, 67n, 71, 95, 115, 121, 122, 135, 136, 137, 145, 146–47, 149, 151, 156, 157, 163, 186, 191, 204, 205, 212–13, 215–16, 219, 221–22, 223
Acoma, N. Mex.: 93–94, 100
Agriculture: 72, 77, 89, 91, 92, 93, 130, 139, 151, 154
Agua Caliente, Calif.: 79
Agua Nueva, Mexico: 143, 155
Albuquerque, N. Mex.: 93
American Association for the Advancement of Science: 66
American Atlas, by Tanner: 19
American Campaigns, by Matthew F. Steele: 209
American Ethnological Society: 85
American Indians: 12, 16, 19, 21, 38, 46, 47–49, 63, 71–72, 74, 77, 79, 98. *See also particular tribes; personal names.*
  attacks by: 75–76, 93, 97, 99, 153, 221
  culture: 90–93
  as escorts: 29, 34, 35, 40, 63
  ethnology of: 85–86
  portraits of: 90, 100
  protection from: 20–22, 33, 157–59
American River: 35
Amnesty: 202
Amphibious operations: 177, 180
Animals: 79, 81, 82, 86, 92, 152. *See also Wildlife.*
  in battle: 124
  food for: 121
  taken on expeditions: 46, 68
  used for transportation: 75, 77–79, 89, 96–99, 128, 151
Anthropology: 70
Apache Indians: 69, 74, 75–76, 77, 85–86, 153
Aqueducts: 18
Aransas Bay: 118, 120
Arapaho Indians: 97
Archaeological observations: 70, 76, 77, 85–86

Arista, General Mariano: 123
Arkansas: 18
Arkansas River: 20, 31, 68, 99
  improvement of navigation on: 17
  surveying of: 26, 30, 46, 48
Armijo: 74
Army General Staff: 10
Army of Occupation: 117, 119–20
Army of the West: 63, 67–87, 89, 92, 101, 127
Artillery: 28, 80, 117, 124, 125, 132, 133, 135, 136, 142, 143, 155–56, 162, 178, 179, 182, 183–84, 187, 188, 189, 194, 195, 198, 208
Astronomical observations: 30–31, 45, 48, 68, 72, 78, 82, 86, 92, 95, 153, 160
Ayolta, Mexico: 194, 195

Bache, Maj. Hartman: 126, 186, 211, 219, 222
Bancroft, George: 26–27, 35–36
Bancroft, H. H.: 41
Bankhead, Col. James: 183–84
Barometers: 46, 67, 75, 86
Bashford, Herbert: 29–30
Battlefield surveys: 128, 137, 145, 189, 204–06
Bear Flag Revolt: 39
Beauregard, P. G. T.: 5–6, 181, 182, 194, 195, 197, 199–200
Bent's Fort, Colo.: 20, 21, 26, 27, 29, 30, 45, 46, 47, 48, 67–68, 71, 86, 89–90, 97
Benton, Thomas Hart: 26–27, 35–36, 37, 38, 43, 45
Bernalillo, N. Mex.: 72
Bestor, Norman: 66, 67, 71, 74, 80
Black Mountains: 75–76
Blake, Lt. Jacob E.: 121–23, 124–25, 126, 136, 137, 216
Board of Engineers for Fortifications: 11
Board of Engineers for Internal Improvements: 13, 14, 15, 16
Botanical information: 86
Boundary surveys: 12, 18, 85, 116, 121, 131, 157n, 162, 179, 192, 206–08, 211–12, 220
Brazos Island: 121–22
Brazos River: 161
Brazos Santiago, Tex.: 118–19, 121–22

Bridges: 127, 129, 152, 183, 207, 215
Brown, Maj. Jacob: 126
Brownsville, Tex.: 126
Bryan, Lt. Francis T.: 149–50, 155–56, 161, 162
Buchanan, James: 35–36
Buena Vista, Battle of: 142–45, 155, 160
Butler, Maj. Gen. William O.: 14

Cacti: 86
Calhoun, John C.: 127
California
  acquisition of: 19–20, 25–42, 63, 80–87
  exploration of: 31–32
  history of: 3, 4, 33–42, 73–75
California Battalion: 39, 40, 42, 84n
Camargo, Tex.: 128, 131, 149
Canadian River: 26, 47–49, 96
Canals: 13, 14, 178, 207, 208
Canon Inferno: 94, 100
Carson, Kit: 29, 30, 34, 35, 74–76, 77, 82, 99
Carson's Sink: 31
Casa Grande: 76–77
Cascade Range: 35
Castro, Don Jose: 33–34, 35
Castroville, Tex.: 152
Casualties: 81, 156, 184, 188, 197, 198, 199
Catholic church: 70, 72–73, 83, 131, 202–03
Cerro Gordo: 187–91, 192, 196, 200, 205
Chapultepec: 197–98, 199, 201
Chesapeake and Ohio Canal: 14
Cheyenne Indians: 46, 90–91, 97
Chihuahua, Mexico: 73, 95, 150
Chilili, N. Mex.: 94
Chronometers: 46, 75, 145
  box: 67
  pocket: 30, 67, 75, 146
Churubusco, Mexico: 196, 200, 201, 209
Cibola, Seven Cities of: 93–94
Cimarron route: 99–100
Civil engineering works
  responsibility for, 6, 13, 15, 16, 17, 18
  surveys for: 17
Civil War, 5–6, 100, 136n, 138, 162, 163, 179, 186, 207, 208, 213, 220–21, 223, 225
Civilian employees: 14, 15–16, 22–23, 26, 29, 66, 74, 95, 213, 215
Clark, Capt. William: 9
Clarke, Dwight L.: 42n
Climate: 68, 118–19, 131, 151, 152
Coast Survey: 12, 16, 179, 180, 191, 208, 212, 214
Coastal fortifications: 11, 17
Collingwood: 39
Colorado: 20, 31
Colorado River: 78
  exploration of: 26, 31
  survey of: 191

Columbia River: 35
Comanche Indians: 47, 48–49, 74, 96, 99, 152, 153, 157, 217–18
Commerce of the Prairies, by Josiah Gregg: 19, 86
Compasses: 145, 146, 205
Congressional Series: 205
Conner, Comdr. David: 181
Conrad, Charles: 221
Contreras, Battle of: 195–96, 200, 201
Cooke, Lt. Col. Philip St. George: 73, 84, 85
"Corps of Observation": 4
Corpus Christi, Tex.: 4, 115, 117, 118, 120, 121, 128
Cram, Capt. Thomas J.: 117, 118–19, 137, 225
Creek Indians: 47
Cumberland Road: 14

Dams, construction of: 14
Davis, Jefferson: 143, 219, 221–22
De Voto, Bernard: 34
Delaware Indians: 29, 34, 35, 40, 63
Dellenbaugh, Frederick S.: 29, 42n
Derby, Lt. George W.: 178, 179–80, 183–84, 189–92, 200–201, 211, 220, 221, 222
Dix, Lt. Col. R. S.: 144
Doniphan, Col. Alexander W.: 73, 94–95, 139, 149
Dredges: 214–15
Duncan, Col. James: 124–25, 194

El Penon: 194
Elevation: 68, 86
Emory, Lt. William H.: 19, 49, 63, 66–87, 89, 92, 100, 101, 115–16, 150, 154, 158, 163, 178, 201, 203–04, 206–08, 211, 216, 217, 219, 221, 225, 226
Engineer Department: 11, 12, 14, 15
Engineers, U.S. Army Corps of: 5–6, 7, 11, 12, 13, 17, 71, 135, 182–85, 222–23, 225
Englemann, George: 86
Erskine, Robert: 9
Ethnological information: 49, 85–86
Expansionism, American: 3, 18–20
Exploration and Survey, Office of: 222
Exploration expeditions: 19, 20, 22
  to California: 27–29
  to Colorado: 26
  across Nevada: 31–32
  of Rockies: 45–49

False Washita River: 47
Ferries: 129
1st Dragoons: 63, 69
Fitzpatrick, Tom: 46, 69
Florence, Ariz.: 77
Florida: 12, 16, 18
Fort Brown, Tex.: 126

INDEX

Fort Gibson, : 48
Fort Holmes, Okla.: 47
Fort Jesup, La.: 4, 115
Fort Laramie, Wyo.: 21, 48
Fort Leavenworth, Kans.: 20, 42–43, 49, 63, 67–68, 83, 86, 89, 97, 127
Fort Libertad, Mexico: 135
Fort Marcy, N. Mex.: 71, 93
Fort Monroe, Va.: 43
Fort Smith, Ark.: 11
Fort Soldado, Mexico: 134
Fortifications: 17, 123–24, 132–33, 134, 183, 184, 196, 198–200
  coastal: 223
  surveying of sites for: 11, 18, 128, 212
Forts
  establishment of: 22, 71, 84
  locations for: 157, 158, 217–18
Foster, Lt. John G.: 194
Franklin, Lt. William B.: 21, 22, 48, 145, 149–51, 152, 153, 155, 156, 160, 161, 162, 225
Franklin Lake: 31
Fremont, Lt. John C.: 6, 8–9, 18–19, 20, 22, 25–44, 48, 67n, 74, 84, 85, 86–87, 100, 116, 147n, 150, 154, 163n, 216, 220–21, 225
  charged with mutiny: 42–43
  court-martialed: 43, 84n

Galisteo Creek: 93
Gallatin, Albert: 85–86
General Survey Act of 1824: 13
Geographic observations: 48, 63, 68, 73, 85, 86, 89, 92, 99–101, 118, 123, 154, 160, 204, 206, 215, 216, 217, 223, 225
"Geographical Memoir," by John C. Fremont: 44–45
Geology: 76, 86, 98, 100
Gibbons v. *Ogden*: 13
Gila River: 76–77, 78, 83, 85, 127
Gillespie, Lt. Archibald: 35–36, 38, 40, 80, 81
Gilmer, Lt. Jeremy F.: 71
Godey, Alexis: 29
Goetzmann, William H.: 20, 222
Gold prospectors: 85, 93
"Golden Gate": 44
Graham, Maj. Campbell: 211, 212, 219
Graham, Maj. James D.: 43, 138
Grant, Lt. Ulysses S.: 196
Gratiot, Col. Charles: 15
"Great American Desert" myth: 12, 44
Great Britain: 26, 27, 36, 39
Great Lakes: 16
  improvement of harbors on: 18
  surveying of: 18, 186, 211–12, 214, 215
Great Salt Lake: 26, 31, 44

Greenwood, Caleb: 46, 47
Gregg, Josiah: 19, 48, 67n, 86, 161
Guerrilla warfare: 163, 192–93, 201–02
Gulf of Mexico: 120, 128, 139
Gunnison, Lt. John W.: 221

Hagner, Lt. Charles N.: 178, 191, 205
Halleck, Henry W.: 5–6
Harbor improvement: 14, 16, 17–18, 117, 121, 140, 142, 162, 178, 179, 192, 207, 211–12, 213–14, 218, 222
Hardcastle, Lt. Edmund L. F.: 178, 180, 183–84, 191, 194, 195, 196, 198, 200–201, 205, 207–08, 212, 219–20, 221
Harney, Col. William S.: 189–90
Hassler, Ferdinand: 8–9
Hastings Cutoff: 31
Hatcher, John: 46, 47
Hawk's Peak: 34–35
Health problems: 131, 138, 151, 152, 186–87, 192–93
Hitchcock, Lt. Col. Ethan Allen: 115, 189
Hubbard, Joseph C.: 45
Hughes, Lt. Col. George W.: 145, 149–63, 178, 183, 191, 201–04, 206, 216, 219, 220n, 221
Humboldt, Alexander von: 116, 205–06
Humboldt River: 31

Ide, William B.: 38
Imperial Valley, Calif.: 78
Indiana Volunteers: 143, 144, 156
Interior, Department of the: 222
Iowa: 18

Jackson, General Andrew: 12
Jalapa, Mexico: 201–03
Johnston, Lt. Col. Joseph E.: 6, 178, 179, 181, 183, 184–85, 188, 190–91, 199–201, 207, 212, 216, 219, 221, 225

Kearney, Lt. Col. James: 211, 219
Kearny, Brig. Gen. Stephen Watts: 20–22, 23, 37, 41, 42–43, 49, 63, 66, 67–68, 69–70, 71–83, 84n, 89, 91, 92, 95, 99, 101, 127, 150, 212, 216, 217
Kenly, Maj. John R.: 201–02, 204
Kern, Edward M.: 29, 31, 32
Kiowa Indians: 47, 48–49
Klamath Indians: 35, 37
Klamath Lake: 35, 37

Laguna, Calif.: 33
Laguna, N. Mex.: 93–94
Laguna de la Madre: 118, 119, 121
Lajeunesse, Basil: 29
Lake Champlain: 16
Land Ordinance of 1785: 9

Larkin, Thomas O.: 33, 34, 35–36, 38, 40
Las Vegas, Nev.: 91
Lassen's Meadows, Calif.: 34–35, 37
Lava fields: 195–96
Lavaca River: 214–15
Lee, Capt. Robert E.: 5–6, 151, 155, 181, 182, 184–85, 187–88, 189–90, 193, 194, 195, 196, 200
Leona River: 157
Lewis, Capt. Meriwether: 9
Light construction: 16, 116, 161, 162, 186, 192, 207, 208, 211, 214, 218
Linnard, Capt. Thomas B.: 140, 144, 145–46, 147, 161
Lipan Indians: 157
Llano Estacado: 47
Lobos Island: 142, 177, 180
Long, Maj. Stephen H.: 8, 11, 12, 13, 14, 19, 43, 44, 116, 212, 214–15, 219, 222
Long Beard, Chief: 97
Los Angeles, Calif.: 40–41, 42, 78, 83, 84
Louisiana Purchase: 19

McClellan, Lt. George B.: 5–6, 182, 183, 194
McClellan, Capt. John: 141–42, 178, 180, 183, 191, 200–201, 205, 207, 221
Magnus Colorado: 75–76
Manifest Destiny: 20, 26–27, 34
Mansfield, Maj. Joseph: 120, 123, 132–33, 134–35
Maps: 20–22, 44, 48, 67n, 84, 225–26. *See also* Battlefield surveys.
   of Mexico: 137, 145, 160–61, 204–06
   military: 19, 115–16, 134–35, 137
   of New Mexico: 84, 95
   responsibility for: 6, 13
   of the Southwest: 63, 71, 85, 116
   of Texas: 119
Marcy, William L.: 4, 127, 221
Maricopa Indians: 77, 85–86
Mason, Capt. James L.: 194, 196, 198
Matamoros, Mexico: 120–23, 126, 127, 128–29
Maxwell, Lucien: 29
Meade, Lt. George G.: 6, 116–17, 118–19, 120, 121, 122, 123, 126, 128–31, 132, 133–34, 135, 136, 137–47, 161, 163, 178, 180, 181, 182–83, 185–86, 191, 200–201, 225
Meritt, Eyekid: 39
Meteorological observations: 30–31, 45, 86
Mexicalcingo, Mexico: 194
Mexican army: 78, 80–83, 124–26, 128–29, 134–47, 155
Mexican Boundary Commission: 157n
Mexican government: 74, 140, 157, 159, 177
Mexican Indians: 85
Mexican National Highway: 187, 194, 201–02

Mexicans
   characteristics of: 69, 158
   mistreatment of: 130, 142, 159, 192–93, 202
Mexico City, Mexico: 128, 138, 141, 160, 163, 177, 218
   attack on: 198–201
   fortification of: 193–94
   march to: 186–93, 201–02, 208
   survey of roads to: 193, 199, 204–05
Michigan: 18
Military discipline: 129–30, 131, 138, 192–93
Military reconnaissance: 13, 15, 21, 71, 122, 124–25, 128, 130, 131, 132, 136, 140–42, 145, 152–53, 155, 187, 188–89, 194, 197, 198, 199, 205, 208–09, 211, 212
Mineral resources: 75, 77, 86–87, 89, 92–93
Minnesota: 12
Missions: 83
Mississippi Rifles: 143, 144, 156
Mississippi River
   improvement of navigation on: 13, 14, 17
   surveying of the lower: 12, 117
Missouri River, 17
Missouri Volunteers: 73, 94, 139, 149
Molino del Rey, Mexico: 197–98, 199, 200–201
Monclova, Mexico: 153, 161
Monroe, James: 13
Monterey, Calif.: 3, 33–34, 39, 40, 42, 73, 94, 213–14
Monterrey, Mexico: 127, 131, 132–38, 139, 140, 141, 143, 149, 153
   armistice at: 136, 138, 153
   map of: 137
   road to: 131, 132, 146
Montgomery, Comdr. John B.: 39
Mormon Battalion: 73
Mount Graham: 76
Mount Turnbull: 76
Mounted riflemen: 127, 132
Mounted Rifles: 41

Navaho Indians: 69, 74, 93–94
Navigation, improvement of: 13, 14, 16, 17, 19, 222
Nevada: 31
Nevins, Allan: 25, 29, 31, 38n, 42n
New Brunswick-Maine boundary survey: 18
New Helvetia, Calif.: 32
New Mexico: 4, 19, 63, 69, 71–72, 89–101, 127, 217–18
New Orleans, La.: 18, 115, 117, 121
Nicollet, Joseph N.: 8–9, 163n
North Platte River: 21
Northeast Boundary Survey: 18, 131
Northern Boundary Survey: 179

INDEX

"Notes of a Military Reconnaissance," by William H. Emory: 63, 84–87
Nueces River: 118, 158

O'Brien, Lt. John Paul Jones: 155–56
Odometers: 205–06
Ogden, Peter S.: 31
Ohio River: 13, 14, 17
Old Bark, Chief: 46, 90
Oregon: 25–26, 33, 35, 38
Oregon Trail: 20–21, 91
Owens, Dick: 29, 30, 34, 35

Pacific Railroad Survey: 222
Pacific Squadron, U.S. Navy: 4, 39
Pacific Wagon Road Office: 222
Padierna, Mexico: 195, 196
Padre Island, Tex.: 119, 120, 121–22
Palo Alto, Battle of: 124–26, 136
Parras, Mexico: 153, 154
Patricio: 181
Patterson, Maj. Gen. Robert: 140–41, 180, 181, 183, 200
Pawnee Indians: 97, 98, 99
Peck, Lt. William G.: 27, 29, 45–49, 66, 71, 73, 74, 89–96, 99–101, 219–20, 221
Pecos, N. Mex.: 70, 100
Pedregal: 195, 196
Perote, Mexico: 203
Phoenix, John: 191
Pico, Don Andres: 41, 82
Pico, Don Jesus: 41
Pico, Don Pio: 33
Pierce, Brig. Gen. Franklin: 192
Pike, Lt. Zebulon: 9, 93, 116
Pillow, Gideon J.: 181, 193, 195, 198–99, 201
Pima Indians: 77, 78, 85
Piney River: 31
Pioneer Advance: 132
Platte River: 48
Point Isabel, Tex.: 120, 121–22, 123, 124
Polk, James K.: 3–4, 19, 26, 35, 43, 120, 124, 127, 138, 141, 177, 201, 218, 221
Pontoon bridges: 127, 128, 129n, 183
Pope, Lt. John: 6, 131, 135, 136, 137, 144, 145, 146–47, 161, 163, 211
Population information: 63, 70, 86, 89, 92, 100n, 151
Portraits: 90, 100
Portsmouth, N.H.: 18
Prescott, William H.: 76
Preuss, Charles: 25, 29, 44
Puebla, Mexico: 192, 193, 200
Pueblo, Colo.: 30
Pueblo Indians: 71, 85–86
Purgatory River: 46, 69

Quartermaster Department: 129n, 214

Quihi River: 157
Quitman, Brig. Gen. John A.: 140–41, 193, 198–99

Railroads: 71, 208
 proposed routes for: 83, 157n, 215
 surveys for routes for: 14, 16, 163, 178, 191, 206, 220, 222
Raton Pass: 46–47, 69, 91, 96
Red River: 74, 95n
 improvement of navigation on: 17, 217–18
 surveying of: 26, 47
"Report and Map of the Examination of New Mexico": 100
Resaca de la Palma: 126
Riflemen, mounted: 127
Rio Grande: 4, 71, 75, 83, 89, 92, 93, 94, 95n, 115–16, 118, 120, 121, 122, 126, 127, 128, 129, 130, 131, 152, 157, 215, 218
Rio de San Jose: 93–94
Rio Puerco: 94
Rito, N. Mex.: 93–94
Roads
 condition of: 75, 118, 123, 140–41, 194
 military: 18, 162
 repair of: 132, 151
 supervision of construction of: 18, 191, 195, 215
 surveys of: 14, 120, 146–47, 150, 208
Roberdeau, Maj. Isaac: 10, 11, 12, 13, 14
Rocky Mountains, expedition to the: 12, 45–49
Ross, George W.: 220n

Sacramento, Calif.: 32, 33, 45
Sacramento Valley: 33, 35, 37, 38
St. Joseph's Island: 115, 117
St. Louis, Mo.: 29, 30
Saltillo, Mexico, and road to: 132, 133–34, 137, 139, 140, 141, 142–43, 146, 153, 154, 155
San Antonio, Mexico: 195, 196
San Antonio, Tex.: 149–51, 157, 161
San Augustin, Mexico: 194, 195, 196
San Bernardo, Calif.: 82
San Diego, Calif.: 80, 81–82, 83, 127, 213–14
San Fernando, Calif.: 41
San Francisco, Calif.: 39
San Francisco Bay: 39, 44, 83, 213–14
San Gabriel River: 83–84
San Joaquin Valley, Calif.: 32, 33, 45
San Pasqual, Battle of: 80–81
Sanders, Capt. John: 135
Santa Anna, General Antonio Lopez de: 140, 143–45, 155, 160, 187–89, 193–94, 195–200, 203
Santa Anna River: 83

Santa Clara Valley: 33
Santa Fe, N. Mex.: 63, 67–71, 73, 75, 89, 91–93, 127
Santa Fe Trail: 46–47, 97
Santa Rita de Cobre: 75
Santa Rita Springs: l53
Santa Rosa, Mexico: 152–53
Santo Domingo, N. Mex.: 71–72
Scammon, Lt. Eliakim P.: 178, 179, 191, 192, 211, 220n, 225
Scientific observations: 68, 71, 85, 150, 152
Scott, Maj. Gen. Winfield: 23, 127, 141, 142–43, 144–45, 155, 156, 159, 163, 177–202, 206, 208, 211
Seminole Indians: 12
Seminole War: 16, 17, 140, 142
Sextants: 30–31, 46, 67
Shawnee Indians: 63
Siege tactics: 182, 183–85
Sierra Madre Mountains: 187
Sierra Nevadas: 31–32, 44
Sioux Indians: 21
Sitgreaves, Lt. Lorenzo: 145, 149–50, 151n, 152, 155–56, 160, 161, 162
Sketches: 48, 84, 90–91, 93, 100, 121, 137, 139, 146–47, 161
Slavery: 79n
Sloat, Comdr. John D.: 39, 40
Smith, Lt. Gustavus W.: 194
Smith, Jediah: 31
Smith, Justin: 40, 41, 42n
Smith, Lt. Martin L.: 178, 191, 201, 205, 208, 225
Smithsonian Institution: 44, 222
Snagboats: 14, 214
Socio-cultural observations: 63, 70, 71–72, 77, 90, 91, 154, 158–59
Socorro, N. Mex.: 94
Sonoma, Calif.: 39
Stanley, John M.: 66, 74, 77, 78, 80
State, U.S. Department of: 18, 116
Steamboat construction: 211, 214–15
Steele, Matthew F.: 209
Stevens, Lt. Isaac I.: 194, 196
Stockton, Comdr. Robert F.: 40, 41, 42, 80, 83
Supply routes: 19, 123–24, 128, 133, 150, 153, 192–93, 201–02
Surfboats: 177, 181
Survey of the Coast: 12
Surveying instruments: 45–46, 213
Surveys. *See* Battlefield surveys; Boundary surveys; Fortifications; Railroads; Roads; *and particular rivers*.
Sutter, John: 32
Sutter's Fort, Calif.: 32 35, 39

Talbot, Theodore: 39, 3l
Tampico, Mexico: 139, 140, 141, 142

Taos, N. Mex.: 73, 93n, 99
Taylor, Brig. Gen. Zachary: 4, 23, 73, 94, 115–47, 149, 153, 154, 155, 159, 160, 177, 180, 182, 186, 212, 215
Telescopes: 67, 145
Texas Boundary Survey: 18
Texas Rangers: 203
Thom, Lt. George: 178, 191, 192, 225
Timpas River: 68
Topographic engineers, duties of: 10, 15–16, 118, 128, 145–47
Topographic equipment: 30–31, 67, 145–46
  damage to: 30, 67
  transportation of: 67, 74
Topographical Bureau: 12, 14–16, 43, 49, 83, 85, 100, 115, 137, 145, 211, 212–13, 221–23
Topographical Engineers, Army Corps of duties of: 17, 19, 66–67
  organization of: 15
Torrey, John: 44, 86
Totten, Col. Joseph G.: 181, 182–83, 208
Tower, Lt. Zealous B.: 194, 196
Trailblazing: 31–32, 44
Trans-Florida canal: 14
Trans-Mississippi West, exploration of: 9, 12
Transit, portable: 30–31
Treasury, U.S. Department of the: 16
Treaty of Couenga: 41
Treaty of Guadalupe-Hidalgo: 100, 218
Turnbull, Maj. William: 178, 181, 182, 183, 185, 189, 191, 193, 194, 195, 198, 200–201, 204–06, 207, 211–12, 219
Twiggs, Brig. Gen. David E.: 122, 140, 181, 183, 187, 189, 193–95, 196, 198, 200–201, 203
Tyler, John: 221

United States and Texas Boundary Survey: 179
United States-Mexican boundary survey: 207–08
U.S. Boundary Commission in the Southwest: 206–07
U.S. Coast Survey, Office of the: 222
U.S. Congress: 13, 17, 127, 129n, 206, 214, 222–23
U.S. House of Representatives: 45, 84, 86, 100
U.S. Marine Corps: 35, 80, 198–99
U.S. Military Academy: 7–9, 11, 12, 43, 66, 100, 116, 117, 121, 130, 131, 140, 142, 149, 150, 162, 178, 179, 180, 183, 192, 209, 212
U.S. Naval Observatory: 45, 222
U.S. Navy: 4, 35, 39, 67, 139, 177, 181
  Home Squadron: 181
  Pacific fleet: 35

INDEX

U.S. Senate: 45, 84, 100, 156, 206
U.S. Supreme Court: 13
U.S.S. *Portsmouth*: 39
Utah: 31

Valverde, N. Mex.: 93, 94–95, 96, 139
Vegetation: 68, 69, 76, 86, 87, 90, 118, 121–22, 123, 124, 154, 160
Vera Cruz, Mexico: 128, 138, 141, 142, 144, 163, 177, 180, 181–85, 186, 192–93, 200–201, 205, 218
Viameter: 75
Victoria, Mexico: 140–42
Voltigeur Regiment: 188, 191, 199, 201
Volunteer troops: 63, 73, 119–20, 129–30, 131–32, 138, 139, 140, 192–93, 198–99, 201, 203, 222

Wagner, Harr: 29–30
Wagon trains: 20–22, 85n, 97, 99, 128, 132, 187, 194
Wagons: 46, 96–97, 146, 213
Walker, Joseph: 29, 31, 34
Walker Lake: 31–32
War Department: 11, 14, 15, 16, 17, 43, 128, 137, 205, 212–13, 218, 222, 223
War of 1812: 10

Warner, Lt. William H.: 66, 71, 73, 74, 78, 80, 81, 93n, 100, 216, 221
Washington, D.C.: 18
Washington, General George: 9
Washington Monument: 18
Water resources: 68, 92, 122, 123, 152, 160, 183
Watrous, N. Mex.: 69
Webber Falls: 48
Webster, Lt. Joseph D.: 215, 220n, 225
Wheat, Carl: 85
Wildlife: 68, 76, 90–91, 93, 98, 154, 158
Williams, Capt. William G.: 130, 131, 132–33, 134–35, 136, 137, 216
Wisconsin: 18
Wood, Lt. Thomas J.: 117, 118, 119, 126, 136n, 225
Wool, Brig. Gen John E.: 23, 95, 127, 131, 139, 140, 143, 144, 145, 149, 163, 201, 212, 215
Worth, Brig. Gen. William J.: 122, 131, 132, 133–34, 135, 136, 137, 138, 140, 155, 181, 183, 192–93, 194–95, 196, 198–99, 200–201, 205, 209

Year of Decision, 1846, The, by Bernard De Voto: 34
Yellow Wolf: 46

☆ U.S. GOVERNMENT PRINTING OFFICE: 1993 298–458

PIN : 068536–000